UNWRITTEN RULES

Dr. Temple Grandin & Sean Barron

OF SOCIAL RELATIONSHIPS

New Edition with Author Updates

Decoding Social Mysteries Through Autism's Unique Perspectives

edited by Veronica Zysk

UNWRITTEN RULES OF SOCIAL RELATIONSHIPS

All marketing and publishing rights guaranteed to and reserved by:

FUTURE HORIZONS INC.

(817) 277-0727
(817) 277-2270 (fax)
E-mail: info@fhautism.com
www.fhautism.com

Cover & interior design by John Yacio III

ISBN: 9781941765388

DEDICATION

This book is dedicated to individuals with autism spectrum disorders who strive each day to understand themselves and the world around them, and to the parents, teachers and providers who help them do so.

Temple Grandin

I would like to dedicate this book to Ron, Judy and Megan Barron: my wonderful father, mother and sister.

Sean Barron

CONTENTS

CONTENTS

INTRODUCTION

SOCIAL RULES

Those guidelines, norms, requirements, expectations, customs, and laws,

Written and unwritten, spoken and unspoken,

That reflect a society's attitudes, values, prejudices, and fears,

And determine the roles we play and the actions we take,

As we interact with other people in society as individuals and as groups.

ACKNOWLEDGMENTS TO
FIRST AND SECOND EDITIONS

We wish to thank Veronica Zysk for her valuable guidance and hard work in putting this project together. We also want to thank Wayne Gilpin who, as president of Future Horizons Inc. when the first edition was released, had the original idea for this book. We are grateful for his vision and to be part of the FH family. Though Wayne has now passed on from this life, we work to keep alive his vision of helping people better understand autism and Asperger's syndrome and the challenges and triumphs of those with it. As Wayne was frequently known to say, "keep smiling!"

A NOTE TO READERS

Three people contributed directly to the final book you are reading. Individual passages written by Temple and Sean are identified with their names throughout the chapters. We owe thanks to our editor, Veronica Zysk, for the rest of the text, which she created on our behalf with our input and direction. It was a true team effort.

We believe in the use of person-first language and have incorporated that styling into the book. However, there are passages where we found it cumbersome or redundant to use person-first language, and the reader will notice the use of the term "autistic." We mean no disrespect.

We also chose to globally use the male gender reference, rather than "he/she" or "him/her." The word "teacher" refers to anyone who works with or has an influence on people with ASD. It is not limited to the formal education system, and professionals and parents alike are all our teachers. Except where noted, the ideas presented in the book apply equally to girls and boys.

Finally, the structure of the book dictated that there be a mixed "voice" within the chapters. The two opening chapters are written in first-person language, as we each authored our own chapters. The remainder of the book represents a marriage of both our thoughts and ideas; therefore, we chose to refer to ourselves in the third person when necessary.

A FEW NOTES TO READERS ON THE SECOND EDITION

The content and structure of this second edition remain largely the same as the first edition, with two major exceptions:

1. Temple and Sean have added content that speaks to some of the social perceptual changes they have experienced over the last 12

years, since the first edition released in 2005. The majority of this content can be found in its entirety directly following the first edition content.

2. Some readers of the first edition found it challenging to track whether Temple or Sean was speaking in parts of the book. As a result, the reader will now see a vertical ruler running down the outside edge of the page. The ruler to designate Temple's content is gray; the ruler to designate Sean's content is black. We hope this visual tool makes it easier to appreciate which author is speaking and when.

3. Some readers thought our editor should have omitted content across the chapters if it was something we already had said. We didn't want this done for two reasons. First, we never assume people read a book front to back. In fact, many don't. Second, some things bear repeating so people of the spectrum, who process differently, actually "hear" and understand things that are important to us.

W hen our publisher, Wayne Gilpin, approached us about writing a book together about the unwritten rules of social relationships, we were both, simultaneously, interested and filled with some degree of trepidation. "There is value," he asserted, "in sharing with the autism community the collective years of wisdom of two successful, socially-adept individuals who struggled with the effects of autism and rose above the challenges of the disorder. You both have insight and experience in the complex arena of social functioning and people want to know how you became the social beings you are."

On a logical, intellectual basis we both could agree with the points Wayne was making. We did recognize the value of broadening the understanding that neurotypical people have of people who are on the autism spectrum, especially in reference to how we think and how that affects our social relationships. We were both able to reflect on the difficult lessons and experiences that contributed to the social understanding we each possess of the world. And, a book like this appealed to us because it is a way of giving back to the world, leaving a legacy of our thoughts on a topic that is ever-present in the minds of parents, teachers, caregivers and people with ASD.

Little did we realize at the time we agreed to write this book what a mirror image of our quest for social understanding it would turn out to be.

While we understood the task at hand, translating ideas into action proved difficult. The farther we journeyed into discussing the content of the book, the more nebulous the theme became. We'd discuss one unwritten rule and a hundred exceptions would instantaneously appear. Anxiety and frustration grew as the project became a giant metaphor for the path our social mastery took as we grew from children to adolescents to the adults we are today. Social rules and exposure to the social world is simple and well-defined at first. As children we are taught "Don't talk with your mouth full" or "Raise your hand in class before speaking."These were concrete rules to follow; they defined what our behavior should be. And it was relatively easy to know when we were—or were not—following them. So too was the initial idea for the book: Talk about some of the unwritten social rules you learned along the way. However, the more immersed one becomes in social situations and social understanding, the more intricate and interwoven are those rules, the more nuanced the interpretation of what to do or say, and the less clear-cut these "rules" become. We descended into that realm of fuzzy boundaries and discovered more exceptions than rules the more we talked about the book. As we marched forward, the light of understanding and confidence in accomplishing the task before us faded.

Luckily a guide appeared in the form of our editor, Veronica Zysk, and we each were handed a flashlight to illuminate our path. Countless conversations provided structure to our thoughts and organization to the ideas we felt needed to be put forth within our writings. It quickly became apparent that our original concept of the book—discussing the myriad and sometimes mysterious unwritten rules of social relationships—was a task so broad neither of us could see a beginning or an ending to the project. It was a gigantic exercise in executive functioning, and that is NOT one of the strong points of most people on the autism spectrum. Giant icebergs of anxiety and stress began to melt away as our wise editor broke down the project into smaller, more manageable steps that made sense to each of us.

Even more importantly, as we talked about how our social awareness had unfolded over the years, our editor started pointing out to us several common bubbles of thought rising to the surface of our consciousness. Our brains started shifting from only seeing the details into appreciating larger concepts. Smaller, specific unwritten social rules started migrating under the umbrella of broader categories that described social behavior. The pivotal nature of these global unwritten rules was both interesting and enlightening to us; they applied across situations and domains, at home, school and in the community, across age groups and cultures. They eventually coalesced into the Ten Unwritten Rules you will find in this book. That people with ASDs think in details rather than generalizations was nowhere more evident than in the process of writing this book.

Early on in the project, during some of our more frustrating months, Sean succinctly summed up the difficulty we were having with defining the unwritten rules of social relationships: "There is the world of the neurotypicals and the world of the person on the autism spectrum. Our perspective and understanding—indeed, our very thinking process—is so very different than yours, yet we are required to conform to your set of rules. For you, social understanding is innate. For us, it is not. Asking me to define the unwritten social rules that help or hinder us in forming relationships is like asking me to write a book about the unwritten rules of the people of France. I'm not French; I wasn't born into that culture and I don't know their rules. The same logic applies here."

Life has a way of completing itself, and by the end of the book we came full circle in realizing that we each did, indeed, have a much richer, fuller understanding of the unwritten rules of social relationships than we did growing up, and we did have things to say that could shed light on working with other people on the spectrum. Perhaps our biggest discovery, however, was *how markedly different was the path we each took in gaining that social awareness.*

There is no mistaking that we each traveled a different road to social understanding, and that the view we each have today of the world is colored by a *different social perspective.* Clearly, there is no single path to social awareness, to being connected to the world; the journey is as varied as are people on the spectrum. But knowledge, to be valuable, needs context. Therefore, we decided to relate our personal stories as a starting point for the book, not only to set the stage for the comments we would make later about the Ten Unwritten Rules, but also to illustrate the very different perspectives we grew up with and the different ways our brains processed information and our experiences.

Parents and teachers who are eager to teach "social skills" to children with ASD may want to take note of our two social perspectives as *different starting points* for instruction. They suggest not only how children with ASD think and learn, but the basic building materials they are born with that contribute to the quality and character of their social awareness. For children born on Path A, their sense of connection to the world, their happiness may always stem from a logical, analytic place of being. They resonate less to emotional-relatedness and more to intellectual pursuits. These are the often-intellectually gifted children who can easily lose themselves in projects and learning, oblivious to the world outside their obsession, for whom facts and figures, problems and patterns are the stuff that dreams are made of, the "little scientists" on the spectrum. For these children, their sense of being and relatedness is tied to what they *do* instead of to what they *feel*. They relate to, and find friendships with, people who have the same shared interests.

Path B children, in contrast, feel emotional-relatedness right from the start. They eagerly, although inappropriately at first, express emotions, make their needs and wants known through emotional channels, they "feel out" their world through their sense of social-emotional connection and are deeply affected when they and their world are out of sync with each other. Emotions infuse their being. They are emotionally demonstrative. These are the children who long for friends, peers with whom they can be emotionally connected. For them, social connectedness is motivating in itself, yet these children can't figure out what to do about the emotional undertow they have to fight just to keep their heads above water.

Temple had "classic autism" right from the start. She was nonverbal until she was nearly four, with regular tantrums manifesting because of her tactile and auditory sensory problems. If left alone, her preferred activity was investigating carpet fibers or watching grains of sand sift through her fingers, over and over and over again. Her impairment was severe enough that institutionalization was recommended, although her mother refused to accept that future for her daughter. However, Temple was also inquisitive, creative, and highly self-motivated to explore her surroundings. It was a world of projects and building things, of being a detective in figuring out how "life" worked. Her sense of self was positive, strong, formed bit by bit by what she did, by the many experiences her mother exposed her to, and the structure within which she learned. Friendships were active, built on shared interests. It wasn't until her early teens that a sense of being out-of-sync with her peers woke up in her brain. By then, a solid foundation of positive self-esteem, strong self-motivation, creativity and flexible thinking had been formed, a foundation that helped her withstand the earthquakes of social misunderstandings that threatened to demolish her world. Through it all, Temple defined herself by what she did. As is now common knowledge, Temple "thinks in pictures" and her mind processes information in a highly logical manner. Temple is a visual-logical thinker. Today she is a university professor and a world-renowned designer of livestock equipment, an accomplished author and strong advocate on autism issues.

Contrast this with Sean's journey, one colored from an early age with a profound sense of isolation, of deeply rooted feelings of anxiety and fear that manifested as extremely rigid thinking patterns, highly repetitive behaviors and rules that absolutely could not be broken. Sean was diagnosed as having autism in 1965, at age four. Like Temple, he was not considered "high functioning" by today's diagnostic criteria, and like Temple, he had delayed language and sensory challenges. He began saying numbers and letters when he was three, but it wasn't until he was well into his fourth year that he started saying other words. His mother recalls his language was more "reciting"— lists of state capitals, radio call letters—than speaking in a form that was functional or conversational. He didn't make eye contact; he had a hard time filtering out extraneous sounds as innocuous as a doorbell ringing, making it appear he was ignoring his parents and adults in his environment, when in reality, all sounds equally competed for his attention. He had a very high pain threshold, but could not tolerate certain sensations, such as sitting in a bathtub, having his head touched and his hair washed or combed. Some of his sensory issues lasted to some degree well into his twenties.

As you will read, Sean's emotions controlled his behaviors. He seemed as though he were living "within a world of his own imagining," within a fog of autism so dense that nothing existed beyond the fog. He was a solitary boy, curious only about things he already knew, but wanted to hear repeated. Order and calm lived only within sameness. As a result, odd rules came to govern his daily interactions. It was a horrible, frightening, out-of-control world; whatever behaviors gave him even a minuscule degree of reprieve became his lifeline to survival. Interestingly, he didn't ask any questions except those about time ("What time is she coming?"). He never, *never* asked how to do something he couldn't do on his own, or something he didn't understand. Some of these challenges continued into his adult life; not asking for help was perhaps the longest lasting of all.

Despite what looked like a disregard for parents and people around him, Sean's nature contained the seed of emotional-relatedness that exists in different degrees within people on the autism spectrum. Looking back now, we realize that his emotional-relatedness capacity was high; missing from the equation, however, was the ability to step outside his own mind, to think flexibly and with what we refer to as theory of mind—the ability to perceive the world from another person's point of view. Every social misstep was a blow to his fragile self-esteem; every misunderstanding a testament that something was inherently wrong with him, that he was "bad." He was self-focused, not by choice but by his autism. Managing the fear and anxiety associated with daily functioning was often too much to bear. Angry explosions were frequent and only dragged him down farther into his black hole of self-despair. Despite all that, today Sean lives independently, is a well-established newspaper reporter and has a wide variety of social relationships and interests.

As we worked on the book, it became obvious how these two very different social perspectives governed our thinking patterns and our behaviors. Temple took a very analytic approach to life, and to the book: research, discuss, evaluate, solve the "problem" and achieve the goal. Her contribution reflects events and ideas that describe how she gained social functioning skills, the logical, methodical way her life has unfolded, and the new thoughts and perspectives on social awareness that have surfaced as a result of her experiences.

On the other hand, Sean's life, and thus his writing, is emotion-infused. The anxiety, fear, longing and pleasure he has experienced as he's worked his way out of his autism, then into and through the nebulous world of social relationships, color every passage.

Our differences are both subtle and overt; they stem as much from environment and upbringing as they do from our unique physiologies. Brain researchers have discovered that autism characteristics manifest when neuronal connections that link up the many different parts of the brain fail to hook up. The frontal cortex is the most affected area and the back part of the brain, where memories are stored, is usually more normal. They have also found that the brain areas that process emotional signals from the eyes are abnormal. Variability in the parts of the brain that are not wired properly would explain why behaviors and feelings can be so different among people with ASD, and why Sean is Sean and Temple is Temple. And, of course, basic temperament comes into play, as it does with all people, whether or not they are on the spectrum.

Two very different paths, yet we both arrived at the same destination: happy independent adults, with satisfying jobs and personal relationships that provide us with a sense of connection and belonging.

Autism is a spectrum disorder, and people with autism are a diverse culture. As with any culture, we have social norms, unwritten rules and a thought perspective all our own. That people with autism have to exist within a different culture on a day-to-day basis in order to survive—one that often blindly insists on conformity rather than respecting our cultural diversity—makes functioning in the world around us exceedingly difficult, often depressing and continually anxiety-laden.

We offer this book in the hope that people of both cultures—those with autism and neurotypicals alike—can gain a deeper awareness of and appreciation for the other. To do that, we can think of no better way than sharing with you how we think about social relationships—this is how we each gain perspective of the other. We could enumerate any number of unwritten social rules offer hundreds of bulleted examples of social behaviors we had learned in a neat and organized manner, but they would have little lasting impression on neurotypical (NT) people until they first understood what it's like to be "in our heads," to hear the conversations we have with ourselves about the people and the situations we experience. Successful social relationships require a healthy ability to take another person's perspective; in most cases, it's teaching the person with autism to take the NT perspective. Within the pages of this book we sought to reverse that trend by explaining *our* perspective on social relationships to the reader. It was an eye-opening experience for each of us, and we share the common bond of autism. Hopefully, it will be a bridge to new understanding between both our cultures.

Despite millions of years of inhabiting this planet together, our social awareness is still in its infancy and there are skills we all can learn to help us coexist in respectful harmony. The more colors on our palette, the more beautiful the world we can create. We each have much to share.

If we are to achieve a richer culture, rich in contrasting values, we must recognize the whole gamut of human potentialities, and so weave a less arbitrary social fabric, one in which each diverse human gift will find a fitting place. —Margaret Mead

Dr. Temple Grandin & Sean Barron
July 2005

SECOND EDITION UPDATE TO THE INTRODUCTION

Since writing the first edition of our book, one observation we've noticed bears acknowledgment. That is the marked overlap between ASD and ADHD. In the last 10 years the way the medical and educational community views autism and Asperger's has changed dramatically. At the time Temple and Sean were born, children who were totally or mostly nonverbal, who were socially out of step with their peers, and displayed marked behavioral challenges were given a diagnosis of "autism." It wasn't until 1994 and the release of the fourth edition of the *Diagnostic and Statistical Manual of Mental Disorders* (DSM-IV) that the professional community officially embraced a "higher functioning" form of autism called "Asperger's syndome" (AS). AS described children who had language—often quite good language—combined with less severe emotional, social and behavioral challenges. Even so, disparity presided in how children were diagnosed, depending on the knowledge and experience level of the professional doing the assessment. Compounding matters was that individuals who had normal or near-normal language yet marked social and sensory impairments were often not diagnosed until age seven or later, when their social developmental challenges became more noticeable compared to their neurotypical peers.

It was during this period that confusion between ASD and ADHD started appearing in earnest. The overlap between symptoms of the disorders challenged parents and professionals alike. Classic traits associated with AS were being noticed in children previously diagnosed with ADHD. Children previously diagnosed as ADHD were being re-diagnosed as AS. Researchers took note and studies started appearing about possible genetic links between the two disorders (Lichtenstein, P. et. al. 2010; Reierson, A. 2008; Ronald, A. et al. 2008).

Then in 2013, the diagnostic landscape around autism/Asperger's changed again with the release of the DSM-V. Gone were the individual diagnoses of autism, Asperger's and PDD-NOS. They were replaced with one disorder: Autism Spectrum Disorder (ASD), further qualified by two domains of functioning (Social Communication, and Restricted and Repetitive Patterns of Behavior Interests and Activities) and three levels of severity for each domain.

More recent research is confirming a genetic influence in the overlap of symptoms between ASD and ADHD with no speech delay (Antshel et.al., 2016; Grzadzinski, Dick, Lord, & Bishop, 2016; Grzadzinsky et.al., 2011; Reiersen, A., 2011). Parents and professionals are noting the social functioning and sensory components of the disorders to require the most attention within treatment programs, as these areas seem to be the most challenging for these individuals. Therefore, we encourage adults involved with either an ASD or ADHD diagnosis to read the information provided in this book in an effort to more completely understand the differences in the way our brains work in processing the social and emotional situations we are faced with every day.

PART ONE

TWO PERSPECTIVES ON SOCIAL THINKING

MY WORLD IS WHAT I DO

by TEMPLE GRANDIN

When I was a child I was a big fan of *Superman* and *The Lone Ranger*. These television shows had clear-cut values of right and wrong. Good guys fought bad guys and good guys won. I understood the messages conveyed in the shows because of their clear values. To learn right and wrong I had to experience concrete examples of right and wrong: You do not hit other kids because you would not like it if they hit you. I understood the rule that "two wrongs do not make a right." An example would be breaking another child's toy because he broke mine.

Roy Rogers' code of conduct was another set of rules to which I could relate. *The Roy Rogers Show* was a popular children's cowboy series. Roy's rules for the western range were also the rules of the '50s, when I was a child.

Roy Rogers' Riders Club Rules:
Be neat and clean.
Be courteous and polite.
Always obey your parents.
Protect the weak and help them.
Be brave but never take chances.
Study hard and learn all you can.
Be kind to animals and take care of them.
Eat all your food and never waste any.
Love God and go to Sunday school regularly.
Always respect our flag and our country.

The 1950s was a time when our society was much simpler, more structured, and a time when following the rules of our culture was more a time-honored tradition than it is today. So many times after giving presentations to parents and professionals in the autism community, I am asked, "Temple, how did you get to be the person you are today? What things occurred along the way that gave you the opportunities to be successful in a job, to have friends, to function so well in the world around you?" Of course, there's never a simple answer to those questions, as the person I am today is different from the person I was forty years ago, ten years ago, or even five years ago. It's not as though I gained social understanding at a certain chronological age, like a light switch suddenly flipped over to the ON position. If these same parents had met me just out of high school, they might have walked away with a different impression. I'm nearing sixty now; that's a lot of years of experiences to learn from, and certainly can't be compared to a child of five or ten who is an infant in his social understanding of the world.

However, in gathering material for this book, and comparing the social understanding I have now with what it used to be at different stages of my life, I can say that certain elements contributed to my success:

- Growing up in the 1950s and '60s
- A structured home life
- Creativity and an inquisitive nature
- High expectations of parents and teachers
- Clearly defined behavior rules and consistently applied consequences
- Positive self-esteem and strong internal motivation

Some of these components are internal; others were external. Some may be applicable to other children and adults on the spectrum; others may be just "me" and the personality traits I was born with.

GROWING UP IN THE 1950S AND '60S

Looking back, I'd have to say that I'm a product of my environment. The social structure of the 1950s and '60s was much simpler than it is today. Family units were strong, people exhibited a higher degree of respect toward each other than they do today, and behavior expectations were more clearly defined. Children were taught manners, consideration for others and to do good deeds in the community.

Despite some rather severe behavior problems in my young years, as I've described in my books, *Emergence: Labeled Autistic* and later in *Thinking in Pictures,* or those that Mother has illuminated in her book, *A Thorn in My Pocket,* Mother never viewed my autism as excusing me from the expectation that I would learn to function within the social structure. Even at age six, I was expected to eat dinner with the family, to behave properly, and to respect the family rules, such as never messing up the living room. Being polite, saying "please" and "thank you" were expected of all children at that time, and most certainly of children in the Grandin household. It was simply assumed, *without question*, that I would learn these social skills.

Mother was strict in her discipline, and applied it consistently. She knew me well, she was a good behavior detective, and I probably inherited some of my acute analytic skills from her, which have helped me throughout my life. She understood the difference between behavior outbursts that resulted from me being tired, or from sensory overload (in those instances there wasn't a consequence) and times when I wasn't trying or was simply "being Temple." I was often a willful child; autism didn't compromise the very neurotypical way I tested boundaries to see how much I could get away with.

One of the reasons she worked so hard on my behavior is she wanted to prove to my father and our doctor that I didn't have to be in an institution. Remember, this is the 1950s and '60s, when knowledge of autism was young and Bruno Bettelheim's theory that autism was caused by uncaring and unresponsive mothers was looming like a black cloud over everything. In her heart, she knew I was capable of learning, as long as the learning was done in a way that was meaningful to me. She worked hard to keep me out of an institution, and it often wasn't easy.

The environment I grew up in was also a natural setting for social interaction and for friendships to form. Absent were hours of solitary activities such as watching television and DVD movies, or playing computer and video games, and this was actually a very positive thing for a developing autistic child. Time was spent making things, building projects like kites or model airplanes, in lots of outdoor activities, and in playing board games or cards. These activities taught me turn-taking. When I was five, I was making things in my room out of cardboard already. These types of activities were naturally reinforcing, they were self-esteem building, and they provided opportunities for practicing all sorts of skills, from language to sensory regulation to behavior control.

While some activities I did by myself, in most cases my days were filled with shared activities, either with my sisters, the nanny, or with other kids—a perfect setting for emerging social skills. My favorite game was table hockey; it required me to learn to play it with another child. And, because Mother drilled into me manners and social etiquette, I developed good play skills at a very early age, like turn-taking and being fair and doing what others wanted to do.

At times I'd get off on one of my jags and just keep talking about something over and over again that the kids didn't really like, one of my fixations. For instance, one of the neighbors had a fake donkey where you'd push the ear down, the tail would go up and a cigarette would emerge from the donkey's butt. In the '50s, this was akin to a dirty joke. I thought that donkey was the funniest thing I had ever seen and I wanted to talk about it and talk about it and talk about it. The kids eventually got sick of hearing me go on and on, but what was good was that they just told me to stop. Plain and simple: "Cut it out; we're sick of hearing you talk about the stupid donkey." That definitely helped. People were pretty direct back then; the kids were direct and the adults were direct if you were doing something inappropriate. There wasn't a whole lot of explaining and trying to be sensitive about feelings. I was told, in very clear language, that my behavior was wrong and if it was Mother doling out the message, there was a loss of privileges for sure. The quality of the interaction was much more up front.

It was also an era where families had a lot of social contact with other families. My class in elementary school had only twelve kids. We all played with each other—it just was the way things were during the '50s and '60s. Everyone got invited to everyone else's birthday parties—there was no exclusion. We played after school with each other. One of our neighbors had a really cool creetor set, another had a pool table—these were activities I enjoyed and I'd often be over there playing with the kids in those families. Socializing was an everyday occurrence and having appropriate social skills was expected. If I acted inappropriately at a neighbor's house, the mom would simply correct my behavior—no big deal—just like my mother did. This is right; this is not right. All the mothers taught kids the same manners and held their kids accountable for their behaviors. It was a much tighter-knit society than it is today.

2017 REFLECTIONS FROM TEMPLE

Many Older People are Great Resources in the Community

There are many people in the community who can be very successful in working with kids, teenagers or young adults with ASD. They do not let a diagnosis scare them away from mentoring and teaching individuals with autism. A 2014 article by Eric B. London, entitled "Categorical Diagnosis: A Fatal Flaw in Autism Research?" states that there is no clear boundary between autism and neurotypicality. "ASDs represent the extreme end of a distribution of traits in the population, placing doubt on the validity of autism as a discrete entity." Children on the spectrum have to learn all social rules by being taught. In my generation, social rules were taught to all children in a more structured way. This helped kids who were mildly on the spectrum to get through school and gain employment later in life. I have talked to many parents and grandparents who have discovered that they were on the spectrum after their children or grandchildren were diagnosed.

Sometimes a teacher can work wonders with students who are labeled as having ASD. An old nun in a wheelchair was able to handle the worst kid in the school who was labeled with both ASD and oppositional defiant disorder. She put him to work as her assistant. He was proud to be her assistant, and he behaved himself.

Many retired people with technical or artistic skills would be willing to teach their trade to students with ASD; someone has to approach them about the idea to do it. This could be done by networking through social media, faith-based groups or community associations. I estimate that a skilled trade would be appropriate for 25% to 30% of individuals with ASD.

There is a huge shortage of skilled trade workers in the U.S., especially in auto mechanics and welding. To get kids interested in a career, it is best to expose them to it before graduation from high school. I became interested in beef cattle because I was exposed to them in high school. The 4-H program also offers some great resources for learning about small engine repair. It is likely that there are bored retired mechanics in your community who would love to teach about small engine repair. Broken lawn mowers are free, and a garage could be converted into a neighborhood shop. Fixing broken phones and appliances is another area where a retired technician could get kids away from video games and headed toward a well-paying job.

I also wasn't a shy kid, and I think that helped me along in acquiring social skills and feeling positive about my life in general. I remember one time as a child going on a trip to Canada with the family. I wanted to go on a toboggan ride, so I just went up to other kids and asked them if I could go on their toboggan. My sister was always too shy to do that. When new neighbors moved into town I would go over and introduce myself to them. I wasn't shy about putting myself in social situations, or anxious about making mistakes, probably because there were so many, many chances to do this that I got all the practice I needed. That, coupled with Mother's insistence on manners, was a recipe for being successful.

I loved building things right from the start; it was a natural outlet for my visual way of thinking. I wasn't interested in "little girl" activities like playing with dolls (hated them, hated them). I wanted to go out and build tree houses, and construct things that flew, like planes and kites. I had really neat parachutes that I made out of scarves and coat hangers. I had a special design so that when I threw them up in the air they wouldn't tangle and they'd open up really nicely and sail a long way.

Mother had my brother Dick when I was about six. While she was in the hospital, I made them a welcome home surprise. I cut a horse out of cardboard, put it on a string and glued a bunch of crepe paper on it. When she came in with the new baby, I lowered the horse down over the banister and all the crepe paper unrolled into big loops. That was my mind at six years old. Another time, Mother was having a dinner party downstairs, directly beneath my room. I took one of my dresses and put it on a coat hanger and then put a paper bag on it as a head and painted some eyes on it. I put it on a string, then lowered it out the window. All the guests screamed as though someone had fallen out the window. It was pretty funny.

I had a really good *visual* theory of mind, instead of emotional theory of mind. For instance, one time when we were playing hide and seek I got the idea of creating a fake person to distract the goal keeper. I thought, now if I take some coats and I stuff them with leaves and I put them up in the tree, the goal keeper is going to go over there and then we can run in and catch the goal. I was doing things like that when I was eight. In third grade I decided that for our school's dog show I would go as a dog and have two other kids show me. I made a dog costume and the two Reece twins showed me. It was pretty funny and went over well with the other kids. I was inventive; they liked that. It helped with friendships because we had shared interests.

Honestly, I doubt that I would have been as creative or that I would have acquired so much self-motivation and self-esteem had I been sitting alone in front of the television or zoning out on video games all day long. Computers would have been equally distracting. Until recently, I still didn't have a computer at home because it can have an almost hypnotic effect on me. I can get caught up watching certain screen savers for hours. As a child, that wouldn't have been conducive to learning skills that would help me later in my life. They would have all been solitary activities, too—you can't learn social skills by yourself. Not growing up in the "electronic age" forced me to engage with other kids and adults; it was positive. Mother exposed me to lots of different activities to stimulate my natural curiosity and refused to let me disconnect from the world. I received praise for the things I did, but not for every little trivial thing I did correctly. Praise had to be earned back then; it wasn't doled out as easily as it is today. People—my family, my nanny, the teachers I had in school—encouraged me to do things I was good at. It all worked together.

2017 REFLECTIONS FROM TEMPLE

Since the first edition of *Unwritten Rules of Social Relationships*, I acquired both a computer at home and an iPhone 6. I do not use them to play video games and neither device has any entertainment features. I use Google on my phone to look up weather reports and flight delays when I am traveling. The desktop computer is mainly used to look up information on the Internet and for searching academic databases. Searching scientific databases takes you into a world of scientific literature. This is especially useful when I am writing papers on either animals or autism. To use these databases, type the names into Google. Several databases I use are:

- *Google Scholar*–Academic and scientific papers on all subjects
- *Science Direct*–Academic papers on all subjects
- *Pub Med*–Medical and veterinary scientific papers
- *ResearchGate*–A site like Facebook for scientists
- *Google Patents*–Look up patents for every kind of invention

Mother clearly taught us that we were responsible for our actions, and that when we acted inappropriately, there were consequences. Home life was structured and the school day was structured, which was better aligned with the autistic way of thinking. I attended an old-fashioned structured classroom, with one teacher and twelve students. Our teacher would have the kids take turns reading. Then she'd have us do math workbooks for a half-hour. Then we'd practice writing for another half-hour. It was also a very, very quiet environment, without many sensory distractions. I think if I were in school today, in a class with thirty kids and all the commotion, I'd need an aide in order to survive.

During the '50s and '60s, there was consistent discipline between home and school. Teachers often tell me that one of the main problems they encounter with kids with ASD is that there isn't consistent application of behavior rules between home and school. Let me tell you, if I had a bad day at school, Mother was called, and the consequence was very simple. She'd take away one night of watching television—not a whole week because she knew that would make me give up trying to be good. But there would be no *Howdy Doody Show* for that night. She wouldn't scream at me or be overly emotional. I'd just come home and she'd very quietly say, "Mrs. Dietch called and told me about school today, and there is no *Howdy Doody* tonight." That was it. Consequences were known up front and were enforced. Period.

Being able to do certain things was also considered a "privilege" and privileges had to be earned. Some were considered "grown-up" privileges and I knew those meant I had to be on my best behavior. I remember going to one of Mother's dinner parties and being asked to pass the hors d'oeuvres—that was one of the grown-up privileges. And I remember another time my aunt let me use her professional oil paints when I was about eight or nine. I was very careful with those oil paints, because it was a grown-up privilege to be able to use them. Mother always knew my areas of interest and used them as motivation to get me to learn new things. But, as I mentioned before, she also knew I had problems with sound sensitivity and other sensory issues. For instance, if I had a tantrum at the circus she wouldn't have punished me for that, because she knew that I just couldn't tolerate the environment after a point. But she still took me to the circus, and other places, so that I gradually got used to them. I liked a lot of the things we did and because she knew me so well, I could try to enjoy them, trusting that when it got to be too much for me, she'd take me out of the situation. I give Mother a lot of credit for her acute understanding of my boundaries and when and how far she could push me.

2017 REFLECTIONS FROM TEMPLE

Learning to Use Money

When my sister and I were ages 8 and 10, we received fifty cents each week as an allowance. In the 1950s, fifty cents could buy about five dollars' worth of stuff today. This money was used to buy candy, comics, and small cheap toys such as kites or toy airplanes. Mother never bought me a ten cent paper kite; it had to come from my allowance. If I wanted a sixty-nine cent toy plane with a wind-up propeller, I had to save for two weeks.

In the summer, my sister and I loved to go to the county fair. For an entire month, we saved our allowances so we could pay for rides and carnival games. Each game cost ten cents to play, and even if you lost, you got one of those paper leis. We loved putting the bright leis around our necks. These leis were not available in the stores; they were a special thing we could only get at the county fair.

Having an allowance and mother's "rules" that my sister and I had to learn to manage what money we had if we wanted something taught me the principles of saving. Many of today's parents think it is "asking too much" for the child with ASD to have to feel disappointed by not getting whatever they want. This is actually doing these children a disservice and preventing them from learning functional life skills they will need as an adult. I have met teenagers with ASD about to graduate high school who are completely unable to go into a fast-food restaurant, place an order and pay for it. Teaching a child with ASD about money and money management is important. Today a child's allowance could be used to purchase video watching time from a streaming service or buy virtual equipment in an online video game.

FOSTERING HEALTHY SELF-ESTEEM

One of the most pivotal reasons I think I was able to succeed in the world as an adult was because Mother fostered a strong, healthy sense of self-worth in me. It's not one particular thing she did or that other parents didn't do. Actually, back in the '50s and '60s, consciously building your child's self-esteem wasn't part of the "psychology" of parenting. Kids did more things and they developed self-esteem from the things they did. But I think Mother unconsciously realized two important things about self-esteem:

- Self-esteem is built little by little through real achievements. For instance, creating beautiful embroidery—that took time, effort and patience to complete—made me feel good about myself.
- The literal, concrete mind of the autistic child requires that self-esteem be built through tangible accomplishments, coupled with verbal praise.

Catha Cohen, in her book, *Raise Your Child's Social IQ*, offers the following list of characteristics of children with positive and negative self-esteem:

Kids with High Self-Esteem
- Have fairly stable moods
- Set realistic goals and achieve them
- Have self-motivation and "stick-to-it-ness"
- Can accept rejection or critical feedback
- Can say "no" to peers
- Are realistically aware of their own strengths and weaknesses

Kids with Low Self-Esteem
- Often blame others for their actions
- Need to be liked by everyone

- See themselves as losers
- Are critical of others
- Get frustrated easily
- Have trouble accepting responsibility for their actions
- Make negative comments about themselves
- Tend to be quitters

The "fix it" mentality that seems more prevalent today wasn't part of my younger years, either. While I did have speech therapy in elementary school, and would visit a psychiatrist once a month, both of these activities were conducted in a manner that to me didn't feel like something was wrong with me that needed "fixing." Most of the physical tests I had were conducted when I was very little, too young for them to create an impression that my autism made me "less than" in some way. Nowadays, kids are being whisked off to one evaluation after another and go from therapy program to therapy program, some five or more days a week. What message is that sending the child other than parts of him are somehow unacceptable, or that his autism is bad? I think the intellectually gifted child suffers the most. Autism professionals and special educators are challenged in that they have to work with such a wide range of individuals who vary from completely nonverbal to genius. ASD children with IQs of 140+ are being held back by too much "handicapped" psychology because programs are not tailored to their individual talents. I have told several parents of brilliant AS children that in the old days the diagnosis was *gifted*, not disabled.

All through elementary school I felt pretty good about myself. I flourished with the many projects I created, the praise they received from family and teachers, the friendships I shared and the new experiences I mastered. When I won a trophy at winter carnival, that made me happy. When Mother had me sing at an adult concert when I was in sixth grade, I felt good about that. Even during the difficult high school years, my special interests kept me moving forward. I could revert to my hobbies when things got tough socially. It helped me get through those years.

Personality has a lot to do with self-esteem and parents need to realize that some kids have a more positive, motivated attitude from the day they are born than do other kids. That has nothing to do with being on the autism spectrum. Fortunately, I was one of those kids, and I admit, it's made a difference in my ability to get this far in life. Some higher-functioning AS kids who know about their diagnosis feel energized after reading about other famous historical figures who had AS or autistic-like characteristics. The book, *Asperger's and Self-Esteem: Insight and Hope through Famous Role Models* by Norm Ledgin (Future Horizons) can bolster self-esteem.

Today, kids are being reinforced for the littlest things and it's setting up a cycle of needing approval for every little thing they do. *The Wall Street Journal* has run many articles lately about young kids entering the workforce who need constant praise from their manager or they can't get their job done. I recently spoke with a senior-level person who works in a government agency and asked her about the summer interns. She said half of them were wonderful and the other half were either lazy or had to have constant reinforcement for every little tiny thing they did. Parents and teachers need to take a look at how they're reinforcing children. Once a child graduates out of the school system, the amount of praise an individual receives on any regular basis falls off dramatically. A child who constantly receives praise for making efforts in the social arena is going to face a rude awakening later in life, which can negatively affect his motivation to stay socially involved. It's a Catch-22, and one that needs more attention than it's currently being given.

I wasn't praised all the time by Mother or my teachers; far from it. Neither were other kids. We were praised when we did something significant, so the praise was really meaningful and was a strong motivator. The everyday things, like proper table manners or eating all my dinner, were not praised. I wasn't praised every time I put my Sunday school dress on properly, or behaved in church or when we visited Aunt Bella. It was just expected that I would behave. But when I made a beautiful clay horse when I was in third grade, Mother really praised that.

It's difficult for most kids with ASD, because of their concrete, literal way of thinking, to acquire a healthy sense of their abilities and their personal worth without the praise being associated with something they can see, touch or smell. Especially when kids are young, encouraging them to engage in activities with visible, tangible outcomes, be it play or in structured education settings, helps them learn the direct connection between their actions and their abilities, and their sense of mastery and control over their world. You can't build things or paint pictures or create anything concrete without making choices, learning sequencing skills, seeing how parts relate to a whole, learning concepts and categories. This, in turn, lays the groundwork for more advanced skills to form, skills indigenous to the less-concrete world of social interactions. Everything builds on everything else. You start simple and slowly get more complex in what you teach a child.

MOTIVATION

A second aspect of my personality that I think factored strongly into my success today is that I'm highly self-motivated to explore the world around me. I do feel an innate desire to do my best, and to contribute something to the world. What was positive for me is that, from an early age, Mother was constantly encouraging me to be involved with different things. She exposed me and my sisters to all sorts of different activities and made us try things. Some I enjoyed; others I hated, but she didn't let autism disconnect me from the world. It was also the 1950s and 1960s, a time when kids got outside and did things and had a lot more physical activity than they do now. Growing up during that era, television was a privilege and viewing time was limited. Popping in a video and watching one-to two-hour movies was not part of my upbringing, nor were endless hours with video games or computers. I think that was good. It forced me to find other things to do, and often these things required me to engage with others, either my sisters or the nanny, or other kids in the neighborhood. Social awareness had lots of natural opportunities to develop under those conditions; there were many daily opportunities to practice.

The "one thing" that was the core of my self-motivation was building things. I've mentioned it often now, and on purpose, as I don't think most neurotypicals understand how much fun building things can be, and how many ways it satisfies innate needs of people with ASD. To the logical, thinking-in-pictures autistic mind, construction (in its many forms, from art to sand castles to sewing) is highly reinforcing. There's a visual, concrete aspect to it that is motivating—you can watch as each part of the project develops, and learn that work = reward. It quenches the need to exert control over the environment and provides a natural opportunity to make our own choices—and visually see how those choices play out. In many cases, we have the ability to recognize and correct mistakes and learn that not every mistake spells disaster. For some kids coming to the realization that making mistakes is okay, or that errors have different levels of importance, is difficult and pervasive and impedes every aspect of their functioning, especially in social situations. That's why we've selected them as two of the Ten Unwritten Rules you'll read about later in the book. Teaching intangible social concepts in concrete ways that are intellectually meaningful to the autism way of thinking spurs successful social interaction. Building things is great practice for developing the skills that permit making more nebulous choices in the social arena later in life. It all starts—literally—with a pile of blocks.

For instance, I made costumes on my little toy sewing machine for our third grade play. I still remember doing that. When I was in fourth grade I wasn't motivated to study, but man, I was certainly motivated to make sets for the school play. And when I was in high school and was having a harder time fitting in, I still was highly motivated to make signs for winter carnival, because people appreciated those signs.

Despite my less-than-stellar motivation to complete my academic work during high school, Mother had certain expectations of me that she clearly conveyed. Slacking off on homework was not one of them. Often she sat down with me and went through my homework. Television was banned until my homework was done. I'm not sure Mother consciously realized the "behavior principles" she was teaching me with, but she certainly had a knack for knowing what would motivate me and what wouldn't.

The most fun times I've had in my adult life have been on some of the construction projects I've worked on, seeing something being built from nothing, watching the progress and seeing the final product. I remember one night I was driving to the airport and came upon a construction roadblock. A crew had been working for almost two years on building big freeway ramps into the airport. This particular night they were going to shut the freeway down at midnight to put up a great big concrete beam. They had five giant cranes there, all these bright lights—man, my construction nerves started tingling. I wanted to stay there and watch them put the beam up; it would have been the highlight of my day.

Think of all the guys in the space shuttle mission control room. Engineers and techie people bursting with enthusiasm over the impending launch. I'll bet there's an ASD guy or two in that group. I remember the Mars rover project and listening to the TV interviews with the engineers. They were so happy about their project—just like a couple of ten-year-olds talking about their model airplane. Find that motivation while your child is young and use it.

2017 REFLECTIONS FROM TEMPLE

Visiting the Jet Propulsion Laboratory and the Mars Rover

In July of 2015 I had a wonderful opportunity to visit NASA and see the Mars Rover. It was really a blast. It was also lots of fun to me to spot all the undiagnosed Aspies who were working on it. We visited the control room where the engineers sat at computers to guide the rocket to Mars. What I noticed was that they liked being individuals and expressing their own style. One of the head controllers had a Mohawk haircut with red streaks, and the head navigator looked like an old hippie with his long grey hair. Seeing these individuals illustrated to me that sometimes people take a winding path toward a career. The navigator majored in theater when he was in college. He then switched to computers and physics. When I visited the Fermilab outside of Chicago, I learned that many of the scientists there became interested in physics because a high school science teacher helped feed their fascination with the subject.

Engineers often have a sense of humor. When the first Rover landed on Mars, it had a sign on it that read JPL (for Jet Propulsion Lab). Since NASA was the funding agency, they wanted their name—not JPL's—shown on the second Rover instead. The engineers followed orders to remove the JPL sign, but the nerds got their revenge by spelling out JPL in Morse code on the wheels. To determine how far the Rover travels, the wheels are designed with holes in Morse code to leave a recognizable mark with each rotation on the dusty Martian surface. If you look at the Rover on Google Images, you can see that the holes form the dots and dashes of Morse code behind it.

Individuals on the spectrum will often be really talented in one area and really bad in another. It is important to develop talents in art, math or music. Talents are also an avenue for social interaction. Other children liked to play with me because I was good at making things; they would overlook some of my other behaviors because of this. Some of the most successful people on the autism/AS spectrum have good careers because their talents were developed. However, talent does need to be balanced with everyday social functioning skills. Future success in life depends on it. I recently heard the story of a middle school boy who excelled in math. His grasp of the subject matter was stunning and his mom was sure he would grow up to become a math wizard. What was unfortunate was that although she regularly supported his math interest, she completely overlooked his basic social functioning skills. This boy couldn't have a basic conversation with another kid outside his area of interest. The mom's response was, "He just doesn't get the social skills. He's not interested in them. We've tried, but he's just not interested. But he's so good in math, I don't push him on that social stuff. His talents will get him by."

Well, my response to that is *"maybe,"* and even if he does become one of the world's best known mathematicians, he still needs to know how to be polite, to act appropriately in public situations, to not be a slob and to handle himself in the world. She'd help her son more by using his interest in math as a motivator for making sure he learns basic social functioning skills. It may be a struggle at first, but it's a necessary struggle that his parents and teachers must engage him in. Without social functioning skills, his future is anything but certain and will more likely be a series of job failures because he can't fit in when it comes to group interaction. People who have heard my presentations or read my books know I'm all for capitalizing on a child's talents, but there has to be a balance of teaching them daily functional social skills, too. Talent isn't enough by itself. One should never attempt to turn an Aspie into a social butterfly, but some basic skills such as manners and politeness are essential.

On the flip side of this issue are the parents and professionals who have blinders on when it comes to social functioning. I have parents approach me all the time after my presentations, all lamenting the same woe: "He'll never be able to find a girlfriend."

"He'll never get married or have a family." Many of these parents have children who are excelling in an academic area that could provide the basis for a successful and rewarding career. However, they're so intent on socializing for socializing's sake that they push the child incessantly over his social development, to the exclusion of focusing on his strengths and making sure he eventually has good career skills. Some of these children just might never develop that strong an emotional connection—yet they may be perfectly happy nonetheless if their innate strengths are supported and developed. Having a boyfriend or girlfriend, getting married, having children are meaningful goals for a large portion of our population—especially for those off the spectrum—but, honestly, there are non-autistic people who choose not to marry or have children, or who get married and have horrible marriages, and I have to ask these parents, "Is this what you want, or what your child wants?" Later in the chapter I distinguish social functioning from emotional relatedness and postulate that this may be an either-or track for some people with ASD; it's an important idea that merits further discussion.

Finding what motivates a child, what makes the hard work worth doing, is largely about being a good detective and really looking at who your child is and what types of things naturally capture his attention. At times this means parents and teachers need to put aside their preconceived notions of what is "meaningful" or "right" in their own minds and really see life through the child's set of interests. Sensory issues can play heavily into this, both as motivators and as roadblocks to motivation. For instance, one girl I read about was always breaking things and her parents came to realize that it was the crashing sounds that were so appealing to her. So they turned that inappropriate behavior into a motivation to support teaching her more appropriate behaviors. They constructed a crash box site and provided her with all sorts of things that she could break in the box. It was used as a reward when she exhibited more socially acceptable behaviors. It satisfied her sensory stimulation needs but at the same time was put to constructive use. As she learned more appropriate behaviors, her need to crash things diminished. Giving her cymbals to crash together may have been an even better alternative. Then she would still get the sound she liked. That's what I'm talking about—instead of judging that breaking things was bad, which of course it is in many situations—her parents turned it into a highly motivating reward to help her learn.

Social skills often have little tangible, concrete reward to the child with ASD that they can directly link to the effort they need to put forth to learn the skill. This is especially true when the child is learning in a rote manner, where the sense of social connectedness is absent. Coupling those nebulous skills with a tangible reward is often a useful, effective strategy in the early stage of developing social skills and social awareness.

Furthermore, parents who start playing detective when the child is very young, discovering what's motivating and using those motivators constructively, provide the repeated opportunities a child with ASD needs to gain a sense of self-directed accomplishment. This becomes critical in the child's ability to "stay the course" when moving into the less-concrete realm of social awareness, and in getting through the difficult-for-everyone years of adolescence. Summing it up is pretty simple: Lack of interest in social situations + low self-motivation = less social development. Substitute high motivation in that equation and the outcome will change, too.

I was very interested in art from a young age. My parents gave me lots of art materials, and I was praised for the art I created. I remember one time I painted a watercolor of a wharf on a beach and Mother had it framed professionally. That was motivating; the recognition I got from friends of Mother's who saw the painting was motivating. But then, I had to sit at the table and have table manners, too. I was not allowed to tear up the living room and if I did, there was no TV that night. She never took away things that fostered my talents such as my paints or sewing machine. Talents can be fragile. I have heard sad stories where a child gave up art or math because it was taken away too often. Take away something that is not talent or career related, such as shoot-'em-up video games or TV.

Qualities like motivation and self-esteem that contribute to social success later in life start in childhood and build, a little bit at a time. It's never too early to start building them in your child.

HIGH SCHOOL: THE WORST YEARS OF MY LIFE

My big problems came in high school. That was my terrible time. Once kids start moving through puberty into adolescence, they are no longer interested in sails and kites and bike races and board games. Attention and interest turns to all things social emotional. For me, that spelled disaster. While I understood how to be polite, and act appropriately in different situations with other kids—that is, my social functioning skills were good—I didn't feel that sense of social bonding that seems to glue kids together in their teens. And, because my peers no longer wanted to do the things that I liked to do, my social circle of friends shrank as those of my peers expanded. I couldn't figure out why I no longer fit in, why I was having a problem with other kids. I had an odd lack of insight that I was different, probably because what I did was more meaningful to me than outward appearance.

While I was interested in cool science projects, the boys and girls around me became engrossed in each other, in dating and movie stars and hair and make-up. The girls would spend hours talking about whether or not a boy's casual comment displayed interest or not—to me those topics were silly and they didn't interest me in the least.

As kids go through adolescence they find comfort in bonding with others who are like themselves. It's part of their normal emotional development as they start to establish their own identity. Noticing who's the same and who's different takes on a new level of importance. If you fit it, life is easy. If you don't, that's when all the teasing and bullying starts. For kids on the spectrum, it can be pure hell. That's why I think it's so important to make sure the basic social functioning skills are in place before then. It's hard enough figuring out the unwritten social rules and the emotions that are often attached to them while keeping a good sense of self-esteem and dealing with all the stress and anxiety. It's one hundred times worse when on top of all that you don't even have basic manners and the ability to act appropriately in public situations.

When I was in high school I was teased all the time. The kids doing the teasing were absolutely not the kids who were interested in horseback riding, electronics club or model rockets—activities I really liked. But there were the "nerdy" kids around who still liked to do those things, so I was friends with them. They didn't tease me because we had things in common. I got teased by the kids who tended to be much more social kids, those whose idea of a good time was just hanging around and talking. It had nothing to do with intelligence—many of the highly social kids were smart, too. It was just a different developmental path we seemed to be on. It's like we were all walking the same road through elementary school (even though we tended to walk in different groups) and then at adolescence we came to an intersection. Some of us turned left—the project-type people whose interest was more on things and facts—while the majority of the kids turned right, onto the Avenue of Social Connection.

As if that wasn't bad enough, transition after elementary school meant contending with a much less "autism-friendly"environment at a big high school. Gone was the structure of one teacher and one main classroom, of orderly, adult-monitored movement from activity to activity. The day became noisy and crowded, having to maneuver among bodies and all sorts of different voices and sounds and smells. From a sensory perspective it was overwhelming and paralyzing on many different levels for me. The teasing was so bad, I became a total goof-off and had behavior problems to contend with. I threw a book at another girl who teased me and got kicked out of the large (four hundred students) private girls' school Mother had enrolled me in. After that, Mother placed me in a special boarding school away from home for gifted, emotionally disturbed children. Remember, this was still 1960—not much was known about autism yet and there certainly weren't teachers trained specifically for this population, as there are today. So options were much more limited. I still spent a lot of time goofing off and not studying until Mr. Carlock, my science teacher, found ways to motivate me again to study. He diverted my fixations into an interest in science and the goal of becoming a scientist. After that I studied because it would enable me to become a real scientist.

My only refuge from the teasing and tormenting was the times when I did things with other kids. My roommate shared my interest in horses, luckily, and we shared that interest in various ways. We had a huge collection of plastic model horses that we would outfit with western parade bridles we made out of shoelaces, with cigarette tin foil glued on for silver mountings. Or we'd ride the real horses together. These are activities we enjoyed and these shared interests were the basis for our friendship. So, I did have friends during high school, but the school day itself—lunchtime, dinnertime, walking between classes—was torture. I didn't really know how to handle the kids' teasing; they'd call me all sorts of names because of the ways I acted, like "Tape Recorder," and I just couldn't handle it. In my childhood Mother or the nanny was around to explain things to me in a way I could understand. However, as

I got older, I was left more to my own devices to figure things out myself. That was hard because the social-emotional encounters of adolescence just didn't make sense. Kids were friendly one day and torturous the next. At one point in school stilts became the craze, and kids were making them out of 2 x 4's. I put my construction skills to work and make a really high pair of stilts and was good at walking on them. The kids thought that was cool, and they didn't tease me while stilt-walking was popular. When the craze ended, so did my acceptance.

The middle and high school environment is much, much more complicated today than it was when I was growing up. Parents are facing challenges that weren't prevalent in my environment back then, like teenage smoking, drinking, sex and drug use. Furthermore, budget cuts are eliminating programs like shop, or drama or music, reducing the options that appeal to kids on the spectrum. What's left? Academic learning within a social environment. I really think that some kids with ASD need to be taken out of this social pressure cooker and allowed to finish up their degree online or within a different environment. A colossal amount of energy is needed just to manage the stress and anxiety that builds up every day in this type of environment; it leaves little left over for academics. And, socializing with teenagers is not a skill I or others will use later in life. I'm not saying everybody with ASD has to be taken out of high school. Actually, I think the lower-functioning kids have an easier time. Their needs are usually more obvious, to both the school (so they receive the services they need) and to other kids (so they understand their challenges). It's easier to control the teasing. The higher-functioning ASD kids, because of their language and often high IQ, are having the most problems. Their challenges are invisible, so teachers are less apt to provide the kind of assistance they need, and peers see them as odd or geeky, not as unaware and uninformed. They don't receive the social skills training they need, so they fall through the cracks. I'm reading more about parents of kids like this who are choosing to home school them for the few years before they graduate, or enroll them in a class at a community college that keeps them motivated enough to get their high school diploma.

The other aspect of high school that really, really bothers me today is that some parents and schools are placing an unbalanced degree of attention on social skills training, to the exclusion of an equal focus on developing career skills. It's great that schools are finally acknowledging the social challenges of people on the autism spectrum, but often the approach is piecemeal and shortsighted. Teaching social functioning skills is important, but as kids enter high school, that emphasis needs to shift to social skills that contribute to success in adult life: how to be an effective member of a study team, time management, dealing with coworker jealousy, selling your talents, the hidden "rules" of the work place, etc. High school is late to be teaching social functioning skills like how to join a conversation, or personal space issues or the importance of good grooming. These really need to be taught at an earlier age so higher-order social skills can be taught during high school. Some of the unwritten social rules we address later in the book can be taught while a child is very young, but then shift in emphasis and tone as the child ages through school and into adult life. Without an understanding of some of these unwritten, pivotal rules, mastery of the more complex, and often more hidden rules of the workplace or of personal relationships will be virtually impossible to comprehend.

COLLEGE AND INTO ADULT LIFE

Gaining social awareness and social understanding is a never-ending journey for all of us who live in contact with others, whether or not we have ASD. Anyone who has browsed the self-help section of a bookstore, read an Ann Landers column, or stumbled onto any of the numerous "etiquette" websites that are now in existence knows what a big business the business of "fitting in" has become. It is no longer clearly defined as it was in the 1950s or '60s. Yet, the desire to belong seems to be innate; to identify with other like-minded people drives us, motivates us. While people with ASD may exhibit this desire to a greater or lesser degree, I do believe they possess it.

As life has become more complex and our social values and morals have loosened, exceptions to the social rules that guide our existence have escalated to the point that it is virtually impossible for any one human being to be cognizant of them all. This idea should be regularly verbalized to people with ASD to alleviate some of the "all or nothing" anxiety they experience when it comes to learning the unwritten social rules. That said, there still exists the unwritten social expectation held by people we encounter, that we exhibit appropriate behaviors—even when we may have no idea of what constitutes "appropriate" anymore. Confusing? Yes. An excuse to put aside the effort it takes to function socially? No. It just means that our social learning never stops.

My exposure to the world of work started at a young age, at thirteen. My very first job was working for a seamstress, hemming dresses and taking garments apart. It was visual, tasks had a clear beginning and ending point, I wasn't pressured and the environment was quiet. Social interaction was limited to small talk and polite conversation, which Mother had taught me. It was a good match for my skills and abilities at that point, and introduced me gradually to the world of work. I could make mistakes and it wouldn't be all that big a deal. While in college, I worked as a summer intern at a research lab and at a school for children with autism and other developmental problems. These jobs taught me responsibility and instilled in me a good work ethic.

My first job out of college was working for the *Arizona Ranchmen* magazine, as a journalist. I worked there part-time for about seven years. Learning the job wasn't difficult: I took notes during a meeting or interview, and wrote up a story. I read back issues of the magazine to get ideas on how to compose an article, what makes it interesting, etc. While it didn't pay a lot, it was a good arena for learning many of the unwritten rules involved with working with other people. And, yes, I made a ton of mistakes. But people were genuinely willing to help me, and guided me along because they recognized my talents.

During this time I also worked for a year and a half for a construction company, designing equipment and handling their advertising. I was responsible for creating all their brochures and making sure articles on their equipment were published in other trade magazines. I became good at both these duties, but in the beginning, they had to really push me to do things. I remember my boss saying to me, "Temple, you pick up the telephone, call that magazine and you get that article in it about the Snake River Project." Of course, I was scared to call up these magazines and made mistakes at first, but I was creative and learned pretty quickly how to do the job.

One of the things I'm realizing today is that very early on, I figured out that certain people could open the door to other job opportunities. And that door led to another, and another, and another. Many people with ASD never seem to grasp this idea; they see only one door if they see any at all. I also realized that I needed to "start at the bottom and work up." That meant doing the things that were delegated to me, even the things I didn't really feel that charged up about doing. Professional respect develops over time and people have to prove themselves in their profession. I quickly learned that I wouldn't keep a job for very long if I refused to do work, or argued with my boss or co-workers over assignments. And for me, keeping my job and doing my best were very strong personal motivators.

Over time I became very good at writing articles and was respected in the field for that. While covering cattle and ranch-related meetings, I'd introduce myself to editors of different magazines and offer to send them articles on research I'd done. I quickly figured out the business-card hunting game and ways that could help get my name around in the field. I started doing a little bit of design work on a freelance basis, and put together a portfolio of my work to show prospective clients. Little by little I built a solid reputation in the field and became more well-known and successful designing livestock systems. It certainly didn't happen overnight.

After I had successfully worked for the magazine for several years, it was sold and I found myself with a new boss. He thought I was weird and was going to fire me. My friend, Susan, the graphic designer at the job, and I made a portfolio of all my articles. The new boss not only didn't fire me, he gave me a raise after he saw the quality of work I had produced on the job.

I cannot emphasize enough the importance of finding and then developing a talent area in children with ASD that can be turned into a viable profession such as drafting, commercial art, custom cabinetwork, fixing cars or computer programming. These efforts provide an opportunity for a person to have an intellectually satisfying career. My life would not be worth living if I did not have intellectually satisfying work. My career is my life. Sometimes professionals working with people with autism become so concerned about the person's social life that developing intellectually satisfying employment skills is neglected.

In my travels to many autism meetings, I have observed that the high-functioning people with ASD who make the best adjustments in life are the ones who have satisfying jobs. A job that uses a person's intellectual abilities is great for improving self-esteem. Conversely, the most unhappy people on the spectrum I have met are those who did not develop a good employable skill or a hobby that they can share with others. With so much of adult life spent in our jobs, it makes sense that people with satisfying jobs will be generally happier and able to respond better to the different situations that arise.

I have met several successful people on the spectrum who program computers. One Aspie computer programmer told me that she was happy because now she is with "her people." At another meeting, I met a father and son. The father had taught his son computer programming, starting when he was in the fourth grade and now he works at a computer company. Many people with ASD are well-suited to this profession because of the way our minds naturally work. Parents and teachers should capitalize on this ability and encourage its development.

Several years ago I visited autism programs in Japan. I met a large number of high-functioning people on the autism spectrum. Every one of them was employed in a good job. One man translated technical and legal documents. Another person was an occupational therapist and there were several computer programmers. One man who was somewhat less high-functioning works as a baker. What I noticed is that the attitude in Japan is to develop skills. These people with autism/AS benefited from that attitude, and would for the rest of their lives.

While developing an inherent skill into an employable position can be work in itself, it is necessary for people with ASD to try hard to do this, and for educators and job coaches to help them through the social aspects of work that are often the roadblocks to success. However, once they succeed, they must be careful to avoid being promoted from a technical position that they can handle well to a management position that they cannot handle. I have heard several sad stories of successful people being promoted out of jobs they were good at. These people had jobs such as architecture drafting, lab technicians, sports writing and computer programming. Once they were required to interact socially as part of their management position, their performance suffered.

Hobbies where people have shared interests are also great for building self-esteem and can often end up becoming financially rewarding. I read about a woman who was unhappy in a dead-end job. Her life turned around when she discovered other people in the world who shared her interest: breeding fancy chickens. Through the internet, she communicates with other chicken breeders. Even though she still works at her dead-end job, because she explored her hobby she is now much happier.

Develop skills in a career that other people value and need, and then become an expert at what you do. I was often the only woman professional working on a cattle project—just me and the guys. They were intimidated at first, but I had developed my talents to the point that they respected the knowledge and expertise I brought to a project. They were willing to overlook minor mannerisms they thought strange because I was so good at what I did. The situation was similar in other jobs I had. You have to become an expert in your field, better than others, to balance out the social difficulties that people around you might notice. A boss might overlook minor social infringements if you're producing better quality work than anyone else on the team. But if you're just doing average work, the social disturbances might be enough to get you fired because there's nothing else to balance them out.

People respect talent and strong talent can open many doors and provide many opportunities. Mentors are valuable in teaching career skills and guiding ASD people in their professional development. I am often asked, "How does one find mentors?" You never know where a mentor may be found. He or she may be standing in the checkout line at the supermarket. I found one of my first meat industry mentors when I met the wife of his insurance agent at a party. She struck up a conversation with me because she saw my hand-embroidered western shirt. I had spent hours embroidering a steer head on the shirt. Post a notice on the bulletin board at the local college in the computer science department. If you see a person with a computer company name badge, approach him or her and show the person work that the person with autism has done.

Since people with ASD are generally inept socially, they have to sell their work or their talents instead of their personality. I learned at an early age the importance of developing a good professional portfolio. At one of my first jobs writing for the *Arizona Farmer Ranchman*, we got a new boss, Jim. He thought I was weird and he was determined to get rid of me. Susan, the nice graphics lady, saw this (even though I had missed the warning signs) and told me to assemble a portfolio of all my articles. Susan helped me save my job. When Jim saw all my good work, he gave me a raise. This is when I learned to sell my work instead of myself. When I showed potential clients my drawings and photos from my jobs, they were impressed. Today a portfolio of work can be easily created electronically on a computer or even on a smart-phone. The portfolio could include photos of artwork, web design, computer programming, pictures of projects, etc. I learned a long time ago that you never know when you may meet the right person who can open a door to a job. When you meet that person, your portfolio should be ready on your phone. Make sure they do not have to scroll through your crazy cat photos first. A portfolio should make a good first impression.

Alongside the process of growing in my professional talents was managing my sensory issues and learning the unwritten rules that are a part of personal and professional relationships. Some of these struggles are addressed in the sections that follow.

Work is more than just a livelihood or a paycheck; it is the key to a satisfying and productive life. For me and many of my spectrum peers, work is the superglue that holds our lives together in an otherwise confusing world. My life is about what I do, and at no time am I happier than when I'm building things. I have friendships that are built on shared interests, that are satisfying and that enrich my life. We talk about autism, cattle, and interesting things happening in the world of science or new insights into the workings of the brain. We talk about our social relationships and brainstorm ways we can solve problems with family, friends or coworkers. We talk about different self-help books or *The Wall Street Journal* columns we read that shed light on social situations and increase our understanding of social relationships. We talk about all sorts of topics, but our conversations always have a purpose and usually take a logical path; we never talk just to talk.

2017 REFLECTIONS FROM TEMPLE

Tips to Help Adults on the Spectrum If They Lose a Job

I have observed two different situations that arise causing people to lose jobs:

1. A young person who has not learned the discipline of work gets fired because he is always late, has poor hygiene or does not finish tasks. This individual doesn't recognize some of the basic social expectations of the workplace. This can be taught, but it will need to be done in a concrete way that is meaningful to the individual.
2. An older person loses a stable job because there is a change in direct management/the person's boss, the business closes or the company gets downsized.

These very different scenarios have to be handled in totally different ways. The first step is to determine why the person was fired. Being late is a common reason. A movie theater manager told me that he loved all the movie knowledge that his usher with autism brought to the job, but he was often an hour late to work. He could not keep an employee who was always late. Being on time was never a problem for me. In the 1950s, all the kids in the neighborhood were taught to be on time, since being on time for school pickup and meals was expected.

Some people annoy co-workers because they nitpick them for disobeying the company rules. I know of two people on the ASD spectrum who were fired from jobs on a construction site for constantly reporting minor safety infractions. There needs to be a clear cut definition of differences between important safety rules that could prevent death or serious injuries and minor bureaucratic rules.

Poor hygiene is another issue that is absolutely not acceptable professionally. Being eccentric and dressing in your own style is fine, but being a slob is never OK. There is a scene in the 2010 HBO movie about me, *Temple Grandin*, in which my boss slams down a can of deodorant on my desk and says, "You stink, use it!" That really happened. At the time, I became very upset when he told me to clean up. Today I thank that boss because conforming to hygiene rules helped me keep my job.

Many individuals with ASD who are living at home need to learn how their food and housing are paid for. In all likelihood, one or both parents have to work. If an adult child is living at home, it needs to be made clear that he needs to contribute to the household expenses. As appropriate, the person needs to be shown ALL the bills that pay for the house, car, and food. There will need to be some requirements applied to motivate the adult child to get to work on time. If the first attempt at holding a job doesn't work out, another approach is to find a different type of job the person may like better. I know a woman who had problems holding more conventional jobs and then she discovered welding. After learning to weld, she got a job through a friend who knew somebody at a construction company. She loves her new job.

It creates a difficult situation when an older person loses a stable job he has had for years. Sometimes focusing on interests outside the work place can help that person find an appropriate new job. Try to find a job where skills used in a hobby might be helpful. Many employers value older employees because they are responsible and dependable. An older colleague of mine got a job at Home Depot when he was between jobs. He is a skilled cabinetmaker, and he wanted to work in the tool section and help customers with their projects. The boss put him in the plant section because he knew that he would be responsible and take better care of the plants. The manager was afraid that a younger person might forget to water the plants. An older employee can be trusted with thousands of dollars worth of fragile plants, which need watering and care. My colleague did not like working in the plant department, but he did it. He knew that it would be a temporary situation and that his boss valued his maturity and dependability.

Romantic relationships have a level of social complexity that I still don't understand today and I consciously choose not to participate in them. My way of thinking and functioning doesn't describe everyone on the autism spectrum, but I think it describes more children and adults than we are acknowledging. I also think it's a way of being that is not yet viewed in a favorable light, especially by people who view the world through a perspective of emotional relatedness.

For some of us with ASD, the emotional-relatedness physical or biochemical circuitry is missing—no matter how hard we try, it's a bridge that may never be built because some of the basic building materials are missing. For others on the spectrum, the building materials that create emotional relatedness are there and it's just a matter of assembling them into a structural whole that forms that bridge. They are different paths, that's all, and people on both paths can lead happy, productive lives. Unfortunately, many people on and off the spectrum still characterize one as inferior, or somehow lacking in options over the other. With this, I disagree. It is a statement that speaks to a lack of understanding of the different way some of our minds work. In some regard, it is more an issue of physiology than psychology, as the next section illustrates.

HOW MY MIND WORKS: DATA ON THE COMPUTER HARD DRIVE MEMORY

Parents, teachers and people with ASD need to always, always, keep in mind that learning never stops, and nowhere is this axiom more applicable than in the realm of social awareness. Trying to teach children the obvious or unspoken rules of social relationships is a long-term project that will span all the years of their lives. It's not a topic that starts at a certain age and then stops; a therapy program that begins and ends. While there are benchmarks along the way that can gauge whether or not learning is taking place, social awareness can't be neatly covered by a single textbook so that when you get to the last page, you can close the book and be "educated." This is a book that has no last page.

My ability to function in the world and develop social relationships has been learned solely through my intellect—by becoming a very good social detective—and use of my visualization skills. After many years I have learned, by rote, how to act in different situations. I can speed-search my picture-memory archives and make a decision quickly. Using my visualization ability, I observe myself from a distance in each situation I encounter. I call this my "little scientist in the corner" and I take note of the relevant details that make up the situation, just like a scientist would observe an experiment. Then all of that data gets put on my "computer hard drive memory" for future reference. Getting the job at the *Arizona Ranchman* magazine was a fantastic experience for me when I was younger. I had repeated opportunities to visit many different places to do stories, and interact with a lot of different people. That put a lot of information on the hard drive; but I didn't start out that way.

When I was young my logical decisions about social situations were often wrong because they were based on insufficient data. That's partly why parents and teachers get the same response from a child in different situations—he only has a small number of visual pictures to recall and associate with any given situation. As the child has more and more experiences, the level of refinement grows and he can make more appropriate responses based on a greater amount of data. Today my responses are much better, because my hard drive contains so much more information that I've amassed through personal experiences, reading books, articles and newspapers, or watching movies and television.

I think one thing that has really helped me is the amount of reading I do. I read extensively, all the time, gathering more information on my hard drive that will help me sort out social situations and be better able to function in my personal and professional life—everything from business to science to articles on relationships and social interaction.

My reading skills were weak until Mother made it a priority to strengthen them when I was in third grade. She taught me to read using phonics and it worked out very well. Other children will learn better with sight words. Use the most effective method that fits the child's learning style. Once I learned to read my interests shot up like a rocket— there was so much fascinating information available to me. By fourth grade I tested at the sixth grade reading level. I did have problems with sequencing ideas, following complex plots with multiple characters is difficult even today, so mystery novels don't hold as much interest for me as do more factual types of reading material.

Neurotypical people have a "social sense" right from the time they're born. Their learning happens through observation, whereas for children and adults with ASD, learning only happens through direct experience. For instance, in the early 1990s, I still didn't understand humor, which made my presentations sometimes flat and monotone. Cattle organizations often invited me to speak because I had excellent slides and visuals. But a "good" presentation takes more than just good slides. Delivery of the information is important, too. To me the logical conclusion was simple: improve my presentation skills. Comments from the evaluation forms that audience members filled out were helpful. I read different articles about public speaking and humor was frequently mentioned, but what people found humorous was nebulous to me. I would add a joke to my lectures. If people laughed, I kept it. If they didn't, I'd remove it and try another. Gradually humor started making more sense to me, and today I have my own file folder of images in my brain that are funny to me. This simple example illustrates how I tackle most social situations. It's very much a scientific approach, based on observation, analysis and conclusions.

I think in pictures; at age fifty-eight my mind is like one giant computer that houses thousands of visual pictures, logically organized in a categorical structure that provides instant retrieval capabilities. When I was younger I had fewer pictures of social experiences, which made socializing more difficult. Socializing became easier as my library of both good and bad social interactions increased. Pictures from memory can then be placed in different categories of different types of social interactions. When a new situation occurs, I can compare it to similar situations from my memory files. A couple of examples of a social category might be "actions that make clients happy" and "actions that make clients mad." A subcategory within the bigger category would be "co-worker jealousy issues" or "how to handle mistakes." I then "look" through the pictures of past experiences to determine which one would be the best template to use in the new situation.

When I think, it's like surfing the Internet in my mind or looking at photos through a viewfinder—one picture after another. It's often difficult for people to understand that there's no word play going on through all of this and no feelings attached to the images—just pictures. I am able to explain my thought processes step-by-step, picture by picture. And, when a situation presents itself that I need to figure out, I do so from a completely logical, non-emotional standpoint. Actually, I think it's much easier to resolve issues that way. A lot of what we do in the world is actually functional, rather than social-emotional, although this analytic approach works well in both realms. I witness many neuro-typical people creating unnecessary stress and anxiety for themselves because of the illogical emotions they attach to situations. I often share my perspective with my non-autistic friends and in many cases, it helps them get through problematic areas of their lives with greater ease.

Here's an example: A friend's mother recently wrote him some really nasty email and we were talking about what his response should be. It was about a family situation and he cared about the outcome, but didn't want to get his life messed up over it, and get drawn into nasty emails going back and forth between them. The first thing I tried to get him to do was to take his emotions out of the situation and look at it logically. Use your cortex, I told him, not your amygdala. (I always accompany that with a little lesson in brain science.) In my mind the picture that came up was crabs in a bucket. The family is like a slew of crabs in a bucket and there's one crab that's starting to climb out, but keeps getting pulled back in. So we talked about that and discussed actions that would push him back down into the bucket and ones that would help him climb out.

Basically that's how I approach most situations in my life: I want to solve the situation rather than get mired down in all the emotional nuances that can never be fully explained—and that often impedes the process. Emotions are hard to figure out; they're not logical. My emotional make-up is simple. Everything I feel falls into one of a few categories: happy, sad, scared or angry. I think part of that is the physical way my brain is built. Other people have more association-circuits in their cortex so they develop highly complex emotional connections. Like women who still love a man who beats them. That's beyond my level of understanding. I can see no reason to remain in that situation except financial necessity. I also think some people get really scared about all sorts of different aspects of life—even of events that have not yet happened and maybe never will. I was never scared like that—it's illogical to me.

Despite the literally millions of social encounters I've had through my life, I'm still discovering new insights into social awareness all the time. I didn't realize that people used eye movements to communicate feelings until I read Simon Baron-Cohen's book, *Mind Blindness*, released in 1997. It wasn't until later in my life that I also learned that for most neurotypical people, information stored in memory has an emotional component; I finally understood why so many people allow emotions to distort facts.

My mind doesn't work that way. I have emotions, and they can be very strong when I'm experiencing them, but emotion is all in the present. Information stored in my memory is done so without the associative emotions. I can recall a time when I got fired from a job. I cried for two days over that, but when I look back on it now, it's just a movie. My mind can always separate information and emotion. Even when I am very upset, I can keep reviewing the facts over and over until I arrive at a logical conclusion, without emotion distorting the facts and interfering with logic.

However, there are certain present-day situations that I can be very emotional over because they are directly tied into my whole sense of being—what I do. When I take out one of my cattle-handling DVDs and hold that little silver disc in my hand, it brings me to tears very easily. Contained on that DVD is all that I am, all my work and all the information I want others to be able to benefit from. None of my DVDs have copy protection on them because I want people to share the information and use it. It's a way for me to live on after I'm gone, for the world to benefit from what I've done. I usually can't even talk about this without getting choked up—there's a strong emotional connection in that regard because it's so representational of my core being.

Even now, some aspects of social functioning remain difficult for me. I try to avoid situations where I can get into trouble because of their social complexity, or I have found ways to compensate for the areas in which I'm weak. I do not have sufficient short-term memory to remember sequences of events. One way I have compensated for this is that I have an accountant. I also have problems with multi-tasking. I can spend five minutes on one task and five minutes on another task, going back and forth like that, but can't juggle multiple tasks at the same time. I have to write a lot of things down that are not visual, creating cheat sheets for myself. Like many people, I couldn't keep my personal and professional commitments straight without a calendar where I can see the entire month. Many people with autism also have physiological problems with attention shifting and find it more difficult to follow rapidly changing, complex social interactions because of their need to move back and forth between auditory and visual comprehension. Even participating in a simple social interaction can be quite tiring, both physically and mentally, because of the tremendous effort required.

Sensory issues must be addressed. Socialization is almost impossible if a person gets overwhelmed with noise that hurts their ears, whether this is on the job or in a restaurant. For some, it may sound like being inside the speaker at a rock concert. Medication saved me when I was in my early thirties. Antidepressants stopped the constant panic attacks I was having and reduced my sound sensitivity. Other individuals with autism are helped by various other sensory interventions such as Irlen colored glasses or auditory training. Special diets, such as gluten and casein-free or Omega-3 supplements help some people. Sometimes the most effective intervention is a combination of a small dose of conventional medication coupled with dietary changes or supplements. I have observed that the most miserable people on the autism/AS spectrum have untreated anxiety, sensory oversensitivity or depression.

Figuring out how to be socially competent is a slow process of continuous improvement. There are no sudden breakthroughs, and there is no single "social skills program" that will make a child become socially aware. It's a team effort and the team changes as children become adults.

However, through it all, the person is the constant. Therefore, it is important that parents and teachers instill three important lessons in the mind of a child with ASD early-on:

1. Social learning never ends, and there are lots of opportunities to practice.
2. Our choices and our behaviors have consequences.
3. Each child is responsible for his own actions.

Without this understanding, as the child grows into an adult, he is apt to feel unable to control his own destiny, to affect his future, powerless over his actions. This fosters a sense of helplessness that drains whatever motivation the person may have to try (or try harder when needed) to be socially engaged. I've witnessed this in many children who don't think social skills are "necessary" and in so many of my peers today who have given up because it takes more effort than they are willing to give. There are other Aspie adults who feel the rest of the world is at fault and that responsibility for their social acceptance lies with everyone else. These are both extreme viewpoints and most of us exist in the middle somewhere. But the important point is that *we are each responsible for our own behaviors.* If our lack of social skills and the resultant behaviors render us unable to live independently, get and keep a job, or contribute to the world in some way, we each are responsible for acquiring new knowledge to change this. Yes, it's much more difficult for us to do so, and that, in itself, causes many an Aspie adult to give up. Level of commitment is a personal choice; choose to stay engaged.

Some of my peers look at me and attribute where I am today to factors outside myself—having had a nanny, going to a private school. They overlook the amount of hard work I had to do to get where I am. Things weren't easy for me, but I stayed involved. It required a constant effort when I was younger and still requires a lot of work today to fit in socially. It all ties into a person's self-esteem, their motivations, and whether or not they have opportunities in their lives to keep learning. Those opportunities are all around us, they are Life, and they have little to do with family income. There's little chance of success in becoming socially aware and learning the unwritten rules of social relationships by sitting in front of a computer day after day and being cut off from the world. People with ASD learn through direct experience. They need to put themselves out in the world and learn by doing.

SOCIAL FUNCTIONING SKILLS VERSUS EMOTIONAL RELATEDNESS

Parents and teachers who are reading this book in hopes of gaining a better understanding of people with ASD, or who are trying to help them with social skills and social understanding should clearly understand the distinction between *social functioning skills and emotional relatedness*. The first is way of *acting*; the second is a way of *feeling*. They are very different from one another, and yet seem to be treated as the same within many of the popular social skills training programs that are developed for people with ASD. They also seem to be lumped together whenever conversation turns to "social skills." This is a disservice to the autistic population and only further complicates for them what is already a complicated realm of understanding. It also muddies the waters in trying to teach social awareness and social competency to a child on the spectrum.

Learning social functioning skills is like learning your role in a play. When I was a little kid, being a child of the '50s, there was a priority placed on manners and etiquette and knowing how to act appropriately in different social settings. Social skills like sharing, turn-taking, playing with other kids—those things were drilled into me by Mother and the governess. She'd take one sled out on the hill and she'd make my sister and I take turns on that sled. Even at a very young age, she was playing Tiddly Winks with us. And if one of us cheated at a board game or tried to move the spinner, there was instant correction. It just wasn't allowed and that was made very, very clear and consistently applied.

I also got plenty of social skills practice at nice Sunday dinners with my grandmother. By the time I was seven and eight, Mother would take me out to good restaurants—very, very good restaurants—and I was expected to behave. It was a treat to eat lobster, or I would get to order my favorite dessert, lime sherbet with raspberry sauce—it motivated me to behave. I was taught to say please and thank you; to not be rude. And it was all done by lots of specific examples and stern and immediate correction. One time my sister and I got to giggling about how fat Aunt Bella was and my mother got on us right away. We were told in a very stern manner that it was just not an acceptable topic to be discussing. They were rules that were drilled into me, and I learned them pretty easily. No emotion was involved.

As I've aged, I've learned to get better and better and better at acting in the play. But it's always a play to me, it's still computer algorithms. It has never miraculously transformed into something else, and as I've lived through more years of my life, I've just accepted that this is the way it is. For instance, I've encountered jealousy among coworkers in many different projects I've worked on. It took me twenty years to figure out how to handle that complex social interaction: pull the person into the project and give him a piece of the action. It works every time. Some parts of the play are harder to learn than others; this one took me lots of years to master.

Emotional relatedness, on the other hand, is all about how people interact emotionally with each other. It is our sense of connection to others, an internal motivation that drives us to form friendships, to identify with other like-minded people, to bond together in relationships, marriage, communities. Emotional relatedness typically involves expressions of affection, outward actions that mirror inner feelings and emotions, consideration of others' points of view—qualities that are often difficult for people with ASD to comprehend. Chapter 3, which discusses in more detail the "autistic way of thinking," sheds light on some of the reasons emotional relatedness seems to be lacking within this population.

A lot of parents ask me, "Does my son love me? Does he feel that for me? Will he miss me when I'm gone?" And, it's really hard to give them an honest answer, because with some kids, they might end up missing their computer more. Mother talks about this in her book, *A Thorn in My Pocket,* and how terrible a thought it is for most parents to even entertain. It's not a statement of the value the child feels for their parent—in many cases it's simply more biology than it is bonding. My brain scan shows that some emotional circuits between the frontal cortex and the amygdala just aren't hooked up—circuits that affect my emotions and are tied into my ability to feel love. I experience the emotion of love, but it's not the same way that most neurotypical people do. Does that mean my love is less valuable than what other people feel?

Brain research is uncovering some interesting findings about the connection between emotions and brain circuitry. It's more physical than we think. An article published this year in the *Journal of Neurophysiology* (see References for citation) described a research study done on the brains of seventeen young men and women who were newly and "madly" in love. The multidisciplinary team found support for their two major predictions: *1)* early stage, intense romantic love is associated with sub cortical reward regions rich with dopamine; and *2)* romantic love engages brain systems associated with motivation to acquire a reward.

Using functional MRI scans, they discovered love-related neurophysiological systems operating in the brain, and postulated that romantic love may have more to do with motivation, reward and "drive" aspects of behavior than it does with emotions or the sex drive. One of the researchers was quoted as saying, "As it turns out, romantic love is probably best characterized as a motivation or goal-oriented state that *leads* to various specific emotions, such as euphoria or anxiety." The researchers also cited their findings as applicable to the autism population:

"Some people with autism don't understand or experience any sort of emotional attachment or romantic love. I would speculate that autism involves an atypical development of the midbrain and basal ganglia reward systems. This makes sense, too, because other symptoms of autism include repetitive thoughts and movements, characteristics of basal ganglia function."

I was one of those people; I never had a crush on a movie star growing up. In high school it was beyond my comprehension why other girls squealed with delight when the Beatles appeared on the Ed Sullivan show. Even today, romantic love is just not part of my life. And you know what? That's okay with me.

Based on lots of observation I've done over the last twenty to thirty years, I'm seeing two different groups of kids with ASD, perhaps resulting from the different ways their brains work, and then lots of kids in the middle. It's actually more like a "social continuum." On the one side are the really smart AS kids, kids who don't have a lot of sensory issues or nervous anxiety. These kids can learn the social play, be taught the social functioning skills without too much trouble. But a lot of them are not emotionally related. I read that MIT—a school traditionally known for the highly skilled technical, engineering-type students who attend and graduate—is offering social skills classes because the students need to be taught these skills alongside the academic classes. Isn't that interesting? You know there's got to be many AS students in that school. But the conclusion I'm drawing is that more than just AS students need social skills training—the neurotypical "techie" students do too. Interestingly, there is a link between autism and engineering. Research by Simon Baron Cohen indicated that there were 2.5 times as many engineers in the family history of people with autism as in their neurotypical counterparts. It makes sense: the really social people are less likely to be interested in building bridges or designing power plants.

Today, teaching manners and etiquette just isn't the priority it used to be when I was growing up. It's an environment that makes growing up more difficult for ASD kids. They come onto the playing field with one strike—a big one—already against them without these skills. The needs of the really high-functioning AS kids, because they're straight-A students, are overlooked. No one even considers that they need services or help in understanding social interactions. Everyone just thinks they're weird and out-of-touch with the rest of the world and that all they need to do is "work harder." So, they never get the help they need to succeed, despite their high academic promise. Right alongside these super-smart AS kids are the really intelligent high-functioning autistic kids. However, these kids have a much higher degree of sensory issues, more anxiety, more physical problems that interfere. There are lots of adult Aspies in the world today who fall into this group. Their sensory problems were never addressed when they were younger, and therefore inhibit them from fitting in socially now. Some sensory overload happens so quickly and is such a constant part of their functioning that working in an office environment is impossible, with telephones ringing, people talking constantly, the fax machine going, the smells of coffee, snacks, people eating lunch at their desks.

The second group is made up of the lower-functioning and the nonverbal kids. From my observation I think a lot of these kids are much more emotionally connected, but they have major interference from all the sensory scrambling going on. When I was young my misbehavior usually happened when I was tired or there was sensory overload. It's like that with this group of kids.

Their sensory issues are acute. They don't learn to talk because what they hear is garbled noise or they can't make out consonant sounds, or their language circuits are disconnected. But they might make lots of eye contact or love to cuddle or have strong emotions, depending on how the circuits are hooked up in their brain. A good program that deals with their sensory sensitivities, that incorporates ABA to help with behaviors and a little floor time to strengthen that emerging emotional relatedness works well with them. Parents and teachers can work with them on developing affection, hugging, emotional regulation, expanding that feeling of connectedness.

The idea of these two groupings is a hypothesis I've formed from observation and talking to tons of parents. For instance, let's use Donna Williams, author of *Somebody Somewhere* and *Nobody Nowhere*, as an example. Donna's right in the middle of the spectrum. She's got very bad sensory scrambling problems— very bad, much worse than mine. And she's much more emotionally related than am I. She's a very social person. As you move toward one end of the autism spectrum, the sensory problems and information distortion gets worse, but the emotional circuitry is more normal. At the other end, intelligence is strong, yet emotional relatedness is weak, or maybe even nonexistent.

Addressing the social education of people with ASD needs to start when they're as young as possible, with parents and educators making the distinction between teaching social functioning skills and emotional relatedness, and realizing that, while both are important, they don't naturally develop simultaneously. Giving kids lots of social exposure is a critical, through natural or contrived social opportunities. In the beginning, social contact may come solely through shared interests. That's okay and should be encouraged. It provides external motivation to stay engaged and learn the skills needed to function among others. The more a child is around other children and adults in a positive, supportive environment, and the more happiness they derive from shared experiences, the more internal motivation develops to continue to interact. That's fertile ground for feelings of emotional relatedness to grow.

As teaching is taking place, parents and teachers can sometimes become so intent on immersing their kids in social situations that they underestimate—or forget about—the impact that sensory issues have in a child's ability to learn social skills and develop social awareness. When sensory and social overlap, social learning won't take place. It can't because the sensory issues are interfering with the child's ability to attend and learn. The anxiety over sensory issues can be acute and can completely fill the child's field of awareness. Nothing else gets through. For instance, for the most part restaurants back in the 1950s were a lot quieter than restaurants are now. It was a tolerable environment and I could concentrate on my social lessons and act appropriately. If I were growing up today, I'd have a lot more problems attending to social skills because my sensory issues would interfere. That's why anyone trying to teach social skills—even basic ones—to a child with ASD needs to first assess the environment from a sensory perspective and eliminate sensory issues that will impede the child's ability to concentrate on the social lesson. Unfortunately, the social-sensory connection is still overlooked in the majority of situations involving children with ASD, and parents and teachers scratch their heads, wondering why the child can't learn basic social skills, or isn't interested in even trying. What do they expect when the child is put into an environment that hurts? Fluorescent lights may be flickering like a disco dance-floor and the sound they make may feel like a dentist drill hitting a nerve. Could you learn under those conditions?

Sometimes the impediment to a child developing social skills lies as much with the perspectives of the adult trying to teach the child as it does with the innate lack of social sense the child brings to the interaction. We each bring to our interactions personal opinions, perspectives and interests. We each have our own definition of what is "important in life," and it acts like a filter through which we see the world. It may be a moment of "A-ha!" awareness for some neurotypical readers that in many cases, the people who are guiding the lives of people with ASD do so through a filter of "emotional relatedness," transferring all the importance they associate with that perspective onto a group of children or adults for whom that perspective may not be equally shared. It's hard for them to see the world through the logical, less-emotion-driven perspective of their child with ASD, and even harder to accept that there are some aspects of autism— especially those that are part of the physical make-up of the brain—that may never change. Admitting that their child may never develop the emotional relatedness of a neurotypical person feels more like failure than it does acknowledging simply "another way of being."

Just recently a teacher was discussing her frustration with not being able to reach one of her AS students and made the comment, "He doesn't seem very emotionally related to me." My response was that he may not be—and may never be—and if she was trying to reach him academically through purely emotional ways, she might never "reach" him at all. I suggested she use his interests in science or some aspect of math or history as a way to relate to him instead. I also asked her to ponder what her definition of "success" was with this child: that she feel liked or that he pass her grade.

I've also had parents say to me, "I don't think my child actually loves me." These same parents seem to overlook the fact that their child excels in an area, or is making straight As, and could have a very good future ahead of him if his interests are channeled in the right direction. However, the parents put all their attention into trying to develop emotional relatedness in their child, resulting in a vicious cycle of effort and failure for them both. I think some of these really smart AS kids lack the capacity to ever "measure up" to the level of social connection their parents want from them. Until parents are willing to see their child as he is—not how they wish he would be—and build from there, the child loses out.

I probably sound like a broken record, but it's worth repeating. On the whole, happy AS people are the ones who have satisfying work in their lives that's connected to an area of strong interest. I realize it's difficult for a lot of parents to understand that their child with ASD may derive greater happiness through work or hobbies than through pure emotional bonding, or that marriage or a family may not be at the top of his list of priorities. It's still happiness, nonetheless.

Since the early 2000s, more and more emphasis has been placed on social skills, without an equal visionary path to developing talents. I recently spoke at a meeting in Wisconsin, where a high percentage of the attendees were educators. Their book table had many good books on ASD, but not one book about how to help students transition out of high school and into college or jobs. I had written a book devoted strictly to careers and talents (*Developing Talents*) that they could have made available! I know they realize that jobs are important—after all, each of them has one—but they don't seem to "get" that kids with ASD need a lot of preparation and training, training that needs to be part of their elementary, middle, and high school education if they're going to have any kind of life after they get out of school. It's too late to be teaching kids basic social functioning skills when they're thirteen or fifteen; that's the time when educators should be ferreting out students' interests and teaching them skills such as working in groups, negotiating a request, multitasking, prioritizing several projects, meeting deadlines, etc. It's as if their vision for the kids stops at age eighteen or twenty-one and they overlook the strategic importance of instilling in students a strong foundation of self-esteem, motivation and critical thinking skills that can lead to a successful career. These qualities are part and parcel of most of the Ten Unwritten Social Rules that affect students' lives.

When you stop to think about it, the school administrators, the guidance counselors, and most of the teachers themselves (except maybe some of the math or science teachers) are all people who work from an emotional-relatedness perspective. They're the "social group" members, who turned right at the fork in the road I mentioned earlier. And yet, these are the people who are making the decisions about the education and training of students with ASD, many of whom need a completely different approach to education and planning for their futures. How many guidance counselors consider *The Wall Street Journal*, or *Forbes*, or any of the corporate-business magazines or newspapers part of their "professional development training" so they can better understand the business world enough to be able to provide the level of guidance our students need? *Psychology Today* is probably higher up their reading list.

Part of this comes from the cultural and social structure of Americans. I can assure you that the emphasis on teaching the high-IQ AS children in China or Japan is much more heavily into areas that will build their career skills and help them become professionally successful than it is on their emotional relatedness. Technical skills are much more highly valued there than they are here in the U.S. I've noticed that parents who are, by nature, more social people seem to have the hardest time understanding their AS child. Mothers who are engineers or computer programmers themselves seem to deal the best with them, probably because their own way of thinking is more closely aligned to their child's. They tend to be very logical and project driven; they innately understand how best to work with AS kids who also share these traits.

It is my opinion that all children and adults—whether or not they have ASD—should be taught social functioning skills and be expected to learn them and use them. These are the mechanics of interaction, the skills we use in daily social situations in all areas of our lives, from home to school to recreation/community settings. Some of the Ten Unwritten Rules that you'll read about later in the book involve some of these social functioning skills. They allow us to blend in with people around us, to move through that all-important "first impression" stage of interaction.

They help us gain acceptance into the "social club." Without these skills, children and adults are immediately, and repeatedly, set apart, and the upward battle to regain acceptance begins. For some, they never catch up; the battle never ends.

Emotional relatedness is an equally important part of a child's social development. But we should not make it an end goal in itself, nor should we lose sight of the child's capacity for emotional relatedness. Make sure a child is taught social functioning skills, and start those early in life. Work with the child on his emotional relatedness, but acknowledge that for some, their capacity may be much more limited than we would like it to be, and *let that be acceptable.*

Mother prepared me to live in the world, but she didn't try to make me into a social being just so I could hang out with other teenagers at the lake, or have pajama parties with other girls. Her eyes were on a bigger prize—giving me the skills and nurturing the talents that would allow me to graduate from school, attend college, find a satisfying job and live independently.

THE WORLD TODAY

I sometimes think about how I would fare if I were a child in today's society. The world is not as structured as it used to be in the 1950s and '60s, where life and social expectations were more clearly defined, people were more respectful of each other, and the overall pace of life was less hurried with much less sensory stimulation. So much of how I turned out today was the result of my upbringing and the environment in which I developed. It naturally supported the ASD child and many undiagnosed mild cases of ASD received enough structure and social lessons that they were able to make it through school, find jobs, and become productive, contributing members of society. Unfortunately, today, that environment has changed, which places an even greater responsibility on parents and educators to artificially create a new environment that meets the needs of children with the social, sensory, language and perception impairments that are characteristic of autism-related disorders.

While affirmative action and special education laws have been instrumental in bringing needed services to people with disabilities, the flip side is that it has also fostered a "handicapped mentality" in some really brilliant people. They feel "entitled" to assistance and are increasingly blaming their success or failure on the world at large, rather than taking personal responsibility for their actions and the consequences of those actions. If we lived in a perfect world, each individual with ASD would receive the support and services needed to be successful. However, our world is far from perfect and we each have to choose if we'll be an active part of it—and do what it takes to survive—or expect someone else to take care of us. Of course, this is an oversimplification of a highly complex situation, but it disturbs me to see so many of my ASD peers growing up with little self-esteem, low motivation and a whole lot of laziness and bitterness. I think people with ASD are more a product of their environment than are neurotypical people. I've always said I could have learned how to be a total criminal just as I learned how to be a good person.

The structure of the era I grew up in, coupled with that of my home environment, instilled within me a sense of doing my best, of right and wrong, and showing concern for people around me. It was a foundation that allowed me to make good choices for myself as I grew up and ventured out in the world as an independent adult. I lived with wholesome family values being stressed by my mother and my friends' mothers, by our neighbors and our teachers. Even the media echoed these values, a sharp contrast to what exists today. Prime time television in the '50s and '60s was Roy Rogers and his code of ethics, *Superman*, *Leave It to Beaver*, and *The Lone Ranger*. Even *Star Trek* offered a code of ethics built on personal responsibility and concern for our fellow man. I really loved the original *Star Trek* series because each show contained an answer to a moral dilemma that was tackled with total logic. Mr. Spock was my favorite character because he was so logical. Everywhere I went, the message was consistent and clear: certain behaviors were socially acceptable and other behaviors were not. Today, children with ASD are growing up watching television shows like *Survivor*, where using tactics like lying, cheating and doing whatever it takes to "win"—whether or not it is ethical or moral—is rewarded with a million dollars.

Gone also is the sense of community that existed in the '50s and '60s. We have slowly become more and more a "me-me-me" society, with fewer people willing to reach out and help their fellow man, to do charitable acts, to value the idea of becoming gainfully employed or giving something back to the world. Families are separated and scattered all across the country, which removes the opportunities for a child to develop a feeling of belonging to a group in its most basic expression. Even the idea of a family dinner has been lost amidst the growing demands placed upon us. How can we expect children with ASD, who need so much more practice in sensory-acceptable environments, to develop the basic social skills to survive when more and more social opportunities are being taken away?

Home life today is hectic, often stress-laden for everyone, and filled with more opportunities for confusion than for clear learning. Children spend hours in solitary activities such as watching movies, rather than being engaged in conversation and learning activities with other children. Children with ASD need live interaction in order for social skills to become "hard-wired" in their brains. They learn by *doing*, through direct experience, much more than they learn by watching and listening.

So many teachers tell me that their students with ASD can't function as part of a group in class; it's a common observation and one that does not bode well in terms of success in college or employment. Or, the children are so filled with fear that it immobilizes them. I was fully autistic as a young child; I didn't start out as a high-functioning child. New situations scared me, as they do many children with ASD. But my mother pushed me into new situations; she had a good sense of how hard she could push me, and she'd make me do things that were uncomfortable. She'd send me on an errand to the lumberyard by myself. She also made me go visit Aunt Ann's ranch even though I was scared to go. After I got there, I loved it. I learned about taking risks, making mistakes, my own capabilities. These were all valuable skills as I was growing up. Even though they caused anxiety, I learned that sometimes I had to do new things that made me scared. And I did.

For various reasons, stemming from cultural inclinations to lack of awareness, adults too quickly make allowances for people with ASD and let inappropriate behaviors slide. They require less from them, probably because they believe they are capable of less. Only a small percentage of people with ASD have jobs today. When I spoke at an Asperger conference in Japan, every single one of the AS adults at the conference had a job. And you know, they were halfway decent jobs. In my meat packing work I see many undiagnosed Aspies who are my age, with good jobs such as a plant engineer. They learned enough social rules to get by. It bothers me greatly to see a sixteen-year-old who is similar to that engineer headed down the wrong path because he was not taught manners as a child.

Low expectations are dangerous for people with ASD. Without raising the bar higher and higher, we arbitrarily cap their potential and rob ourselves of the chance to learn what they are actually capable of learning and doing. I recently attended a school talent show being put on by teenagers with ASD, and was appalled by the way these student performers were dressed: sloppy jeans and t-shirts, unkempt hair, some looked like they hadn't had a shower in days. How will these teenagers learn to dress appropriately for work, or a job interview if we do not hold them to a higher standard in situations like this talent show?

I am quick to pull other Aspies aside in social situations where they look like slobs or have bad grooming habits, and tell them to get control of how they look. Granted, sensory issues can impact this, but there are so many different options available now, from softer fabrics for clothes to unscented hair and bath products, that there is no longer an excuse for not looking your best when in public. Having a personal dress style that is different is acceptable; being dirty or smelly or unkempt is not. It's just that simple. I was very angry when one of my bosses walked into my office and put a bottle of Arid deodorant on my desk and told me I'd better wear it if I wanted to keep my job. But now I thank him for it. Yet we are increasingly willing to make excuses for the socially unacceptable behaviors of people with ASD. No matter how grungy or uncooperative they become, there are people who tout that "true acceptance" means letting them live in whatever way they choose. I think this is hogwash. We need to give them the services they need, but within an environment of high expectations and a real belief in their capacities to succeed.

My life story seems to provide education about people with ASD to some people and for others, I hear that it gives them a sense of hope for their own child's future. While people with ASD are similar in many ways, we each bring to the equation a unique personality that contributes as much to our development as do the characteristics of autism we manifest. In relating my personal story, it is my hope that readers take stock of the factors that contributed to my social abilities: my upbringing, the era in which I grew from young child to young adult, and the different "parts" of my personal make-up that helped me become the adult I am today.

The one point I want to emphasize is that people with ASD are more than the sum of their parts. We are not assembled into a whole in such a way that each part can be singled out and "fixed." We are not people made of Lego blocks that can be taken apart and put back together in a different fashion so that autism is no longer part of the puzzle. Our autism is not distinct from our being; it is infused in us down to our cellular core. It is like a color or flavoring interwoven into our make-up.

I notice a lot of professionals whose approach to treatment starts from this compartmentalized viewpoint. He needs speech therapy for his verbal deficits, ABA for his behavior problems, enroll him in a social skills class so he learns to play with other children. The unspoken assumption is that through some miracle all these lessons and interventions will effortlessly gel together and make sense to the child. This is especially true in the realm of social skills and social awareness. Meeting the individualized needs of a child is necessary and should not be overlooked. However, attending to the parts, without respect for the interrelationship of the parts to the whole, dilutes our efforts to help the person with ASD understand his own relationship to the world. While we each are individuals, our goal is to work in concert with the rest of the people around us.

Parents of children with ASD have always been concerned about creating the best environment within which their child can learn and grow. It would behoove us to consider that the environment we create outside of our children is the world we foster within them. In that regard, what we see is really what we get. Let's see our world, and our children, differently.

2017 REFLECTIONS FROM TEMPLE

Aging with Autism

In my work designing livestock equipment, I have worked with at least six people who were likely an undiagnosed individual on the autism spectrum. They were designers, construction people, metal fabricators or plant engineers. Figuring out how to build stuff was so much fun. This was our social life. Today, twenty years later, where are these people? Two of them still own successful businesses, a third one is still employed as an engineer with the same company and a fourth switched from construction to counseling. There are two others I have lost track of: one was fired from a successful long-term job after he was transferred to a new city with a different boss, and I have no knowledge about where the sixth one is. All of these people are from my generation and they are either past retirement age or will be approaching retirement age.

Some older people with autism are having a really hard time. Some of them have criticized me because I emphasize the positive aspects of autism and do not discuss the negatives. One of the reasons I do this is because I want to motivate students with ASD or other learning challenges to be successful. The day before writing this section, I talked to a middle school student who was doing a school project on autism. She repeatedly asked me questions about how people perceive autism, and I told her that many famous scientists and musicians were probably on the spectrum. There is no way I am willing to tell a thirteen- or fourteen-year-old child negative points about autism. My public face must be positive.

Helping Older People on the Autism Spectrum Feel Fulfilled

I have talked to several people with ASD who lost a place to live when their parents died. They were totally depressed and had a negative outlook on life. Several older people who have contacted me had advanced academic degrees, and they were not able to get a job in their field of study. When I suggested that they engage in volunteer work or tutor students, I received a hundred reasons why they could not do it. Some of these people have found support in online communities where they can talk to each other. It is good that they can find others to communicate with, but they also need to be in contact with people who can view the world more positively.

There are some older people on the spectrum who have retired from good careers and have gone into fulfilling second careers. One of them was an engineer who became a counselor for college students. He decided to do this after he was diagnosed with autism later in life. He told me that the diagnosis gave him relief. In my book, Different Not Less, I relate the stories of older, successfully employed people who were diagnosed later in life. A diagnosis gave them insight into their problems with marriages and relationships. One admitted that, if he had been diagnosed earlier, he might have been less likely to work hard in his career. Autism could not be used as an excuse when he started his career. Later in life, after a career was established, the diagnosis helped these individuals understand other people.

The best way I can think of to help a person who harbors negative feelings about autism is to get them started on doing something that gives them a sense of purpose. Having a sense of purpose is very important to me. My sense of purpose improves when a project is successful or one of my students is doing well in his or her career. Dr. Jim Ball, a certified behavior analyst who has a nationwide consulting business working with individuals with ASD, told me about a case in which he was able to help an older non-verbal individual with autism, who was in an institution, have a better life. He taught him how to make coffee and got him a job making the coffee in a convenience store. Performing tasks that others appreciated gave this individual a sense of purpose. When he retired from the convenience store, he made coffee and served it at the retirement home. He is a person who will always have to live in a supervised living situation, but now his life has purpose. Other people appreciated the good coffee he made.

Kids on the ASD Spectrum Must Stretch

For kids on the spectrum to grow up with the skills they need to succeed, they MUST stretch themselves just outside their comfort zone. Since writing the first edition of this book, I have observed that it is increasingly important to give them CHOICES of activities to stretch their mental processing. The choice could include Boy Scouts or karate, robotics, a maker club with 3D printers, or theater or music. To use a visual analogy: you wouldn't throw them into the deep end of the pool, but they have to venture toward that deep end gradually. To develop, they must stretch in various ways: how they think, how they interpret the world around them, how they handle new situations, changes in routine, etc.

Within the last five years, I am seeing more and more kids who are being overprotected by their parents. Kids who are perfectly capable are not provided with enough opportunities to learn living skills such as creating shopping budgets and cooking. Recently I met a fully verbal, smart 13-year-old who had never gone into a store by himself to buy something and then pay for it at the cashier. When I told his mother that he had to learn these skills, she started crying. She said she could not let go. Over and over I have seen this pattern of parents sheltering kids and doing tasks for them.

The 2013 revisions of the DSM-5 have caused many problems. According to the older guideline, a child is labeled as having autism only if an obvious speech delay is present. The child would be labeled as having Asperger's if he/she was socially awkward with no speech delay and either normal or possibly above-normal intelligence. In the 2013 revisions, the Asperger's label was removed. This has created a huge spectrum ranging from a child who could be working for Google to a child who cannot dress himself. Parents and teachers tend to over generalize, and they often do not see the huge differences between individuals on the ASD spectrum. Based on my talks with many parents and teachers, I estimate that 50% to 60% of the children who are diagnosed with autism are fully verbal by age 6. They are usually capable of performing work on par with their peers in at least one subject at school. Part of the increase in kids labeled with autism over the last 5 years or so is due to the increased detection we have today. I went to school and college with students who were socially awkward, and today I'm certain they would be labeled as ASD. All of my socially awkward school friends have gotten and kept good jobs. Many parents have told me that, after their child was diagnosed, they have learned that they also had mild autism. These parents all had good jobs because they were taught both social and working/life skills. Other labels that share many characteristics with autism or Asperger's are specific learning disorders, ADHD and sensory processing problems.

Learning Work Skills

Kids with ASD need to learn work and life skills. Learning the skills necessary to function within a work environment BEFORE graduating from high school makes the transition to the work force much easier. It is never too late to start. An adult who is not working can be gradually weaned off video games, movie watching, or other reclusive activities.

Work skill training can start with kids doing chores at home. During middle school, they can start doing tasks on a schedule OUTSIDE the home. They could walk the neighbor's dogs or volunteer at a church or community center. As soon as they reach the legal working age of 14 to 16, depending on your state, they should get a job. A position within a company that has some direct contact with the public is a good starting point. They need somebody to teach them the many social skills involved in knowing how to approach customers, converse with them, offer assistance, and meet the customer's needs. Before I graduated from high school, I had lots of work experiences, such as sewing for a seamstress, cleaning horse stalls, engaging in carpentry and helping Aunt Ann on her ranch. She had guests, and I had to wait on the children's table. All of these activities taught me the discipline and responsibility of having a job. I was proud and had self-esteem, because I managed the horse barn and cleaned eight stalls every day.

I have given talks at many large tech companies, such as Google, Microsoft, SAS and NASA. These places are full of people on the ASD spectrum. At Colorado State University, where I teach, the incoming honors freshmen read *Thinking in Pictures*. About 75% of the honors students were in a STEM (Science, Technology, Engineering, Math) field such as computer science, and it is likely that a high percentage of them were on the ASD spectrum. Some of these kids wind up in college and some don't. For instance, one day I talked to our honors students, and the next day I saw a kid with similar intelligence/functioning capabilities at an autism meeting who was being overprotected and was not learning basic skills. This overprotection of kids with social and processing challenges creates a handicapped mentality. They are often much more capable—provided good instruction is given to them—than many adults assume.

Video Games Must be Limited

During the ten years since I wrote my sections for this book, I have observed increasing problems with excessive use of video games. A child or adult who spends hours each day playing video games is not going to learn new social or life skills. In the 1950s when I was a child, TV watching was limited to one hour per day during the weekdays and two hours a day on the weekends. The same rule MUST apply to video games. When video game playing is not controlled, I have moms tell me that they cannot get their 18-year-old child to leave his or her bedroom. If an older person is playing hours of video games, they have to be slowly weaned off. Video games MUST be gradually replaced with other activities such as learning coding or fixing cars.

In our book, *The Loving Push*, Debra Moore and I discuss problems with video game addiction among ASD youth. The results of scientific studies are ugly: Some individuals with ASD can get so obsessed with video games that they shut out other activities. Too many smart talented individuals are playing video games while living on Social Security instead of getting a good job with a tech company. Some people will call me old fashioned for being so critical of these habits, but if these video game players got good jobs, I would not be so critical.

A DIFFERENT PERSPECTIVE ON SOCIAL AWARENESS

by SEAN BARRON

O n June 2, 1975, I was very angry. The bottom of my stomach felt as if I had swallowed a dumbbell: I spent much of my childhood and teenage years dealing with that emotion and getting to know it intimately. That day stands out because of how vividly I remember sitting in seventh-grade study hall with an ugly scowl on my face—perhaps looking to any observer like I was ready to kill someone.

Killing a person wasn't on my mind, however, but had it been possible, I would have liked to inflict serious damage on the situation that I found so infuriating, to alleviate the anger directed at one of my teachers.

Miss Jillian (a pseudonym) was monitoring the study hall group that period in Boardman Glenwood Middle School's cafeteria, and I purposely faced her with my menacing look— designed for her to see— without looking directly at her. After she slowly walked toward where I was sitting, she said, "Sean, you look mad at the world."

I responded by not responding; rather, I kept the expression on my face the same and refused to meet her eyes, hoping she would get the message. Instead, she gave up and moved to another part of the cafeteria, which only increased my fury. She obviously doesn't give a damn about me, I reasoned, or she would have tried to find out why I felt this way. Since she's the object of my wrath, it's her responsibility to do her part to make the situation better, I now realize I was thinking.

It was close to the end of seventh grade for me and Miss Jillian had been my science teacher that year. She was a young and energetic woman in her late twenties or early thirties with dark, shoulder-length hair and a wide smile, and this was her first year of teaching at the school. The pert instructor had a loud, booming voice that grew even louder when she lost her cool. This usually was when she found she was competing with the voices of several disruptive pupils, something that happened almost daily because Miss Jillian had difficulty controlling her classroom. Nevertheless, none of this did anything to diminish how incredibly attracted I was to her; I spent the bulk of the school year with a crush on her. Every day I could feel the rush of excitement inside building to a fever pitch as the final period approached, and I couldn't wait for the final bell to ring. At the end of the school day, while the other pupils were rushing through the halls to get to their bus, I was scrambling through the same halls to reach Room 114, where she and I would have time alone. Excitement and euphoria quickly turned to resentment, though, when I would arrive outside her door only to find one or two other pupils inside talking to her. How dare they have the audacity to keep Miss Jillian from me, I thought, but more troubling was the faint but growing feeling that if she truly cared about me, she wouldn't have allowed them into her room during "our time" in the first place.

Harboring such intense feelings and keeping them secret from everyone turned out to be monumental tasks. I don't know which was more difficult: working so hard to ensure no one found out how I felt, or going through life sensing that my feelings were not mutual without understanding why. Perhaps not surprisingly, I spent many weekends and holidays quite maudlin and depressed, since those times represented long stretches away from her. Such time blocks were trying and pressure-filled for me because I had no way to channel or get rid of depression and anxiety that were often palpable without opening myself up to a new set of problems.

My world came crashing down on this lovely June day—it did that a lot, and I guess I took the cliché "Taking on the weight of the world" to new heights (and weights). I learned that Miss Jillian was going to be getting married the following summer. Without understanding the specific reasons, I knew there was something wrong with being in love with a woman who was going to be marrying someone else. On some primitive level I realized that she would never return my feelings. I viewed Miss Jillian's getting married as an indignation and personal affront. To my mind, announcing she was going to be walking down the aisle with somebody else and her rejecting me outright meant the same thing.

I quickly concocted a plan to avenge the "wrong" she had done to me. I was going to "undo" my feelings (although I had no idea how one just suddenly stops having a crush on someone) by ignoring her as much as possible and denying her existence. And I would carry through with that strategy if she returned the following year as Mrs. Robinson. It wasn't that I didn't want to have contact with Miss Jillian or have her see me. Quite the contrary: in a perverse way, I wanted to cross paths with her so there would be as many opportunities as possible to get back at her. My unrelenting anger needed expression and at that stage in my life I could figure out no other outlet. I didn't know how to attach words to my complicated emotions, let alone articulate a narrative to my parents or others that would be effective in getting at the root of my anger, fear and isolation. Besides, to admit such feelings in this case would force me to reveal my closely guarded secret and face what I thought would be tremendous shame and embarrassment—not a worthwhile trade-off, in my estimation.

Undoubtedly I remember the precise day and time all of this played out because it was a turning point in my life. Many of us have defining moments in our lives that seemed insignificant at the time. Most of the time, I don't remember a given event or situation that triggers anger, fear, uncertainty or any other negative emotion partly because I don't experience those feelings too often anymore, but also because I've developed ways to diffuse those situations, something that took me years to master. But in June 1975, I had no perspective as I watched nearly everything I had invested my emotional energy in evaporate with a single announcement before the class.

IN THE BEGINNING

About ten years before I sat sulking in that study hall, my parents sat in a doctor's office forty-five miles away and listened as they were told that their three-year-old son had been born with autism. Mom and Dad had never heard of the condition before and the Akron doctor's lack of reassurance, compassion or empathy did little to help matters. He viewed the condition and diagnosis as tragic events and said that my ending up in some institution was not only likely, but inevitable. Autism was a hopeless situation, something to which mental retardation would have been preferable, he told my stunned parents.

Fortunately, my folks refused to swallow his grim prediction. Mom and Dad vowed to work through whatever challenges my condition presented and would use whatever reasonable means they could to break through my odd and unusually repetitive behaviors, lack of responses and general unhappiness. Looking back now, I am convinced that without their single-minded devotion to a path that was fraught with challenges unimagined at that moment, I would neither be sitting here today writing this book nor have the emotional depth of experiences to feel the gratitude I do to them.

My autism brought me much misery and unhappiness, and in essence robbed me of a childhood. I was born with a pervasive fear that never seemed to diminish, so I spent most of my earliest years devising ways to lessen the unrelenting terror, if not get rid of the chronic dread completely. To that end, I tried to find ways to look at and take in the world that would make sense to me and be less overwhelming while at the same time, provide a measure of comfort, control, balance and security—all of which were missing from my life. Isolating and manipulating objects while tuning out people; fixating on repetitive motions; asking the same questions over and over; developing stereotypical movements, arbitrary rules and rigid thinking; and focusing to an extreme degree on one item or event to the exclusion of everything else were among the ways I found some control and security, while temporarily sidestepping my fears.

As I got older, however, it became apparent that I would get little mileage out of using these methods. As I learned shortly after starting school and having a frame of reference by which to compare myself to other kids, I not only was different from my peers in negative ways, but I was also the perfect target for ridicule. Many of those who did not make life harder for me chose instead to avoid me as though I was a leper.

Despite the many language, social, perception, perspective, psychological and other problems my autism created, I was able to maintain decent grades throughout my school years. I consistently held between a B and C average. I think part of the reason was because I compensated for areas in which I was lacking, which seemed to be everywhere—something I would do a lot later on as I fought my way out of my shell.

Memorizing dates, making up math problems and solving them, pointing a telescope toward the heavens and declaring that I saw Saturn's rings (when I thought no one else at Boardman High School could say that) were some of the things that allowed me to feel empowered over my tormentors.

Still, these activities did nothing to help me learn about relationships with people.

It took a 2,500-mile move to California at age sixteen, as well as many years' worth of trials, setbacks, triumphs, gains, pain, heartache, hard work, determination and practice, for me to gain the upper hand on my autism.

I am convinced that the groundwork for my emergence was laid back in 1965—the same year I was diagnosed and my parents were told that a mental institution awaited me—when my mother and father refused to accept the doctor's terrible prediction. They worked hard to reach me through the hazy, fuzzy world I lived in and to make the "impossible" possible. And I give my family as much credit as I give myself for creating the conditions that allowed me to come out.

FEAR, FEAR AND MORE FEAR

Even from a young age I remember wanting desperately to win a revered place in others' hearts, a desire largely incompatible with having heavy fear in my own heart. This Catch-22 of social functioning caused a circular chain of events to unfold as years went by, starting as early as age five.

I entered nursery school with feelings of intense fear, far beyond the typical separation anxiety my peers felt. I was afraid much of the time in school because of the different environment, the many challenges school represented and an overall fear of the unknown. The fear prevented me from being able to fit in and keep up with many classroom activities.

I remember a teacher's aide in Mrs. Kreidler's nursery school room, who assigned an art project that was unlike anything I had ever done. Part of the activity required us to use a pair of blunt scissors to cut out whatever we drew on the paper. Before that day, I had never used a pair of scissors, and I was almost physically sick at being in a situation that required me to do so. I had no idea how to correctly handle and hold them, let alone cut with them. The aide must have thought I was being stubborn, and challenging her authority, because she yelled at me for not being able to cut out whatever I had drawn. I also recall the other kids' silence as she made clear her scorn.

I think even as early as nursery school, other children sensed there was something different about me, something odd they couldn't put their collective finger on. Since my class was quite small, my reputation spread quickly and cast me in a negative light in their eyes.

My inability to correctly use a pair of scissors and the aftermath that followed were fleeting, and the kids in my class and the woman who reprimanded me probably forgot about the entire episode by the next day. What was not so quick to be resolved, and what haunted me far longer than a knack for cutting on the lines was how to make them my friends.

I spent most of my first five years pretty much living in a vacuum of my devising. I did many repetitive, stereotypical and often destructive and antisocial behaviors because I sought to find relief and security from the constant fear I felt. It wasn't the kind of fear that is situational and that all children experience. Instead, it was constant, nagging and persistent—and it hung over and around me like smog. I developed a tunnel-vision approach toward processing information. Allowing in only tiny tidbits of information was the one way I knew to make some sense of my environment. It was so much easier for me to fixate on an individual carpet fiber, even if it meant missing everything else going on around me, simply because such an activity made my world seem less overwhelming.

The problem with going through my early years like this was that I was missing experiences that I needed in order to develop the social skills I so desperately wanted. I became so engrossed in detail that I missed the larger picture that gave detail its context. Time marched on and, like the soldier who unquestioningly follows orders, so did my way of functioning, from nursery school right into the elementary classroom.

As I began to discover, my deficiencies extended far beyond an inability to cut out a piece of paper and make shapes. It began to dawn on me that I had no idea how to relate to the other kids in basic ways. I didn't know how to say hello. I preferred to be left alone in school, and my aloofness must have been apparent to the other kids. After all, I had spent most of my early life fixated on things like the spinning motions of a washing machine and a toy top, following with my eyes where telephone wires went, tossing things up into the backyard tree and intensely watching their trajectory and a host of other solitary actions. All this left me with little interest in playing with the other neighborhood kids at or near my age, so I certainly didn't come to school magically transformed with the ability to socialize with kids I had never seen before. It didn't take long for me to realize that a virtual Grand Canyon separated me from everyone else.

First and second grade are punctuated by memories that most children would prefer to forget. I was a challenge and discipline problem for my teachers both years. The larger classroom space, longer school day and many more children bouncing about was overwhelming from the start. Each day was filled with fear and anxiety, as though I was a caged tiger on display at the zoo.

I had no concept of context, and this was the late 1960s and early '70s, a time when little was known about autism. The emphasis—especially in Miss Johnson's second-grade room— was on conformity and following the rules. You didn't speak unless called on; you followed the instructions the way you were told to; you did everything in an orderly fashion. She ran a well controlled classroom and had certainly established reasonable expectations, except that I didn't yet know how to conform, and the comfort that resulted from predictability had not yet taken effect.

Not surprisingly, I was reprimanded a lot by my first and second-grade teachers. Both probably thought I was testing their patience, but neither could make the distinction between willful misbehavior and my inability to follow directions. Exacerbating this situation was the fact that I had great difficulty concentrating for any length of time and found it excruciating to sit for long periods.

The antidote to my problem was perched on a wall in the back of the room. For much of the 1969-70 school year, I must have carried with me pencils that were sharper than Einstein because I spent an inordinate amount of time using the manual pencil sharpener. This behavior was a major source of irritation to Miss Johnson and was perceived by her as a violation of classroom rules. But from my socially-limited, perfectly self-relevant perspective, getting up to sharpen already pointed pencils gave me a break from endless sitting and focus and allowed me to derive comfort by engaging in, and being mesmerized by, the repetitive, slow-spinning movement required to turn the crank. To this day, I have the report card Miss Johnson gave out in the middle of the year on which are inscribed the words, "He needs constant supervision."

UNHAPPINESS AND TURMOIL

In addition to my constant fear, I felt deeply unhappy as well. I rarely smiled and almost never laughed unless I did something that fed into my need for stimulation. One effect of my negative emotions was that I hated to see the other students enjoying themselves.

A girl in my class, Denise, appeared to be me in reverse—she was as happy and full of life as I was miserable. Every time she laughed aloud in class I resented her a little more. So I found a way to punish her. When the teacher returned our math work, she marked off points for the problems we'd missed with an "x." I began to use her method—I made an "x" on a piece of paper every time Denise laughed, adding up the total each day. It was my way of subtracting something from her for having the nerve to express feelings I thought I would never have.

Besides being trapped in my dark and gloomy world, my odd behavior built a reputation that would haunt me for years to come. The other kids couldn't help but notice how strange I was. I rarely interacted with other people. The few times I played with anyone during recess, I tried to engage them in a game I'd devised that incorporated my own rules and fixations. I became the kid to make fun of and, since most of my classmates accompanied me through middle and high school, they acquired more sophisticated ways of tormenting me as we all grew older.

For some reason, parts of the school experience suddenly "clicked" by the time I entered the third grade. I was finally able to understand the concept that home and school were two different environments and that some behaviors were acceptable in one place and not in the other. And by that time, I had a fairly good handle on what to expect in school, so the most obvious transitions, like being in the same room Monday through Friday, began to jell. This new understanding allowed me to function in third grade so I was no longer a discipline problem. I did my best to keep my compulsions and repetitive desires under control. I had little difficulty following instructions and completing the math, English and other subject lessons. I didn't flourish, however, on the social front. I could still see the Grand Canyon from Ohio.

I was now starting to feel much more comfortable in the classroom than at home. I was settling in and finding the school day's structure to be exactly what I needed. Like many children with autism, I did much better in a highly structured environment. During all four years of elementary school, I had one teacher per grade. Also, the arithmetic, reading and other lessons happened at the same time each day, as did lunch and recess. Even the lessons themselves—such as the programmed reading materials in which we read a story and filled in the answers to the questions on a plastic fold to the right of the passage—were highly structured and concrete. I functioned well and was able to complete most lessons successfully because they were set up the same every day.

The situation at home, though, was far different. My parents were having tremendous difficulty understanding what was going on with me and, despite their best efforts, had little success breaking through my compulsions, robot-like behavior, anger, and arbitrary, self-created rules. They couldn't get me to communicate in any way besides those that were repetitive, and I was almost always unhappy. Despite having moved into a larger home a few years earlier, and into a neighborhood with more kids my age, I had little desire to be with them. I still had few social skills, so most of the time I played with them only after being forced to; otherwise, I would have been content to spend the time alone in my bedroom.

Meanwhile, at school, the chasm between academic and social success was widening. By third and fourth grade, bonds between various kids had been formed. However, I found myself being left out and the older I became, the odder I seemed to others. I talked to myself. I satisfied a need for stimulation by twirling the front of my hair as tightly as possible around my index finger. I made strange humming noises. I spent some of the outdoor time during the spring and fall harassing honeybees by kicking and swatting at them and making odd sounds as I did. In the cafeteria I could be seen picking apart my sandwich, eating one ingredient at a time. My appearance was, to say the least, out of step with what the other kids were used to seeing. Sometimes my hair was unkempt and stuck straight up, especially after twirling it (imagine a clumsy, uncoordinated and too-tall Alfalfa). More often than not, my shirt was buttoned wrong, or I would emerge from the restroom with my pants still unzipped. I hated pairs of pants that created too much pressure around my waist, so I often wore pairs that, if accompanied with a belt, would have fit. Instead, I would refuse to put on the belt and would venture off to school in pants that were too loose.

No matter how you look at it, neither my behaviors nor my appearance endeared me to my peers. Instead, they further isolated me and gave certain kids more ammunition to use against me, increasing my stress, anxiety and embarrassment. As a result, I retreated inward and this only isolated me still further. I felt like a freak of nature.

RULES AND RIGID THINKING

From grade school to high school, I was trapped on this merry-go-round. As I got older and my reputation grew and spread, the merry-go-round spun faster and faster. Each time I attended a different school, the pool of prospective tormentors grew, and by high school, it seemed everyone was privy to the "accepted" knowledge that I was a person to be singled out for persecution. Getting decent grades through the school years and knowing that I was "making it through" each year wasn't enough emotional armor to make me immune to my peers' tormenting. Although I was able to follow the classroom and school rules, complete the work and study for tests, I remained woefully, socially inept.

Sometimes I added to my own misery by teasing a few kids in various ways. This wasn't so much because of a desire to deliberately hurt them—even though that was clearly the result—as it was a way to reinforce my insatiable need for predictability. I needed to see for myself over and over again that if I sneaked up and flicked the ear of a certain child, repeated the same phrase each time I saw a particular person, etc., that the response would be the same every time. If I got a different response, or if the person ignored me, that just intensified my need to keep at it until the child gave me what I needed.

Of course, none of this justified what I was doing, nor did it make me any friends. It had the chilling effect of further widening the social gap between me and nearly everyone else in my grade, as well as confirming for my "enemies" that their treatment of me was okay—as if they needed further confirmation.

My middle school debut, like that of my nursery school year, got off to a rocky start. I began the fifth-grade year in November 1972, two months later than everyone else. I had just left Beechbrook, a residential treatment facility near Cleveland for children with severe problems, which had been my home during the weekdays for nine months. My parents sent me there because they had run out of ways to deal with my increasingly aberrant, destructive and negative behavior. They thought it would provide help for me individually and for our family while giving them a much-needed break. The thought of starting fifth grade so late paralyzed me with fear. Not only was my need for routine broken (the real first day of school is always the Wednesday after Labor Day), but I knew those in my classes would be curious about my long absence. I was now in a school in which pupils had homeroom and different classrooms for different subjects. Some of the kids from elementary school would inevitably be in my classes and would, I was sure, start asking questions.

I couldn't say I had moved, nor could I make the other kids believe I had suffered from a two-month cold or flu. The most daunting aspect of the November transition from Beechbrook to Boardman Glenwood Middle School was coming up with something plausible that would safeguard my secret. If anyone found out that I had spent time in a school for children with mental problems, I was certain they would either laugh or run me out of school.

Fortunately, the issue didn't grow into the monster that I had anticipated. A few people asked where I had been, but I brushed them off by saying "I was sick" or simply changed the subject. Either because I refused to answer or because other distractions came up, the issue eventually died down. And I was able to get on with the business of being an unhappy, but academically determined fifth-grader who had miles of social distance separating him from his peers.

I was desperate to have friends, to have people like and admire me, to be like everyone else. However, everything I did seemed to set me apart. One morning, I went into my sister Meg's bedroom, picked up an eraser, tossed it into the air and tried to kick it. Instead of hitting my target, my foot hit the top of one of her bedposts, resulting in a broken foot and a four-week walking cast. I couldn't believe that I had to go to school with a cast on my leg, making me even more unlike everyone else. Amazingly, though, many kids signed my cast and expressed get-well and other positive sentiments. Four weeks later, I got the cast off. Two days later, as I was going into the school building, I jumped in the air, landed between two steps and broke my other foot. I was so frightened that the other middle-school kids would make fun of me for breaking both feet that I went the rest of the day keeping the increasing pain to myself. Finally, the pain became unbearable and I could barely walk. I approached my last-period English teacher and whispered to her that I needed to see the nurse. "I want you to see your seat and sit in it," was her incredulous response. It wasn't until I got home that I realized that it was Broken Foot II, the sequel. The teacher apologized the next day for not believing me, and the kids once again signed the cast with sympathy and humor.

At least the leg casts were temporary and my clumsiness was soon forgotten by my classmates. Other behaviors of mine created more lasting memories, however. My eighth-period classroom faced the school's rear parking lot, something that served me well but posed another challenge in terms of keeping me focused on the fifth-grade lesson at hand. Such a vantage point was terrific because it offered me a clear view of the school buses that lined up there toward the end of the day. The buses began trickling in about fifteen to twenty minutes before the dismissal bell rang and, more often than not, the last bus arrived after all the others had pulled out.

This situation coincided with my growing fixation with school buses that tapped into my need for sameness and predictability. For the most part, the school buses started filling the parking lot at about the same time each afternoon and in the same order. I loved to see the angle at which they parked and to gauge the spaces and see the lines between the buses. I took note of what was going on outside the room and paid close attention to the arrival of my own school bus. On the way home each afternoon, I also became aware of some other buses' routes and visualized them in my head, taking note on a daily basis where a given bus should be at a precise time.

As was common in my thinking patterns at that age, I created a rule governing my school bus fixation: I wanted the bus on which I rode home to be one of the last, if not the last, to pull in.

This way, I could see the angle at which it parked after all the others left. Even more importantly, a late bus would mean a late arrival home —and less time to be yelled at, stopped and punished for doing many of the things I felt compelled to do once I arrived home. School was orderly; home was not. These seemingly "inappropriate" behaviors were my daily attempt to make sense of an environment that often had chaos instead of control and structure at its core.

Most of the time, however, my rule and the real world were not in sync. My bus was nearly always one of the first, not the last, to arrive on the scene, causing my school day to end on a very negative note. Actually, most of my weekdays had anger as their bookends; I went to school furious that family members didn't come to the breakfast table in my prescribed order and at the end of my school day, the same feelings roiled when my bus driver violated my rule by arriving too soon for my liking. I was well aware that I could not control the timing of the buses' arrival, nor was there any way that I could convince my bus driver to acquiesce to the necessary changes I wished to see. Since my bus was never one of the last to come each afternoon, I did what, to me, was the next best thing: I made it a point to be the last pupil to board the bus.

At this age the most trying times for me were the minutes spent between classes and the twenty-five minutes in the school cafeteria. I was very uncomfortable in the large, square-shaped room and in the school's hallways because both locations had a concentrated number of students. The noise and commotion were taxing to my senses. Thirty kids in an enclosed room was one thing, but ten times as many in a wide open echo-y space or room was overwhelming because I felt naked, exposed and on display—even if no attention was on me.

I often dealt with the lunch periods by not eating. Going hungry was a small price to pay for getting out of having to share a common room and table with pupils I thought hated me or wanted no part of me. But for that half-hour, I was anything but idle. I spent the lunch period roaming the middle school's halls on a fixed route I had devised. After charting my route I made several trial runs, then refined, shaped and polished it so that it would take precisely the entire lunch period to complete. This activity allowed me time to be by myself and away from various tormentors while simultaneously satisfying some of my compulsions. In addition to my lunchtime routine, I had mapped out another, entirely different route that I took as soon as the last bell of the day sounded. This one was carefully devised to allow me just the right amount of time to be the last person on the school bus, but not long enough to cause me to miss the bus. Neither orchestrating nor timing it were difficult; instead, the real challenge was doing it covertly so that my being the last one to board the school bus each day would be seen as simply coincidental. I was able to maintain my lunchtime route for close to a year until one of the teachers caught on and threatened to send me to the principal's office if I didn't go to the cafeteria like everyone else. But his threats didn't deter my late afternoon ritual.

A NEW THOUGHT

The older I got, the more apparent it became that something was seriously wrong with me, although I still didn't realize it was autism despite the fact my parents had discussed it with me. I simply didn't take it in. I just lumped together all my problems under the moniker "Bad Seed Syndrome"—my belief that, for reasons unknown, I had been born inherently evil. I believed this for years. My literal, concrete, black-and-white thinking patterns and ways of relating to the world only supported and confirmed this. Most of the time, I was corrected, yelled at, teased, tormented, ignored and shunned. All I knew was what I saw—consistent negative attention. The deduction was simple: Sean was bad.

When I was in my early teens, my perception of myself began to change. I realized that something profound was wrong with me and I began to want to change it. This caused certain inner priorities to shift. I wanted to make friends and somehow reach beyond myself. But as this socially-positive desire grew, so did the strength and grip of the compulsions. In fact, by now these compulsions had become so ingrained that they were as vital to my life as was the oxygen I breathed.

True to form, my peculiar behaviors kept me isolated from other kids instead of drawing them to me, and new fascinations cropped. In sixth or seventh grade, I developed a fixation with pencils (no relation to my unusual need to sharpen the same years earlier), and a need to manipulate them. I often brought several with me and drew on my school desk slanted lines that paralleled the buses' parking spaces. Then, during any down moments, I "drove" each of three or more pencils with my hand—making the low-pitched, throat-clearing sound meant to emulate the sound of the bus—slowly between these lines.

When not writing with them, or driving them as "buses," I used pencils to test whether gravity still worked. Thankfully, each time it did. I dropped the pen or pencil off the desk and followed its descent with my eyes and noted how it landed. Each time I did this made we want to do it again. If I was satisfied with both how and where it ended up on the floor, I increased the number of times I repeated the behavior to try to get the pencil to land the same way and in roughly the same spot.

Because I wanted people to like me, I tried to satisfy the compulsion, yet not draw negative attention to myself. Indeed, it was a tightrope without the wire.

Repeatedly, I created the social conditions I so desperately wanted to avoid. Other kids started noticing my pencil-dropping pattern and knew that it was not accidental. I remember one time Miss Owens' classroom was eerily silent, at a time when she was out of the room for some reason. Right on cue, I dropped my pencil and the room broke out into laughter—and my face glowed red. It wasn't long before my seventh-grade English teacher got wind of what was going on. One day, she gave us a small writing assignment in which we had to create a character and write a narrative about that character. Since this was also a time in my life that I deeply desired a sense of humor, I became convinced that success with the assignment would be my ticket off Heartbreak and Isolation avenues. I really had no idea how to create a story or develop characters, so I invented one that I thought would satisfy the assignment's requirements, incorporate my fixations in a positive way and, most importantly, showcase whatever sense of humor I had.

I fused all three elements together by creating a character I called Count Pencildrop. I patterned the first part of the name after the famous vampire and, thinking I was onto an unprecedented blaze of originality and creativity, came up with the second part of the name to match the fixation that consumed me. The story was little more than an act of transference, in which I created a fictional character to channel my own compulsions that were, paradoxically, frightening and funny. In the end, this assignment provided me with an unintended and unpleasant introduction not to the world of humor, but to the world of sarcasm. When Miss Owens returned our papers a day or two later, she wrote on mine, "Very funny." I received a D—and a blow to my fragile and fleeting self-esteem.

Eighth grade was also filled with many subtle misinterpretations of other kids' intentions. There were two girls who seemed to like me and would say hi to me and act giddy when they saw me. Unfortunately, their behavior contradicted my past experience and conditioning; I interpreted their actions as negative and assumed they had ulterior motives. *No one likes Sean Barron*, I thought. There has to be a catch.

Around the same time, a mild-mannered pupil whom I did not count among my tormentors called me at home one evening—an unprecedented event—to ask if I knew how to do an American History homework assignment. Instead of telling him or even being simply cordial, I responded the same way I had to the two girls' displays of interest: Quit bothering me or I'll call the police. Not long afterward, all three students gave up on me.

Toward the end of eighth grade, existing problems seemed to magnify, as did my overall anger and unhappiness with life. I was still constantly being corrected, yelled at, stopped, reprimanded and punished at home while it seemed nothing but positive attention was being doled out to my sister, Meg. Translation: Meg's good, Sean's bad; Mom and Dad love Meg, Mom and Dad hate Sean. Despite what they told me countless times—that my parents hated many of my behaviors, yet loved me in spite of them—it was much too abstract a concept for me to comprehend. I couldn't even begin to fathom that their negative attention arose precisely out of the love they had for me. They corrected me out of love, not out of hatred.

Just as frustrating and aggravating for me was my inability to recognize and respond to the positive attention I did get from them. On numerous occasions during my childhood and teenage years either one or both of my parents came to me, nearly begging me to talk to them about what I was feeling or thinking. This was especially true when I came home from school visibly upset, angry or on the verge of a meltdown. Despite their best and most soothing efforts, I never answered. I can only now begin to imagine the level of frustration, anger and sadness that must have caused them. Even when my mother held my shoulders, looked into my eyes and pleaded with me to tell her how she could help, I said nothing.

There were several reasons I responded to her in such antisocial ways. My literal thinking prevented me from being able to form an accurate picture of what had happened. I knew I was being tormented, bullied, ridiculed, hit, slapped, punched, and tripped. But having that knowledge was different from knowing what to do to put a stop to those things—or knowing how to talk to someone who could.

Another reason I kept silent and looked everywhere but in my mother's eyes was that the pain was so fresh from these experiences, saying all the bad things would have increased the pain. Lacking perspective as I did, I also believed my parents would conclude that a certain amount of what happened at school was my fault anyway. After all, I was always getting reprimanded at home for things they said I had done wrong. Why would school be any different?

Also, talking about other kids' cruel misdeeds would have meant having to face instead of deny them. I knew I didn't have the ability to verbally describe the situation, so taking the paths of least resistance—denial and masking—seemed the best and only options. Why bother trying to discuss a bad day when my inadequate abilities would likely only cause me further aggravation? Another, perhaps subtle but more pervasive, reason for my unresponsiveness was directly tied into my self-image. My self-esteem was very low; it felt as though a Herculean effort would be needed to rectify these wrongs. They were intricate, interrelated events that branched out in a dozen directions, without a clear-cut starting or finishing point.

A NEW PERSPECTIVE

One thing that made a huge difference in my social emotional under-standing was what I refer to as "talk therapy." After we moved to California when I was sixteen, and I had settled into a new school, I spent many evenings in our California living room—sometimes until 1:00 or 2:00 AM—with one or both parents. They would often spend several hours trying every way they knew to explain the most basic concepts of how relationships worked. I was in my late teens and still didn't understand why, for example, it wasn't okay to "absorb" people who took a genuine interest in me and showed they cared about me—that is, why it wasn't acceptable to spend all the time I wanted with someone who was much older and had family and other personal obligations.

During our talks in the wee hours, Mom and Dad pointed out to me how destructive my unrealistically high expectations were regarding other people. I expected the people we associated most closely with at the time (most of whom were in the music business, since my folks worked with singer Maureen McGovern) to treat me as they did my parents. I wanted to be the centerpiece of their lives. When they failed to fulfill my expectations, I became deeply hurt and enraged and denied their existence. I retreated to my bedroom and refused to deal with them. I still felt they were as responsible as I was for how I felt, courtesy of the black-and white thinking and lack of perspective that were some of the main themes of my autism.

By the age of seventeen, I knew I was a lot better off than I was before moving to California. However, I still had a lot of anger and bitterness bottled up, and those charged emotions would stay inside me if I didn't do something about them. I still wanted more than ever to be a hero and do something exceptionally well. It was during that year that I watched the made-for-TV movie *Son Rise*, about Raun Kauffman's recovery from his autism. For several hours afterward, Mom and I talked. I realized for the first time that I had autism. Something broke inside me. I understood for the first time that I was capable of working to become the person I wanted to be.

I started turning my gaze outward; my world became more than myself.

Over time, I slowly started coming out of my shell and even small accomplishments loomed large and made me feel ten feet tall (in this case, I didn't mind being tall). I began to break my habit of ignoring people I thought didn't pay enough attention to me. I forced myself to talk to them and be as friendly as I could. Not surprisingly, they were friendly in return. Also, I started paying attention to my appearance, making sure my shirt was buttoned correctly, that my hair was combed rather than sticking out in tufts that attracted negative comments. My curiosity about things outside myself was developing and, tentatively at first, I began asking real questions instead of those connected to my fixations. As time went on, such successes became more common and my desire to reach out to others increased. Everything I learned made me feel good about myself.

In my last year at high school, I made my first friends, all girls. They invited me to sit with them at lunch, included me in after-school plans and asked me to parties at their homes. Two years earlier, I had felt like an alien and now people were beginning to accept me. I was ecstatic.

During the late 1970s, my parents saw me making progress, which is part of the reason they sacrificed so many hours of sleep to try to reach me and explain the most basic concepts of relationships to me. My father told me years later that at that time he thought of my brain as a complex set of wiring. All the circuitry was in place and working; it was a matter of getting the wires to connect. The longer and more persistently we talk, my parents thought, the more likely the connections will finally be made.

Over time—and thanks largely to my parents' patience—I started developing a sense of critical judgment. I began asking questions and probing underneath what I saw. I began to actually recognize ulterior motives. I compare developing critical thinking and common sense to exercising a set of muscles that aren't used to being stretched, bent and flexed. It took years of listening, absorbing, watching and asking questions to lose my naiveté and to develop some insight into human nature. The process was slow and difficult, but my parents continued to guide and help me. They never gave up on me, and as a result, I didn't give up on myself.

When I graduated from high school, I had mixed feelings. School had always been the source of teasing and torment, but during my senior year I was happier than ever before. Just when I had begun to fit in, it was over. On the other hand, I felt triumphant. In ninth grade, I would never have believed I'd make it through school, but now I had my diploma in hand, everyone was congratulating me and we had a large party at my home.

All my life, I had thought higher education was completely out of reach. However, as a successful high school graduate, I suddenly realized going to college was not impossible. There were free two-year community colleges in California and I decided to enroll at Los Angeles Valley College, the nearest school, and chose three courses that interested me (psychology, geometry and English).

During the summer I felt apprehensive about attending college, but my parents found an on-campus class for people with disabilities designed to help them learn to take notes, recognize key phrases in lectures and develop good study habits. I attended the class in August. It gave me a boost of confidence and when the semester started, I felt surprisingly relaxed. I was pleased that my coursework was easier than I had feared; after my first semester, I had a B average.

A NEW DAY

I moved back to Ohio in 1984 and worked at a variety of minimum-wage jobs—a janitor at a doughnut shop, a dishwasher at a fast-food restaurant and a mouse at a pizza place (wearing the costume, I had to maintain the video games). After several years, I decided I needed to do something that helped people. When a friend told me that a local nursing home was hiring, I applied for the job of rehabilitation aide and got it. I felt it was my first real job; I felt great respect and affection for older people partly because of my wonderful relationship with my grandmother.

In 1992, *There's a Boy in Here*, the book my mother and I wrote about my emergence from autism, was published. Its success added fuel to my desire to be a writer and I started to think about going back to school to get a degree in journalism. Despite a lifetime of hating and resisting change, and even though I was in a job where I was perfectly comfortable, I resigned after twelve years at the nursing home and enrolled at Youngstown State University for the second time. To me, journalism was exactly the opposite of being autistic; it required looking outward, thinking of others, being objective, having perspective and seeing things from several points of view.

After two semesters of course work, I applied for and got an internship at our local newspaper. Though I had never used a computer and resisted even approaching one, I now had a job in which a computer was essential. Rather than hiding my ignorance, I asked for help and got it. I had been assigned to the copy desk where the other employees worked with me, taught me my first computer skills and were extremely supportive. Despite being new on the job, my co-workers made me feel accepted and valued. For the first time, I felt like a peer. My confidence soared when the paper extended my internship for a second semester, and after my first year, I was kept on as a freelance writer. I still have that job today.

For too long through my twenties and early thirties, having anyone in my life—even someone who was destructive, manipulative and harmful—was better than the absence of friends, mainly because I'd spent years feeling isolated, ostracized and alone.

In my late thirties I decided I would no longer allow people who dragged me down to occupy a spot in my life. Trying to "rescue" troubled souls—something that happened a lot during my years of recovering from autism—made me feel needed and special, but always ended up bringing me down. Now I know that connecting with others is a choice that is available to me—it is a capacity that lies within, and I can exercise it or not, at will.

An ability to let go of the past has gotten much easier as my range of experiences has grown. The more situations I live through, the better able I am to put them into perspective and let those that are inconsequential fall by the wayside. The more I connect with people—my family, friends, coworkers, even strangers—the greater appreciation I have for each person who is in my life.

One evening last year, a friend and I had made plans to go out to dinner. However, we were unable to decide on a restaurant and we went back and forth several times before I finally said, "Wherever you would like to go is fine. Where we go is secondary to my wanting just to be with you." That response is an example of my new perspective on social occasions. If I'm with someone whose company I enjoy, I now get tremendous satisfaction and pleasure from doing even the simplest things.

I often look back at those years of constant struggle and, in a strange way, I'm glad to have gone through such experiences. Had it not been for my autism, my life would likely not have been as rich and meaningful as it's turned out to be. Writing collaboratively with my mother on our book wouldn't have been possible, nor would travels that have taken me across the U.S. and to Europe. And most importantly, I would not have met the thousands of wonderful people who work with or are parents of someone with autism—some of whom have become friends. Even though I would never wish to return to an autistic state, my attitude toward it has changed considerably. I no longer think of what I did in terms of right or wrong (hence, either-or thinking) and now see my autism for what it was: a different way of relating to and trying to make sense of the world.

Forming and maintaining healthy relationships is difficult for most of us. I'm constantly reminded of this fact when I go out to eat and see how many couples sit together in a booth and barely look at each other. They sit like stones, rarely smiling as they wait for their food, and speak more to the server than to their partners. I don't pass judgment, but often end up wondering what their private lives must be like.

I've talked to friends over the years who have gone through many relationship problems, including dealing with an alcoholic and abusive spouse, being in a marriage that is one-sided, coping with financial problems and their effects on the marriage, and the list goes on. And there is one rule I've learned about relationships that is in opposition to my way of thinking when I had autism: *there are no hard, fast rules that will guarantee 100% success with relationships.*

There are, however, some overarching "unwritten rules" that I have picked up on as I've become more connected and in tune with society. These broad frameworks stand as sentries to the gates of my social functioning and social awareness, opening doors that have made these the best years of my forty-one years of life.

My autism was quite a journey—and an often painful one at that. Feeling at ease in social situations and having confidence in handling whatever comes my way were not things I learned in a single "A-ha!" moment of ultimate social transformation. It was, and continues to be, a process that unfolds in its own time, layer by layer.

I have changed in many ways since I began my struggle against autism. I have a deeper appreciation for things I used to take for granted. I thrive on ideas and concepts, and am comfortable in the abstract realm. Interestingly, the less autistic my behavior, the more I'm unable to recall and retain rote information. I'm terrible with numbers, dates and lists now, but to get along in the world and with others in it, that's a tiny price I'm more than willing to pay.

Thankfully, the social connections I so desperately wanted growing up have been made. My relationship with my family is extraordinary. I have a network of wonderful friends, a job as a newspaper reporter that satisfies me on an intellectual level and a woman whom I've been dating since 2003. All the people in my life affect me in positive ways.

I am the happiest I have ever been. I feel deeply connected to the larger world and have many things to be thankful for. Recently I heard "New Day," a song by Patti LaBelle, on the radio and found the lyrics highly inspiring and personal.

> "It's a new day, open my eyes and the path is clearer,
> New day, pushing ahead till my goal gets nearer,
> New day, spread my wings I'm doing things my way,
> It's a new day."

PART TWO

TWO MINDS: TWO PATHS

HOW THE AUTISTIC WAY OF THINKING AFFECTS SOCIAL UNDERSTANDING

Rene Descartes' infamous line, "I think, therefore, I am," aptly describes the manner in which the person with autism spectrum disorders perceives his world. His mind is one of absolutes, of thinking patterns that are rigid and repetitive, where minute details become focal points of obsessive attention, and self-involvement takes precedence over exploration. How each person thinks, from a physiological, emotional and cognitive framework, impacts his ability to make sense of his experiences, to relate behavior and consequence, to function in the world. And nowhere is this more evident than in the realm of social thinking and behaving.

Before embarking on any effort to teach a child or adult about the unwritten rules of social relationships, people who sit outside the world of ASD must become intimate with the autism mind, with the thoughts and perspectives of the specific child or adult with ASD. Sean and Temple describe the workings of their minds in the passages that follow. They illustrate two very different ways of thinking and perception—two people who, while both diagnosed on the spectrum, gained understanding of the world around them through markedly different styles of relating. Their ability to describe their inner thoughts in such detail is a window of opportunity for parents and teachers in gaining this understanding, in stretching the NT mind past the edge of comfort and into the realm of "different thinking." In a sense, it's a willingness to go "out of your mind" in order to truly appreciate the autism way of thinking that governs their actions, reactions, thoughts and feelings.

Sean Starts:

I remember the large, twenty-four-inch television in my parents' upstairs bedroom and how temperamental and quirky it was. It was a black-and-white Zenith and the set seemed like an ancient relic—even though I had little idea of what state-of-the-art TVs were supposed to look like in the mid-1970s. I'm not sure when they bought it, but what stands out in memory was how old and cranky it became. I never knew what the picture would look like when I turned it on. This seemed to depend on factors that were a mystery to me.

Sometimes when I turned on the set, the picture was rather clear. More often than not, though, I got more than what a discriminating viewer *should* see and hear: a merger in which the program I meant to watch would be complemented with sound from a show on another station. I might turn on the set intending to watch an episode of *Gomer Pyle* only to hear staccato trotting sounds from a movie on another channel as John Wayne galloped off into the sunset. Oddly enough, to correct this I had to stand about four to five feet away from the TV, stomp my foot and hope for sound and image to become one. Over time, an inverse relationship developed between frequency of stomping and harmony of picture and sound. And during the TV's twilight years, there was usually sound minus any picture.

I recall just as clearly the increasing frustration I felt. I also see, more than two decades later, the similarities between the TV's behavior and mine during that time. Both were erratic. Both were frustrating. Both were unpredictable. And both seemed hopelessly inconsistent to other people.

THE THREE Rs: RULES, REPETITIONS AND RIGIDITY

My ways of relating to the world and the people in it were devoid of shades of gray. Because of my autism and the shell I lived in, I felt much more comfortable taking in my environment in tiny doses than seeing and trying to make sense of the big picture, which at the time was most overwhelming to me. Having autism meant living daily life under a dark cloud of unrelenting fear that I came into the world with—and for which there seemed to be no cause and no long-term relief. Developing a tunnel-vision way of relating to people and most things provided a measure of comfort and security. Manipulating objects, turning lights on and off repeatedly, focusing on minute details to the exclusion of everything else around me and doing numerous other repetitive acts typical of autism was my channel to feeling in control of my world. At the same time, this approach allowed me to deal with intense fear more effectively by focusing my mind so squarely on something else that it made daily life more bearable.

CAUSE AND EFFECT: CONTROLLING FEAR THROUGH REPETITION

I have no idea how many ways there are to deal with a level of fear so great that it hangs over you like a storm cloud. The three remedies I chose and that made the most sense to me in all areas of my life were repetition, repetition and repetition. Nowhere was this more evident than in my thirst for predictability. For me, one of the things that separated autism from more typical behavior was not so much that I threw objects down the heating duct, tossed them into the backyard tree to watch their trajectory from branch to ground, became transfixed on a top's spinning motion and a score of other behaviors. Instead, it was the *frequency* with which I did these things, propelled by a deep, unrelenting need to do them. Also at work was what I call the "melting effect."

By that I mean any feelings of joy, comfort, security or control I got from the many repetitive behaviors were almost always fleeting and seemed to evaporate shortly afterward—quickly replaced by the awful feelings of dread and fear again. It was a circular path I couldn't step off.

Until I was about seven or eight, we spent some time during the summer swimming in the pool at the home of family friends. It was seven feet at the deep end; the shallow part was three feet deep. I had a ritual from which I almost never deviated: I would "test" the depth at the shallow end each time I got into the pool. Afterward, I spent much of the time in that section because I was terrified of being in water over my head and of going under the surface. I thought the water would somehow swallow me, so I clung tenaciously to the edge of the pool for most of the time I was in the water.

A little later, my grandparents bought us a membership to a nearby swim club. There, I somehow got over my fear of going underwater and enjoyed venturing into depths over my head, even up to twelve feet. But what didn't change was my need for predictability.

Despite my newfound confidence that catastrophe did not await me if I went underwater, I still needed to test the waters, to know that certain conditions would remain unchanged every time I got into the water. It was common for us to spend several hours at the club on nice summer days, and I spent most of that time measuring the water's depth by bobbing up and down or going over my head to see and feel, for instance, how deep six feet was. And I needed to know that six feet felt the same every time and was in the same part of the pool every time. When this information was confirmed to my satisfaction, I did my part to share my glee and temporary comfort with others. "Five feet! Six feet!" I would announce to anyone within earshot each time.

Therein lies part of the autistic experience at work. I realize that my autism wasn't so much defined by what I did, what I was interested in as a child and teenager, or even the fixations themselves. Lots of children revel in making "discoveries" like the ones I made at the swim club; such forms of play are quite healthy. Similarly, many kids have certain rituals that help them make sense of, and find organization in, their environment and lives. We all need predictability and structure and it's hard to imagine the chaos that would result without them. Even repetition itself really isn't a precursor to autism.

It's been my experience that the addition of certain *extremes* to this mix—and the absence of processing abilities—acts to set apart children (and adults) with autism from their typical counterparts. For me, that meant acquiring what I call "islands of knowledge," that is, learning things piecemeal and having great difficulty taking cues or information from one situation and connecting them to the same, or a similar, situation. For instance, one of my fixations was speedometers. As I walked up the street with my mother, I checked all the speedometers in the cars parked in neighbors' driveways to see the position of the needles. However, when I saw a car coming down our quiet street, I would pull away from my mom and dash into the street to look into the car window and see the speedometer moving. No matter how many times I was reprimanded, scolded or punished, I never remembered those negative effects. The next time a car came down the street, I would do it again. My repetitive action eased for a little while the constant fear I felt. I was unable to grasp that the consequence of my running into the street could be me being struck by a car. Quenching the fear overshadowed everything else.

BLACK-AND-WHITE THINKING AND ITS IMPACT

When I was about twelve or thirteen, I spent one afternoon in my bedroom, while my parents and a family friend visited downstairs. I was building from Tinker Toys a large airplane that I was eager to show the friend. After at least an hour of assiduously following the instructions and diagram, I finished the elaborate project and called the friend to my room to show her my accomplishment. However, as soon as I let her see the plane, I noticed that I had forgotten to add one blue rod. I became enraged and wrecked the plane in her presence, throwing the parts all over the room. I never thought for a second that simply inserting the missing part would solve the problem, a process that would have taken a split second, and it never dawned on me that she would likely never have noticed the piece missing anyway. Instead, in my mind it had to be an exact replica of the airplane depicted in the instructions; anything else was wrong and bad, period.

It also never occurred to me that most toys, objects and other items had more than one use and that a person could improvise. When I was four and five years old, I used items like Tinker Toys in manipulative and destructive ways—such as pouring them onto a bedroom closet floor, closing the door and pretending the closet would spin like a washing machine. This helped in my quest to live a less fearful existence by providing a level of control (the toys were on the floor and "spun" because I made that happen). More often than not, however, that meant using the items in ways contrary to their intended purposes. I broke hundreds of dollars' worth of toys, games and other items over the years, but rarely saw my actions as destructive and inappropriate. Instead, I did all of this so I could focus on something other than fear and experience a level of comfort, control and security.

All of this served as a benchmark for how the first five years of my life played out—five years that, by and large, were devoid of social contacts with other children. Unbeknownst to me then, these scenarios were cultivating and enriching the fertile soil from which new sets of problems and challenges would sprout, fester and grow into monsters.

Objects such as Tinker Toys were a lot easier for me to deal with and make sense of than people. People were impossible to control and didn't seem to follow any predictable patterns; they rarely did the same things at the same time in the same manner. Since I couldn't exert control over others, I did what to me was the next best thing: I devised a series of arbitrary, *unwritten* rules I expected them to follow that was in line with my black-and-white thinking patterns. When they failed to perform according to these rules—rules they were largely unaware of—all hell broke loose in my world and theirs.

As I grew older and my use of words became a bit more sophisticated, I used conversations to exert control. To that end, I had the strong need to ask other people repetitive questions based on whatever my fixations were. I asked things like, "Which switch turns on this light?" "What is the capital of Wyoming?" "Have you ever been to Alaska?" "Alabama?" I went systematically through all fifty states in this manner. If I learned that someone had been to another city, I might follow that up by asking what the city's TV or radio station call letters were, as well as where on the dial the radio station could be found. I asked dozens of other similar questions and interestingly, none were open-ended ones. I controlled the conversation's flow and was drawn more to its rhythm and predictable outcome than to a need for information. My thoughts and expressive language were contained in a black-and-white box I built to insulate me from the fear of the big, unpredictable world just outside its walls. My behavior hung out there, too.

All of this limited my ability to make sense of the confusing world around me; yet a limited amount of comfort beat no comfort or security at all. Yes, I hated being stopped so often by my parents and teachers for doing what I felt driven to do and yes, I detested being yelled at and punished. It was a spiral whose end always pointed down. However, taking the extra step to link the punishment to the behavior was beyond me. My mind ran on a single track; my whole being was engrossed by those behaviors I felt an extremely pressing need to act out. Nothing else mattered.

People with ASD experience the world with literally a different mindset, one that is sometimes difficult for neurotypicals to truly understand. While readers may relate to many of Sean's thinking patterns, what is enlightening is the extent to which his thinking controlled his ability to connect with the people and events around him. His fear was pervasive; his need to control his environment through repetitive acts consumed him. Little else mattered but achieving some sense of calm—no matter how small the measure.

Equally enlightening, although from a completely different perspective, is the manner in which Temple thinks, and how her thoughts affect her ability to be socially connected, as illustrated in the following passage.

Temple Speaks:

One of the things I'm noticing more and more as I get older is that the way I think is markedly different from most of the world. It continues to surprise me how illogical people are in their thinking patterns and how much emotions and being social drives people and even distorts their thinking. The more highly social people are much less logical in their approach to situations.

In one of my columns in 2001 for the *Autism Asperger's Digest* magazine, I wrote that I've always thought that genius is an abnormality. If all the genes and other factors that cause autism were eliminated, the world would be populated by very social people who would accomplish very little. The really social people are not motivated enough by "making things" to spend the time necessary to create great art, beautiful music or masterworks of engineering that require a great attention to detail. It's just not part of their mindset. Yet, that's often where people with ASD excel.

I keep returning to this idea that kids on the spectrum loosely fall into two groups when it comes to their social-emotional capabilities: the kids who are more like me—the super high functioning ASD kids who tend to be more logical and less emotional—and then the kids (some high-functioning and others with less-verbal capabilities and more behavior issues) with the sensory issues, but a stronger emotional make-up. That's why I'm so adamant that sensory issues be addressed in this population. When the senses are distorted, the child's true potential will never be discovered. He'll always be seen as incapable, when in fact, he's just expending all his energy trying to deal with the invasive world around him.

The minds and bodies of people with ASD are wired differently. More and more research is uncovering the extent to which biology affects behavior, and the impact our senses have on our ability to interpret our world. Yet, professionals across the country still take a negative or passive approach to sensory processing problems, and many flat out refuse to believe that they impact behavior. How's that for "rigid thinking"? People just don't seem to "get" that these sensory problems are real and they have an *enormous* impact on our lives. There are thousands of verbal Aspies who testify to this over and over—why aren't people listening? I think it's that people's brains are so rigid in their own way of thinking and perception that they just can't imagine that a different way exists. Rigid thinking is not just an autistic trait—apparently it's hardwired in all of us. But neurotypical people seem to think and feel that it's okay to be rigid as long as their ideas are shared by enough people. Imagine if Galileo or Albert Einstein succumbed to that line of thinking. Where would we be today? Different thinking is where progress and invention and discoveries lie.

When a person thinks in pictures and the rest of the world relates on a verbal basis, it's nearly impossible for the verbal thinkers to imagine our perspective, although I think it's easier the other way around, i.e., for people who think in pictures to learn to think with words. As I've grown, I now have a better sense of what that's like.

I notice this same visual/verbal thinking in the cattle industry. The people who seem to really understand what I have to say about animals are the really good "intuitive" trainers—and I find they often have a few learning problems themselves or they're dyslexic. The highly verbal people in the field often deal with animals strictly from a behavioral, operant-conditioning framework. They can't seem to think about animals in any other way and they tend to deny genetic differences among the animals.

I think one of the reasons why ABA has gained such popularity is that it appeals to the verbal thinking people. And it's also why they can't seem to appreciate the more "whole-child" social-emotional, cognitive teaching methods like Stanley Greenspan's DIR (Developmental Individual-difference Relationship-based)/Floortime model or Steven Gutstein's RDI (Relationship Development Intervention) methods.

Learning is more than operant conditioning, whether it's cattle or people we're working with. We have to look at the physical biomedical/biochemical workings of the person, assess their sensory issues, determine whether they think from a logical or emotional framework, and then create programs that take into consideration all of these factors if we're going to teach social functioning skills and emotional relatedness to people with ASD. Yet, many programs with a social or behavioral basis teach good/bad behavior and expect behavior conditioning to produce social understanding. That's exactly the stage where much of our programming sits now with people with ASD—a piecemeal, compartmentalized approach to treatment.

If there's a basic physiological reason that social awareness is not developing in a child—their brain wires are not connected— no matter how many ways parents or professionals try to teach the child, success will be limited by that physical impairment. If his sensory systems are going haywire all the time, or stress and anxiety levels are pervasive, until those issues are addressed and alleviated, forget trying to teach more advanced aspects of behavior and sociability. Equally ineffective are mismatched teaching methods, such as appealing to the logical-minded child through emotional reasoning, or vice versa. Until we address the whole child in our teaching—whether we're teaching language or social skills or play skills—we're doing disservice to the child or adult. We're expecting a lot of effort from the child, but setting him up for limited success right from the start. It all comes back to appreciating the different ways that people with ASD think.

The intensity of the AS individual's adverse response to change is directly related to his desire for routine, sameness and being in control. In all cases where AS individuals become upset with change, it is because they haven't developed an efficient mechanism to exert socially appropriate control over themselves or the situation. Change causes anxiety and fear; it was this way for me and it is this way for many other ASD individuals.

Some people with ASD think in very rigid patterns, and see a particular behavior in an all-or-nothing manner. When we are asked or expected to change a behavior, we think that means we need to extinguish it. Most times, this is not the case. It is more that we need to modify the behavior and understand times and places when it is acceptable, and times and places when it is not. For instance, I can still dress like a slob in my own house, when no one else is around (a trait I've learned is shared with many neurotypicals). Finding a way to compromise so that we keep our personal nature, but conform to some of the unspoken "rules" of society, is where our efforts need to be.

2017 REFLECTIONS FROM TEMPLE

Since the first edition of this book released, I've learned about another social-behavioral early intervention program for children with autism, called the Early Start Denver Model. Developed by two well-known psychologists in the field of ASD, Sally Rogers, PhD and Geraldine Dawson, PhD, the program combines a relationship-focused developmental model with the behavior-based teaching practices of ABA (applied behavior analysis). It can be used for children ages 12-48 months and the best part is that it is not tied to any specific setting for the delivery of services. It can be used by therapy teams in group settings or by parents or professionals in individual therapy sessions in a clinic or a home setting. Even though we typically view ABA as "teaching at the table" and focusing on social skill performance, the Denver Model expands that to include a strong emphasis on interpersonal exchanges, shared engagement, joint attention and activities, and language and communication taught within a relationship-based context. The authors wrote a book that explains the model well: *Early Start Denver Model for Young Children with Autism: Promoting Language, Learning, and Engagement* (2009).

THINKING AFFECTS BEHAVIOR

Residing within all people—to a greater or lesser extent—are the "sociabilities" that Temple mentions. They are the tools with which we become socially aware, feel socially connected, and learn basic social functioning skills, like manners and social etiquette. These abilities exist on a continuum and develop throughout our lifetimes, as we pass through the different stages of social-emotional growth. We've all encountered the person who can't seem to "feel" for others, who rarely displays an empathic reaction to a dismal turn of events in another's life, the person who seems uncomfortable around people, who doesn't "fit in." We each are gifted in some skills and deficient in others—the capacity is there, even in people with ASD. Despite the seemingly innate nature in which social skills and emotional relatedness develop in typical people, they can be learned.

Impacting the ability to learn the unwritten rules of social relationships or any aspect of social behaviors is the literal-mindedness of people with ASD. Earlier Sean related how his black-and-white thinking patterns wreaked havoc. Here he recalls another situation that supports how the autism way of thinking interprets simple behavior-consequence relationships.

Sean Speaks:

I didn't have a clue about why some *school*work had to be done at *home*. What we did at school was supposed to stay there, period. I remember one evening watching *The Mod Squad* and about halfway through the show, Dad came in and suddenly switched off the set. He sternly told me that my homework had to be done before I could watch TV, and that he was going to see to it that this happened every evening. I saw this as punishment, pure and simple, because he was stopping me from doing something I wanted to do for reasons I could not articulate nor fully understand. Even as a first-grader, I loved to watch television because of the visual stimulation and the predictability. Following the rule my dad laid out was too abstract; I felt I was being punished and deprived for something that to me, *made no sense.*

Temple Adds Her Perspective:

Mother had very strict rules about where I could "act out" and where I couldn't. For instance, she'd let me wreck a lot of stuff in my room, but destruction of the living room would result in very severe consequences. I only remember it happening twice and in both cases, in my way of thinking—which could be very literal when I was younger—I wasn't really disobeying. One time I walked up and down the stairs with a pencil against the wall in the front hall. In my mind, this was the "front hall," not the "living room." When Mother had parties and I'd serve hors d'oeuvres at the parties I don't ever remember misbehaving at one of those parties. I did misbehave above the party though. I made the distinction between at the party and *above* the party. My bedroom was directly above where the party was held. So I decided to scare the guests by tying a dress on a coat hanger and dropping it out the window. The people who saw it screamed but I pulled it back up and they didn't figure out what happened. That was above the party—it wasn't at the party. Of course, part of this behavior had nothing to do with my autism—I was just being precocious and testing the boundaries of what I could and could not get away with.

People with ASD think specific-to-general while typical people think general-to-specific, and this difference in thinking pattern tips the scales heavily on the side of misunderstandings for ASD kids. Their whole world is comprised of details—thousands of little bits of information that at first don't necessarily have any relationship to each other, because concepts are not yet a fluid part of their thinking patterns—especially in very young children. Furthermore, all those myriad little bits of information each have equal importance in the mind of an autistic child. Their ability to assign various levels of meaning to the information they're amassing is a skill yet to be developed, and in its early expression can often be wrong.

Imagine what life would be like if, at a young age, each experience, each simple interaction, be it with family members, at the grocery store, playing in the back yard with the dog, all those details were stored in your mind as separate bits of information and you were clueless as to how they all related to each other. No concepts, no categories, no generalization—just details. The world would indeed be an overwhelming place to live! Shutting it all down or off, or retreating into silence to escape the sheer volume of unrelated details bombarding your senses would be understandable. So would a behavior outburst when the mass of images at any given moment became too much to handle.

Temple Contributes:

I figured out how to take all those details and put them into categories, and then form subcategories within categories. Organizing the information this way helped me make sense of the world. When I was little, I categorized dogs from cats by size.

When a small dog came into our neighborhood, I realized I could no longer use size to differentiate the two categories of animals. I looked for a visual feature that dogs had, that cats didn't: all dogs have the same nose regardless of size. Another person might use a sound category: dogs bark, cats meow.

The NT world thinks just the opposite. From an early age we effortlessly and neatly understand the broad categories and concepts that all those millions of details fall into. We don't have to play detective in our heads, scanning all the hundreds or thousands of bits of information to find pictures of a four-legged animal (there are lots of them), of a particular size (still lots), with ears and a tail (still many), that barks (more narrow), and has a certain shaped nose to "learn" the concept "dog." For us, "dog" is a generality that has meaning right from our first experience with the animal. The brain automatically creates an image labeled "dog" and codes it in a specific location of the brain. Each time the child sees a dog again, the information taken in through the eyes travels along the neuropathways to that location and makes the cognitive connection. NT kids don't stop and scratch their heads each time they see a different color dog or a different breed of dog, or pick apart each individual detail of the new animal, saying to themselves, "Hmm, is that animal a dog? Does it meet the criteria for dog?" They just know it is.

Apply this different autism thinking pattern to the nebulous world of social interaction and it can set the mind spinning! Each social interaction, even those brief and unimportant, contain a multitude of obvious and not-so-obvious clues to understanding the situation in context and responding in a socially aware manner. The concepts and categories of social interactions lack the clear defining characteristics that are present with things, or places or the more logical academic subjects like math or physics. However, for the visual thinker, they are nonetheless concrete pictures.

Temple Comments:

Defining the characteristics of "dog" in order for the broad concept to be understood is very different than is trying to explain or teach the concept of "friendship" or "compassion." When I say the word "friendship" I see pictures of doing really fun things together with another person. All the images are specific, such as building cattle corrals with my friend Jim or going to the movies with Mark. When I think about "compassion" I see images of Mother Theresa taking care of the poor, or doctors and nurses in hospitals trying to keep people alive in the aftermath of Hurricane Katrina. From experience I have a large library of images I can put in the friendship or compassion files.

Our social world is filled with intangible ideas that cannot be neatly broken down into unique parts that can be easily categorized. The social world is fluid, ever-changing, the same yet different in subtle ways. Perhaps that's one reason why children and adults with ASD can often be very good in academic subjects where the relationship between facts is logical and direct, and do poorly in areas that require extrapolation, interpretation or integration. The brain pathways that facilitate the crossover of category to category, or that illuminate the possible connection of one area to another are undeveloped or under-developed in the autistic mind. It's like having a million pages of information on various subjects, but not having a cross-referenced index.

Compound this scenario by thinking in pictures, rather than words, and the possibilities for misunderstanding and miscommunication rise exponentially.

As Temple Shares,

I didn't feel I could think really, really well until I was in my forties. I didn't feel that I had enough information on the hard drive to really understand a broad range of topics and social situations and think about them intelligently until I was in my late thirties, early forties. Before that I thought much more rigidly, much more with symbols. As I discussed in detail in my book, *Thinking in Pictures,* when I was in high school, there was a little attic door that went out onto the roof. I used to go through that door—literally and within my mind—to practice getting ready for my life after high school. This transition was so abstract that I could not think about it unless I could visualize the door and going through it. At the age of sixteen, I did not have enough experiences to use images from my memory. Today I no longer use door symbols because over a period of almost fifty years I have many images in the vast Internet inside my head. These images serve as guides of how to act in a new situation. To understand a new situation I have to relate it back to a past experience.

Basically my mind works like Google for images, and for other people like me, the number of images on our hard drive controls whether or not we can formulate an appropriate response. I can't solve a problem without adequate information on the hard drive. That's why personal experiences are so important in helping children make sense of the social world around them. It's like this: when I was younger, let's say I had fifty images on my hard drive. Every situation that came up, I'd access my hard drive and the only resources it had to draw from were those fifty images. One would come up—one had to come up because for me, that was thinking. In the beginning, it didn't matter whether it related or not to the situation or topic at hand. If it was related it worked—and my response was correct, or as close as the picture's information allowed it to be. If it was not related, my response was incorrect, or my logic or social understanding was faulty. When I was young and the number of images on my hard drive was limited, my responses were generally incorrect. However, Mother was smart in that she constantly make me interact—as long as I wasn't tired or in sensory overload—and those experiences put more and more information on the hard drive. And, because life was so structured, many situations were learned easily because they occurred in the same way, over and over. Whether I was eating at my house, a neighbor's house, or attending a classmate's birthday party, talking with my mouth full was not tolerated by any of the mothers. It really helped me learn social functioning skills more quickly.

I can remember my father giving me *The Wall Street Journal* when I was in high school and I started reading about business dealings and employee issues and CEOs getting in trouble for this and that. I thought, man, if I keep reading all these articles about business I'm going to really understand business dealings and professional relationships and learn some of those unwritten rules of professional life. I did, but I had to read it for five years before I felt like I had enough information on the hard drive where things really started to make sense.

Reading and personal experiences put information on the hard drive. Some people with ASD can decipher the meaning from a situation with one experience; for others it takes a lot more practice. I got fired *once* from a job and that was all it took for me to learn that keeping my job was a priority and I needed to do whatever it took to keep that job. I just talked to a lady about an adult with AS who's been fired about thirty times for telling clients they were fat, or ugly—factual but socially inappropriate comments. It keeps happening and he still doesn't understand the inappropriateness of his actions. Obviously there's some different brain wiring going on in his head than in mine, and no one's giving him the structured teaching he needs to learn the difference between honesty and diplomacy (one of our Ten Unwritten Rules). I suspect it's that way across the spectrum—everyone is wired a little differently, yet the impact of that faulty wiring is immense.

I also find that guys tend to be more rigid in their thinking and seem to have more trouble with authority than do girls with ASD. The first time I ever got a traffic ticket I was Miss Polite, yes sir, yes sir, I'll get my license sir—nothing that could be misread as oppositional behavior. Girls are more flexible in their thinking overall, whether or not autism is present. I think that's part of the reason they work in groups more naturally, which in itself, provides more opportunities for social interaction to develop.

People on the spectrum who think in pictures process data much differently than do the people I call "verbal-logic" thinkers. We tend to be associative thinkers and we associate things together that other people wouldn't normally think are related. Many NT people perceive our thinking as linear, but it's not. It's associative. It's like the Google search engine—put in a keyword and the matches can relate in any way, as long as the keyword in part of the mix. For instance, if I have to prob-lem-solve, my mind has to sift through a whole lot of little details that my Google search returns. It's like someone giving you a jigsaw puzzle in a giant bag, without a picture for reference. Once I put 20% of the puzzle together I have a pretty good idea what the picture might be. I certainly would know whether it was a horse or a house or a motorcycle. Every bit of information is a clue, and every bit of information has value. It's almost like being Sherlock Holmes, looking at every little minute detail and its relevance. But it requires that I wade though a zillion other details to find the ones that belong to the puzzle. It's a process of picking out the relevant details. Maybe that will help people understand why responses can take longer for a person on the spectrum. There's so much that has to happen in our minds before we can determine what to say or do.

I have observed that there are actually three types of thinking minds on the spectrum. People on the spectrum tend to have a specialized brain, good at one thing and poor at other things. The three types are:

1. *Visual thinker mind.* Thinks in pictures. Often poor at algebra; good at drawing.
2. *Music and math mind.* Thinks in patterns. Good at chess and en-gineering. Instantly sees the relationship between numbers that I do not see.
3. *Verbal logic mind.* Poor at drawing and good at memorizing facts or translating foreign languages.

Some individuals are a combination of the minds; there are also dif-ferences in emotions. Simon Baron-Cohen calls the two different types "systematizers" and "empathizers." I score really high on the non-emo-tional systemitizer mind; I think with intellect. Others think more with emotion and feelings.

I think some people with ASD have a visual thinking nature, and others tend to be verbal-logic thinkers, who are still associative in their thinking but have a more rigid processing style. They still have strong logic, but it's a different processing style. I've met Aspies who are very strong in their mathematical abilities, but they are pattern thinkers. They try to convert everything they encounter in life, including social relationships, down to a final mathematical proof. Things aren't quite that simple. That's not how the social world functions. So, stress and frustration result, sometimes to the extent that it impairs their ability to be social and work in a social environment. They tend to just withdraw, rather than find ways to work through it, mainly because they can't perceive any other choice on their own. They need other people involved who can show them alternative ways of thinking and behaving.

Dr. Nancy Minshew works extensively researching different aspects of the autistic condition. One of her research participants—a fairly intelligent man, a verbal logic thinker—had a bad reaction to a medication and he refused to try another medication. Dr. Minshew spent more than a half-hour explaining to him the differences in the medication, why taking the new one would be a good choice, offering the science behind the new medication, etc. You know how she finally got him to take it? She simply said, "The pink pills made you sick; these are the blue pills." His response: "Okay, I'll try them." Even though people with ASD may have high IQs, sometimes the communication needs to be simple and basic in its logic.

Growing up I learned social functioning skills through examples—a whole lot of concrete, clear, examples. Stealing a toy fire engine was stealing; that was bad. Whenever my sister Izzy and I were being rude, Mother got right on us. If we made impolite comments about fat people, or about the size of Aunt Bella's boobs, Mother would immediately interject and very firmly tell us to stop that behavior and that you don't talk that way. That's all she'd say. If she had tried to appeal to my sense of logic or explain why our comments might hurt other people's feelings, I don't think it would have worked as well with me. All those words would have interfered with the lesson and confused me; it wouldn't have made as much sense to my visual thinking brain. It was the experience itself and being able to clearly categorize it as "inappropriate" that helped me learn.

As I was able to put more and more experiences onto my hard drive, I could start forming categories with an increasing level of refinement. I made smaller and smaller categories because there was more and more information to put into categories. It's similar to a computer programming chart—there's logic to its organization. Broader categories are at the top with smaller and smaller ones beneath it. But what's different is that my mind doesn't have to retrace up the tree to think. I can jump to any other part of the tree or any other tree because of the associative thinking ability.

In talking with parents and professionals, even in talking with other people on the autism spectrum, I'm now realizing how difficult it is for people who are verbal thinkers to really understand how the mind of a visual thinker processes information. Verbal thinkers can have visualization skills—some are even good at imaging some scene from the past, or being able to visually walk through their house. Some verbal thinkers, however, have horrendous visualization skills—they can't even imagine something as familiar as their own car as a picture in their minds. People with strong verbal abilities but low visualization skills will find it extremely difficult understanding the autism mind, especially the visual thinking-in-pictures mind. It's so foreign to them it has no meaning.

Yet, to teach people with ASD who are visually-oriented, these NT parents and teachers need to better understand our thinking; otherwise, treatment programs will be ill-matched to their way of learning. Perhaps a very specific example of how my mind works will help. Suppose someone at one of my conferences asked me, "Temple, what's the optimum size of water troughs for animals?" Here's a picture-by-picture response of how I bring up the information in my mind:

To start, I'm starting to see different water troughs, from very large ones I saw in Arizona to little small ones I've seen on jobs or in books. So that tells me that the optimum size depends upon the situation you're in. In a situation where you can't fill the water trough that often, you better have a big one so you don't run out of water. But those are hard to clean. You also have to have enough water troughs for the number of animals you have and so now I'm seeing feedlot cattle waterers. I'm seeing watering troughs out on a ranch. You've got a lot of different situations where you're going to be watering animals out of water troughs. Now I don't think you even said "cattle" so now I'm seeing pig waterers. And I see nipples; I'm seeing a small bottle waterer for a mouse. I retrieve so much information for a general question like this. So then we could modify the question to narrow it down. You might ask me about water troughs for feed lots in Colorado. Now I see something much more specific— that stopped all the pictures of water bottles for rats and pig waterers. In Colorado outside water freezes in winter, so we need a water trough that would have a continuous flow of water or would be electrically heated or I see a picture of a fiberglass-insulated trough that prevents them from freezing. Now I'm seeing another picture, more than one trough next to each other in a pen, because a steer can just stand next to the water trough and not let another animal drink. That's bad. The pictures go on, all qualifying different aspects of water troughs.

Now, if you had asked me about these cattle waterers when I was in elementary school, the only picture that would have come to mind would have been a water bowl we had for our dog. That's really inappropriate, but that's all that would have been on my hard drive. So, my mind would have turned to something else to try to figure out the question. And, because I was pretty inventive, even at a young age, my attempt might have made pretty good sense. For example, I might have thought, cattle are a lot bigger than horses, they're bigger than a dog. They're going to have to drink a whole lot more water. So, the container needs to be bigger—and at that point my investigative/problem solving skills would kick in. I see a picture of the *Encyclopedia Britannica*. I would have gone to the encyclopedia to try to learn how much water cattle drink. The Internet didn't exist when I was growing up; we used the encyclopedia or the library to search for information. That's how my mind works.

Temple's scenario of how her mind works may be mind-boggling for the person who thinks predominately in words. It illustrates the extent of processing that has to occur before a response can be generated by a person who thinks that way. It's a window to understanding why at times there may not be any response to a question if there's not enough relevant information on the hard drive, or why inappropriate responses are given (again, not enough information).

Where does emotion fit into all of this? The answer may surprise you. Pause for a moment and recall some favorite memory. No doubt, woven throughout the memory will be the emotions you experienced, a sense of the tone and flavor of the situation that bonds the event in your consciousness. The memory has a quality that goes far beyond a mere picture in your mind, even if the intensity of the emotion is different from what was originally experienced. "Time heals all wounds" has stayed the course because of its truth: time does lessen the impact of pain and suffering in most of us. What's interesting is that feelings of joy can be recalled in like intensity. Perhaps our will to remember or forget partially controls the level of intensity we use to store emotions in our memory banks.

Emotions formed, from an early age, the backbone of Sean's way of thinking and responding. They were infused into his social skeleton and overshadowed his ability to function in socially appropriate ways. There is no doubt that at the very heart of Sean's every encounter was a sea of emotions—a torrent out of control in his early years, a tamed tempest as time went by. But nonetheless, a fertile ground for emotional relatedness to grow.

Contrast This to the Way Temple Describes Her Emotional Make-Up:

As I'm thinking and pictures are going through my mind, I have control of the search engine, meaning I can stop and focus on a particular picture or move on, at will. Some Aspies tell me that they don't have that control. They say the pictures just come on their own and they can't stop them. However, the pictures that do appear are all relevant to the topic I'm searching on. For example, if I Google myself on the category "evil," all the images reflect evil, such as Hitler or the image of a jet plane being deliberately flown into the World Trade Center on September 11th. The NT thinking pattern would naturally also bring up thoughts of "good"—the opposite of evil. This is a fluid process that allows people to quickly compare and contrast, skills that are often difficult for the person with ASD. I would have to punch in another key word, "good," to change my image set.

Searching is done absent an emotional response—there is no emotion associated with the images I see in my mind. My emotions are experienced all in the present and they can be very intense. For instance, if someone treats me badly, I experience sadness or anger at the time of the incident or, depending on the intensity of the emotion, for a few days afterwards. However, then the emotion dissipates and the memory is stored on my hard drive as a picture. When I recall that memory at a later date, the emotion is gone—it's like looking at a snapshot of the situation. My choices in relating to that person who hurt me or made me angry are now logic driven. It's difficult for most people to appreciate how my mind works like this, since most people have emotions glued into their memories.

Emotion presses the "Save" button in my brain and stores what I see or experience as data on my hard drive. For example, I was in an emergency landing in an airplane, and you'd better believe I remember that. On the other hand, I don't remember every hotel room I've ever stayed in because I don't care about hotel rooms. Now, I do remember the really weird ones or the really awful ones, or those that were very pretty. The ordinary Fairfield Inn room I do not remember. "Save" is not an automatic process. It's just like operating a computer. If you type out a ten-page document and turn off the computer without saving the document, it's not there the next time you start up the computer. Where there is either an intense emotional reaction or an intense level of interest, the situation is stored to memory. Where there's not, it's as though it never happened. I've done some little tests on myself, looking at houses on the way to work and the next time it's as though I never saw them, because they are of no interest to me. I do remember the Whole Foods store and King Supers because that's where I shop; they have meaning. Sometimes I wonder if this is part of why some kids with ASD need so much repetition to learn. If an experience has no real interest to them, and there's no emotion connected to it (meaningful reinforcement or intrinsic motivation), it never gets stored to their hard drive. It also explains why intense interests are learned with so much ease. Every little bit of information that's interesting presses that Save button. This is an important concept for parents and teachers to grasp—that information is not automatically stored in the brains of kids with ASD. Figuring out what presses that Save button is the key.

Despite the growing awareness of the characteristics of autism spectrum disorders, little is really known about the intricacies of the autism mind. Higher-functioning adults with ASD are slowly becoming more vocal in explaining their personal perspectives; at issue is the extent to which the parents and teachers are willing to listen—really listen—without judgment or preconceived notions.

The NT world would do well to consider that they approach the task of teaching social awareness to people with ASD with some measure of bias and with what could be characterized as a "faulty logic system." The social science term, *observer bias*, is defined as error that is introduced when researchers notice a behavior and interpret it according to what it means to them, failing to take into consideration that it may mean something entirely different to the person exhibiting the behavior. They look for the behavior they expect to find and often fail to notice that which is foreign to them. In the autism community, parent and teachers, therapists and caregivers all perceive the world through a filter of social understanding. The myriad social rules make sense (mostly), are learned largely through observation; assimilation of verbal nuance, body language and facial signals all happens effortlessly, without the need for direct instruction. They seek to teach people with ASD from a framework built upon this innate social awareness, not taking into account that these people do not possess this same framework.

While we are in complete agreement that teaching needs to take place—without it individuals with ASD will never achieve their full potential—teaching must take into account the different ways that people with ASD think and be based on whole-child needs, not just on developing social functioning skills or emotional relatedness. A child who has learned the social functioning skills that gain him entry into social encounters, whose sensory issues have been addressed to an extent that his attention can shift to social awareness, and who is being supported in venturing out into the world around him, is one who is less stressed and has a better chance of fitting in.

The perspectives put forth in this chapter by Temple and Sean demonstrate two markedly different thinking patterns. Yet, one constant stands out: teaching persons with ASD in a way that links their thinking and behavior helps individuals understand their behaviors in the context of the social expectations of the world around them. Peter Dobson (2001) pioneered much of the current thought that forms the basis for cognitive-behavior approaches, and suggests that all cognitive programs share three fundamental premises:

1. Thinking affects behaviors
2. Cognitive activity may be monitored and changed
3. Changes in a person's thinking patterns (cognition) can bring about the desired behavioral change

Temple Supports This:

When I was in my twenties, my Aunt Ann successfully used cognitive therapy on me. When I was depressed and complaining, she gave me objective reasons why I should be happy. She said, "You have a nice, new truck and I have an old, crummy one." She also gave me other examples of things that were positive or were going right in my life. It perked me up when I compared the pictures in my mind of the two trucks. It concretely helped me understand that some of my thoughts were illogical and not based on fact. Emotions can do that; they confuse thinking.

It's interesting to note that the pivotal Ten Unwritten Rules discussed next in the book all reflect these three premises.

Temple Continues:

As our understanding grows of how the brain works, one day we may discover that savant skills are indeed resident in every human being, but that the use of language masks our ability to access these parts of the brain. Research by Dr. Bruce Miller shows that damage to the frontal cortex and language parts of the brain by Alzheimer's disease will unmask artistic and musical talents. Perhaps this understanding will promote acceptance of people who, while lacking social skills, can make meaningful contributions to society just the same.

Parents and teachers who involve themselves with people with ASD need to realize that you cannot turn a non-social animal into a social one. Make the distinction between social functioning skills—what every child and adult should be taught—and emotional relatedness and acknowledge that perhaps not all individuals with ASD are social animals, even though you would like us to be. For some, we will become expert actors on the stage of life, but it will always be a part, one we just learn to perform more skillfully as years go by. Our happiness will be derived from the things we do, not the emotional connections we form.

For others, true emotional relatedness is a seed buried deeply under sensory issues and unmet physical needs, but one that can blossom into happiness of a different sort. Define "success" by teaching people with ASD to adapt to the social world around them, while still retaining the essence of who they are, including their ASD. Not all of autism is bad; capitalize on their talents and teach them to compensate for their deficiencies. Then happiness and fulfillment can be a common experience among us all.

2017 REFLECTIONS FROM TEMPLE

I want to stress even more the importance of problems caused by sensory over sensitivity. I know individuals on the ASD spectrum who are so sound sensitive that they cannot tolerate a dinner in a noisy restaurant. It is impossible to be social if the sensory environment of social places cannot be tolerated. In my case, I can tolerate the noisy environment, but listening to conversations in such a setting has become difficult. Since the first edition I have lost hearing in one ear, and this has made hearing conversations in a noisy environment harder to do. Often I have to say, "This ear has stopped working, so talk into my good one." To hear, I have to turn my good ear toward the speaker and not look directly at him/her. I am now almost 70 and am finding aging to be difficult. It is similar to being an older car with parts that stop working. My mind is the same, but my body doesn't work as well.

I get asked all the time, "What is your number one priority for autism research?" I would love to see researchers discover treatments for sensory over sensitivity. For young kids, loud sounds can often be better tolerated if the child has some control, such as wearing headphones or ear buds to mask out some of the noise. The child can keep the headphones with her to use as needed. However, if she uses headphones, encourage her to only wear them when she really needs them. If headphones are worn all the time, problems with sound sensitivity will become worse. If a child has difficulty tolerating a noisy supermarket, allow her to have control of the time she is in the store.

Overprotected Kids

Since the first edition of the book released, I am seeing increasing problems with kids being overprotected by both parents and professionals, and they are not learning basic social skills such as shaking hands. Too many parents think that, since poor little Tommy has autism, we will make his life easier and order his hamburger for him. Little Tommy needs to learn how to order it himself. As he gets a little older, he can learn to pay for it himself also. In another case, a fully verbal 15-year-old was becoming a recluse. His mother liked having her son edit videos for their church, but she became upset when I suggested that he should do it in the church office. She admitted that she could not let go. When I was seven, I bought things in stores, and at 15, I was cleaning horse stalls every day. Teaching children to be more independent does not happen overnight or all at once. Parents need to incorporate teaching these life skills into their family's daily routines, start simple, and build more complex skills over time.

Suggested Ways to Teach Basic Skills

Ages 7 to 8—Children can serve as hosts or hostesses at their parent's parties; the child must greet and shake hands with each arriving guest. They could usher at a church or community event where the child must greet and shake the hands of arriving guests. If the child is a teenager or in his/her twenties and has never done this, he or she must start learning these skills now. Other skills that must be learned include ordering food in restaurants and shopping. I also had to learn not to keep telling the same story over and over. Today I have a rule: you can only tell the same story twice. It is NEVER too late to learn new skills.

INTERLUDE

We'd like to introduce a brief interlude at this point in the book. Just like an intermission during a play or movie-marathon, it's a chance to get up and stretch—in this case your mental muscles—and let some of the ideas and viewpoints we've shared in part one settle in and take hold so that seeds of understanding begin to sprout.

Some of you may be surprised, delighted or dismayed at this juncture by what you've read thus far. That's understandable, and frankly, we experienced those same emotions in putting together this book. Sean was surprised by the way Temple thought and at times found it difficult to imagine what thinking in pictures was like. Temple, in turn, found Sean's emotion-infused thinking patterns to be very unlike her own thought processes and found further evidence for her "visual versus verbal thinkers" theory that she puts forth throughout the book.

The real value of this book springs from the in-depth and personal insights offered by Temple and Sean. A growing number of books on social skills and social awareness focus on the mechanics of the process; each is valuable and needed because social functioning is a very necessary part of leading a happy, independent life. However, *Unwritten Rules* goes where few, if any, books have gone before: it delves deeply into the minds of two people and shares not just their thoughts, but their *ways* of thinking. It unlocks doors to understanding how autistic thinking affects social behavior, and why social awareness can be such an uphill battle. It lays the groundwork for appreciating the pivotal nature of the Ten Unwritten Rules of Social Relationships that follow in the chapters to come. Without understanding the perspective from which people with autism view the world, the rules will seem like ten common thoughts that are almost too simplistic to have any real relevance. But if you're starting to "think like a person with autism," these rules become your ticket to opening up the social world for them. All aboard yet?

Little did Sean and Temple know—or even suspect—at the time they embarked on this journey that each would find their own revelations in understanding people with ASD. By the end of the process they both agreed: understanding of the autism mind is truly in its infancy.

Revelation #1:

The child or adult who thinks in pictures sees the world through a framework so different that it is difficult—and sometimes impossible—for many people to appreciate. Parents and professionals who work with this segment of the ASD population need to find ways to teach in a manner aligned with their thinking patterns and be cognizant of the impact this way of thinking has on behavior and the ability to achieve emotional relatedness.

Revelation #2:

There exists a value judgment within the NT world that emotional relatedness is a prerequisite to achieving happiness and success. The authors ask you to consider that this judgment may be actually *preventing* some ASD children from becoming happy, functioning adults.

Revelation #3:

Achieving social success is dependent upon certain core attributes of the person with ASD; we refer to them as the Four Cornerstones of Social Awareness:

1. *Perspective-taking:* the ability to "put ourselves in another person's shoes"; to understand that other people can have various viewpoints, emotions, and responses from our own. At an even more basic level is acknowledging that people exist and that they are sources of information to help us make sense of the world.

2. *Flexible thinking:* the ability to accept change, and be responsive to changing conditions and the environment; the ability of the mind to notice and process alternatives to that which is concrete and directly observable.

3. *Positive self-esteem:* a "can-do" attitude that develops through experiencing prior success and forms the basis for risk-taking in the child or adult. Self-esteem is built upon repeated achievements that start small and concrete and become less tangible and more complex. It is not built, however, upon receiving excessive praise for behaviors that are more expected than extraordinary, such as saying please or thank you.

4. *Motivation:* a sustained interest in exploring the world and working toward internal and external goals despite set-backs and delays. Often the best motivation is to use the child's fixation and broader it out into other activities. If the child loves trains, then teach reading, math and writing with train-centered books, examples and activities. Play train-themed games to motivate social interaction.

Based on the social understanding we have achieved in our lives, we emphatically agree that *perspective-taking, being able to look beyond oneself and into the mind of another person, is the single most important aspect of functioning that determines the level of social success to be achieved by a child or adult with ASD.* Through doing so, we learn that what we do affects others—in positive and negative ways. It gives us the ability to consider our own thoughts in relation to information we process about a social situation, and then develop a response that contributes to, rather than detracts from, the social experience.

In her book, *Inside Out: What Makes the Person with Social Cognitive Deficits Tick?* Michelle Garcia Winner outlines the attributes of perspective taking (PT). These attributes illuminate the level of interconnectedness that exists among the Four Cornerstones of Social

Awareness, how each combines with the others in building a foundation of understanding that allows a child or adult to accept and respond to different perspectives, to feel emotional relatedness, and to appreciate the need to learn social functioning skills.

1. Recognizing the thoughtful presence of another person
2. Recognizing the individuality of another person
3. Recognizing that another person has his or her own personal set of emotions
4. Recognizing and responding to the fact that another person has his or her own set of desires and motives
5. Recognizing that another person has his or her own personality
6. Having an intuitive desire to learn about others' interests and personal histories
7. Developing and using memory of a person to facilitate and sustain interpersonal relationships, as well as create a base of understanding about that person's potential actions
8. Formulating language to inquire about another person's interests
9. Understanding social conventions surrounding specific environments
10. Understanding social conventions specific to social contexts
11. Staying aware of the shifting internal states of the communicative partner through eye contact.

Perspective-taking works hand-in-hand with flexible thinking; it provides opportunities for experiencing success in social interactions, which in turn fosters positive self-esteem. It can also act as a source of internal motivation, especially as children grow into adults and the type and quality of social interaction expands. Michelle's book and others that help parents and professionals teach and develop PT in the autism population are mentioned in the Resources section at the end of this book.

Unwritten social rules probably number in the billions—a staggering thought for anyone, an inconceivable image for a person who has any level of impairment in social understanding. An exaggeration, you suggest? Surely, it's not in the billions? Ponder this: social rules govern situations that are experienced solo, between two-people, or among groups small to large to gigantic. Different rules apply based on the cultural or sub-cultural similarity or differences among group members. Unwritten social rules among the very private Japanese are markedly different than among the more liberal natives of the Scandinavian countries. Age groupings, public versus private settings and personal versus professional environments all have different social nuances that further confound and confuse. Clearly, fostering social awareness and social connectedness is a train ride with no final destination. At each stop along the journey people get off and new people get on—each an opportunity to hone existing skills, learn new ones, and stretch our social muscles in new directions.

In discussing a vast array of unwritten social rules, we discovered that many seemed to be aligned with others, and some seemed to be pivotal in nature, i.e., a focal point around which other unwritten rules revolved. The more we talked about them, the more they made sense to us; new meanings surfaced. In a way, they helped us restructure some of our own thoughts on unwritten social rules, which in turn, unlocked new doors of understanding. These pivotal rules became the basis for the second half of this book.

We've selected the ten rules we think every child or adult with ASD should be taught. These are rules that will be taught over time, they are rules that will grow with the child as his social understanding blossoms. They are rules that apply across chronological age, across areas of functioning, in single and group settings. They are akin to the "Golden Rules" of social understanding—the big guiding principles that govern our social actions.

How they are taught will vary from child to child, teen to teen, adult to adult, based on their predominant thinking pattern (visual versus verbal) and a careful and comprehensive look at other brain and body-based challenges present in the person. As we've mentioned several times already, the seeds of social awareness can't burst forth and thrive amidst conditions that detract from, rather than nurture, their growth. Each child will require a different mixture of nutrients for social understanding to ripen. Attend closely to sensory issues, build positive self-esteem, cultivate perspective-taking, discover what motivates and excites the child. Within this rich environment, social awareness will flourish.

PART THREE

THE
TEN UNWRITTEN
RULES OF SOCIAL
RELATIONSHIPS

THE RULES

RULE #1 Rules Are Not Absolute. They Are Situation-Based and People-Based.

RULE #2 Not Everything Is Equally Important in the Grand Scheme of Things.

RULE #3 Everyone in the World Makes Mistakes. It Doesn't Have to Ruin Your Day.

RULE #4 Honesty Is Different Than Diplomacy.

RULE #5 Being Polite Is Appropriate in Any Situation.

RULE #6 Not Everyone Who Is Nice to Me Is My Friend.

RULE #7 People Act Differently in Public Than They Do in Private.

RULE #8 Know When You're Turning People Off.

RULE #9 "Fitting In" Is Often Tied to Looking and Sounding Like You Fit In.

RULE #10 People Are Responsible for Their Own Behaviors.

RULE #1:

RULES ARE NOT ABSOLUTE;
THEY ARE SITUATION-BASED
AND PEOPLE-BASED

Always *and* never *are two words you should*
always remember never to use.

—Wendell Johnson

Webster defines the word *rule* as a "prescribed guide for conduct or action," a "usually valid generalization," a "standard of judgment" or a "regulating principle." Inherent in each of these definitions is that rules affect behavior, whether that behavior is internal (the way we think about ourselves and others) or external (our actions and communication). Missing from each of these definitions is the implication that rules are absolute and unchangeable; indeed adjectives such as "guide" and "usually" suggest otherwise.

Many rules are written and/or shared through oral conversation. "No elbows on the dinner table" or "It's not polite to stare" have been uttered by mothers, fathers, aunts and grandparents for many generations. However, the majority of social rules are unwritten—and in many cases, unspoken—guidelines shared through the raise of an eyebrow or a tacit but stern look that clearly sends a nonverbal message. Well, it may be clear to everyone except children with ASD, whose neural networks can't process this information, and often don't even realize that nonverbal communication is taking place.

Neurotypical individuals have an innate sense of these rules and start learning them, largely through observation, starting in the first years of life. Early rules govern interaction within the home/family setting. As typical children venture out into an ever widening social circle and hone their social skills through trial and error, they realize—by about age four—that rules vary across settings and consequences are often not uniformly applied.

To the literal thinking mind of children and adults with ASD, however, rules are carved-in-stone codes of conduct, commandments of social interaction that control actions across settings. The black-and-white manner in which spectrum individuals think restricts their ability to realize that other people—with unique minds of their own—may interpret rules differently. Or, that some rules are more important than others, and minor rules can be broken often without repercussions. A rule to a person with autism is like a song burned to a CD: no matter when and where it's played, the words and music never change. It's a one-track tune playing over and over in their brains.

Some people with ASD cling desperately to rules because they provide predictability and a measure of control over their world. Temple points out, in the passage that follows, that most children are rigid about rules because their thinking is narrow and inflexible. They lack self-confidence in their ability to react successfully in changing social interactions, and can fear the panic that change causes within them. Once their skills are more developed, they can accept that rules fluctuate over settings and within different groups of people.

Temple Shares:

Generally, people with autism can learn rules, especially those that fall under the heading of social-functioning skills. Most kids can be taught to wait in line, say please and thank you; most adults can learn basic social conversation, to let people know when they're running late to work or an appointment (operational social skills). Where children and adults with ASD have problems is learning flexibility in applying rules to different people and different situations and that context (the situation and the people in it) affects how we think about and interpret different rules. *Flexible thinking is what's difficult, not learning the rules.* While both need to be taught—and both should be taught starting while children are very young—it's flexible thinking that will move the child along and allow more advanced levels of social understanding to grow. Yet, it's the rote social skills that are given more attention, probably because they're easier to teach. Understandable? Yes. Effective practice? No, not if the goal is a socially-aware child or adult.

Rigidity in both behavior and thinking is a major characteristic of people with autism/AS. They have difficulty understanding the concept that a rule can apply in one situation but not in another or that sometimes it is okay to break a rule. I heard about a case where an autistic boy had a severe injury but he did not leave the school bus stop to get help. He had been taught a rule to stay at the bus stop so that he would not miss the bus; he could not break that rule. Most people would know that getting help for a severe injury is more important than missing a bus. But as simple as that process may sound, it's actually quite a complex thinking process, one that involves a LOT of social interpretation. To the autism mind, a rule is absolute.

A good way to teach flexibility of thinking is to use visual metaphors, such as mixing paint. To understand complex situations, such as when occasionally a good friend does something nasty, I imagine mixing white and black paint. If the friend's behavior is mostly nice, the mixture is a very light gray; if the person is really not a friend then the mixture is a very dark gray.

Flexibility can also be taught by showing the person with autism that categories can change. Objects can be sorted by color, function or material. To test this idea, I grabbed a bunch of black, red and yellow objects in my office and laid them on the floor. They were a stapler, a roll of tape, a ball, videotapes, a toolbox, a hat and pens. Depending upon the situation, any of these objects could be used for either work or play. Ask the child to give concrete examples of using a stapler for work or play. For instance, stapling office papers is work; stapling a kite together is play. Simple situations like this, that teach a child flexibility in thinking and relating, can be found numerous times in each day.

They lay the groundwork for the more complex flexible thinking required as children grow and encounter different people and different social situations.

Children do need to be taught that some rules apply everywhere and should not be broken. To teach an autistic child to not run across the street, he has to be taught the rule in many different places. The rule has to be generalized and part of that process is making sure the child understands that the rule should not be broken. However, there are times when an absolute adherence to the rule can cause harm. Children also need to be taught that some rules can change depending on the situation. Emergencies are one such category where rules may be allowed to be broken.

Parents, teachers and therapists can continually teach and reinforce flexible thinking patterns in children with autism/AS. The trick is to do it in a way that accommodates the visual manner in which they think. For many kids, verbal logic won't get through to them. As their thinking becomes more flexible, it will start making sense to them that rules can vary according to the situation or the people involved. The two are interwoven: to the child with inflexible thinking, a rule is absolute. Until the thinking becomes flexible, parents and teachers may need to exercise caution in using rules within behavior and social programs. Constantly use phrases such as "In this situation ..." and "In a different situation ..." to demonstrate how rules apply. Stress the importance of the context and the people in it as a means for thinking about how the rule does or doesn't apply at that time, in that place, and with those people.

Flexibility of thinking is a highly important ability that is often—to the detriment of the child—omitted as a teachable skill on a child's IEP. It impacts a child in all his or her environments, both now and in the future: school, home, relationships, employment, recreation. Parents and teachers need to give it more attention when developing a child's educational plan. It's a precursor to understanding social rules and convention.

Just how important is flexible thinking? Sean is able to recall how his inflexible thinking made it impossible for him to understand the rules his parents and teachers were asking him to learn. His black-and-white interpretation of rules prevented him from appreciating that rules are context driven and that what was acceptable to do or say in one situation (for instance, at home) could be frowned upon in a different situation (for instance, at school). For Sean, as with most individuals with ASD, a rule was a rule, period.

Sean Speaks:

I don't remember too much about my first and second-grade years at school, except that I was a challenge for both teachers. I do recall, however, being overwhelmed right away by the largeness of the classroom space and the number of students; there were about twenty-five pupils instead of the ten I was somewhat used to. Spending seven hours in the same classroom with that many kids sent my anxiety levels skyrocketing; I felt continuously on display. Add to the mix that it took little to embarrass me, and those ingredients were a recipe for disaster.

It took several years for me to feel comfortable in any way at school, and for the first two years I had a lot of trouble handling even the simplest and most routine transitions and adjustments. I lived a half-mile from my elementary school, which meant I walked to and from school each day. It took little time for me to get used to making the ten to fifteen-minute walk past the field that stretched along most of the route. It was after class got underway at 8:00 AM that trouble began.

I was a challenge to my teachers during this time because I had no concept of context. I knew some rules, but didn't realize what other rules meant—especially those that governed the unspoken behaviors that were strictly school-related, like how to act at lunch or during recess. I didn't understand the unwritten "rule" that *certain behaviors were okay at home, but were inappropriate at school.* The result was, to borrow a phrase from author Isaac Asimov, "an immovable object meeting an irresistible force." In other words, both conditions can't exist at the same time because one is the contradiction of the other. It was impossible to follow the rules of the classroom and continue with behaviors that were unacceptable there. Yet, I persisted because my perspective was still very self-involved and I didn't yet understand the nuances of social interaction.

Sean's mindset would prevail for many more years, and its impact would mushroom beyond his ideas about himself and his own abilities to flavor his perception of others around him. Rigid thinking again made it impossible for him to understand that rules were not absolute codes of conduct, and that consequences were often dependent upon which rules were being broken, by whom, how often and what impact breaking the rules had on others involved in the situation. It also speaks to the inconsistent manner in which adults enforce rules, and its resultant impediment to social understanding for autism spectrum children.

Sean Continues:

I recall as a ninth-grader walking into a boys' restroom and seeing what looked like a fogbank hovering in the air and being appalled. The "fogbank" was not composed of fog at all; it was the result of several students deciding that the restroom was the perfect venue for lighting up and having a smoke break between periods. There were three or four kids smoking hurriedly, either from a fear of being caught or being late to class. My reasons for wanting to yell at them were twofold: I had always hated cigarettes, and I knew they were harming their health. Didn't they know how to read the warnings so clearly printed on their packs?

Confronting them wasn't an option because I knew a little about simple arithmetic—there were several of them and one of me. Under those conditions, that likely meant my choice of several forms of physical harm—and none of the items on that menu seemed palatable. So I decided I would defer getting them back for their abominable act.

A few days later, I again used the same facility and saw the same few kids doing their thing. But this time, one of the teachers walked in and interrupted their smoke break. Good, I thought, they will now get what's coming to them. Much to my shock, however, the teacher instead reprimanded the boys and told them to put their cigarettes out and "get to class." The guilty parties filed out, a few with smirks on their faces, and the teacher lagged behind. Not wanting to appear too curious, I too walked to class.

I decided at that moment that I would dislike that teacher because he didn't punish those kids severely enough—indeed there was no punishment at all other than the verbal reprimand. Surely something as important as underage smoking and ruining one's health warranted more severe penalties? Why did the school have this rule if students were so easily let off the hook? What kind of teacher would overlook the indiscretion and permit these students to break the rule? My disdain for the teacher was only reinforced over the following weeks as I witnessed him catch these same students a few more times and in each instance fail to use his authority to mete out more serious punishment, such as suspension. Smoking in school, I clearly knew, was punishable by being kicked out for three to ten days. Why didn't he follow the book?

By this time, I had few friends and had no idea how to make and keep them. As a high school freshman, I quickly felt more comfortable around teachers and office staff than peers. After all, it was the other kids, not the adults, who were making my life miserable and confirming what I believed to be true: that I was a terrible person.

So it made sense to me to play the role of an adult and report the kids to a higher authority than what that one teacher represented. The school had three vice principals, two of whom handled boys' discipline problems and one who took care of difficulties pertaining to the girls. It wasn't long before I saw one of the assistant principals in the hall during lunch and told him of the terrible acts going on almost daily in the first-floor restroom. I figured it was my duty to mention to him what was going on because a rule was a rule. No smoking meant no smoking and no exceptions. If the teacher wasn't going to fully enforce it, it was up to me to do my part. And besides, I reasoned, the smokers will be thankful toward me because my actions now will save them myriad health problems later.

I felt empowered after confiding my "find" to Mr. Sampson, the nicer of the two vice principals. Not only was I enforcing a school rule, which to me was a positive behavior trait, but I was doing a good deed for the kids. Two good results with one act, I thought.

A week or two later, though, one of the kids made it clear to me that he didn't share my perceptions on the matter. I recognized him as he walked toward me, seemingly oblivious to my presence. Suddenly, he swerved in my direction, grabbed my shirt and said, "You better quit talking to Mr. Sampson. I know you told him about us."

Even though I was shaken initially, the repercussion that lasted much longer than the wrinkles in my shirt was an even deeper sense of confusion. I couldn't reconcile my way of seeing the situation—wanting to do something good—with his violent reaction. Didn't he know smoking was detrimental to his well-being? And after all, rules were meant to be followed. My perspective was the only perspective that existed in my brain; that others thought differently—and to such a degree as this—was foreign.

Years later, I realized that my autism and rigid thinking patterns prevented me from seeing the nuances in this social situation, and that while a rule is a rule, some rules could be broken and others could not. And I didn't realize this very basic unwritten rule of social interaction: *people are individuals, each with their own ideas, perceptions, strengths and weaknesses.* Broad generalizations, rules that should apply to everyone, always be followed by all, didn't take into account each individual involved in the interaction. Yes, the teenagers smoking in the restroom clearly violated the school's nonsmoking policy. Yes, inhaling carcinogens was undoubtedly hurting their lungs. And yes, I was being honest when I set out to act like the Lone Ranger and do something good for someone. But what I didn't get was that it wasn't my place to take on an authoritative role—regardless of how noble my intentions—and how by doing so I would create resentment among my peers.

It was a long time later as I fought my way out of autism that it began to dawn on me that few rules are absolute and should be enforced exactly the same way in every situation. Some situations do require strict adherence and honestly should always be practiced. It's never all right, for instance, for people who work with money (bank tellers, Brinks armored car drivers and so on) to steal any amount for any reason. Rationales like "The company can afford to miss a few bucks," never justify theft. Likewise, people who break the law should always do the honest thing and turn themselves in and face the consequences. In those situations, honesty is always the best route and it will likely get you out of trouble faster.

Temple, ever the social scientist even at a young age, approached social situations from a logical viewpoint rather than with Sean's emotionally-laden perspective. By high school she had developed a rule system that guided her behaviors within social interactions. The more data she put on her hard drive— through direct experiences, trial and error—the more refined her rule system became. Notice how logic, rather than emotion, steers her thinking about social rules and that becoming flexible in her thinking patterns was a prerequisite to having the capacity to understand that rules can change across environments and with different groups of people.

Temple Explains:

Children and adults on the autism spectrum are generally concrete, literal thinkers. Ideas that can't be understood through logic or that involve emotions and social relationships are difficult for us to grasp, and even more difficult to incorporate into our daily lives. When I was in high school, figuring out the "social rules" was a major challenge. It was not easy to notice similarities in peoples' social actions and responses because they were often inconsistent from person to person and situation to situation. Over time, I observed that some rules could be broken with minor consequences and other rules, when broken, had serious consequences. It perplexed me that other kids seemed to know which rules they could bend and break and which rules must never be broken. They naturally had a level of flexibility of thinking that I did not have.

However, I knew I had to learn these social rules if I wanted to function in social situations. If I had to learn them, *they somehow had to be meaningful to me, to make sense to me within my own way of thinking and viewing the world.* I started observing social interactions like a scientist and discovered I could group the rules into an organizational format to which I could relate: into major and minor categories. By the time I was a senior in high school I had a system for categorizing some of the social rules of life, comprised of four rule categories, and everything—absolutely everything—fell into one of these categories. I still use the same system today.

1. *Really Bad Things.* I reasoned that in order to maintain a civilized society, there must be prohibitions against certain highly destructive or physically harmful behaviors, such as murder, arson, rape, lying under oath, stealing, looting and injuring other people. The prohibition against really bad things is universal and all cultures have them, otherwise a civilized society would collapse. Children need to be taught that cheating—in all forms, not just on tests—is bad. Learning to "play fair" will help a child grow into an adult who will not commit really bad things.

2. *Courtesy Rules.* All civilized societies have courtesy rules, such as saying please and thank you, not cutting in line at the movie theater or airport, and not spitting on others. These rules are important because they make other people around you more comfortable, help demonstrate respect for your fellow man and prevent anger from arising that can escalate into really bad things. I don't like it when somebody else has sloppy table manners so I try to have decent table manners. It annoys me if somebody cuts in front of me in a line so I do not do this to other people. Different societies have different courtesy rules, but they all serve the same function. In most countries, some common courtesy rules are: standing and waiting your turn in a line, good table manners, being neat and

clean, giving up your seat on a bus to an elderly person, or raising your hand and waiting for the teacher to point to you before speaking in class.

3. *Illegal But Not Bad.* Rules in this category vary greatly from one society to another, among subsets of a society and on down to the family unit. How an individual views these rules will be influenced by his or her own set of moral and personal beliefs. These rules can sometimes be broken depending upon the circumstance. Be careful though: consequences still apply and while some are minor, others are major and may include legal ramifications or monetary fines. Included in this category are slight speeding in cars and illegal parking. However, parking in a handicapped zone would be worse because it violates a courtesy rule. Running a red light would not fall into this category, however, because doing so carries the possibility of injuring or killing someone; it belongs in the first category, Really Bad Things.

   I define which behaviors fall into this category by looking at the original reason for the rule. Take speeding on the highway, for example. The original reason for the rule is to prevent car accidents. So I can bend the rule by doing a little bit of speeding, because I'm not doing anything risky that's going to cause a car accident. Along those same thinking patterns, I'm not going to run a red light because if I run a red light I really risk causing an accident. I also judge situations using probability scales or using percentages—which are logical and visual for me. Back to the example, my chances of causing an accident on the freeway with a little bit of speeding, say five miles over the limit, might be 0.01%. If I run a red light the chances of causing an accident are high; they might be 10-20% or even higher. I also run the risk of violating Rule #1 here too— wrecking property, killing or hurting people is a Really Bad Thing.

One rule I often recommend breaking is the age requirement for attending a community college. I tell parents to sign up the child so he can escape being teased in high school, or to encourage and develop talent in an area that can turn into a career. However, the parent must impress upon the child that this is a grown-up privilege and he must obey all the courtesy rules.

4. *Sins of the System (SOSs).* These are rules that must never be broken—although they may seem to have little or no basis in logic—because the penalty is so severe it may have life-changing repercussions. SOSs vary from country to country and culture to culture. In the U.S. two major sins of the system are sexual misbehaviors and drug offenses. A small sexual transgression that may result in your name being added to a sex-offender list in the U.S. may have little or no consequence in another country. Being caught smoking marijuana here in the U.S. may result in years in jail; in another country the consequence may be a small monetary fine. I have chosen to accept and not challenge SOSs, simply because it avoids many socially-complex situations that would require an exorbitant amount of effort on my part to figure out. This is one of the reasons I chose celibacy. The majority of my social contacts come through work and attempting to date a professional peer is too socially complex for me.

Growing up, behaviors that can be categorized as Really Bad Things and Courtesy Rules were consistently drilled into me, day after day, month after month, by my mother, the nanny, and our neighbors. Those categories formed pretty easily in my mind because examples occurred on a daily basis that I could add to my hard drive. The interesting thing about courtesy rules is they were so ingrained into me as a child I almost didn't look at them as rules; they were just the way you did things. Originally when I set up my rule system I only had three categories—the courtesy rules weren't included. But as I got older I needed the category for new adult courtesy behaviors I learned as I engaged in new social situations.

I came up with Sins of the System during high school, at my boarding school. That's when I really became a social detective. Whenever I saw something that didn't make sense to me, like my roommate rolling around on the floor in elation after seeing the Beatles, I'd say to myself, "interesting sociological phenomena." I used to call it ISP. Then I'd try to figure out why she was doing what she was doing. My involvement was investigative, rather than emotional.

There were two sins of the system at that time: sex and smoking cigarettes. I figured out that once the teachers knew they could trust me, that I wouldn't run off in the bushes and have sex with some boy or smoke, they would tolerate my doing some things they wouldn't let other kids do, like go out on the hill by myself and fly my kite. I also watched what happened to other people when they broke rules, and I started categorizing in my mind a list of behaviors that really got them into trouble. Then through trial and error I tested the system to see what I could get away with and I learned that if I didn't commit sins of the system, I could get away with breaking quite a few other of the illegal but not bad rules. I was always testing the system to put more information on my hard drive and help me understand when rules applied and when they didn't. It was a logical puzzle to me—I'd do certain things just to see if I could do them.

In college, I wondered if I could make a master key for the whole campus out of any ordinary key. So I sent away for a book on lock-smithing and made a grand master key that would open every door on campus. I made another master key out of an empty Budweiser can. I was pretty clever at that time, always testing the boundaries of my abilities, just to see if I could do what I set out to do. But I never actually did anything harmful or unlawful with those master keys. One Sunday I did insert the key I made into the Dean's office door and turned the lock to see if it worked. I didn't even open the door—I just wanted to see if it would turn the cylinder. (It did.) That inquisitiveness was part of my basic personality; climb mountains because they're there. It was a good trait to possess because it helped me become a strong social detective, too.

As I got older and went through more and more social situations, and my thinking became more flexible, I started developing sub-categories under each of the four main categories. For instance, I put killing someone in category #1, Really Bad Things, but I also put smashing somebody's computer in that same category. Obviously, murder is much more serious than destroying property and carries a different penalty. Today my categories each have different sublevels, based on severity or levels of importance.

I felt a lot of anxiety during these years because social phenomena didn't make sense and I was having a hard time figuring them out. For a long time I thought all my anxiety was caused by my inability to learn the meaning of life. It wasn't until I was in my early thirties that I discovered that the anxiety was caused by faulty biochemistry, and was correctable with medication. Life would have been a heck of a lot easier if I had learned that earlier and had been able to get rid of what was sometimes all-consuming stress by taking a little pill each morning. It would have created an internal environment much more conducive to social understanding.

I've had many, many years of practice and lived through thousands, or maybe millions, of different social situations and even today, when I refer to my categories to help me with a social situation, it's still like acting in a play. These are the social rules and this is how I act—it's as though I'm sometimes one step removed from the interaction. I've learned how to do the meet-and-greet social interaction at the start of a business meeting. Or chitchat over coffee with business associates. I tell myself, "Okay, I have to be nice now, I have to go to the conference room and shake hands and be polite." It's a learned behavior, and the way I am today took a lot of learning.

The truth is, not all people with ASD want to put the effort into becoming socially proficient. What are we going to do, force them? I think not. Now, some adults just aren't hard-wired for this social understanding to happen. Some are, but despite a lot of effort on their own part to learn to fit in, their repeated failures have left them feeling anything but motivated to keep trying. Instead, they're angry or socially withdrawn. Then there's a small group who have an oppositional streak to their personalities. It's not necessarily their ASD that's the impairment—it's their basic personality. Some people with autism have to learn, and accept, that certain behaviors will not be tolerated, period. They will have negative consequences that will drastically affect their life and their ability to live independently. For instance, you will be fired, no matter how good your work may be, if you commit a Sin of the System at work. People with ASD need to accept that idea if they want to keep their job—it's one of those rules of the workplace that applies to everyone, even people with ASD. Yet, some adults keep making the same mistakes over and over and think everyone else is responsible except themselves. Lack of flexible thinking and perspective taking are the culprits here; they can only see their situation from their own perspective. And it hurts their chances of being successful. That's why teaching flexible thinking should be such a priority.

Most neurotypical people don't have to stop and think about handling routine day-to-day social situations, or stop to evaluate whether or not a rule applies from one situation to another. But people on the spectrum do. A good analogy for understanding and appreciating the level of effort this takes is to imagine yourself going to a professional symposium in another country. You know some, but not all, of their social rules. You're cognizant that your language translation skills might not be perfect, and you have to monitor what you say and do continuously so you don't offend another person or make a fool of yourself. So, every experience is anxiety-laden. You want to fit in, you want to interact, but even a simple introduction is unnerving. Now, take that feeling and multiply it over hundreds of daily interactions, times 24 hours a day times 7 days a week times 52 weeks a year times year after year after year. That's what it can be like for people with social deficits—even seemingly "simple" interactions can require a lot of effort on our parts for us to look like we fit in.

I think that as a child or young adult becomes more proficient in social skills, teachers assume the behaviors have become "natural,"that some innate sense has finally "woken up" and that's not necessarily true. For many adults with ASD, socially appropriate behaviors have a "use it or lose it" quality and regular—perhaps daily—practice is needed. It doesn't become effortless "second nature" for many of us. The same skills continue to require daily effort to act them out appropriately.

This method of categorizing social rules has worked well for me. However, each person with ASD may need different rule categories that make sense to him or her—it has to be personally meaningful for it to work on any long-term basis.

One of the most difficult unwritten rules of social relationships for children with ASD to understand is that *nearly all rules have exceptions.* Some rules are concrete and specific enough that parents or teachers can point out the exceptions to the rule. In most cases, however, this exercise is both exhausting and misguided. A better use of that time and effort would be to concentrate on teaching the child to think flexibly. Michelle Garcia Winner's Social Thinking Methodology has materials that help teach about perspective taking and flexible thinking at different ages/ stages in a child's life. While children with ASD can have encyclopedic memory capacities and develop highly structured logical databases of rules, sub-rules and exceptions to rules, helping them work through a literal, black-and-white thinking pattern to a mindset that can process information flexibly will, in the long run, enhance their social awareness more.

A few last words to parents and teachers: be flexible in your own thinking; become aware of how frequently you bend/break the rules you expect the child with ASD to follow; and model the type of flexible responses you hope to teach the child.

Inflexible thinking patterns are not attributable solely to people with ASD . Parents and teachers can easily get so caught up in their own ideas about programs and lesson plans for spectrum children that they become rigid in their own thinking and overlook obvious signs of miscommunication and misunderstanding on the part of this population. Often the source of frustration, anxiety and inappropriate behaviors exhibited by a child reside not in the child, but in the adults' words or actions. So, be cautious when using Rules as part of any behavior and/or social skills training. If you know a child understands a rule, but his actions are opposite, look for contextual reasons. He may be doing exactly what you are asking him to do, or following a literal interpretation of the rule as you've presented it.

Rebecca A. Moyes, in her book, *Incorporating Social Goals in the Classroom*, offers this charming example of the literal way children with autism relate to rules.

Rebecca writes:

> One mom relates that despite many requests to her son to not track dirt into the house, via the rule, 'Wipe your shoes before coming into the house,' every day he'd tromp into the house, leaving a trail of mud behind him. This frustrated her to no end and despite repeated requests and escalating measures involving consequences and even time-outs, she finally realized that the source

of the problem was her, not him. She happened to be at the door one rainy day as her son came in, and watched as he bent down and ever so diligently and thoroughly, wiped the tops of both shoes before entering the house. She realized that he had been following directions as he interpreted them. When she explained that she wanted him to wipe the dirt from the bottoms of his shoes, the problem was solved!

Jennifer McIlwee Myers, a socially-adept high-functioning woman with ASD who has a knack for articulating the autism condition with clarity and straight-to-the-point insight, offers her own comments on rules and rule-breaking.

Jennifer shares:

> The nastiest set of hidden social rules for me were the ones that directly contravened the rules that were formally taught. Some teachers would, for example, tell the class repeatedly that there was no talking, when in reality there were strange and intricate rules about those times during school when one could get away with talking softly or passing notes quietly as long as you didn't disturb others.
>
> One set of hidden rules that make me nuts was the rules for gym clothes. Each year we got a handout that said all female students had to wear a solid colored t-shirt with no writing or logos and shorts with an elastic waist with no pockets, snaps, buttons, or zippers. Each year almost all of the other girls wore logoed shirts, shorts with pockets, etc. The real rule was: you can wear any t-shirt and shorts in gym as long as they provide modest coverage and don't interfere with physical activities.

Not only did it drive me crazy that every week all of the other girls violated the rules with impunity, but it also drove my respect for the teachers to an all new low. Why trust or believe a teacher who is so dumb as to be either unable to comprehend their own rule sheet, or who is so unaware of blatant violations? It was just one more thing that told me that the teachers weren't on my side and could not be trusted.

Jennifer also speaks to the power of rules to bolster self-confidence and help children persevere despite what can seem like overwhelming odds against them.

Jennifer continues:

The most important hidden rule my mother took the time to teach me got me through my childhood alive. It literally saved my sanity repeatedly.

My mother often explained to me that *the skill set for childhood is not anything like the skill set for adulthood.* She told me that I just didn't have the traits that would make me excel at being a kid, especially in social life, but that I did have a lot of traits that would be great in an adult. She pointed out that many of the kids who were popular and seemed to have it all were going to undermine their hopes for adulthood by the end of high school (or college at the latest) with binge drinking, experimenting with drugs, maltreating their bodies to achieve fashionable thinness, causing themselves permanent physical damage in pursuits of sports glory, and so forth. Many others would simply find that all of the traits and skills that they had so carefully honed throughout high school simply didn't work in adult life.

She told me that when those people were sitting around at age forty, drinking and remembering those few years of perfection, I would have a life.

In short, my mother was fond of reminding me that childhood is a temporary state. Both of my parents admitted that childhood is essentially very stressful and that most of the traits prized in children have little to do with adult achievement or functionality. Without them impressing the importance of this little secret on me, I might not have been able to keep going through high school.

As we come full circle with Unwritten Rule #1, *Rules are not absolute*, we leave you with Sean's final passage, a promise of sorts that success can be achieved. People with ASD can be taught to think flexibly, they can learn why rules exist and what functions they serve. By judiciously monitoring how we teach social rules and through constant vigilant attention to pointing out the exceptions to the rules we teach, social awareness and understanding can grow.

Sean Speaks:

Albert Einstein once made the seemingly innocuous observation that all things are relative. Of course among the "things" he had in mind were the scientific laws that governed the creation of matter and other similar ideas. His statement extends beyond scientific principles to nearly everything in life—something it took my getting rid of autism to understand and appreciate. It's just as true whether it applies to matter, distinguishing between the "absolute" versus "relative" truth, or in some cases, to even something as simple as eating a salad.

One evening when I was seventeen or eighteen my parents and I visited the home of some family friends who worked in the music business with my parents. They were delighted to give us a tour of their spacious home with numerous gardens overlooking the Los Angeles basin and to have us to dinner. Everyone talked for about a half-hour while I spent most of that time by a bay window mesmerized by the view. I was still staring out when our gracious hosts had us sit with them at the dining room table for our meal.

The smell of the food got stronger as they brought everything out from the kitchen. Before serving the main course, the friends brought beverages, salads and a variety of appetizers to everyone. For years I rarely touched vegetables or fresh fruit, relying instead on a diet filled with starches and carbohydrates. On this evening, however, I vowed that I would at least try my salad, which contained not iceberg but organic lettuce as well as cucumbers, chopped tomatoes and bits of cabbage. After they returned to the kitchen, I took a large forkful and found that I could barely swallow the bite.

Eyeing me first as she returned to the dining room, the woman asked me, "So, how do you like it?"

"I hate it," I said matter-of-factly. "I don't do salads."

An awkward split-second silence filled the room as Mom and Dad shot stern looks my way. Later, the salad was the source of conversation between me and my parents, not a source of Vitamin A.

"Sean, you don't say that to someone," my mother explained. Yes, you may not like the salad, but you don't bluntly tell that to people who made it as an act of graciousness and kindness, my parents tried to get me to see. As we pulled into our San Fernando, California, driveway thirty minutes later, the conversation about the effects such harsh words have on people was still going on.

I went to sleep that night still at a loss as to why on one hand I was taught to tell the truth, yet when I had done so earlier that evening, I was reprimanded. The contradiction made no sense. It wouldn't click for several more years that such social situations were neither contradictions nor absolute rules, but that *rules were relative and based on time, place and people.*

Most children, autism or not, are taught early certain absolute rules, such as the idea that it's always wrong to tell a lie. But as children turn into teenagers and adults, the immutable nature of rules softens and becomes more malleable as children develop a broader view of life. They learn that each social encounter is made up of numerous elements involving different perspectives, thoughts and emotions, and that appropriate actions are often dependent upon factors beyond the pure issue at stake. As children gain social maturity they realize, for example, that the rule "always tell the truth" may not apply when the truth hurts another person's feelings. My autism prevented me from consistently making these adjustments until much later—until I was in my twenties.

With this in mind, I plainly see why the atmosphere changed so drastically when I told our California dinner hosts that I hated the salad they prepared. I was being completely forthright at the time; she asked how I liked the salad and I told her the truth. In that situation, as well as countless others, the key my autism masked from sight was basic logic. How on earth would our dinner hosts know that I didn't eat salads, never having had me to dinner? When I responded to people in these and similar ways, I ended up with truth and few friends. And friends are a lot more fun to hang out with than absolute truth.

Today, I still prefer plain salads. But when it comes to always telling the truth, my recipe for success is this unwritten social rule I learned the hard way: that *it's better to stretch the truth a little than to hurt someone a lot.* It took a while to learn—but I did learn it—that the only absolute rule of life is that there are few absolutes. In the smorgasbord of social relationships, it's the one rule I can't live without.

2017 REFLECTIONS FROM SEAN

At a recent autism conference, I shared with my audience a situation that took place a few years ago during which a county sheriff pulled me over for speeding. He was quite friendly and courteous as I explained that I was in a hurry, and he responded by making me aware that I had been traveling 45 MPH in a marked 25-MPH zone. I knew I had no counterargument to make and, worse, had blatantly broken the law. I felt terrible about my transgression but accepted full responsibility.

"I know I was speeding, and I make no excuses. I fully blame myself and apologize for having done so," I said before the deputy returned to his cruiser's computer to check to see if I was wanted on any warrants, as part of standard procedure.

I engaged briefly in deep-breathing exercises to calm myself as I watched him come toward my car, absolutely certain I would receive a ticket carrying a hefty fine, a stern warning and a possible court date. Much to my surprise, however, the deputy issued me a written warning instead of a ticket and then mildly admonished me to slow down whenever I drive through that section of town.

How was I able to sidestep what seemed to be the inevitable—especially given that I had gone a whole 20 mph over the speed limit? Did I have connections with one or more important people in the area who would likely get me out of my predicament? Did I curry favor by being a friend of a friend? Or was I prominent enough in the community that he felt compelled to simply look the other way? The answer to all three was a resounding no. So how did I get such a lucky break? The answer was internal.

I acted on the idea that societal rules and laws are situation and people-based. In other words, players' interactions with one another in nearly any given instance in which the rule's voracity, strength and endurance are challenged and broken are crucial in determining how the outcome will play out. This tenet holds true sometimes even in the most egregious cases. For example, two people with similar evidence and case parameters could be convicted of murder but receive different sentences based on intangibles such as the level of remorse shown and responsibility taken. The defendant who expresses sincere sorrow could be treated with slightly more leniency than the person who lacks empathy and remorse.

This brings me back to getting stopped for speeding. Long before I learned to drive, I spent my younger years following a pattern in which I did everything I could to deny, deflect and cover up mistakes I made, mainly because I perceived that my worth as a person was directly tied to how well I did something. If I failed at a task, I was a failure—period. There was no negotiating with my internal logic or reasoning and no consideration for the importance of the task. And the more I dug in, the bigger the problem became.

So against that backdrop, it's not a giant leap to figure that, if I had been belligerent with the deputy, I certainly would have gotten a ticket, which probably would have carried a steep fine and perhaps an embarrassing mandatory court appearance.

I think this also serves as a good example to bolster a teachable moment to those on the spectrum: Just as mile markers and signs on a highway serve as tools for making a long trip easier, rules can be viewed as guideposts that make navigating life easier and more manageable. To put it another way, individuals on the spectrum can be taught that flexible thinking and interpretations, coupled with rules that look unbending and inflexible, are actually complementary of each other, not contradictory.

That means it's vital to show them that society's rules and laws have two parts: the letter and the spirit. The first explains the conduct expected of people and consequences for violating such expectations. The second implies variance in how the rule is enforced as well as the sanctions for breaking it. The two go hand in hand.

POINTS TO KEEP IN MIND:

- Social rules change as time goes by; a social rule in the early '60s might be too strict for today's culture.
- In teaching kids with ASD, consider using a different word than "rule"; try something like "guideline" that has a less-absolute meaning.
- Avoid using the words "always" or "never" in explaining rules.
- Social rules are a reflection of a society's attitudes, values, prejudices, and fears. Teachers especially should consider the cultural environment of the child/parents and whether this impacts social-behavior expectations at school.
- Social rules are a source of comfort as well as constraint; they can help organize a child's thoughts and reduce anxiety over being uncertain what to do/how to act in a given situation. Just use them wisely.
- Appropriate social behavior changes as children age. Teach social rules in a way that will apply over various situations and still retain their "validity" as the child grows up. It's confusing to the child to learn a social behavior that is appropriate at age five and then be taught that it is inappropriate at age ten and needs to be "unlearned." Think forward before defining a rule for today.
- When posting formal rules, keep in mind the literal thinking style of people with ASD. Some students with ASD will not "get" that rules not posted may be in effect, too, or that the posted rules apply in settings outside the classroom. "No hitting, biting, pushing or shoving

children"is acommon classroom rule. So is tripping therefore appropriate behavior, or is throwing things at a child acceptable behavior? It's not on the list! Make sure to explain that other rules exist that define acceptable and unacceptable behavior besides those on the chart. Check for comprehension that rules on the chart apply/don't apply in different school settings. For instance, the no-hitting rule may also apply in Art and Music class, but the rule to keep shoes and socks on at all times might not apply during gym class when students change into sneakers.

- Get in the habit of frequently repeating a short "social mantra" to help the child learn flexible thinking. Saying something as simple as "Every rule has an exception" can cue the child to look at the situation from a different perspective.

- Avoid inconsistent application of rules and their consequences: between family members, between home and school, between different teachers in school. While Uncle Joe may think he's helping when he responds to a social miscue with, "Well, we'll let it go just this one time," his behavior can confuse, rather than help, the child or adult with ASD. Frustration and anxiety can result, rather than learning. Teachers may unconsciously have their own set of personal "hidden rules" that can confuse a child with ASD, especially when these rules oppose the "formal" rules they share with the class at the beginning of the school year. "Be in your seat when the bell rings" is a common rule teachers cite, although many teachers will overlook infringements on a regular basis. It's a breeding ground for mistrust to develop. Consistently applied consequences reinforce learning; inconsistency creates an environment that hampers, rather than facilitates, learning social behaviors.

RULE #2

NOT EVERYTHING THAT HAPPENS IS EQUALLY IMPORTANT IN THE GRAND SCHEME OF THINGS

S top for a moment and imagine what life would be like if your thoughts and emotions were black and white. It's difficult to grasp, because the world outside autism is anything but a two-toned experience, but really give it a try. You wake up to discover that your four-month old adorable puppy chewed up every favorite cook-book in the kitchen, including all those time-tested recipes you wouldn't share even with your sister and your reaction is absolute—it's either no reaction or a full-blown rant and rave. On the way to work, the ATM machine is out of cash, you realize you left lunch sitting on the counter back home along with your umbrella and it's started to rain so hard you get soaked walking the twenty feet from the parking space to your office. In each instance, no "ifs" and "buts" color your perception of the experiences. Your emotions swing wildly, in an all-or-nothing manner. They're either off or on; nothing in between. Thoughts like "that's okay" or "no biggie, I can grab a sandwich from the deli downstairs" are absent from the self-talk you use to gauge the relative importance of life events. Even your thoughts are unconditional. The more likely comeback is see-ing yourself entirely at fault: "I must be the stupidest person walking on this planet to forget my umbrella." You just don't think that—you believe it. Now, play this scenario over and over a hundred or so times, each time with that same non-categorical response to events, and ask yourself, "How do I feel?" In truth, you probably can't even imagine how an entire day of thinking this way would make you feel; it's that foreign a way of thinking. Welcome to the world of the person with ASD bound by black-and-white thinking!

Sean vividly recalls what life was like when "making mountains out of molehills" aptly described his demeanor.

Sean Remembers:

I recall many times feeling stressed out and overcome with anger—feelings that often accompanied events, places or settings that most of us would equate with emotions far removed from these.

One such place was a Dairy Isle that we often went to on the way home from the local swim club. My order never deviated from chocolate ice cream in a dish or a chocolate milkshake. All went well until I got the shake. It violated a rule I held sacred: Drinks were to be filled to the top.

Instead, I got my treat in a cup that had the dreaded words, "Fill to here," printed just under a line two-thirds of the way up indicating how full the drink was supposed to be. To me, it was 30% empty, causing 100% fury. And, fury is what I felt—not disappointment, not irritation, not even mild anger, but seething fury. My response was to either continually stir the shake and make it appear as if I was drinking it, buying time until we got home and I could get rid of it, or to refuse to touch it and dump it out at the earliest opportunity.

It infuriated me that they would make a beverage and only partially fill it; a cup or glass was supposed to be full. Otherwise, why manufacture the cup that large? My rage still brewed inside me even after I got home and disposed of the drink. I recall ripping the cup and/or stomping on it until my fury abated.

The milkshake is but one example that demonstrates the all-or-nothing way of thinking that was a hallmark of how my autistic mind worked. I devised rules that helped me get a grip on the confusing morass of stimuli that was my world. They were guardians that stood at the gates of experience, trying to keep fear and anxiety out. And in my mind the rules were quite reasonable; everyone should follow them. The fact that no one but I knew them had no relevance at that time. That would have required me to understand others' different perspectives, and my way of thinking was so clear-cut to me, I assumed it was thinking that everyone else shared too. When the outside world didn't conform, when people did things like take a cup and fill it to only 60% capacity, depriving me of a drink I looked forward to having—my anger and stress catapulted.

All the rules I devised and expected the world to conform to were equal in importance. Why? *Because each time a person followed a rule I felt a measure of control and security, regardless of the rule or situation.* It mattered less what the rule was than whether or not it was executed. I lacked the ability to think about any single rule out of context and weigh it against anything else. So when my parents would point out to me, for instance, how unhealthy it was to have such a strong reaction to something as minor as having a semi-empty cup, their argument and attempt to get me to see reason didn't register. My thinking overall was black and white and literal; seeing shades between the extremes was nearly impossible.

It took me many years to learn that when it comes to social interactions among people, and even understanding these social encounters in relation to myself, an unwritten rule was understood by everyone but me: that *not everything tips the scales evenly, and I needed to weigh things against each other in importance.* When I look back, I realize that this skill developed in proportion to how much I overcame my autism. In my late teens and early to mid-twenties, I worked very hard to see beyond my own comfort needs, to acknowledge that other people thought differently than I did and learn to appreciate the perspectives of others. As my thinking expanded beyond myself, so did my ability to interpret the hierarchical nature of the world.

This was anything but easy, however. I often compare it to being in a coma and having to fight to learn to walk, speak, and function again. Only in my case, it was an emotional coma of sorts. While it did gradually get easier, I had to force myself to fight the very things that gave me comfort in order to learn a better way of functioning. The more I looked past myself, the more my thoughts, reactions and ways of relating to the world flexed."

At the heart of Rule #2, which in its essence acknowledges that our world is composed of "shades of gray" and has a hierarchical structure to it, are two presuppositions that the individual can:

1. Sort into categories the myriad details that qualify our experiences, and
2. Appreciate that different levels of importance can be assigned to these categories.

Categorical thinking is not inherently strong in people with ASD, but it can be taught, starting with children who are very young. The good news is that it can be illustrated in very concrete ways and across a vast range of settings on a daily basis, with relative ease. Personal interests can be used to keep the child engaged and make lessons motivating and fun.

Temple Points Out:

When I was a young child, everything pretty much got me equally upset. My thinking patterns were rigid, more black and white than shades of gray. I was fortunate in that our home life was structured and Mother and the nanny were consistent in their expectations of me and the consequences they attached to my behaviors. That sameness was calming to some degree, it allowed me to experience a sense of order and control. However, a lot of anxiety existed nevertheless.

I got upset over things that other children didn't even notice. One night it rained really hard and the roof leaked, leaving a small water stain on the ceiling of my room. I became terrified, fearing the ceiling would collapse. The pictures conjured up in my visual mind were of all the upstairs furniture crashing down on me.

Even as I moved into high school, I was still experiencing giant anxiety attacks over very minor events—my reactions were still out of proportion to what was happening. I recall finding out that the high school planned to change the daily schedule. Classes ended at three o'clock and sports activities followed. They wanted to reschedule some sports earlier in the day and extend classes later. That resulted in huge anxiety for me. Now when I look back at it, it seems ridiculous that I would react the way I did. But at the time, it was a very big deal because my thinking was still very literal and inflexible and I didn't have a lot of data on my hard drive that could even begin to allow my mind to compare/contrast one thing to others. It's like a computer that stops on one image—it doesn't realize that housed on the hard drive are other images that might relate.

There are three basic levels of conceptual thinking: *1)* learning rules; *2)* identifying categories; and *3)* inventing new categories. Category-forming ability can be tested by placing a series of objects on a table, such as pencils, notepads, cups, nail files, paper clips, napkins, bottles, CDs, and other common objects. An adult with autism can easily identify all the pencils, or all the bottles. He can also easily identify objects in simple categories, such as all the objects that are green or all the metal objects. Conceptual thinking at this basic level is generally not a problem. Most autism programs attend to this quite well, starting with children who are very young. Teaching colors, shapes, animal sounds, etc., are building blocks for developing this skill. There are lots of good products on the market today, in video/DVD format that parents can use at home, too. Teaching this level of category formation skill is generally not a problem.

Where the person with autism has extreme difficulty is inventing new categories, which is the beginning of true concept formation. For example, many of the objects in the list referenced above could be classified by use (e.g., office supplies) or by shape (round/not round). To me, it is obvious that a cup, a bottle and a pencil are all round. Most people would classify a round CD in its square plastic case as not-round; however, I might put it into the round category because of the CD inside. My associative-thinking skills are strong, and many people on the spectrum share this trait. We see associations that typical people miss—and may consider "wrong" because of their own thinking style.

One of the easiest ways to teach concept formation is through playing category-forming games with children. For example, a cup can be used to drink from, or to store pencils or paper clips. Notepads can be used for note taking, for art drawings, or, more abstractly, as a paperweight or a coaster for a glass. Activities such as these must be done with a high degree of repetition; it will take some time for the person with autism to learn to think differently. However, with perseverance, results will occur. Practice is the key, in structured lessons and natural settings. The opportunities to facilitate category formation are endless when adults look around them. Think of the grocery store—what a natural setting for teaching new categories. In the beginning, the simple act of verbalizing what the adult sees can be helpful. "I see a red tomato, a red radish and a red onion. They're all red. They're also all vegetables ... they're all round ... they can all be eaten." Starting with the concrete, visual object is good. The young child can see it, feel it, and experience it through more than once sense. Even if the child can't yet independently recognize the different categories, pointing them out reinforces that they exist. I loved to play the game "Twenty Questions," which helped me learn to form new categories. One person thinks of an object, such as a fork. The other person has to guess what it is, by asking twenty or less questions. The first question is usually, "Is it animal, plant or mineral?" Parents can help guide a rigid thinker by suggesting questions at first; with enough repetition (and this is a fun way to learn) categories will eventually form in their minds.

Helping children "get into their head" different and varied ways of categorizing objects is the first step in developing flexible thinking. Alongside this is exposing children to change, starting at a young age. Structure is good for children with autism, but sometimes plans can, and need to be, changed. When I was little, my nanny made me and my sister do a variety of activities. This variety prevented rigid behavior patterns from forming. I became more accustomed to changes in our daily or weekly routines and learned that I could still manage when change occurred. Without that variety, my rigid thinking would have prevailed. It's an unwritten rule of social relationships, and of life itself: *change is inevitable.*

Mother also instilled in us an understanding of compromise, in very concrete terms. Sometimes we did what my sister Izzy wanted to do, and sometimes we did what I wanted to do. Mother didn't tolerate a behavior outburst over something like this, unless I was tired or there was some sensory issue involved. It just wasn't acceptable behavior to yell and scream and act out because I wanted to do something different. On a conceptual level what we're talking about is teaching compromise, along with a sense of what's fair/unfair. It doesn't have to be as complicated as some parents and professionals see it. It's as simple as putting two glasses of juice in front of two kids and giving one a whole lot more than the other. Kids can understand this, they know how that feels. Then, the next time you give the other child more. When simple things like this are repeated over and over it does start to make sense to kids with autism. Doing it over and over and over is the key. It was drilled into me that *sometimes I had to do what somebody else wanted to do, that*

I wasn't always going to get my way. It's one of the unwritten rules we all live under. I got it; I learned to compromise.

The metaphor I use that makes sense to me is, once again, mixing paint. There's a can of black paint and one of white paint; they're opposites. Compromise means mixing the two. A good compromise for me would be more black paint in the pot than white paint—a very dark gray. If the compromise goes the other way, it ends up looking light gray. In my logical-based thinking, I'd rather have 80% of my black paint in the mix than none, so I make an effort to compromise. I learned through my experiences in early adult life that sometimes compromise is the only thing that's achievable when dealing with people. As a child, it was simply an expected behavior.

I also had good problem-solving abilities even from an early age, which I think helped me learn to think more flexibly. All the projects I built strengthened those skills. Everything from building a simple cardboard house to building snow forts reinforced a systematic way of thinking and relating details to the "big picture." I had to learn that you have to build walls before you can attach a roof. That may sound simplistic, but it's an early level of learning to prioritize actions and that one action may have more value than another. The child doesn't realize he's learning to prioritize actions, to think in ways that will eventually play out with emotions and in social relationships. To him, he's learning the mechanics of building a house. Parents should never underestimate the value of play for young children, and especially playing games that involve one or two other children. There's so much opportunity for basic social interaction that lays the groundwork for more advanced social thinking skills to develop later on.

I've noticed that some adult Aspies who still think in rigid ways have the hardest time in social situations. It's like their mind has just one big category, one box or only a couple of boxes into which all their experiences go. They haven't learned to subdivide the data down into smaller categories, so they regularly misinterpret the experience or the intentions of the other person. It's that black and white thinking again, coupled with not having enough experiences, enough information on their hard drive to form meaningful categorical subdivisions. As adults, they're looking for the one ultimate key to unlock their confusion, to give them the meaning of life. Well there isn't one. The result is a lot of confusion, huge amounts of negativity directed at themselves, and stress and anxiety.

I want to reiterate that thinking flexibly requires a lot of practice. It's not going to develop in a thirty-minute, twice-a-week session. The more examples the child is given, the more flexible his or her thinking can become. The more flexible the thinking, the easier it will be for the person with autism to learn to develop new categories and concepts.

This is all a precursor to being able to understand social relationships. Once the child has acquired some flexible thinking skills with concrete objects, parents and teachers can begin to expand their conceptual thinking into the less concrete areas of categorizing feelings, emotions, facial expressions, etc. It's all a part of developing social awarenessand social problem solving.

All those details! The "little professor" mind of children with autism amasses so many details. Every situation, every encounter, is broken down into minute pieces, all equally important. What happens to all that data? Categories provide a logical structure inside their mind. For those readers who use a computer on a daily basis, imagine a year's worth of your files stored on the hard drive all in one file folder. Each time you need to refer back to a bit of information, you have to sift through thousands of files to find the one you're looking for. Year after year you add thousands more files—maybe you've been able to eke out a handful of folders to organize them into. But it's still an overwhelming amount of data, all still viewed with equal importance. Are you beginning to get a better sense of how important it is to teach young children about categories and promote flexible thinking? Are other behaviors you see in children with autism also starting to make sense, like their delayed responses (so much information to go through to come up with a reply) or tuning out (too much information to wade through all the time)? And, can you now better appreciate the value of values?

Good news again! Help is available to teach individuals with ASD the second part of Rule #2, that different levels of importance can be assigned to the various categories of information they have stored in their brains. The process is similar to teaching categories: start with the concrete and gradually expand to more conceptual arenas, like emotions. Visual representations like charts, circles, point scales and thermometers are meaningful to children with ASD. For instance, sitting in your seat while the bus is in motion may rate a "5" on a five-point scale of importance, while staying seated while watching a movie at home might rate only a "1." In a similar vein, talking at length about your favorite interest may be okay at a level of "5" with parents, "3" with your teacher or the babysitter, and only a "1" with peers at school.

Books such as *Navigating the Social World* by Jeanette McAfee and *The Incredible 5-Point Scale* by Kari Dunn Buron and Mitzi Curtis offer excellent practical, visual tools that can be used to teach children with ASD to distinguish levels of importance in their thoughts, actions and especially, with their emotions.

Relationships and emotions are inseparable associations to individuals who are highly social individuals. But as Temple pointed out earlier, this is not necessarily valid for all people with ASD, especially those who think in pictures. Nevertheless, success in understanding the obvious and more nuanced rules of social relationships is dependent upon individuals with ASD understanding the categorical nature of emotions: a variety of different emotions exist, and each emotion can be expressed in varying degrees. This is a more advanced level of mental processing that requires not only flexible thinking, but perspective taking, appreciating that different minds share different values, dependent upon personal, familial, cultural and social norms. Lack of perspective and lack of experiences robs a child of a frame of reference for understanding emotions.

To neurotypicals, the realm of emotions is a richly colored, detailed inner canvas. To the child with ASD, it may be a stark white canvas, devoid of paint. Children with ASD have trouble recognizing, expressing and controlling their own emotions. Some individuals display few emotions, which is termed having a "flat affect." Temple describes herself has having no more than a handful of emotions. To the untrained eye, the emotional reactions of spectrum children may seem varied and complex. It makes sense; a typical person can effortlessly experience different levels of emotions, different nuances of emotions, so a parent or teacher assumes that ASD kids feel this too. That assumption is faulty, though, even for individuals in their teenage years and into young adulthood. Their understanding of emotions may be much more basic.

Sean Briefly Explains:

Autism has a way of affecting one's ability to character judge, thereby making it harder than solving a Rubik's Cube with both eyes closed to judge others' motives. Unless someone's facial expressions were blatant, or unless the person forcefully expressed, say, anger, I had great difficulty deciphering people's feelings. Even in my early teenage years, I didn't know that people can and almost always do feel more than one emotion at a time. I couldn't reconcile how someone could experience "conflicting" feelings, such as sadness and happiness, at the same time. It just didn't make sense to me. You were angry or not angry, sad or happy, confused or with it, at a given time, but not both.

Emotional expression, and emotional control, can be difficult for spectrum kids. Their emotions have only two settings: none or high. Because their emotions can be so volatile, some children are hesitant to engage in situations where their emotions may erupt, where unpredictable situations will sap their ability to stay in control. Couple this with the out-of-proportion emotional outbursts that were described earlier in this chapter and emotions are a mighty scary monster for many children unable to control them.

Temple Shares,

I have a problem with modulating emotion. It doesn't matter whether I'm feeling anger or feeling sadness, whether I'm crying or laughing—the feeling is "all on" or "all off." A while back I was on an airplane, watching a movie. In one of the scenes there was a giant snake under a fancy table in a ballroom. I was laughing so hard that everybody in the plane was turning around to look at me. I can now control it, but in the beginning, the emotion was either off, or it turned on full force. It got me into trouble sometimes, because my emotions were inappropriate responses to situations, like when Mother would reprimand me for laughing out loud at a fat person.

Personal experiences have taught me that I needed to be able to control my emotions, and my tantrums, especially my anger, which has been my biggest problem. It's that logical thinking part of me, how to solve the social dilemma. After I blow up in a fit of whatever emotion I'm feeling, it's over very quickly and the feelings are gone. I have learned, however, that the repercussions are very real. *Your behavior has consequences*: it's another unwritten rule. In school, when the kids were teasing me I'd often lash out. One time I threw a book at the girl who teased me and I got kicked out of school for that. In high school, my angry outbursts resulted in the loss of horseback riding privileges for an entire week, and I really loved riding horses. Keeping that privilege was highly motivating for me, so I forced myself to figure out a way to not get angry. That's when I switched anger to crying.

As I entered the workforce, I knew I had to control my anger or I'd never be able to keep a job. If I had a tantrum at the Swift plant, it would have been bye bye career. I did lots of crying out in the cattle yard when I felt my anger escalating. I'd go off by myself and let it go.

The only way for me to control anger was to switch it to another emotion; you can't get rid of emotions, you have to change your reaction—in this case, to one that would not result in me being kicked out of the plant. Crying wasn't always an option, though. I remember working on a cattle project when the equipment started malfunctioning, and the plant manager started yelling and screaming at me. I had to come up with a way to diffuse the anger on the spot, to see the situation differently. Trying to work this out through social understanding would have been meaningless. So, in order not to get mad I viewed him as if he were a two-year-old having a tantrum. It worked—I didn't get angry. But sometimes, it worked so well that it was all I could do not to laugh instead. I knew that would make him mad, too.

Because complex emotional situations are still so hard for me to decipher, I've learned I'm just better off trying to avoid them altogether. When I was using crying as a substitute emotion, I'd have some pretty severe crying jags. Crying was still all or nothing, too. Lots of times I'd get physically sick from the crying. Now I look for warning signs and then I tend to get out of the way, or remove myself from a situation like that. It's what I call "psychodrama" and I try to avoid it. Of course, some things I can't avoid, and I can handle it now. If a plant manager is having a tantrum because he thinks an equipment malfunction is my fault, I let him rant and rave, and then I appeal to his logic. Once he's calmed down, I might take him up to the conference room and explain to him that I hadn't really broken his equipment, that start-up was actually going quite well and it was not reasonable to ask for 100% production in the first five minutes. Neurotypical people interject so much psychodrama into their social and professional interactions; they let their emotions take over their intellect. It causes a lot of problems that a little logic and common sense could prevent. Highly intelligent Aspies can often remain calm and focused in situations that drive more socially-oriented people off the edge of reason, because they can keep their emotions separated from their thinking. It's actually a good trait when channeled appropriately.

Both Sean and Temple experienced intense emotions; however, *how* they perceived their emotions differed, as did the residual effect. Whereas Temple exploded and then the attached emotions would quickly dissipate from memory, the emotional fall-out for Sean would cling for hours, days or even years.

Sean Speaks:

In sixth, seventh, and eighth grade, I had a fixation with school buses and would watch them line up at the end of the day in the school's back parking lot. I noted which ones arrived early and late and loved to see the angle at which they parked. Soon I invented a card game I called "Buses," in which I would move the cards across a rug I had in my bedroom that represented the rectangular-shaped parking lot and simulate the movements of the school buses from arrival to departure. I picked about twenty cards—the number that corresponded to the number of school buses—and had them slanted on the rug at the exact angle of the stationary school buses. After about ten minutes, I would have most of the cards "leave" the rug before one or two others "arrived"—the same situation that played out in the school's parking lot.

In time, I added a variation to my game. Instead of simply using a deck of cards to represent the school buses, I chose to use, to the extent possible, people—specifically, myself, my two parents and my sister, Meg. Each weekday morning before Meg and I left for school and my parents left for work, we gathered for breakfast at the kitchen table. Eventually, I saw this daily gathering as another means by which to satisfy my insatiable fixation on school buses. I "assigned" each person to a seat at the table, as well as an approximate time and exact order in which I expected them to come downstairs. I was to be first, my parents second and third and my sister last. I remember many mornings in the kitchen actually listening for stirring upstairs and becoming worried if I heard what I thought was Meg getting up before it was her time to come down. Sometimes I would wolf down my food and try to finish and leave the table before her kitchen arrival—in the same manner that some school buses exited the school property before others arrived.

Everything went smoothly in the morning unless someone violated this precious family rule. When that happened—and it did more often than not—I became agitated and my morning would be ruined. If Meg came down early, sat in someone else's seat or both, I often left for school in a foul mood that sometimes took hours to diminish. My family knew I was unreasonably angry because of my rule being broken. They just didn't know how to break through those feelings, nor did I have the ability to explain why the violation led to such strong fury. I wasn't yet able to link my need to control the situation (and those in it) with my feelings of being powerless over the world around me. At that point in my life, the ends justified the means. I was functioning at a simpler level of response, based on action-reaction. If each person arrived in the kitchen and conformed to my desperate need for order, I felt empowered; if, on the other hand it was violated, I left the house feeling powerless, angry and helpless.

In time, however, just as Temple devised ways to control her anger and her emotions, Sean was able to gain control of the helm too, steering his life and his emotions to a greater extent in the direction he wanted them to go. However, the process was anything but easy and the effect it had on his parents and his own self-esteem clung to him for years.

Sean Continues:

My black-and-white pattern of thinking meant I dealt with lapses in judgment, mistakes and so on in one of two extremes: complete and utter denial of my actions or with enormous rage—anger that was way out of proportion to the event itself. Since my autism made it difficult for me to weigh the importance of many things, my anger was huge regardless of how large or small the situation that had caused it (and 99.9% of the time it was quite small). *All* mistakes were equal in their ability to reinforce in my mind that I was a "bad" or "stupid" person. To make up for my "badness" I crossed the line from striving for perfection to expecting it, thus setting up for myself an impossible task. When I failed—which was of course inevitable—I felt even worse. It was a circle of doom with no beginning or end.

Whether I resorted to falsehoods or flat-out rage, the result was the same: It made a tiny situation much bigger than it should have been while causing undue hard feelings in myself and others.

And it was something I did not only as a teenager, but also as a young adult.

One time, when I was in my mid-twenties and my mother was visiting, we ran several errands. While in the car, I incorrectly used the word "gregarious" during a conversation with her. The word means sociable or fond of others' company, but I used it in another context and in so doing, caused her to point it out.

"Sean, I don't think that's the word you meant to use."

"I'm such a retard. Are you sure I wasn't dropped as a baby and my brain deprived of oxygen?"

"Oh come off it. Now you do sound stupid," she said, anger rising in her voice.

"I sound stupid because I am."

By this point, the level of ire had moved up several notches when my mother said, "Stop feeling sorry for yourself."

There were several more angry exchanges during this conversation—each one carrying more emotion than the last—as frustration on both our parts continued to escalate. Both of us were seething by the time we arrived home and neither wanted to be in the company of the other.

Did it have to go this way? Were there better choices I could have made in response to having such a minor mistake brought to my attention? I emphatically answer both with a "no" and "yes," respectively.

Some things I could have done that would have led to a different—and far better—outcome include:

- Laughter. Yes, laughing at the error of my ways or words works wonders (alliteration unintended). There really is truth to the worn-out saying that laughter is the best medicine. It releases endorphins in the brain that are good for you and have a positive effect on your mental status, and it helps you and those around you feel better right away. Most importantly, laughter has the added power of diffusing otherwise unpleasant situations. I know that had I been self-effacing or made a joke of the fact that I used the word wrong, both my mother and I would have had a good laugh, I would have felt better and the whole thing would have been over in seconds. However, at the time my autistic thinking didn't allow me to see other options. As it turned out, a bad mood developed in the car, solidified and persisted for hours—all because of my single-minded thinking and reaction, not because I misused "gregarious."

- Going MOR. "MOR" is an acronym for the '70s expression "middle of the road." It basically means just what it implies: taking a neutral stance on something. To again use the car example, I could simply have said something like, "Oh, okay. I didn't realize I had used that word wrong." Such a response may not have gotten my mom and me all warm and fuzzy, but it too would have ended the situation right then and there. Any bad mood would have been, to borrow another acronym, DOA (dead on arrival).

- Even swallowing it. Nodding in agreement or saying nothing and simply letting it pass would certainly have been preferable to hours of a dark mood complemented with indigestion. This approach may not have diffused it as quickly as the other two, but it would have been much better than allowing the situation to spiral out of control.

2017 REFLECTIONS FROM SEAN

It is my opinion that this is one of the more vexing rules for those on the autism spectrum to understand, internalize and apply, because the notion that not everything is equally important can easily be at odds with the literal and concrete thinking patterns of many with ASD. The implied disproportionality that the rule suggests, in the minds of many on the spectrum, also may challenge their sense of equality and balance and, in some cases, a desire to do things chronologically. A student on the spectrum may reason, "I must always do my schoolwork for first period before finishing my assignment in second period, because first period comes before second period." But what happens if the second-period work is due the following day, but the student has several days to complete the first-period assignment? Such a situation would naturally disrupt the person's chronological flow pattern and require rethinking his or her ingrained priorities.

This concept can even be highly difficult for neurotypical people—and institutions—to follow. Recently, I have witnessed what I feel are the harmful results of what can happen when the media (of which I'm a part) attempts, intentionally or not, to reflexively equalize two or more sides of an issue in the name of maintaining journalistic balance.

During the recent divisive 2016 presidential campaign between Hillary Clinton and Donald Trump, the major media outlets continually reported on Clinton's controversial handling of emails while she served as secretary of state and juxtaposed that with a video showing Trump bragging about having sexually assaulted women.

In Clinton's case, the FBI's investigations twice concluded that she used poor judgment and had been careless in handling sensitive and classified information on her server, but nothing she did rose to the level of criminal conduct. On the other hand, we have uncontroverted proof of Trump's transgressions.

It's my view that, in an ill-fated effort to be fair to both sides, the major media outlets treated each situation equally in their coverage, creating in many people's minds the impression that Clinton's lack of judgment regarding the email server was equal in magnitude, scope and importance to Trump's track record of misdeeds. The problem here, as I see it, is that equality should not be the only deciding factor when trying to exercise sound news judgment.

Equality is far more dependent on fairness than fairness is dependent on equality. If someone steals a T-shirt from Wal-

Mart on the same day another person goes on a shooting spree and kills ten people, should both events receive equal coverage and be viewed as equally important? No.

Therefore, we can easily see the importance of teaching young people in general, not just those on the spectrum, the value of prioritizing—that not everything that happens carries the same weight in the bigger picture.

Understanding the unwritten rules of social relationships requires an ability to not only blend black and white into shades of gray, but also to realize that other interesting, vibrant colors make up our world. It's not surprising that a social framework comprised of few emotions, that can erupt at will in an all-or-nothing manner and inhibit rather than enhance personal relationships might be an unattractive avenue of experience for an individual with ASD. Why work at social skills and emotional relatedness when the result is feeling worse than before?

Not everything is equally important in the grand scheme of life. It's such a simple statement, one that is so infused into the thinking patterns of neurotypicals that the idea that it may need to be verbalized and even taught can be in itself a revelation. Teaching children and adults to be able to recognize and invent categories, associate categories with each other, and appreciate the different values that exist within and between categories are the precursors to social awareness. The hierarchy provides intrinsic structure and motivation: with it they can recognize their own progress and, in turn, gain the self-motivation that is needed to be successful in social relationships.

POINTS TO KEEP IN MIND:

- Although it can seem foreign to parents and professionals, all—and we mean all—situations may be experienced with the same intensity of emotion by a child with ASD. When working with a child, stop and remind yourself of this again and again.
- Actively engage children, starting from a very young age, in building categories.
- Use visual representations as much as possible in teaching categories and emotions. "Today I'm Feeling" charts help kids learn about different emotions and distinguish one from the other. Scales, thermometers, colors or numbering systems help kids learn about levels of emotion in concrete terms.
- Talk your thoughts "out loud" during the day to help children appreciate that everyone has different emotions and experiences them in different ways. "Mary is feeling nervous about meeting her new teacher today." "Daddy is disappointed it rained today; he was looking forward to playing golf with his friends."
- Learn to recognize the signs of impending overload or outburst—they are there.

RULE #3

EVERYONE IN THE WORLD MAKES MISTAKES; IT DOESN'T HAVE TO RUIN YOUR DAY

Sean Explains:

I was twelve years old, but didn't need a lot of introspection to realize that I had a past littered with wrongs. The three big ones, as far as I could see, were *1)* my behavior, *2)* my inability to make friends and *3)* everything else I did. I was a failure, and there was no thinking about it otherwise. So, with all this going on inside me, the last thing I needed was to be told that making errors was an inevitable part of what I was trying to accomplish. I hated making mistakes because I felt *that I was a mistake.*

Sean describes, in the above passage, how many of the more emotionally-related children on the autism spectrum feel about themselves and the impact that error-making has on their self-esteem. Keep in mind that for individuals whose emotions are so intricately interwoven into their overall functioning, the black and white thinking patterns will also be stronger. They will view their abilities as abhorrent or excellent, their mistakes as nothing other than complete failure. Absent from their thinking is the recognition that comes so easily to neurotypical children: that *mistakes fall into different categories of importance, based on the context of the situation.* They demand no less than perfection from themselves, but as Sean illustrates in the following passage, perfection without the benefit of learning over time.

Sean Continues:

Around age twelve, I had started listening at night to classical music on a local FM station and had an idea of what great piano playing sounded like. I envisioned what others who listened to such music must think of those who played it so well and I thought: Why can't I be among the great musicians? So I decided to learn to play the piano. After expressing my desire to my parents, they found Mrs. Simon, who was a friend of my grandmother's, and I took two years' worth of weekly piano lessons from her. I remember the color-coded Finger Power workbooks, the easiest of which I used during my first lessons. Right away I viewed as an insult the fact that I had to play these lessons— which were made up of chromatic scales and other mundane warm-up exercises—instead of "real music," and I resented that professional pianists got to be heard by the public while I was stuck doing things thousands of times easier. Much to my chagrin, reality was intruding on my goal, which was to do something extremely well and be deeply admired for doing it. Soon, a new thought took up residence in my brain—*If they can play so well without effort, then why can't I?*— and stayed for years to come. The underlying rule of life, that *practice makes perfect*, was lost on me.

The few feelings of accomplishment came when I advanced from an easy lesson book to a slightly harder one. I knew I was getting better, but my resentment continued to build and clouded any pleasure I felt from my progress. And what I saw as a gross injustice—the fact that I had to practice while others got to play—cast a pall over every lesson and the six days in between.

As a result, fewer and fewer notes were heard in our house. Initially I spent about a half-hour each day at the ivories, but that turned into thirty-minute practice sessions a few times a week and then dwindled to once a week for perhaps ten minutes. Often, I went an entire week sitting on lots of surfaces, but never a piano bench.

Our household soon began to fill up not with piano harmonies, but with conversations that went something like this:

MOM: Sean, did you practice today?

ME: (A prickling sensation starting to overtake me) Yes. MOM: When? I didn't hear you.

ME: Well, I did.

MOM: Sean, come downstairs and practice. You're never going to get better if you don't practice what you went over during the lessons we're paying for.

ME: Why the hell do I have to practice all the time? Every time I hear a professional piano player, they play perfectly. If they can play so well, then I should be able to.

MOM: It took them years of practice. They didn't just sit down and start playing. The only way to get better is to practice every day. You can't just play once a week and expect to get better.

ME: That's not true. I want to play, not practice.

I had painfully learned that the only way I was going to get closer to setting the music world on fire and using my piano talents to kindle it was to go through the painstaking scales, exercises and simple, sparsely noted tunes. And, I now knew, before I could play all the right individual notes, I was going to have to play plenty of wrong ones. That was how it worked.

Therein was the rub: Wrong notes. I was twelve years old, but it didn't take a lot of introspection to realize that I had a past littered with wrongs. The three big ones, as far as I could see, were 1) my behavior, 2) my inability to make friends and 3) everything else. I was a failure, and there was no thinking about it otherwise. So, with all this going on inside me, the last thing I needed was to be told that making errors was an inevitable part of what I was trying to accomplish. I hated making mistakes because I felt that I was a mistake.

Sure enough, no practice session was mistake-free. Each "bad" note I played did more than sound incorrect. Each one was bitter music to my ears because it served as a sharp reminder that I had failed yet again. After two years, I quit.

By the early 1980s—after my negative experiences with the piano were behind me, or so I thought—my interest in jazz had blossomed and, feeling a lot more self-confident, I was now driven by a desire to one day play in a Dixieland band. I saw myself playing in the type of band that was popular years before my time. So I began taking trumpet lessons in 1982, vowing to myself that I would not make the same mistakes—wrong notes notwithstanding that I had made eight years earlier. I was far more mature now and many of my attitudes toward myself were different. I was not the same person I was as a twelve-year-old and my life was a lot better. For one thing, I assumed the trumpet would be a much easier instrument to master, since it had three valves, as opposed to eighty-eight keys to worry about. And I didn't know that the three valves always produced the same combination of notes; I thought I could just play and invent ideas as I went. So, I figured, all of this would factor in not only on my playing, but also on the reasons for placing myself back onto a musical avenue.

The biggest difference was that a healthier perspective would now blanket everything surrounding my playing, both inside and out. Now, I told myself, I would be content to simply get good enough to play in a local jazz band, as opposed to striving for world fame. I would go through the pain of rebuilding my musical foundation by learning chromatic scales, etc. and when the time came, I would just ask my instructor, Mr. Miller, "How do you improvise?" About a month or two into my lessons, I asked him that question, thinking I was ready to advance to that level.

But old demons don't go down without a fight. Several weeks into my lessons, I encountered challenges that I hadn't anticipated and despite higher self-esteem, the effects were eerily similar to those of my piano playing days. I still played wrong notes, but I started noticing other deficiencies, such as I was often unable to finish the exercises and simple tunes he gave me because my embouchure gave out. Apparently, I had developed a bad habit of placing the instrument's mouthpiece incorrectly; I created too much pressure against my lips, cutting off some of the blood and replacing it with lactic acid, a term I came to despise. I remember playing a solo of "When the Saints Go Marching In," as part of a 1982 recital Mr. Miller held and, toward the end of my piece, being unable to hit two Ds above middle C because my lips had gone numb. What I did feel was the audience's polite but tepid applause.

Just as years before, my weekly practicing diminished, but not my desire to play like Dizzy Gillespie (and be equally admired) without having to practice. One evening, I decided I was going to "tough it out" and, if necessary, pretend that I had no physical limitations and continue playing even if I reached the point that only air, air and more air came from my horn. Not surprisingly, that's just what happened. Anger increased with the acid reaching my lips and gathering in my stomach. One E flat that should have been E natural later, rage consumed me and I slammed the trumpet against the floor, slightly bending its bell and making it unplayable. I hadn't been able to do that to a piano—something to do with its being too heavy.

A few years and no Dixieland band offers later, I sidelined playing altogether. Because of these experiences—and somewhat similar ones when I tried out for various school sports and took tennis lessons—a razor-sharp link was established between my failures and competitive situations in general. Such situations have for years had a corrosive effect on me. Even now, I am affected to some degree. I play volleyball and softball on occasion, but am sharply tuned into the teams' attitudes and approach. If I sense that things are moving too far from fun into the "win at all costs" side of the ledger, I'm outta there.

I now know I looked at success as being linear; the more notes I play "right," the better I am as a person. However, I would fall into the destructive trap of starting a new venture with expectations that were too high, setting myself up for disappointment and getting wounded when I inevitably fell short. I still wanted to be well known and capture the hearts and admiration of millions because I was convinced that fame would negate a lifetime of struggle, pain and autism. Cheers rather than criticism, raves instead of reprimands, seemed a better way to go.

Even at a very, very early age children appreciate, without being told, that mistakes are part of the human condition, and that no one is perfect. Through trial and error, young kids gradually add situation upon situation to an ever-expanding hierarchy, understanding that mistakes occur for all sorts of reasons, some entirely out of the range of personal control, and society dictates that our responses be gauged to each situation accordingly.

Contrast Sean's early thinking patterns to those of Temple; you will notice the stark difference in how they understood their own shortcomings. The long term influences cannot be underestimated.

Temple Shares:

As far back as I can remember, I was not a child who had to have everything perfect or it would send me into a tantrum. I know that some children with ASD are like that, but that wasn't my thinking pattern. Mother made us do so many different activities, and a lot of those activities involved other family members or other kids, that making mistakes was really no big deal. It happened and we just moved on. I didn't take it personally, probably because my logical mind and thinking in pictures kept emotions one step removed from most experiences. The way I viewed it, the mistake was in my thinking, in my problem-solving; I didn't automatically feel worthless when I made a mistake because it wasn't as tied into my sense of self. And all those experiences kept putting more and more information on my hard drive, so that when I did make mistakes, I'd have many chances to go back and do it again and learn to not make the same mistake.

Having lots of experiences also built my self-esteem in natural, positive ways, rather than the contrived "good job sitting" type of reinforcement that some of the more structured programs dole out today. Mother and the nanny would compliment me on my accomplishments and because I was so motivated to build things—and good at it—I pretty regularly received positive praise for what I did. My self-esteem developed through my accomplishments. When I did nice artwork, it was praised. I remember singing a solo in an adult Christmas concert one time. I was about nine and sang "America the Beautiful." The people really liked it and everybody clapped. That raised my self-esteem. Of course, when I acted inappropriately Mother and the nanny would get right on me for it, too, but most of the time they were giving me genuine praise. I don't remember thinking or feeling that I was a bad person because of my mistakes. There was enough positive praise to balance it out.

One of the things Mother did when I was doing something wrong was to always tell me the right way to do things. In today's language, that's good "positive behavior programming" principles, and it works well with the autism population. She did this all the time with table manners. Instead of scolding me for leaving my knife and fork in the wrong position on the plate, she'd simply say, "Temple, put your silverware in the four o'clock position." It was always the same, always consistent. It really helped me learn what I was supposed to do, rather than drawing attention to what I was doing wrong.

As a young adult, working for a magazine early in my career was an extremely good learning environment for me. I had the chance to go to all sorts of different meetings, experience all different types of people—I gained a lot of social knowledge while on that job. Most adults with social problems don't have a chance to get a whole lot of good experience, either because they're not interested in learning social skills, or the fear of situations runs so deep they cut themselves off. But in order to be social, you've got to have enough information on the hard drive so that when you surf the Internet inside your mind, you can problem-solve to an appropriate solution. Their hard drives are like the Internet when it first started—not a lot of information was there. It takes a tremendous amount of data before social relationships start making sense.

Obviously I made mistakes on that job, but they were minor enough that I didn't get fired over them. My thinking was flexible enough that I could distinguish between minor mistakes and more major ones, although I couldn't always control my emotions. I attribute an even bigger part of my ability to keep my job to the fact that I had most of the basic social functioning skills that would get me by. This demonstrates an unwritten rule of relationships: *people keep "social history" in mind; they weigh your good points and bad points when it comes to mistakes you make in determining their own reactions.* I knew how to be polite, to make small talk, I had good manners and could follow directions. That, in itself, was a big plus. So, the mistakes I made were tolerated because my social work skills were decent. Plus they realized I was smart; I was intelligent enough to learn the aspects of my job quickly, so I usually didn't repeat mistakes over and over.

Anxiety was part of my functioning at that time, and affected how I acted, but it wasn't because I was making mistakes or needing things to be perfect. It was all physiology. My mind was pretty flexible when it came to understanding that everyone makes mistakes.

But I still did have what I call the "perfectionist syndrome" to contend with at times. What's interesting is that early in my career I almost quit designing cattle corrals entirely because one client unfairly criticized my work. There was nothing wrong with the corral and today I would just put him into the "jerk" category (yes, that's definitely a category firmly ingrained in my thinking). But back then, with big projects like this one, I still wanted my work to be absolutely perfect. Since the client was not totally pleased, I thought I would have to quit doing cattle handling design. Fortunately, my good friend Jim Uhl, the contractor who built the corral, talked me into continuing my career.

Jim was instrumental in helping me understand the concept of doing work to a specific quality standard, and appreciating that performance standards range from low to high. Some type of work requires a higher quality standard than does others. Building a bridge requires a higher standard for safety than does building a coffee table. That concept was explained to me in a concrete manner and it made sense. Today I approach mistakes using the same thinking process. I will tolerate a small number of grammatical errors in a paper because if I kept correcting, the paper would never get done. However, too many mistakes and the project would then move into the "sloppy work" category.

It's an unwritten social rule: *there is a difference between honest mistakes and careless work.* This is a distinction that I had to learn through experience, because I exhibited both a desire to be perfect with some projects and a careless attitude toward others. The perfectionist syndrome was only active in me on projects that were really important to me. It wasn't a factor with things I didn't care about. Depending on the situation, that trait is not welcomed within the work force. When I was twelve I was asked to wash a car and I did a really sloppy job; I just did not care. At the construction company I worked for I can remember doing a really sloppy job photocopying some sales material. It was a job

I didn't want to do.

Being perfect or being sloppy—neither extreme is practical and as I gained social awareness, I learned these two unwritten social rules:

- *I needed to do my best* when asked to perform a task at work, even on jobs that were unimportant to me.
- On those jobs that were important to me, I had to learn that *perfection is not always possible.*

What these passages so clearly illustrate is that people on the autism spectrum will relate to Rule #3—Everybody makes mistakes, it doesn't have to ruin your day—in quite different ways depending on how they think and process information. The more logical thinkers will process mistakes as faulty problem-solving abilities; the more emotionally-related, verbal thinkers will view mistakes as indications of their personal value and worth.

Temple Provides Additional Insight:

Some kids who want the world around them to be perfect, to function according to some rigid plan they hold in their minds, have a hard time accepting any kind of mistake they—or others—make. I think these are the children and adults who are more emotionally related, because they can't separate their actions from their emotions. They're all tied in together, and when you add in their low perspective-taking abilities (which are common among these individuals), they naturally think that all the mistakes they make, all the social blunders that happen to them are because of something they did or didn't do.

They expect perfection from themselves, and what parents and teachers need to realize is that they expect this same level of perfection *from everyone else around them.* So, all day, every day, all around them they experience people failing to live up to the unrealistic and impossible rules they've set up in their heads. The confusion is dense, and thick and pervasive and ever so debilitating, which sets these kids up for a lot of self-inflicted stress and anxiety. That's why it's so important for parents and teachers to *constantly* repeat Rule #3 to these kids: everyone makes mistakes; it doesn't have to ruin your day. Put it on visual schedules, write it on their notebooks, add it to homework directions given to them. It's so critical that this Rule gets drilled into them, so that even before it starts making sense from an emotional perspective, they at least have learned it from an intellectual stand point.

Rule #3 is a two-component rule, a two-step learning process. Kids can come to appreciate that everyone makes mistakes and that mistakes are tolerated, to a greater or lesser degree depending on the error made. They can gain that perspective and learn which mistakes have minor consequences and which carry more severe penalties. There are rote ways it can be taught.

The second part, "it doesn't have to ruin your day" can be harder to learn because it involves some level of emotional awareness and per-spective taking. They often can't appreciate the rule applies to them-selves as well as others. It also requires them to appreciate different de-grees of emotions, another aspect of social skills that may need to be taught alongside this rule.

Kids who have bad social experiences burned over and over onto their hard drives get in a rut; the same negative thoughts keep spinning over and over and over again in their brains. Sometimes it takes mak-ing their environment very "socially simple" to turn things around—sort of like reformatting the hard drive in the social section, and repeated-ly introducing new, positive experiences—for them to gain some sort of social balance. This is easier done during elementary school, when kids are more malleable and their peers are more interested in being helpers. Once kids move into the in today/out tomorrow, quickly shifting social arena of middle school, especially those kids who attend larger schools, the odds of creating a socially simpler environment drastically decline, unless parents choose to home school the child. That's why so many ASD kids regress or lose ground during middle school. Social capabilities develop fast and ASD kids just can't keep up. The social gap keeps getting bigger and bigger between the child with ASD and his/her neurotypical peers unless parents and teachers do something to break the cycle and help them regain some control. Depression is frequent; it's no wonder.

I live for what I do. When I was younger it was projects, not people, that made me feel in control and good about myself. Even though my adolescent years were hard and I was constantly feeling anxiety and living through a lot of teasing from kids around me, I still had my projects—and the self-esteem I felt from them—to ground me, to keep me balanced to some degree so that I didn't completely go off-kilter.

So, while it's important to teach social functioning skills and give kids opportunities to develop emotional relatedness, doing that without also providing them some sense of stability and accomplishment, can in the long run make them less social, rather than more. Concentrate equally on developing talents. These skills provide a rudder that helps guide the individual through the seas of social turmoil, and keeps their sense of self-worth healthy, despite all the social mistakes they're making as they navigate through middle and high school.

That middle school environment can be especially treacherous for the ASD student who takes every mistake to heart. To keep the constant feelings of failure at bay, defense mechanisms become their life preservers.

Sean Describes.

I regularly used denial as a handy, but unhealthy, tool to cover mistakes I had made. Having no perspective caused me to take personally nearly everything bad that happened to me. Every mistake was my fault, stemming from some defect in my character. I often reacted with denial, saying things like, "Oh, I meant to do it that way," "I did it on purpose," "I was only kidding," and so on. That method never worked; instead, it always magnified the significance of what should have been an insignificant error.

My parents spent most of my twenties trying, among other things, to get me to see the importance of admitting my mistakes and learning to laugh off some negative situations that made me so angry. Other times, I reacted with rage that was out of proportion to the event. If Mom showed me another way to do something, for instance, I read her suggestion as "You're always wrong," and I would explode, since I had no ability to see that doing something in a different way does not necessarily imply a judgment.

In some ways, much of the rage I felt in my late teens and early twenties was the result of what I saw as simple math. I was becoming more aware of the world outside my sphere and one of the negative consequences of this growing awareness was being faced with how my aberrant behavior affected others. As my awareness of the world around me grew, the anger, resentment and guilt turned inward. I developed a phobia of making mistakes simply because I began to feel that I had already made enough of them for two or three lifetimes. I had to make up for such a dismal track record by being perfect and anything short of perfection proved over and over that I was as defective as I felt inside."

Even into my mid-twenties, I still had trouble telling the difference between situations that were hard for me because of my autism and those that were challenging for everyone. "No one learns without mistakes," Mom would say. That was an unwritten rule that everyone but me seemed to understand. I still didn't realize that everyone goes through learning processes, that *everyone makes lots of mistakes at first and then gradually perfects their skills*. By this time in my life I was more than ready to be in the "normal" world; instead, I felt as if I were still walking down an endless corridor filled with twists and turns toward it. I wanted a straight-ahead path with no detours and a bright light at the end guiding my way. This fixation often prevented me from learning because I could not take in information when I was enraged and shut down, so of course I made even more mistakes.

I still had some ironclad rules of my own devising and they were still illogical and ill-matched to what I was trying to accomplish. If I perceived something I should have already known in the first place, I had to perfect it. I would accept nothing less of myself. Yet, I still was removed from understanding processes—of going from ignorance to mastery of whatever it was I presumed I should know. There were things everyone else seemed to know automatically, and now I insisted that I know them, too. With each change, I wanted instant results rather than yet another struggle. I knew everyone made mistakes; accepting that as okay in myself was something that would yet take years to master.

What is interesting to note is that for children, adolescents and adults with ASD who have a stronger degree of emotional-relating ability, their intellectual abilities can be so clouded by the emotional chaos that even some of the simpler social interactions—like asking for help—need to be formally taught, and constantly reinforced.

Sean Continues On:

I got my first paying job when, at age nineteen, I walked into the Los Angeles Valley College placement office and scanned the three-inch-by-five-inch index cards listing various job openings available in the San Fernando Valley. On a whim, I took the first one I saw, which described an opening for a teacher's assistant at a private preschool in nearby Northridge. I talked to Frank, the director, a young, soft-spoken man.

"Are you currently taking any child development courses?" he asked.

"No, but I plan to take basic child development next semester," I responded.

"Okay. Well, come in this afternoon after your classes for an interview," he said.

After filling out an application and taking part in a half-hour interview, he hired me. I was amazed and flattered that I was handed the position on the spot and that Frank, with his innocent face, was such a decent person. All I had to do was promise that I would take a child development class.

I received the minimum hourly wage of $3.35 to work for three hours a day as a teacher's assistant with children ages two to five. It wasn't long, however, before the part-time job turned into a full-time nightmare. It became apparent that Frank disliked me and that he singled me out for special criticism and did what he could to make my life miserable. This isn't the way it's supposed to be, I thought.

Less than a week into the job, I was informed that a complaint had been brought against me for going to use the restroom and leaving the teacher alone with all the kids. The next day, Frank mildly admonished me in front of the class full of children and two teachers. But the reprimand was mild compared with what was to come.

Soon I was the one being left alone for an hour every day with the preschoolers who hadn't gone home before the last teacher left for the day. I even was responsible for two and three-year-old children and had to change their diapers if they had an accident. I had no idea how a diaper worked. I was in charge of the children and if anything went wrong, I would be responsible and would suffer the consequences.

After about two months the director demanded I work full time, saying it was either that or lose my job. Full-time work meant also receiving an hour-long lunch break. Most days I spent that time at a restaurant within walking distance (I hadn't yet learned to drive) and I passed Frank's office as I left the building. Frequently, I noticed Frank staring at me through his office window. His stares were so unsettling that I sometimes got physically sick and was unable to finish my meal. One day, he did a lot more than stare.

It was a hot, smoggy afternoon and the kids were scattered on the playground. Two or three teachers had reported in sick and nobody was called to fill in for them. I was one of two staff watching thirty-five children and I positioned myself at one end of the yard to see as much of what was going on as I could. I had my hands full dealing with various fights and scuffles that were taking place and was somewhat aware that several children were climbing on a picnic table behind me. I knew they were not allowed to do that and that they could fall, but I was trying to handle other situations at the same time. As I turned around, I saw a classroom door swinging open and Frank hurrying toward me. His face was as red as a sugar beet as he walked up and stood inches from my face.

"You know the kids aren't allowed up on the picnic table," he said loudly with clenched teeth. "I've been watching you from my window and noticed that you didn't do anything to stop them. They could get hurt and I would be responsible. If I see one more child up on that table, I'm going to fire you."

Without giving me a chance to respond, he walked briskly into the building.

I was mortified and embarrassed. I looked at the ground for several seconds before mustering the courage to resume watching the playground. I noticed several children had stopped what they were doing and were still eying me. I picked up my heavy eyelids, forged a smile and thought about ways to stab myself with a sharp knife until my workday was finally over.

Not once during that instance or other similarly trying experiences on that job did one of the cardinal rules of workplace relationships enter my thoughts: that *if I don't know what to do, or can't handle the situation, that I could ask for training or advice.* I still did not have the concept of asking for help. So absolute in my mind was the idea of avoiding mistakes that admitting I needed help meant admitting I was not perfect.

Being able to acknowledge and accept your own mistakes and those of others is truly a life-preserving perspective for the person with ASD. Not only does it alleviate much of the daily stress that people with ASD live under, it opens the door to other equally transformational abilities to widen that perspective, such as risk-taking. Sean, in this next passage, and Temple in the one that follows, speak to the whole new world of experiences that open up once people can reasonably assess their shortcomings.

Sean Begins:

After watching the movie, *Son Rise*, about Raun Kaufman's journey out of his autism, and enjoying the brief honeymoon period that followed the knowledge that I was not an inherently "bad" person, I began to understand—intellectually and emotionally—that my lifetime of problems would not instantly evaporate. Despite my high expectations, I would have to learn Life 101: Looking and Reaching Beyond Myself and Other Practical Matters for Getting Along in the World and With Others. Its syllabus included many things like smiling at and acknowledging people when I saw them, figuring out people's real intentions beneath the surface, understanding others' motives, being able to look a few steps ahead of an action and anticipate what its likely consequences would be and on and on. There would be no quick mastery of this curriculum and I would undoubtedly make mistakes along the way. But the unwritten rule that many millions of people who had come before me had acknowledged and accepted was not making sense: that *I had to learn to do what was socially appropriate—even if it meant making mistakes, taking great risks and placing myself in many uncomfortable situations.*

Temple Echoes Some of His Thoughts:

One of the keys to becoming socially adept and being able to understand the social rules of relationships is getting out in the world and gaining experience. And, that means taking risks and making mistakes. It's just something you have to accept and push yourself on, even though it might cause some anxiety. I remember talking to a young man with autism about fifteen years ago. He spent his days locked away in his room reading all sorts of magazines, because he thought if he took in enough information he'd be able to think in social ways. He didn't realize that he had to get out and experience the world first-hand, and that no amount of book learning would be a substitute for face-to-face interaction.

The only way you're going to learn is by doing. You've got to get into the world and act, even if it means making mistakes. You could look at that as an unwritten rule of social relationships specifically for people with ASD. I don't know how much this is actually verbalized to children with ASD because neurotypicals can learn by observation, by watching the experiences of others. Not so for the majority of us on the spectrum.

When I was young, it wasn't easy for me to venture out into new situations because it caused great anxiety, but Mother pushed me to do things. She had to push me to go to the ranch and stay with Aunt Ann. I didn't want to go, but instead of letting me stay home, Mother told me if I didn't like it I could come home in two weeks. I ended up staying the entire summer. I was nervous because I didn't know what would happen—but every child is nervous to some extent about new situations. That's natural, normal behavior; that's not autism.

Another time Mother was remodeling our kitchen and I was helping. She asked me to go to the lumberyard myself and I didn't want to do it. She made me go. She said, "I don't care if you're going to cry. You're going to go to the lumberyard and you're going to buy these things we need." It sounds harsh, but she knew my capabilities and didn't let me get out of doing things because I was afraid of making a mistake. Each time I did something like this, it bolstered my self-esteem; it proved to me I was capable of handling new situations.

She knew when to push and when not to push, and in most instances, she wasn't pushing me into situations that were hugely social. Yes, I had to talk to the clerk in the lumberyard but that was pretty basic conversation that I had been taught and was capable of handling. Going out to the ranch was not a purely social thing either; I had lots of different things to do.

I think a lot of today's social anxiety comes from parents who prematurely put their kids into highly social situations before they're ready, before they've mastered social functioning skills and before they're feeling any sense of capability and self-esteem. Many parents underestimate just how difficult—and complex—being in a social situation is for most kids on the spectrum. So the information that goes onto their hard drive is mostly about what they're doing incorrectly; it's all counter-productive to the child succeeding. If he's not taking in information regarding where he's being successful, the only thing he can do is keep replaying what's there—all the inappropriate experiences—and he keeps getting the same (inappropriate) outcome. It's like a bad programming loop he can't get out of. He doesn't have a model to reference what's positive and effective.

This problem is more common within the ASD population than I think parents and teachers realize. The kids' information bank has mostly inappropriate experiences to call up. It's depressing; it's de-motivating for them. These kids just give up on mastering social skills because they can't see a way out, a way to make anything different or better—and the adults around them aren't changing the way *they* do things so the child can experience success. That's why formal *positive* teaching is so important—people with ASD need to be taught how to act and what to say, over and over until they get enough good information on their hard drive that the mistakes start happening less and less. The earlier this training starts, the better. It works most effectively when started with very young children. Teach them what to do, as opposed to focusing on what not to do; maybe if parents and adults made that an ALWAYS rule for themselves, kids would be more motivated to learn social skills. Again, I'm not trying to bash adult efforts, but to point out that again and again and again, what I encounter out in the trenches are adults who don't understand the thinking patterns of people with ASD and still try to use punishment-based behavior systems to work with them. Until that mistake gets corrected with the adults, children and adolescents on the spectrum will suffer.

Skills and self-esteem have to come first, or any chance of feeling good about learning social rules will be squashed. Pretty soon the child is so anxious and afraid of venturing out that he resists even the simpler social interactions. Remember, to a lot of kids with ASD all mistakes are HUGE in their minds. So, even minor mistakes make them feel badly in BIG ways. Start with building self-esteem within a positive, supported environment. That foundation will carry him through the rough spots later when the social relationships rules are so much harder to decipher and understand.

As with all the rules and the personal experiences offered throughout this book, our goal is to open your mind to new ways of understanding people with ASD, how we think and how that thinking affects our ability to function within the social framework around us. The goal for most parents and teachers in doing so is to guide spectrum children toward an adult experience that includes independence, a satisfying job and meaningful social relationships. We'll all make mistakes along the way, and hopefully, we'll all keep in mind this unwritten rule of social relationships: *what matters more than the mistake you make is what you do once you realize you've made it.* For Sean, he's learned that in many instances, laughing at our own mistakes puts them in perspective quicker than anything else.

Sean Shares:

I want to add a few points about laughter with regard to mistakes. I'm not talking about situations for which a serious response would be appropriate. Obviously, if you're in a supermarket, for example, and you accidentally clobber someone coming around a corner with your shopping cart, laughing it off would not be the right thing to do. Apologizing and making sure the person is okay are the right ways to handle such an incident. Once you have done that, then laughter may be all right, depending on the person's response and frame of mind.

It's also important to distinguish between what I call good versus bad laughter. By this I mean the difference between laughing *with* someone (or at what the person said when humor was the intent) and laughing AT the person.

To dig up one other cliché (and quickly return it to its resting place where it belongs), laughter is contagious. I've been in festive social situations where the mood is jovial and people are having a great time laughing, conversing, etc., and have found myself doing the same—even if nothing funny was said to trigger it. I get caught up in the mood and respond in kind. Likewise, there have been countless occasions at which I have laughed when someone was trying to be funny. Laughter is one of those things that has a way of feeding off itself.

Laughing at someone, on the other hand, usually causes the opposite reaction. This is hurtful and inappropriate. It's when, for instance, you laugh at a funeral. It's when you laugh after a person trips—or any situation and set of circumstances that causes a person embarrassment or other negative feelings when that person wasn't trying to be funny. Laughing at people is akin to making fun of them, and nobody enjoys that.

By and large, however, most garden variety mistakes and situations in our everyday lives lend themselves to a little humor if we're willing to "let our hair down." And making fun of yourself in a humorous way is always more attractive to people than subjecting them to your self-righteousness or your heavy negativity. I find it hard to be around someone who is angry, sullen or upset most of the time and who often complains but does nothing to change anything. It's not that I don't care about such a person; it's just that it zaps my energy and affects me similarly. Laughter may be contagious but unfortunately, so is chronic negativity. No matter how hard you try to hide a bad mood, those around you can feel it, even if they don't say anything. So I think it's best to deal with it on the spot, and even better to take steps to prevent it in the first place.

These are things my parents explained over and over to me for years. Finally it's sunk in that nobody cares about an inconsequential mistake; we all make them—autism or not. But others do care about how you handle and react to it. That's what has the longest and strongest impact.

In closing, Sean also wanted to point out the value of finally accepting your past mistakes, forgiving yourself for them, and finding ways to move on. Many people with ASD carry around huge amounts of guilt and remorse for the errors they've committed in their lives. Genius minds that can remember and recall details about hundreds of topics also equally retain memories of mistakes large and small. Guilt isn't only reserved for mistakes with people, as these final passages from Sean demonstrate.

Sean Speaks:

For more than fifteen years, I carried guilt and shame that stemmed from my days as a teacher's aide with children. I had many conversations with my mother about this and after one talk, she came up with a brilliant idea.

"Why don't you look into becoming a Big Brother," she suggested.

"I don't know," I said. "I'm not sure I would be any good at it."

For a while, I was reluctant to pursue the idea. Finally, I relented. After completing the paperwork, I was matched to a nine-year-old boy whose mother had died when he was four and whose father was absent. For the first few months I felt tense with Ron because I was fearful of saying or doing the wrong things. I also took great care not to respond to him in ways that echoed the methods I used as a teacher's aide. But old habits don't go down without a fight.

The local Big Brothers/Big Sisters organization had an annual Christmas party in which gifts were given to the kids. Ron and another child got into a big argument and I tried to mediate. When it became obvious that my attempts at peacemaking weren't working, I ignored the situation and pretended not to notice the growing hostility between the two boys. That didn't work, either, and I resorted to yelling—the same pattern I had often used when I worked with children years earlier.

Tension filled the car as I drove Ron home. He was angry with me for the way I had handled the fight and I was enraged with myself. The agency required Big Brothers to see their Little Brothers at least once a week, but for three weeks after that incident, I pretended to be out of town. I just couldn't face Ron because my poor reaction at the party convinced me that I was still the failure I had been before.

I couldn't remain "out of town" forever, though. I realized I had to get over what had happened and in the process learned this unwritten social rule: *avoiding a problem doesn't make it go away.* I called Ron and suggested we go to a nearby roller rink and to a Dairy Queen so we could have one-on-one time. We had a good time together and after that my relationship with Ron improved. The more I relaxed, loosened up and made adjustments, the better our friendship became. In 1998, I was named Big Brother of the Year for the Youngstown area. Since he is now past age sixteen, I'm no longer Ron's Big Brother, but we remain good friends.

When I was a child, I wanted a dog, partly because I thought I would be able to better relate to animals than I did to people. I had spent time with my grandparents' dog; their dog obeyed me and didn't respond negatively when I interacted with him. So I was thrilled when, at age seven, we went to the home of our family dentist and brought home not floss or a new toothbrush, but a puppy. At first, I treated Molly with great affection, but as I grew older, she too became an object I used to satisfy my compulsions. When I was ten or eleven, I started teasing her for the same reasons I occasionally teased people: to get a predictable response. Molly had a favorite spot in our dining room where she liked to lie down partially under a chair and it became a game to sneak up, lightly push her from behind and watch her run into another room. The more I did this, the more predictable her response, which, of course, only fueled my desire to continue.

My parents soon caught on and told me to stop tormenting the dog. A fear of being caught did nothing to deter me and despite my parents' warnings, I continued. Even though on some level I knew it was wrong, my compulsions were so strong that I felt driven to satisfy my need to see a predictable outcome and exert control over the outcome. Over time, my parents grew angrier and forbade me from having contact with Molly.

A similar pattern played out when we got our second dog, McGill, a German Shepherd. He was lovable and affectionate, and I felt drawn to him initially. But the clouds soon darkened when I saw the enormous difference between how my parents and sister responded to the dog and to me. We got McGill when I was twelve and he was part of the family for a decade. During those ten years he was the object of my family's love and affection, whereas I was the one receiving constant reprimands, scorn and punishment. I soon thought that my parents—especially my mother—loved our dog more than me, and jealousy and rage brewed inside me.

Within a year, I grew to dislike the dog intensely. Affection turned to anger and, on occasion, mild abuse. I became so resentful of McGill that I yelled at him to get out anytime I came into my bedroom and found him in it. Sometimes when I caught him there, I hit him on the back, causing him to yelp in pain. Despite my cruel treatment, McGill still sought my love and attention and I responded by ignoring him.

Shortly before I moved to Ohio in 1984, he developed arthritis in his hind legs and died soon after. By the time he died, I had made progress in my fight against autism. My anger toward him had diminished, but guilt at my treatment of him had increased. The guilt stayed with me and one day, eight years after his death, I came across a photo album containing several pictures of him and wept.

After the tears dried, I realized that I needed more than time to assuage the guilt. I had to channel my negative feelings in some way, so I looked in the phone book for numbers of local animal shelters. After a few calls, I found one that temporarily housed dogs and cats waiting to be adopted. After learning that the agency needed volunteers, I signed on.

Eight years later, I still get tremendous satisfaction and joy from going there once a week to take care of the dogs. I make sure they have enough food and water, and I find time to give individual dogs plenty of love and kindness—both of which I still wish I had dished out to McGill. An unwritten rule of social relationships is that *forgiveness is something we do for ourselves.* Harboring guilt for years on end can be extremely self-destructive. In some cases we can't repair the mistakes of our past, but in many cases we can heal the wounds in ourselves they created.

Of course, I can't bring our German Shepherd back. Working for the shelter, however, has let me channel my sadness and guilt in a constructive way and has been healing for me. I still get pangs of sadness when I think of how badly I treated him, but also feel comfort in knowing how I would treat him now. With McGill, I learned a very important unwritten social rule that stands sentry over the one we introduced at the beginning of this chapter: *We all make mistakes; they don't have to ruin your life.*

2017 REFLECTIONS FROM SEAN

It's often been said that, when celebrities, corporate types, athletes or other wealthy and prominent figures run afoul of the law, they get into more trouble for attempting to cover up their bad behavior than they do for the acts themselves. Numerous examples lend credence to that notion. And the pattern is a far-reaching way of creating a corollary of this all-important third rule: The mistakes we all make are as unavoidable and normal as breathing and eating, so the true important piece lies in knowing how to effectively handle the aftermath.

As a child, teenager and young adult, one of my biggest, most nagging fears was that I would drown in a sea of mistakes, regardless of their size and reach. My self-esteem was so fragile and precarious that any error I made, coupled with the perception that I was already defective, validated in my mind that I was deficient and unworthy. So, given that baseline, a minor mistake such as missing math problems on a test might as well have been equal to the inability to keep up on a car assembly line resulting in the entire operation temporarily shutting down. As a result, I almost always dealt with my mistakes by vehemently denying or covering them up, which, as my mother and father repeatedly pointed out, only made things worse. Ironically, I often created the catastrophe that I so valiantly tried to avoid.

To this day, I still have some fear of making mistakes, but little by little, such trepidation has decreased in proportion to the point that I have been able to escape the grasp of autism in my adult years. In this context, perhaps, being a journalist is an ideal profession for me for two reasons: Firstly, it continually places me in a position to keep my social skills sharp because I obviously have to interact with a variety of people in a variety of contexts and, as such, I have to make constant adjustments. Secondly, no two events I cover and stories I write are exactly alike, so the potential for mistakes (big and small) is always great. At any time I could get a fact, date, dollar figure, name or narrative wrong in a story. Yet for me, the field is self-reinforcing, because each time I get a story published in the local paper with few or no edits, it reaffirms that I did my job at least competently.

Of course, that's not to say that, over my sixteen-year career, I haven't erred. Like everyone else, I'm imperfect. But what has changed markedly is that I've gained a much healthier attitude when dealing with the occasional gaffe.

A few years ago, I covered a very sobering annual ceremony honoring local police officers who had been killed in the line of duty over the past 100-plus years. Because I wanted our readers to remember the names of these fallen men, I decided to complement my story with a graphic that listed each name and the department on which he had served.

The day after the story ran, I received an email from one of my editors mentioning that an attendee who was a fellow police officer called to say that I had listed the wrong department for one of the deceased men. My mind immediately went into overdrive, my pulse quickened and I felt a wave of panic sweep through me. And I must admit that the old temptation to cover it up or "pass the buck" temporarily kicked in.

After reading the gentleman's email, I still felt bad—especially since I feared that, in the eyes of the complainant, I had disrespected the late officer. But once I got my bearings and rational thinking returned, I called the man and admitted having gotten it wrong. I assured him that my mistake was a mere oversight, nothing more, and I thanked him for bringing it to my attention so I could take corrective action, all of which he greatly appreciated.

Needless to say, taking such an approach diffused the situation and, coupled with a retraction that appeared in the paper the next day, led to the best possible resolution—an outcome far different from my previous habit of denial and defensiveness.

"Right and wrong doesn't mean good versus bad. These things are teaching us something; they will happen and help us become the person we should be," says Jennifer Schmidt, an educator at Beavercreek High School in Beavercreek, Ohio, who started a social-skills training course for students with autism called Peer Spectrum. "That's at least how I explain it to my students who need the 'why.'"

I've also learned, and am trying to more thoroughly internalize, the reality that sometimes doing all one can to correct a mistake may not always be enough for the aggrieved party. I know a time may come when I make an error and do everything in my power to make it right, yet the person still angrily holds it against me. As difficult as it may be to accept and as bad as such an instance would make me feel, I have come to realize that I can't control anyone but myself. If some people hold bitterness and grudges after I do my best to right a wrong, that's something they have to deal with, not me. I can't make another person do anything; as I've grown, I have slowly absorbed this life lesson. And I think it lends itself to a teachable moment for our friends on the autism spectrum.

In sum, as wonderfully refreshing as it is, unfortunately, it's all too rare when someone who errs admits having done so, without pretense, self-aggrandizement or self-fulfilling purposes. Yes, owning up to one's mistakes can often be unpleasant. I compare it to undergoing a temporarily painful shot or taking terrible tasting medicine, neither of which many of us enjoy. But we accept short-term discomfort if we know it will lead to long-term wellness, which is what admitting our mistakes will bring.

POINTS TO KEEP IN MIND:

- Striving toward perfection is a goal many people share; *having* to be perfect is the mindset that makes social functioning difficult for the child or adult with ASD.
- There's a function to every behavior; repeated mistakes may signal lack of understanding of the request or the appropriate behavior. Probe for comprehension.
- Be positive and proactive in teaching: Show the child what to do, demonstrate the appropriate behavior.
- Make sure consequences are meaningful and fit the intensity of the mistake.
- Help children learn the difference between mistakes that occur when they are trying their best and careless errors that occur when a child is not trying. Social reactions are different between the two.
- When in new or different situations, people with AS need extra time to cognitively process the experience. Help them along by pointing out the important details that can aid in problem solving.

- Separate the person from the behavior: help children with ASD understand that the mistake is in what they are saying or doing, not in who they are.
- Indecision stemming from a real fear of making a mistake often leaves an AS person "spinning his wheels and getting nowhere." Reinforce risk-taking, even if the outcome is less than perfect.
- Monitor your own behaviors: how do you react to your own mistakes? Kids model what they see!

RULE #4
HONESTY IS DIFFERENT THAN DIPLOMACY

O ne of the most frequently-experienced, near universal character-istics inherent in children and adults with ASD is the absolute honest response they will genuinely provide when asked, and even when not asked. Every parent, teacher, SLP, OT, behavior therapist or school administrator who has spent time within the autism commu-nity undoubtedly has a story or two about times when a child's utter honesty has resulted in laughter and amusement or hurt feelings and profuse apologies on behalf of the child.

We encourage spectrum children to engage in social situations. We reward them for their attempts at verbal communication. As a society we value honesty and in our attempts to pass along our values to our children, we often teach them, "Honesty is the best policy," or some vari-ation of the timeless axiom, such as, "Always tell the truth." Lurking behind these simple words, however, are a host of variations and excep-tions to the rule that wreak havoc in the lives of people with ASD.

Understanding the difference between honesty and diplomacy hap-pens so naturally within the typical person's social development that making a formal distinction through structured teaching is often over-looked in social skills programs for children and adults with ASD. Adults talk about perspective taking and understanding others' emotions and feelings during social interaction, but rarely do they draw a clear enough distinction that makes sense to the younger child with ASD.

Temple Speaks:

From a very young age, Mother drilled into my sister Izzy and me different social functioning skills. Included in these "courtesy rules," as I later named them, were behaviors that required me to acknowledge that other people had thoughts and feelings different from my own. These courtesy rules weren't negotiable; it was the socially-accepted behavior that was expected of me and other children growing up in the 1950s and '60s. It didn't matter whether or not I understood why I should act that way; I was just expected to follow them.

When I was young, I pretty much verbalized the obvious in front of me, like going up to a stranger and asking him why he had a big wart on his nose, or pointing at the fat lady in the grocery store and laughing. I'd make all sorts of impolite comments and got into trouble a lot for doing so. Mother labeled that "rude behavior" and was very clear that it was not polite or nice to do. Being courteous had nothing to do with honesty.

Mother drilled into me that you don't stare at people who have disabilities; you don't laugh at fat ladies; you don't point out people who have a big wart on their nose or their face—things like that. Mother was so strict about it that it was pretty easy for me to distinguish appropriate versus inappropriate behavior when it came to interactions with other people in public settings. And, she took us so many places that I had frequent opportunities to practice. I learned the courtesy rules through trial and error; when I was being impolite there were consequences that I didn't like. It wasn't like learning table manners, where she would simply correct me and tell me what the appropriate behavior was. Situations involving other people always carried with them consequences—bigger consequences, because they involved other people's feelings.

Being honest, on the other hand, had to do with lying or deceit, trying to cover up something you did that was wrong, like when I stole a fire engine from a neighborhood boy's birthday party. That was where the honesty rule came into play in our house. I remember when my little ten-year-old brother stole a light bulb from a hardware store. Mother marched him right into the hardware store, told the owner that my brother needed to talk to him, pushed him in the office and shut the door. She left my brother in there with the store owner to explain that he had taken a flashlight bulb. That was the consequence.

The way I was brought up, talking about people's appearance in a derogatory manner fell into the rudeness category and stealing or telling a lie fell into the honesty category. So, honesty and diplomacy were different in my way of thinking right from the start. I think that made it easier to learn the courtesy rules, because they were more cut-and-dried behaviors than having to process complicated concepts like honesty or falsehoods. And the courtesy rules really helped me fit in with other kids, and act appropriately in different social settings. By themselves, social courtesies are little things that go unnoticed when kids or adults do them right, but capture a lot of attention and make people stand out when they're not followed. That's why I think it's so important for parents to look at basic social functioning skills as distinct from emotional relatedness, and make sure the functioning skills are drilled into kids from an early age. They open a lot of doors to social interaction that will give emotional relatedness a chance to develop.

Sean too was raised within a family environment that encouraged honesty and being polite and respecting the feelings of others. Unlike Temple, however, Sean's highly literal mind coupled with an eagerness to stay true to the policy of being honest, resulted in behaviors that, more often than not, were regarded as rude or inappropriate.

Sean Speaks:

As a writer, I hate to use clichés more than I do their opposites. So when I say that honesty is not always the best policy, not only am I taking pleasure in turning such a trite saying on its head, but I'm uttering a truth: being honest in all situations really can make mountains out of molehills.

Most of the time, it is best to deal with social situations and people in honest and forthright ways. If you do something wrong, it's certainly best to be honest about the mistake, offer apologies and correct it if possible. But there are other times when a pinch of diplomacy runs circles around a cupful of honesty.

Even years later, my eleventh birthday stands out in my memory. What I recall more vividly than anything else associated with the day was my reaction to one of the gifts I received. At that time, I loved getting board games more than any other item, and I often shook the unwrapped present before opening it so I could get a sense of what was inside. I took delight in hearing a familiar clattering that provided a good clue that this was a game of some kind.

On that day, I shook a rectangular package and heard the sounds I welcomed. With anticipation, I opened the gift as family and a few friends—including the one who bought it for me— watched. My excitement quickly turned to anger, though, when I saw what I had gotten. It was a new Monopoly game.

I knew there were countless board games on the shelves of any toy store, so of all the available choices, why did this person have to buy me something I already had? Anger and disappointment fully engulfed the sheer joy and excitement I had felt only moments earlier.

"I already have this," I said, flinging it aside.

Mom and Dad, under the pretense of wanting me to help them in the kitchen, took me aside out of earshot of our guests and angrily told me that it was not okay to react that way when the person was obviously trying to do something nice for me.

After returning to the room I apologized, but the atmosphere was different. The friend sheepishly said, "That's okay," and slowly the mood in the living room brightened. But it needn't have been darkened in the first place—and wouldn't have been if I had used some diplomacy.

In my warped, autistic way of thinking, I was being truly honest in my response to the friend in two ways: I did already have a Monopoly game in my bedroom and I really was angry and disappointed that I didn't get something else I wanted. A response was clearly warranted when I opened the gift, and my expression of emotions, as well as the factual information about the gift itself, was rooted in pure honesty. But this social situation also clearly demonstrates how sheer, unchecked honesty without any diplomacy can lead to another person's feelings being wounded. I was unable to see beyond my own feelings and that, combined with literal and black-and-white ways of seeing the world, prevented me from understanding how my inappropriate response could affect another person.

2017 REFLECTIONS FROM SEAN

I vividly remember our annual family trips to Florida to visit my paternal grandmother and her husband in the early and mid-1970s when I was a teenager and preteen. They had a series of friends with whom we all went to dinner and met on other social occasions, and I liked all of them. I was particularly fond of a husband and wife who were very kind to me and didn't seem to know or care about my often odd behaviors. But of grave concern to me was that they, especially the wife, smoked heavily. And, worse, she smoked those terrible non-filter Lucky Strike cigarettes that had the highest levels of tar and nicotine.

I also recall my parents' mild admonishments that followed when I bluntly expressed my concerns to Mrs. B. by saying something like, "I wish you wouldn't smoke because you're going to die of lung cancer." In her southern genteel way, Mrs. B. kindly acknowledged knowing that smoking wasn't good for her, and she seemed to appreciate my worries regarding her health.

For a long time after we no longer saw Mr. and Mrs. B., my mother and father reprimanded me, and I thought it was because I had somehow stepped over the line by expressing such concerns, and it was inappropriate for me to have done so. But I came to realize that my worries pertaining to Mrs. B's health and well-being weren't the issue: It was how I approached her—specifically, how I had used brutal honesty at the expense of a little diplomacy or knowing not to say anything.

As an adult, I greatly appreciate the distinction between honesty and diplomacy in social relations. At the time, however, like many people on the spectrum, I failed to realize that the two are not mutually incompatible—they intersect in many areas, but not across the board. The situation with Mrs. B. and her smoking habit was just one of many instances in which I had to learn (often embarrassingly) the difference between them. Consequently, I've ingrained a rather simple concept of when to be 100 percent honest and when diplomacy is the better choice (which is most of the time).

Sheer honesty should be reserved for situations that by their nature are black and white, carry negative consequences and for which any other alternative would reasonably result in someone getting hurt or a wrong going unaddressed. When I was eleven or twelve, I stole a small, square packet of yeast worth about 15 cents from a local grocery store. For some reason, I had developed a fixation with those items, and it was this fixation, not malice or a dare, that drove me to steal. But regardless of the reason for having done it, what I did was unjustifiable. So when my father learned of my transgression, he not only made me walk the three miles round-trip between the store and home to make restitution, but made sure I apologized to the storekeeper, which I did. And I've never stolen anything since. This incident carried no room for equivocation; I had done something that was clearly wrong by societal standards, and honesty was the only remedy for making it right.

But most interactions in life aren't so clear cut, and this is where diplomacy has its place. Another key piece that has made this distinction easier for me to appreciate is that I'm always working to improve my ability to actively listen to others, something I feel is one of my biggest strengths. When I truly listen to people with my mind, heart and ears (as opposed to falling into the trap of waiting until they finish so I can respond), I get a fuller picture of where they are coming from and how they are feeling, both of which make it much easier to respond diplomatically and empathetically. As a general rule, people who seek an opinion, who are experiencing difficulties or who may simply need help and encouragement neither want to be told what to do nor want advice, because intellectually they know what to do. Instead, they need validation that someone cares, and diplomacy is a much more effective way to go in this case.

If one looks carefully enough, at least a grain of truth or positivity can be found in nearly every situation, a fact that provides a way to fit diplomacy into the crevices. For example, a server at a restaurant may be having an exceptionally bad day. She may have dropped a tray of hot food, brought a meal in which the chicken was cold and overcooked, and unintentionally made a family of four wait twenty minutes before getting around to taking their order. A co-worker on the autism spectrum realizes that, despite this terrible day, the server is generally friendly, affable and a good worker. Since diplomacy goes hand in hand with empathy, a distinction between diplomacy and honesty might go something like this:

HONESTY
Co-worker: "You have had a really bad day. Normally, you're very good at your job, but today you really screwed up."

DIPLOMACY
Co-worker: "It seems that you're having a rough time of it today. We all have our off days, but that doesn't change the fact that I think you are a really good, hard worker."

The two examples in this simple social interaction essentially say the same thing, but highlight how the two techniques can lead to radically different outcomes.

To make the distinction between honesty and diplomacy clearer for her students on the autism spectrum, Jennifer Schmidt, who teaches the Peer Spectrum course, uses film clips, including one from the 1997 Jim Carrey comedy Liar, Liar, as instructional aides for teaching when it's appropriate to tell a harmless white lie. Recognizing that none of her students have a desire to intentionally hurt people's feelings, she uses the clips to point out that sometimes making such utterances in the name of being polite or tactful is acceptable and appropriate so as to avoid hurting others.

"I even go so far as to tell them to tell their parents that I taught them to lie that day in school," she goes on to say. "While this comment is tongue and cheek, I'm also trying to open up the dialogue between the students and their parents."

Kids with ASD want to excel and be good at what they do. This extends to telling the truth or upholding a rule about honesty that adults may have taught them. In some cases, telling the truth is simply the only thing they know how to do; it becomes a rule that springs forth from their black and white thinking patterns, they have no other choice. The verbal, emotionally-related, interactive child often falls into the role of "truth police"— upholding these rules in absolute fashion, without regard to context or other people's feelings. In their minds, this is a positive quality that should be welcomed and praised by those around them. However, without being able to appreciate how social context affects the rule, the resultant social repercussions to their absolute honesty are anything but positive.

Can children and adults with ASD lie? Is it part of their mental and emotional make-up to be able to do so? Opinions differ among professionals in the ASD community as to whether or not this ability exists.

Temple Comments:

One of the things I hear often is the inability of people on the spectrum to lie. I agree that with some kids this is true; it depends upon their functioning level. Those who are really black-and-white thinkers, who don't have a lot of perspective taking and few categories built on their hard drive will be pretty rule-bound when it comes to telling the truth. For some, even the thought of lying will be very, very stressful, as we point out in the passage that follows this one. But as their level of functioning increases and their thinking becomes more flexible, the capacity to lie expands too. I've heard Tony Attwood comment that ASD kids can learn to lie and once they do, they're very good at it.

Personally, I know the difference between a truth and a lie, and I can lie if I want to, but I cannot do it on the spur of the moment. Lying requires more intricate sequencing of thoughts and I can only lie if I plan it out very carefully beforehand. I pride myself that I don't ever lie about anything that's of consequence, or that might hurt someone's feelings, unless, of course, safety issues are involved. For me, lying is never about personal gain at the expense of another; most of the time it's about circumventing some of the bureaucratic rules that our society imposes on us that are actually really stupid. One time I deliberately missed a connection at an airport because I wanted to visit with someone. Some airlines charge a $100 fee to change flights, even when seats are available, which I think is just bureaucratic nonsense. I went up to the service counter at the airport and told them I couldn't walk fast enough through the airport and missed my flight. Well, that was a lie. But I'd planned it out beforehand.

Anytime I lie it causes me anxiety; that hasn't changed as I've aged or as my thinking skills have progressed. But as I've learned to think more flexibly and can put actions into a more detailed hierarchy of relative importance and values, the anxiety isn't as severe with some things as it used to be. Because of that categorical thinking, I can understand the concept now of white lies, or that disguising the absolute truth is sometimes a better choice than is being 100% honest.

Lying can indeed be stressful to many children on the autism spectrum. The stress can be so severe as to be immobilizing for them, which reinforces the need for parents and teachers to clearly distinguish honesty/lying from being courteous and diplomatic in situations involving other people. Patricia Rakovic, a speech/language therapist in Rhode Island, has been running a social skills group for boys with ASD for several years now within one of the school districts in the state. The students range in age from twelve to fifteen, and the group includes typical peers. In developing material for this chapter of the book, we asked her to query her students on the subject of honesty. As an experiment, she broke the group into ASD students and non-ASD students and individually asked each group their opinions on the subject of honesty, telling the truth, white lies, etc. Their different reactions demonstrate the disparity that exists between people with ASD and their NT counterparts when it comes to the subject of honesty.

Pat explains:

> Wow! I had no idea what would happen when I approached these two groups on the subject of honesty and lying. The group of typical boys immediately latched onto the subject. They all began talking at once, quickly organized who they would lie to and what they would lie about. They even broke into role play as they demonstrated what might happen in different situations. For the most part, they lie to their parents, teachers and other adults about misdeeds. They spoke about white lies and when they would tell them and why. They also talked about not lying about big things such as someone they saw doing drugs. When they mentioned their friends, it was interesting in that they said they would lie to them pretty much about everything—they thought it was pretty funny. They LOVED the exercise and were animated in describing how they can tell if someone is lying by their tone of voice, eye contact, posture, rate of speech, etc.
>
> Contrast their reactions with the same question posed to my group of ASD students. They did *not* respond the same. Many of them were adamant that they never, *ever* lied. They had rules for themselves: "You never should lie to anyone" and "You should tell the truth." In their minds these rules were absolute; there was no hierarchy to honesty.

They had a very hard time with the concept of a "white lie" and we heard "I'm confused" several times as we tried to explain it. I invited them to play act with me—something we often do in our social skills group—and asked them, "Do I look fat?" and other similar questions. Even in the role-play they were very reluctant to voice something that was not true. Some of this role playing they understood from commercials on television and a few of the students were able to respond appropriately. However, they still had difficulty with accepting the fact that someone would lie, or that it was a socially acceptable behavior based on the context of the situation.

They also didn't seem to understand or be able to discern even the most blatant lying among their peers. There is one student in our mixed group who is a great fabricator of stories, to put it mildly. If a boy said he watched NASCAR on TV, this boy would respond that he built a race car, and was in a race, the car exploded but he still won the race. If the kids are talking about going to the school dance, the boy will say he's playing in the band (mind you, the school dance doesn't have a band). The boy's classmates are quick to recognize his stories and call him on his blatant lying; the students withASD are not. They don't seem to realize he is lying, even when he is directly questioned by the staff. Example: when we were talking about the school dance, I asked the boys if there was a band at the dance. Although they said no, they still didn't "get it" that the boy was lying about being in the band.

While talking about honesty and lying was noticeably stressful for the students with AS, the only situation in which they seemed not to be as upset about lying was if their parents asked them what was happening between them and their sibling (e.g., "No mom, it wasn't me.").

What was most startling to those of us who run this social skills group was the emotional toll just talking about the subject of honesty and lying had taken on the ASD boys. One boy related he had, at one time, lied about going outside to play because he wanted to look for his cat. His face crumpled and the color drained from it before my eyes. I thought perhaps the cat had been run over, but the overt uneasiness was his reaction to having lied, as when I asked about the cat, he said it had been under the bed all the time. The student then collapsed into tears about the incident and lying. Another boy related that in the first grade (remember, these kids are teenagers now) students would get stickers for reading books. He hated to read books so he would say he read them when he had not. No sooner did the words leave his mouth then he put his head down and began to wail. The group discussion quickly dissolved with the students saying they had had enough of the topic. Another ASD student insisted that lying would never, ever be talked about in group again.

This is one of the few times we have experienced such a strong, anxiety-ridden, emotional reaction from the students in our social skills group when discussing any topic. Obviously, to the child or teenager with ASD, honestly and lying is a highly charged issue that must be handled delicately and within a caring, trusting environment.

Telling the truth is an "easier" response, from a social perspective, than is being diplomatic, which involves putting the response in context, judging the perspective of the other person, looking for nonverbal clues about the person's motive, etc. This type of mental processing is difficult for the ASD child and it often takes time for him to sort through all the pieces to develop a socially-appropriate response, even when his perspective taking abilities are good. In most cases in social interaction, replies are expected quickly, so out pops the truth or the child remains silent.

As children grow into adulthood, the people around them often misinterpret their naiveté or gullible nature with being stupid. Many AS adolescents and adults are very intelligent yet shy away from social interaction because they lack the ability to perceive others' motives or they recognize the social environment is just too complex for them to decipher. They know their behaviors are looked upon as odd by others; they just can't figure out why and what to do about it. Rather than lie or risk looking weirder than they already feel, they may remain silent in a situation. Others will venture beyond their comfort zone in an attempt to gather information that can help them better analyze the social situation. If their problem-solving skills are adequate, the return can be worth the risk, or it can backfire just as easily.

Temple Points Out:

I learned some hard lessons about honesty versus diplomacy when I had my early interactions with people at work. Two instances come to mind. What benefited me in the long run was that in both cases, people got on me hard for my behavior right away; they didn't overlook it or let it slide until it became such an issue that it could no longer be tolerated.

During one of the first projects I ever worked on I made the mistake of criticizing some welding. I said it looked like pigeon turds, in front of a lot of people. It was a very undiplomatic thing to do, but I hadn't yet figured out how many of the courtesy rules I'd learned from Mother growing up applied in the work setting. The guy's welding wasn't the greatest but that wasn't the right way to criticize it. Harley, the plant engineer brought me right up into his office and told me, real straightforward, that what I had done was wrong and that I needed to go up to the cafeteria right away and apologize to the welder. He used a good metaphor that visually made sense to me—he said he needed to "nip these little cancers (meaning my rude behavior) before they metastasize." It didn't take me long to figure out that while my comment may have been accurate, it didn't make any of the other people on the job like me very much, which would make social interaction more difficult.

When I get in situations like that, where I've made a social blunder, I don't want to compound the situation by lying, so I usually think carefully about what I can say that will repair the situation and still maintain my own sense of integrity and honesty. I didn't go up and tell Whitey his welding was great, but I did go up to him and apologize for using that kind of language and that my comment was rude and inappropriate. We smoothed it over pretty quickly, because construction guys weren't all that social to begin with back in the 1970s.

The second time the honesty versus diplomacy issue came up, there were more serious consequences. Some senior engineers designed a project that contained some mistakes, obvious only to me. Not knowing any better, I wrote a letter to their boss, in this case the President of the Swift company, citing in great detail the errors in their design, and calling the engineers "stupid." It was not well received. Even though my comments were honest, I learned that within the job environment, one of the cardinal unwritten rules is that *you simply cannot tell other people they are stupid, even if they really are stupid; especially your boss.* First, it's not good "business etiquette"—there's a whole set of unwritten rules specific to the workplace. To keep a job, people with ASD need to learn them. Second, most typical people have their emotions all wrapped up in what they do. With adults, jealousy and control issues are often involved in the choices they make, the things they say or do, or not do.

Jealousy is a difficult social construct to learn about and it took me until my forties to just start to figure out what was going on and how to deal with it. With ASD adults just entering the workforce, it's better to just do your job and never criticize your boss or other employees, until you become better able to interpret their motives and understand their different personalities. It takes a lot of time to do that.

In this second instance, I was technically right in my comments about the project, but I was socially wrong in acting upon them the way I did. Honesty was definitely not the best decision in that particular situation, and it did cost me my job. Through that experience I also learned another critical rule of social interaction that has become more and more important in this technical age: *Be very careful about what you write*. I still follow that rule today. Anything on paper, or even sent via email, can come back and bite you later. Unless I think something I'm putting on paper could be published and distributed worldwide without repercussion, I don't put it down on paper. That's how I ward off some big social mistakes that other Aspies frequently make. I just don't do it, period.

KNOWING WHEN TO SAY WHAT YOU REALLY THINK

Part of wisely knowing when 100% honesty is needed, and when diplomacy is a more socially responsible behavior is figuring out the motives or real intentions of the other person before responding. That means looking for clues and, most of the time, actively probing for additional information in order to get a good read of the situation. It wasn't until I was a young adult in the work place and was exposed to many different types of people in various professional settings that I gained sufficient data on my hard drive to analyze and problem-solve people's motives and intentions. It's complicated and involves a lot of nuance, both in people's language and their nonverbal style of communicating.

I gradually learned about body language and how those different facial expressions, voice tone or gestures provided me with clues as to what was going on. And, it all had to work within my logical way of thinking to make sense to me, so it took on an algorithm of its own.

Let's say I'm working with a client doing a remodeling job on the stockyards at his plant. I'm not sure how honest to be about what needs to be done. I start by asking myself, "Does he really want me to tell him that his plant is a piece of crap, or do I need to be a little more diplomatic about it?" In most cases, I've learned diplomacy goes farther than blunt honesty, so now I pretty much assume up front that I need to start there. So, I might ask the plant owner a series of questions: What level of remodeling does he want? Does he want just a few band-aid jobs, like some minor repairs, or adding some new gates? Does he want minor surgery—that might be ripping out a few pens, changing things around a bit, or does he want major surgery, knocking down sections and rebuilding from the ground up? Through experience and a heck of a lot of social analysis, I've learned that people who only want band-aid repairs don't want to hear that their facility is a wreck. Those who want major surgery already acknowledge the condition, and I feel more comfortable talking frankly to them about the state of their stockyard.

I ask questions and listen to people's responses; this helps me judge not just the mechanical end of the project, but also how logical or emotional a client is in dealing with me. I developed this process once I started doing more consulting work—it's like Sherlock Holmes gathering clues so he can put the whole picture together and solve the crime. Social interaction is like a puzzle I have to figure out; I've learned how to gather information that helps me know how to act and fit in better. It's easier to figure things out when you're talking about a building project or something concrete than when you're talking about personal issues, but the process I use is pretty much the same no matter what situation I find myself in. An unwritten rule of social interaction that seems to ring true more often than not is this: *where people are involved, err on the side of being too diplomatic, rather than too honest.*

HOW TO GIVE CONSTRUCTIVE CRITICISM AND SUGGESTIONS

Despite the old adage, "Sticks and stones can break my bones, but names can never hurt me," I learned that words could indeed hurt. When I was called names by the other kids in school, it was anything but pleasant. But as I got older I learned another unwritten rule of relationships: that words could also heal, and *it was up to me to wisely choose what I said in each and every social encounter.* Let's say my Aunt Bella came up to me wearing a hideous hat. I'm not going to volunteer a compliment unless I can do so in honesty; I'm not going to just spontaneously say "I think your hat is nice, Aunt Bella" if that's not how I really feel. And I'm not going to blurt out that the hat is hideous, or looks terrible on her, because I know that would hurt her feelings. But let's say she asked me directly what I thought of it. I might make the comment that it's a pretty color, or that it matches her outfit nicely, or that it had pretty red cherries on it. I'd find something positive about it to say, but I wouldn't lie.

How do you know when to be completely honest and when not? That's where the ability to construct new and more refined categories is useful. Aunt Bella's hat is not very important in the scheme of things, so the degree of honesty of my response can be lower, if needed, and I'd only offer a comment if directly asked to do so. But suppose her hat was constructed of poisonous materials that could make her sick. I'd be frank about that, because it might injure her. Her hat moved higher up the scale of importance because of the materials it was made from.

I have had clients who had a spot on their face or body that looked like melanoma, like it could be cancerous. I don't want them to die, so in this instance, I'd make an unsolicited comment: "I know this may sound rude but I don't like the way that spot looks on your face. Have you been to a doctor and had that checked out?" I'm not rude in how I do it—I don't say it in the middle of the conference room—but I might pull them aside in the hallway after a meeting and ask them about it. Yes, it might hurt their feelings but I take that risk if I think somebody may have a serious medical problem that needs attention; life threatening issues transcend rudeness. I have a hierarchy for that type of decision-making.

Most situations in my daily life fall someplace in the middle though; they're not way over on one end of the Honesty category or the other. So, one of the sub-rules I've developed for responding to questions that require me to gauge diplomacy or how honest I am is *"Good news always comes first."* For instance, let's say I attended a conference and one of the other presenters asked me what I thought of his presentation. If I was 100% honest, I'd tell him I hated the talk. But I know that's rude, and it's also not constructive social interaction. There's a high probability that a comment like that would alienate the person from ever talking to me again. That's not my idea of a successful social interaction (unless I really do want to stop the person from ever talking to me again!).

In framing my response I first ask myself: how well do I know this person? Unless the person is a friend, I start with very general comments. Then I'd analyze my thoughts about the talk. A bad talk can be boring, but have good content; it can be delivered well but have bad content; or it can be both—boring delivery and bad content. If it's a matter of presentation style, like they had crappy overheads or they talked in a monotone, I'd try to be nice and find something positive to say first. My response might be something like, "I really loved what you had to say. You made some really great points. I want to talk to you about how you can fix up your slides to make your presentation more effective." It's honest, but it's also diplomatic. But if their information was inaccurate—they made the statement that sensory problems in autism are just nonsense—I would be challenging them from the floor, not waiting until afterwards.

I've learned through experience a couple more unwritten rules: *never start a conversation or presentation with negative or controversial comments*, and *most people don't like to hear negative comments about themselves or their work*. People need to become comfortable with you before they'll be receptive to talking about anything controversial, or discussing anything that might put them emotionally on edge. I once gave a talk in an agriculture engineering meeting, about stress in cattle. I started out the presentation with a picture of a guy beating the crap out of a steer—it went over like a lead balloon. So the next talk I did on the same subject I started out with all the non-controversial information first and used that same picture at the end of the talk. People had a much better reaction to the presentation that way.

The last opinion we share with readers has indirect reference to honesty and diplomacy. It is more a "sister rule" that we hope parents and teachers will teach alongside Rule #4. Whereas honesty is mainly about *what* to say, and diplomacy is mainly about *when* to say it, it behooves every child and adult to learn that *offering unsolicited comments isn't always welcomed*, as the following passage from Temple echoes. In our eagerness for our children to be socially engaged, we encourage them to talk, we reinforce them when they respond, so they get in the habit of offering their opinions without being asked—and we delight in their social participation. But not all situations warrant a verbal comment; it's an unwritten rule in certain social relationship settings, both personal and professional, that *keeping silent is preferable over offering an unsolicited opinion.*

Temple Speaks to This Idea That Your Opinion Is Not Always Needed:

As I got older I could appreciate the different levels of thoughts, ideas, and feelings that other people had and compare/contrast them to my own. My courtesy rules became more refined, based on situations and context. But along the way I had to learn an important unwritten rule of social interactions that at times went against my autistic thinking: that *sometimes my opinion didn't matter and that volunteering information wasn't always in my best interest.* I also had to learn that when asked a direct question that involved being honest, there were different ways I could respond—there were different levels of honesty—and that sometimes silence or "no comment" was the most appropriate one. Trial and error impressed upon me that certain ways of responding were more positive overall than others, and some would flat out alienate the person to whom I was talking. It comes back again to perspective taking—I had to realize that other people weren't always interested in what I had to say.

This is where some kids and adults with autism/AS get in trouble; they dole out unsolicited comments without realizing how they affect other people. At a young age they might have been taught the honesty rule and it's become ingrained in their thinking. Along the way, no one taught them the difference between honesty and diplomacy, or tempered that rule by teaching them to choose their words carefully before offering comments. So talk they do, when asked their opinion and when not, and even when no one is interested at all in what they have to say.

I often talk with adult Aspies who still apply the honesty-is best rule in an absolute manner, and feel they are right doing so—anytime, anyplace. One girl with autism I knew was bluntly honest with her co-workers about their weight or how they looked and her response to me when we were discussing the issue was, "Honesty is best." Her behavior became a problem on her job, yet she couldn't get it that maybe this rule wasn't working in her life. What I say to people who parrot the honesty phrase to me is this: your co-workers don't need your opinion on personal issues; keep them to yourself. You're hired to do a job and offer your opinions on job-related issues, not on people's hairstyles or their fashion sense.

Many Aspies think all their opinions matter and don't realize that some opinions are best kept to themselves, especially in social or job-related settings with people who are less than close friends. That's most of our social encounters. Offering unsolicited opinions can often get you into social trouble. My opinion about another person's personal attributes or their comments or their actions are really not that important and being 100% honest in a way that's rude will probably hurt someone's feelings. That's bad in the scheme of things; it reduces my social options and alienates me from others. I've learned to keep my comments mostly work-related or project related until I really get to know people and establish friendships with them. The only times I'm 100% honest are when safety issues are involved, where people could be physically hurt or killed, or when there's a law enforcement officer involved in the situation. And even then, there's a polite way of offering information and a rude way of doing it.

Honesty isn't always the best policy; as a general rule, being diplomatic is much more applicable across people and settings than teaching kids to always be honest. Being conscious of other people's feelings and acting in ways that facilitate, rather than alienate social interaction, can be taught as rote skills to a large extent. However the skills are taught, the process is one of trial and error and learning from mistakes. The key is to use the information from each situation intelligently and try another approach when something doesn't work. And remember the age-old saying: "If you can't say something nice, don't say anything at all."

POINTS TO KEEP IN MIND:

- Having to "un-teach" a previously established rule is difficult. Teaching young children to "always tell the truth" is tempting, but think twice about doing so. It's not always true nor is it the best choice in all situations.
- Set the stage for success: don't ask a question such as "Are you enjoying the birthday party?" in front of the host if you're not 100% sure the response will be something everyone wants to hear.
- If rules are important to a child, develop some general rules about knowing when/when not to voice an opinion, especially an unsolicited one on things such as other people's appearance. This works equally well with rigid-thinking adults.
- The likelihood that a child with ASD is telling the truth (or will tell the truth) runs parallel to his (developmental) age; younger children more often will tell the absolute, unvarnished truth when asked, or as a voluntary contribution.
- Be clear on what you're trying to teach, and teach one social skill at a time. Adults often unknowingly set up conditions that are confusing for a child who is working on social skills. Are you teaching a child to obey your requests? Are you teaching a child to respond to questions in order to keep a social conversation going? Or are you teaching him how to be diplomatic in his responses? A generic "Kyle, what do you think of this nice dinner that Aunt Mary has prepared for us?" can be confusing. For one child the issue is whether or not to obey (answer the question); to another it's a decision to tell the truth or lie; a third child may have the theory of mind skills to understand that being diplomatic is the order of the day. And you thought the question was innocent and easy?
- Topics such as honesty, diplomacy, and socially approved white lies have no clear-cut boundaries; personal ethics and morals dictate our

opinions and even within social groupings, what is "wrong" or "right" can differ tremendously. As a result, many adults adopt a very "autistic-like" rigid response to the social misbehavior of their children. It's much easier to give them a rule, to take the shortcut and say "always tell the truth" then to merge onto the Road of Lifelong Learning that involves the responsibility to explain the "when," "why," and "with whom" aspects of social relationships. Be honest with yourself if you see your reflection in this mirror and get off that shortcut as soon as you can. Social relationships are complicated; there is usually no easy answer. As you take the high road and work through situations with a child on an ongoing basis, you reinforce to him that social understanding doesn't occur in a flash of wisdom, but is a continual learning process for everyone. That's putting him on the road to social success.

RULE #5
BEING POLITE IS APPROPRIATE IN ANY SITUATION

t's an unwritten rule of our social culture that *being polite and having good manners gains you entry into group social interactions*, whether that interaction is personal or professional, between two people or among many individuals. Even before uttering a word, exhibiting polite and appropriate physical manners demonstrates to others that you understand the boundaries of "group behavior" and gains you "Level 1" acceptance. Good manners are relationship-building behaviors; they facilitate continued social interaction. While they vary from culture to culture, from one social group to another, can be looser or more formal, and can change literally overnight, people still notice when they are *absent*.

Temple described her four rule categories in an earlier chapter, one of them being Courtesy Rules. As she points out, these rules may vary from culture to culture, but they all serve the same functions. They exist in order for people to feel comfortable around one another, they demonstrate respect for your fellow man, and define the boundaries of socially appropriate behavior in group settings.

Inherent within manners is the ability to appreciate that differences exist among people, in their thoughts, feelings and actions, and yet accept that group guidelines are necessary in order for people to exist together in a civilized society. That's where the difficulty starts for children and adults with ASD; their perspective-taking ability can be so challenged that it prevents them from understanding when they're being impolite to others. However, as Temple strongly suggests in the passage that follows, having autism is not an excuse for bad manners or no manners. As she points out, Rule #5 is more about behavior modification than it is about understanding the emotional underpinnings of social relationships. While both are important, mastery of the basic social functioning skills should be given priority and taught from a very early age through behavior modification techniques, or if the child's level of functioning is such, via therapy programs that are based on social-emotional principles. Without these skills, children will miss out on the opportunities to engage with others that provide the fertile ground from which perspective taking and emotional relatedness can blossom.

Temple Speaks:

As a whole, people in our society have become ruder and cruder than ever before. People behave in social settings today in ways that would have been considered really impolite when I was growing up in the '60s and even in the '70s and '80s, and it's tolerated. Over the last twenty years or so, having good manners and being polite in social interaction—the whole idea of there being a "right" and "wrong" way to act in social settings—has become less and less important. Fewer and fewer parents are taking the time to instill manners and teach proper social etiquette to their children. It's having a ripple effect. Young parents today aren't even conscious of some of Miss Manners' rules which used to govern society when I was young and growing up.

Typical kids are able to deal with this shift in emphasis on teaching social functioning skills—they have the brain capacity to learn by watching other kids and still pick up manners if they need them, despite not being directly taught. But the ASD kids can't learn by observation;

they need direct teaching, direct experiences—they need that structure that used to exist in the social world. It's not there at home or at school, and they're lost as a result.

I think that raising kids with ASD is much more difficult today than it was when Mother was raising me. "Good manners" and being "polite" were much more clearly defined. All parents pretty much taught their kids the same manners, so the same rules applied from one family to another, from one social setting to others. There was a lot more conformity across social settings, so it was easier for a person with ASD to understand what behaviors were appropriate and inappropriate.

Even typical kids and adults have trouble these days understanding and interpreting their social culture and making sense of what's appropriate to do or say. Just check out the etiquette section of any large bookstore; there are tons of books out now written specifically for kids, adolescents and adults about good manners and social graces; some of them are really good. There are all sorts of Miss Manners-type websites, too. Fortune 500 companies have etiquette classes as part of grooming people for high-level management positions, because there are so many really intelligent young adults with really poor manners and social skills. The idea of "appropriate" behavior is so context driven now, and the nuances of context are so much more complex, that it's no longer an easy part of life for anyone to figure out. It's a minefield for kids with ASD who, by their very nature, have difficulty with social context and think in rigid, black-and-white patterns.

Because social expectations are no longer clearly defined, I think some parents are afraid to even tackle the subject of manners with their ASD kids. It no longer lends itself easily to strict rules, because there are so many more exceptions to the rules than there used to be. For instance, when I was in school, we had a dress code; today, just about anything goes. On the one hand, that's good: it opens up avenues for a lot of self-expression. But it lends a whole different level of anxiety to a simple task like getting dressed for school each day. Understanding the basic social functioning skills that constitute being polite is hard enough on its own for people with ASD. Our looser social structures pile on additional levels of nuance that pump up the stress quotient of daily life for these kids and adults.

TEACH MANNERS FIRST, BEING SOCIAL SECOND

That said, autism is no excuse for rude behavior and some basic social functioning skills should be drilled into kids with ASD, like Mother drilled them into me when I was young. This is where parents and teachers need to again be cognizant of the difference between social functioning skills and emotional relatedness. Rule #5 is first and foremost about behavior—teaching a child basic manners and social skills that are the in-roads to social interaction. When children are young, these can be drilled into them via rote teaching methods, like ABA, if needed. It's simple behavior-consequence teaching—adults don't need to incorporate emotional understanding into it. That's confusing to the child.

Emotional relatedness takes much longer to develop in a child. It involves perspective taking and thinking in flexible ways, which can develop in the child, but happens gradually as the child has more experiences. In the meantime, unless kids with ASD have certain basic skills that ingratiate them with their peer-group, like knowing to say please and thank you or "I'm sorry," knowing how to share, take turns, how to compromise during play, they'll never get a chance to spend time with other kids so the emotional relatedness can develop.

Working on manners and being polite has to come before trying to teach them to understand the emotional backdrop to "being social," yet I too often notice programs that are trying to do both at the same time. For some kids, it's too confusing and they lose out on both fronts. Some kids need social skills taught in a very structured manner, so it's very clear what is "good behavior" and what is "bad behavior" when it comes to interacting with other kids and adults. The more rigid their thinking patterns, the more structured the lesson should be. Even kids who seem emotionally connected at a younger age will benefit from a more structured teaching style when it comes to social functioning skills. As kids start developing theory of mind and can see other perspectives than their own, then the "why" behind the lessons can be explained, the emotional aspects of interaction can be explored and explained. Mastering the social functioning skills has to come first, though; it needs to take priority over emotional relatedness.

Little kids should be taught all the courtesy rules, to the extent their mental and physical functioning permits. These are things like table manners: you say please and thank you, you ask people to pass the food (you don't just reach or grab it yourself), you don't talk with your mouth full of food, no elbows on the table, etc. Then there are manners and etiquette for interactions in the school environment: you address the teachers with respect, you raise your hand and wait to speak in class, you don't push in line, you don't walk up behind people and poke them, you don't make fun of someone when he makes a mistake, you don't interrupt other kids. There are all sorts of social functioning skills for different settings and situations; they're too numerous to even begin to address, and listing them is not what this chapter is all about.

Good manners and proper etiquette were taught to me as a very little child as behaviors I needed to learn—not as "ways to make friends." Maybe today it's going a bit overboard to teach kids to put the knife and fork at the four o'clock position at the end of the meal, but I advise parents it's better to err on the side of too formal than to err on the side of sloppiness. I'd start out teaching them what used to be called "old-fashioned manners" through lots and lots of repetition. Most of these ways of acting have stood the test of time and apply generally across all social groups and settings. When children make mistakes, just correct their behavior in a non-emotional, factual manner by demonstrating and/ or telling them the appropriate behavior. One day Mother told me to keep my mouth closed when I chewed. I could see no logical reason for doing so until she told me that it made her sick to see chewed food because it looked like the inside of a garbage truck. She also pointed out that seeing my "mouth garbage" produced the same reaction in her that watching my classmate's disgusting food-mixing habits produced in me. That type of graphic, concrete explanation made sense; I kept my mouth closed when I chewed food after that.

Mother expected me to perform when it came to basic manners— she didn't view my autism as a reason to lower her expectations of me. It was a behavior issue; it had nothing to do with being emotionally connected to people. It was good behavior versus bad behavior when it came to manners and she called it being polite or being rude when it came to conversation or verbal comments. She did realize when my autism was affecting my ability to control my behaviors, though. When I was tired or the setting was noisy I'd lose it, and she made allowances for that. But simple manners like saying please and thank you, there were no allowances for bad behavior there. Now, I did have my bad days; it wasn't always as simple as I'm describing it. Remember: I wasn't "high functioning," I was classic autistic. That was a factor Mother kept in mind, but overall she still held me accountable for my behaviors.

With young kids and up toward the end of elementary school, social functioning skills are more related to whether or not another child will play a game with you, or work on a project with you, or talk about something. Shared interests, doing things together, exploring the physical world dominate the social landscape during those years. When children move into middle school the hidden rules of social relationships get really hard to figure out. They're much more related to feelings and concepts like belonging and social relatedness. "Hanging out" becomes the preferred activity and exploration is into the world of emotions, inner thoughts and feelings. It's difficult enough as it is; the kids who haven't mastered the basic social dynamics of group interaction will be completely lost, unable to catch up. Even worse, they'll become the object of teasing and bullying because they haven't learned how to even navigate a simple social interaction with another kid.

ASPIES FROM MY ERA FARED BETTER

I see a lot of ASD adults my age out in the workforce, with decent jobs living independently. Why? Because they grew up in the '50s and '60s and their parents probably drilled the social functioning skills into them, as my mother did with me. Then I see the junior version of myself today, and while some of these young adults are really brilliant, they can't keep a job because of their poor social skills. As a society we're failing to teach them the social functioning skills they need to be successful. As an autism culture we are perhaps putting too much emphasis on emotional relating to the exclusion of making sure they master basic social skills.

When teaching manners and etiquette was a priority in our society, we didn't notice how much they impacted a child's ability to grow up, become independent and achieve success; everyone just acquired these skills. But now, since they're no longer being taught, we're seeing the negative effect that not having these skills has on a person's future. It's social skills, not academic success, that determines how well children with ASD will able to function as independent adults.

This is the real tragedy for ASD kids: our society isn't giving them the opportunity to become proficient in basic social skills. As parents and teachers, we have the tools and the know-how to teach these skills (some of us may need to brush up on our knowledge!), and individuals with ASD can learn them with enough practice and reinforcement. The pace of our society is so fast nowadays, academic expectations are so much more intense, and our attention spans have become so short, that the type of learning environments these kids need—structured, positive behavior oriented, sensory-friendly programs with extended opportunities for practice—are being found less and less. How many parents make it a priority for their family to sit down to meals together? Even just one meal a day? Even just on weekends? I grew up having to interact properly at three sit-down meals every day. I was expected to have table manners and to participate with appropriate conversation. That's a lot of practice on basic skills that benefited me in all sorts of different social settings, practice that kids miss out on today because something as integral to family life, like mealtimes together, is no longer a priority. It's easy to blame school systems for not doing their job, and I realize that there are lots of single-parent households today with moms and dads struggling to make ends meet. But for children with ASD to grow into socially functioning, socially aware teens and adults, some of the ways of "simpler life" need to become a priority again. Adults need to make conscious choices to create these learning situations for the child. These skills open the doors for them to social interaction. Without them, the doors stay locked forever.

Mastery of the various basic social functioning skills takes time, practice, and patience, and social blunders will be part of the journey. Fun, engaging programs and meaningful rewards will keep motivation strong in most children, but there may come a time, or there may be a subset of children, for whom learning the basic social functioning skills becomes, well, a drag. They disengage; motivation wanes. What do to?

Temple Says:

"With some social behaviors, or with some kids, a strict approach will be required. Some kids won't be at all interested in learning social skills; they have to be taught that learning these skills is not a choice, but a necessity. Parents and teachers who are tuned into a child, who know what sparks his interest, what really gets him going and what turns him off, who know his thinking patterns, can generally keep him interested in social skills too by using these interests and motivations. For some, though, keeping them interested will be a challenge, so a direct 'you just have to learn this' approach is best. Doing things we don't like to do is part of life. To function successfully as an adult, he'll need to accept this. Don't let him off the hook on learning the social skills because he's not interested."

Sean, on the other hand, points out that learning the value of two words, "I'm sorry," is an equally important skill to be taught alongside the other social functioning skills. "Situation repair" skills can turn social blunders around so that the door to further social interactions remains open, rather than slamming shut when inappropriate words or actions interrupt the social flow. An unwritten rule of social relationships is at play: when you're not polite in any given situation, a polite apology is the next best thing.

Here's What Sean Has to Say:

People with autism can be so wrapped up in their own thinking that they fail to see the effect their words and actions have on the people around them. At times my own need to control my environment was so strong that whenever the rules I created in my mind were broken, even in the slightest way, it was an earthquake of gigantic proportions. Autism does not give a person a license for displaying poor manners and hurting others' feelings. Allow me to explain further.

I came home one May afternoon from school and, like most eighth-graders, I was looking forward to a three-month break and the advent of summer. I walked through the front door and found my mother in the living room grading papers. As a sixth grade reading teacher, she too was undoubtedly excited about the approach of the end of the school year.

For most of the day, I had been looking forward to our trip to the township park. That morning, we had made plans to leave the house at 4:30 PM, which was perfect because I got home shortly after 4 PM and would have enough time to unwind and change clothes. After I came back downstairs, I realized the time to leave was quickly coming up.

"Mom, it's almost 4:30. Aren't we going?" I asked.

"You know what? I still have some more papers to grade, so I'm not quite ready. How about if we leave at 5:00 instead?"

"What?" I said, as anger gathered and consumed me in seconds. "You said we were going at 4:30 and it's 4:29."

"I know, but I need another half hour to finish this stack of papers," she said, trying to stay calm. "As soon as I finish, we'll go."

"You didn't say 5:00," I responded, enraged. My voice was much higher and louder. "You said 4:30, and 4:30 means 4:30."

"Look, we will go when I'm through ..." I don't know what else she may have said, nor do I remember her explanation beyond this point. The increasingly tense dialogue ended because I was screaming, yelling and storming through the house. I thought a blood vessel might burst somewhere. I was so furious that I blocked out anything but the fact it was now past 4:30. Mom never said 5:00 and she had violated one of my basic rules: that once plans were made, they weren't to be changed, period. The rule, along with my sense of security, was shattered.

By the time I re-entered the living room a few minutes later, an unusual and very disturbing sight caught my eye. My mother was crying. My rage ebbed for a second as she said something barely audible through her tears. But, just as quickly, it intensified again as I ran full speed upstairs to my bedroom and slammed the door so hard the house shook.

After the bite-sized earthquake, I jumped onto my bed and buried my face in the sheets and cried. I wanted to end my life and never see Mom that upset again. By now, several layers of fury had been added to the pot, in addition to what I felt regarding the time violation. I hated myself for being such a low-life as to cause my own mother to cry. At no time during this ugly episode did I intentionally try to hurt her. I was just so caught up in what I wanted and the perceived wrong that had been done to me (and I still had no comprehension of how or why my behavior or reactions affected other people, or how to stop either). And blind rage, like depression, has a nasty way of feeding on itself. By being consumed with the cause of my anger, I became angrier and the situation ballooned—it became that much harder to think clearly, let alone know how to do damage repair. I stayed in my bedroom cut off from the world until my dad came home and dinner was ready. A generous helping of tension went with the meatloaf.

And we never made it to the park.

How could this whole odious incident have been avoided, or at the very least deflated, and the tear ducts kept dry? Two simple words would have done the trick: "I'm sorry." I could still have been upset that our trip didn't begin when I wanted it to (people have a right to their feelings), but had I apologized at *any* point during the escalation, it wouldn't have spread further. Saying I was sorry would have been like depriving a developing fire of oxygen. It would have changed my outlook, causing me to feel better in a short time, and Mom would certainly have been understanding.

And we would have made it to the park—what I wanted to do all along.

At the heart of the meltdown was hard-core rigidity as well as the firm belief that it was my mother's fault for changing plans. I still hated change (unless I initiated or in some way controlled it) and at that time I felt that what I wanted was completely reasonable.

Now, however, I realize that my rigidity drove my mother crazy and that the reason she cried was because she was so sick of it and worn out by it all. During that painful day and well into the night, I felt terrible that I had caused my mother to react that way. Intellectually, I knew that saying I was sorry was the only way to fix it. But I didn't know how to get myself to say that precious sentence.

So what is it that makes saying those two words so difficult? For me, it wasn't mean-spiritedness or machismo that kept them from leaving my mouth. It was being so caught up in trying to preserve some semblance of order in my life and having little ability to deviate from it. It was also an inability to see something through someone else's eyes. When something or someone violated my house of cards—and it happened a lot—I became so filled with fury that it consumed me. I couldn't apologize under those conditions—there was no room in my thinking processes for anything other than the rage.

But anger and rage don't have to be all-consuming, and you do have control over your feelings. Apologizing is valuable for many reasons, not the least of which is its ability to heal. It:

- Makes you attractive to other people. It's an unwritten rule: *If you have done something wrong or hurt another person, saying you're sorry is the quickest way to make it right.* Remember, if the other person refuses to accept your apology (assuming, of course, that it's sincere), then at that moment it becomes their problem. The only person you can control is yourself; you aren't responsible for someone else's response.
- Diffuses bad feelings. In the park example, I could have said to my mother, "I'm really mad that we're not going at 4:30 ... " and apologized at any point during the screaming match. If I had calmed down enough, say, after five minutes to switch gears and take stock of the situation, I could have told her how sorry I was for acting

the way I had. It might have taken us a little while to "deflate" and move past it, but bad feelings would certainly have gone to bed before sunset, not after. Apologizing during the height of negative feelings might not get rid of them instantly, but it sure beats keeping them fed and nourished.

- Puts you on a path to take constructive and corrective action to right a wrong.
- Shows the other person you care enough to want to take positive steps toward repairing it.

You're never too old, macho, big, small, smart or "perfect" to apologize if you have wronged another person, made a mistake, hurt someone's feelings or shown bad manners. Saying you're sorry extends beyond race, creed, age, religion or background— or being diagnosed with autism.

In his concluding passage, Sean also wants to share that first impressions are built upon more than the cursory please-and thank-you manners and encompass all the niceties of reciprocal conversation, as he learned the hard way.

Sean Shares:

Manners can make all the difference between an interaction moving forward after that crucial first impression or being stuck in park (and perhaps sent to the junkyard). Sadly, during the early days of dating, my inability to understand this rule led to the latter.

The year after I graduated from high school, I met a woman in one of my classes at the junior college I attended in Van Nuys, Calif. I acted solely on physical attraction, which was strong enough for me to overcome my fear of approaching girls. I asked her on a date, but since she knew me only casually, Lisa made it clear that she wanted to go out as friends.

I stammered when I called her the next day because I had forgotten to mention that I hadn't learned to drive, that I needed her to pick me up. Nevertheless, she agreed, and we went to dinner. However, the food and the conversation were on opposite sides of the pleasure scale: the meal was great; my manners weren't. This was evident from her diminishing level of enthusiasm as the short evening wore on.

I remember that I failed to look in the mirror before the knock on the door came and that I left the house without being sure I looked presentable. My prominent memory regarding my attire is my wearing shoes with holes in them.

What's worse is that I spent most of the meal pontificating on specialized knowledge I had without taking her interest level into consideration. Nor did I think to steer the dialogue to include her interests, etc. Instead, I discussed obscure jazz musicians, what they played, which band they were with and the years they played with those groups. I resorted to a variation of the "What if" questions I asked as a child. I asked her numerous times, "Have you ever heard of …?" And I asked knowing there was a good chance she wasn't familiar with the person.

I recall that Lisa was polite throughout the dinner, but she seemed to grow tired of such conversation. After dropping me off, she just said, "I'll see you in class." That was the last time I saw her outside the classroom, and even in class she was noticeably more distant.

I know that things didn't go well that night because I violated the unwritten rule that points out *the value of being inclusive*. I asked her about the musicians because it validated my self-esteem and gave me a sense of power—power that I knew this information and she didn't. But I did so without taking into account what her reasonable reactions would be, such as boredom and, eventually, resentment. I realize that my quest to feel big and powerful came at too high a cost.

The rule of displaying good manners extends beyond please and thank you. It's also not enough simply to make eye contact and be sure the shirt is tucked in. *Good manners also incorporate inclusive conversation.* By that I mean shifting gears away from yourself and displaying an interest in the other person.

At any time I could have done so with Lisa—with humor, perhaps— by saying something like, "So, I've yammered on enough about myself and given you the history of Sean Barron. Let's hear all about the life and times of Lisa." The straightforward approach works, too: "Well, I've talked enough about myself. I'd like to learn more about you."

Either method would likely have led to a better outcome—and maybe, down the road, to an actual date. So it's critical to know that manners and good first impressions fit together like a meal and good conversation.

2017 REFLECTIONS FROM SEAN

In his famous 1971 musical hit, "American Pie," Don McLean expresses what he felt was a loss of innocence in American society at that time.

"Basically in 'American Pie,' things are heading in the wrong direction," McLean said in 2015, as reported in the *Newcastle Herald* of New South Wales, Australia.

Several times throughout the epic 800-plus-words song, he uses the line, "The day the music died," in a gloomy reference to the February 3, 1959, plane crash that killed singers Richie Valens, Buddy Holly and J.P. Richardson Jr., better known as the "Big Bopper," and, arguably, permanently altered the rock 'n' roll landscape.

Today, it seems that things are continuing to head in the wrong direction on many fronts. It's difficult to shake the sense that this is a time in which overall civility and general politeness in our society have died, or are at least on life support and have nearly flat-lined. It's hard to miss; you see this lack of civility—which goes hand in hand with an overall sense of personal entitlement—at political rallies, on cable news talk shows and even at a local restaurant. The Internet, to a significant degree, has fed into this phenomenon by giving bigots, xenophobes and others who choose to be hateful another powerful platform for espousing their poisonous views, rants and rhetoric.

Not long ago, I had a meal at a restaurant and sneaked a series of glances at a family of four seated across from me. The mother and father seemed engaged in a normal conversation with each other, but the two teenage children were engrossed in their iPhones, so much so that for nearly a half hour, neither one looked up. When the server came to take everyone's order, one of the teens in a monotone and a detached response stated what she wanted, without a smile or acknowledgment of the employee, as if to say, "How dare you interrupt me." At the same time, the parents were enabling this rude behavior by failing to intervene. I can state with near 100 percent certainty that, if smart phones and iPhones had been around forty years ago and I acted as those two teens had, my parents would have scolded me—and rightly so—for being downright rude.

Am I saying that we should get rid of all technological devices and return to an artificially bucolic 1950s *Leave It to Beaver* kind of society? Certainly not. Today's technological capabilities have done a lot to enhance communications as well as make it much easier and faster to get, use and exchange ideas.

Facebook and other social media websites have allowed most of us to do everything from sharing recipes to finding lost loved ones. All of that is wonderful, but the problem comes when technological tools are used as a substitute for true communication with one another instead of another means of achieving it.

Estimates say that slightly more than 90 percent of our communication is nonverbal. So someone who relies heavily on emails, text messages, iPhones and social media for communication miss the other person's facial expressions, body language, eye movements and so on, all of which are crucial to getting closer to the person's soul and relating effectively to one another. In short, when people spend all of their time texting and little or no time talking and listening, civility suffers.

It's no accident that communication techniques, rules of etiquette and general good manners, even though some of them vary over time and across cultures, have been around in one form or another for thousands of years. The reason they have survived the test of time is simple: They work and have allowed us to advance and develop as a species. Regardless of how smart we become in a technological world, it will never be a smart idea to abandon being polite, adhering to good manners and simply being kind to one another.

It's also important to mention that precautions should be taken to resist subscribing to the assumption that those on the spectrum who have difficulty responding appropriately to others or who only see life through their own eyes also lack empathy. Good social-skills programs such as Jennifer Schmidt's Peer Spectrum incorporate theory of mind elements that give those in the course sharper ways to improve their ability to see things through lenses other than their own. Deficits in this area can easily adversely affect one's peer relations and interactions in groups, along with interpersonal and business relationships. Being impolite, unintentionally or otherwise, or lacking the means to differentiate between honesty and diplomacy, can have severe negative implications for a person on the spectrum, whether on the job or in a serious personal relationship, regardless of the person's cognitive skills and intelligence.

"Most people don't lose their jobs because they're incompetent; they lose their jobs because they can't get along with other people," Schmidt observes.

One last point about being polite and having manners: you're going to run up against a lot of people who don't have good manners and act in ways that are impolite and disrespectful. Some people exhibit these behaviors because they were never taught otherwise; some people feel the need to "challenge the system" for a host of personal reasons; some people are just plain rude. Parents and teachers working with younger children on the spectrum or with those who have very limited perspective-taking skills can employ Nike's "Just Do It" strategy in obtaining compliance. But as children grow to become adolescents and young adults, as their minds become more flexible and they are increasingly conscious of the thoughts and feelings of people around them, the discussion will inevitably turn to why some people have good manners and others do not, beyond the question of training. As Temple describes, this became an issue for her once she entered the work force and was exposed to more and more people. What is interesting to note is that while Temple's mind works in very logical, analytic patterns, the sentiment that echoes throughout the following passage has a decidedly emotional tone. She expresses the sense of remorse that many people today share about the declining social ethics of our society. Her mode of thinking, visual and in pictures, may set her apart from the verbal processing thinking style of most people around her, but one unwritten social rule is shared between them: being polite and having manners is "good behavior" anywhere in the world.

Temple Shares:

When I first started working, the unwritten rules of social behavior in the workplace were easier to understand than they are now. Most of the manners that were appropriate in social settings were equally appropriate on the job. The theme behind most of them was about treating your fellow man with respect and courtesy, so they applied across settings. Workers didn't challenge the system as much as they do now. People took pride in their jobs and being part of a team was valued, whether the team was a family unit or a work unit. People respected the chain of command on a job and took personal responsibility in doing their part to keep a team intact. People overall were more tolerant and respectful of each other.

Plus, I worked in an industry that was 98% males, which actually was easier for me to adjust to than would have been a predominately female industry. Men tend to be more logic driven and less emotional in their social relationships than are women. The men I worked with were much more direct in telling me when I was acting in a socially inappropriate way, and their comments were mainly about my behavior, not a statement of my value to the project or the company. That made a difference. I was very project-loyal, so when I was told that something I said or did might negatively impact the overall success of the project, it made sense to me. It didn't lower my self-esteem because it was simply a behavior I needed to work on, not a different person I needed to become. People who are highly social wrap everything in emotions, and tie behavior into judgments about self-worth and self-esteem. That type of thinking can spiral downward quickly and deflate motivation. If I made a social blunder it meant I needed to learn a different behavior; it didn't mean I was a bad person. It's an important distinction to teach, especially to kids and adults with ASD.

Aside from the basic polite/impolite behaviors that govern social interactions on the job for all employees, I created some basic work-related courtesy rules and manners to guide my own actions. Some of them were a result of getting into social interactions that were just too emotionally complex for me to decipher. There are certain subjects I still avoid today, because they are so illogical that I can't find a way for them to make sense to me.

Reading *The Wall Street Journal* and articles in business magazines helped me understand good versus bad work behaviors. But beyond that, I learned that I functioned more successfully if I kept my interactions pretty simple: be civil, make small talk, stay away from discussing controversial subjects like religion, politics or personal issues like sex with coworkers or the boss, keep a low profile, and concentrate on doing the job rather than gossiping and talking about other people.

I had to learn a few other unwritten rules of the workplace in order to keep my jobs and develop my career: that *many people you work with act in inappropriate ways, that some people won't like you despite your efforts to be cordial, and there was nothing I could, or should, do about it.* That meant not offering my opinion or criticizing them or talking about them to other co-workers, and especially not tattling to the boss about what other co-workers were doing.

I got to the point where I had to just accept—and I'm almost cynical about this now—that some people have bad social behavior and it's tolerated by others; not only tolerated, but almost considered "normal" nowadays. Looking at it from a logical perspective, especially as it plays out over months and years, it doesn't make sense to my way of thinking. Yet it's a reality I encountered over and over again. All I could do was learn to work around it, and I developed ways to do that as long as the people with the bad behaviors were not my direct supervisors. In that case, if the problem got bad enough and we couldn't find a solution, I'd have to quit a project. Actually, that's an unwritten rule of social relationships inside and outside the workplace: *sometimes you just can't find an amicable solution in a social relationship and it's time to severe the relationship and move on.* This is especially true when it comes to dealing with people with bad social behavior.

Once children with ASD grow into adults with ASD, their impolite ways of treating people, their bad manners or their lack of manners is much less tolerated, and another unwritten rule kicks in: *the expectation is that once you become an adult, you should know how to act appropriately.* The "free passes" get taken away, it's no longer acceptable to act rude or impolite to others; the old adage "Three strikes and you're out!" is the more common response from other adults, meaning your chances to get things right are limited. That's why drilling basic social manners and rules of etiquette into children with ASD is so important: they have lots more opportunities to practice and make mistakes while they're young than when they're older. In elementary school being impolite might mean a buddy doesn't want to play with you that afternoon. Once you're in the workforce, it can cost you your job. The consequences get much more significant.

POINTS TO KEEP IN MIND:

- Rules of etiquette and common manners—the list is exhaustive and changes all the time. Each generation has new "rules" about manners; however, some basic ones stand the test of time.
- Good manners make people feel comfortable around you. They are a nonverbal signal that you understand the boundaries of the social group.
- Learning polite/impolite behaviors can be a bore and a chore for many kids with ASD. Keep it fun, teach in natural settings as much as possible rather than in a lesson format. Use cartoons, movies, drama, skits and exaggerations to keep it interesting and light.
- With younger children, or those with low perspective taking skills of

any age, teach manners via a behavioral approach. Tying emotions into the behavioral lesson can be too confusing for some kids. Teach the skill first to mastery, then add in the "why" behind it.

- Put emphasis on the behavior, not the person: "This behavior is rude," rather than, "You're being impolite." Don't tie self-esteem/self-worth into what is essentially a behavior issue.

- Behaviors have a function; rather than trying to extinguish inappropriate social behaviors, find the function it serves and then teach an appropriate replacement skill. For instance, a child who constantly interrupts may be eager to show others he is smart. By giving him opportunities to "show off" what he knows, learning to wait his turn to speak may come easier.

- Keep in mind at all times that children with ASD don't learn by observation, but by experience. It's tempting to slip into the mindset, "They must be able to get this— it's so obvious/simple/straightforward." Give them lots of opportunities to practice, and probe often for comprehension. Put aside your own ideas and judgments about what he "should" be able to do and really look at what he understands or doesn't.

- Use visuals to reinforce learning!

- Teach the difference between formal and informal manners; the context of the social situation will often dictate the level of formality.

- The manners you teach will, to a degree, need to be peer-appropriate, especially as the child moves into middle/high school. Some manners that are welcomed by adults will be laughed at by teenagers. Make sure the ASD child understands "when, where, and with whom" to use different manners.

- Keep in mind the child's native culture, especially in teaching bilingual children whose home environment retains strong cultural ties. Their manners and customs may be more or less formal, and lessons can be doubly confusing for these children. Reinforce the concept of different manners for different places.

SOME BASIC MANNERS:

- Say "please" and "thank you."
- Be nice to people regardless of their social position. The janitor should be treated with the same good manners as a boss or teacher.
- Use "formal" manners with adults in positions of authority.
- Don't stare at other people.
- Don't call other people derogatory names.
- Don't laugh at or make comments about people's weight, appearance, age, etc.
- Don't discuss family matters in public settings.
- Don't ask people you do not know well personal questions such as why they got divorced or fired from a job.
- Don't ask people questions about their financial status or how much their things cost (e.g., their house, car, clothes, computer, etc.).
- Don't interrupt people while they're talking, either verbally or by walking between them.
- Don't talk with your mouth full or chew with your mouth open.
- Don't scratch your private parts in public.
- Don't crowd people (i.e., personal space issues).
- Use "Mr." or "Mrs." or "Ms." when addressing adults you don't know well.
- Don't grab things from others (food, toys, books, etc.).
- Don't make obscene gestures.
- Don't point out others' mistakes, laugh or make fun of them.
- Don't tattle on others unless personal safety issues are involved.
- No elbows on the table.
- Don't wave your eating utensils around while talking at the dinner table.
- Don't pick your teeth in public.
- Don't spit, burp, belch or pass gas in public settings.

- Cover your mouth when you sneeze or cough.
- Don't eat with your hands (unless it's 'finger food' or things like hot dogs, burgers, etc.).
- Display polite telephone manners, including cell phone usage
- Don't tell people they're stupid in front of other people.
- Control your temper in social settings.

RULE #6

NOT EVERYONE WHO IS NICE
TO ME IS MY FRIEND

H ow do you define a "friend"? Ask one hundred different people and you'll probably get one hundred different answers. Age, gender, political, economic, religious and cultural differences will flavor the response. Some may ask for clarification: Do you mean an old friend or a new friend? An acquaintance, a buddy, a work friend, a romantic friend? A go-to-the-gym-together friend or a tell-all-your-deepest-secrets-to friend? While we may all define friends differently, the common thread that binds us together is the desire to have friends and be friends. And that's no different for people with ASD.

What is different is their ability to intuitively feel who's a friend and who's not, to sort through the various and varying internal and external clues that signal whether a person's smile is a sincere gesture of friendship or is a social mask, hiding true feelings, intentions or motives. Is he a friend or foe? The lines are often blurred for people on the spectrum.

Temple Shares:

Young kids pretty much buddy-buddy around with each other because of their shared interests. You like to fly kites together, or build snow forts, or ride your bicycles, or play board games. When I was young, my friends and I did these sorts of things together; our friendships were based on shared activities. At that age, emotions are simple and happen at surface level; they come and go quickly. You laugh at all sorts of things and bursts of anger quickly melt away, all within a matter of minutes.

In adolescence, all that changes. Kids' emotions take center stage and young teenagers start looking inward. They align themselves with other kids who share their thoughts, their feelings and their fears more than with those who share their passion for catching frogs or building things. The "nerds" are the kids who continue to be jazzed about solving complex math equations, chemistry experiments or delving into the molecular structure of the universe in physics. For the rest of the kids, social interaction becomes the stuff that dreams are made of.

Most kids with ASD entering middle school lag behind their peers in social-emotional development; in many cases it's *way* behind. Yet they still feel the need to belong. Their bodies keep growing in ways similar to their same-aged peers, so in their minds, everyone's still the same; there's one big group and everyone belongs to it. On the inside, too, they still measure friends by simplistic measures that defined the group structure in prior years—shared activities, people who say hello, people in the same class together. They miss the shift in group structure that occurs at this time, when friendships are defined by smaller and smaller social groups based on selective differences, rather than broad similarities. The one big social group of elementary-school peers breaks down into individual cliques in which some kids with ASD never belong. For others, even that awareness fails to develop.

I had problems well into college understanding who was a friend and who was not. Once I left elementary school, it was a lot more difficult to decipher. I could pretty easily catch on that someone didn't like me if he or she was obvious with words or behavior. Mother had equipped me with some of the unwritten social rules that are important to young adolescents: *don't be a tattletale, if someone tells you a secret, don't go blabbing it to another person* (unless it involves their safety or well-being), *not all teasing is bad teasing*—some people tease you in friendly ways because they like you. I wasn't oblivious to those, and since I also knew the basic social skills that you need to get along with others, like turn-taking, playing in a group, respecting other people's feelings, I could at least function in school. I also had decent conversational skills, and that gained my entry into some social groups.

Where I got confused as a teenager and young adult with regard to Rule #6 was appreciating all of the more complex social-emotional issues, like jealousy, or recognizing that other kids had ulterior motives, or were feigning affection just to be mean. I learned some very hard lessons very early in my first year at college. I met a girl I'll call Lee and she acted like she was really my friend, spending time with me, talking with me, asking me questions about myself—all the behaviors that on the surface indicate budding friendship. After about a week I confided in her about my autism, and told her about the squeeze machine and the door symbols I used in my head, things like that. A little while later I found out she had blabbed it around and that students were making fun of it and laughing at me. I was really upset; I felt betrayed.

It took about three instances of getting burned like that (and the three instances didn't take that long to happen) before I changed my tactics and decided that I would talk about the personal parts of my life with only a few close friends, and only once I knew for sure they were to be trusted. As I explained in the first chapter, I feel the emotion associated with an event, but then it gets stored on my hard drive in pictures without the emotion. It becomes a logic puzzle to figure out.

I learned two very important unwritten rules of social friendships from those situations: *1) there's a difference between someone acting friendly and someone being your friend*, and *2) trust has to be earned*. I still remained friendly with the students and talked with them, but I learned to keep conversation on safe subjects, like studying for exams, or homework assignments, or events going on at the school. They were acquaintances, but the majority of them didn't become friends.

The real downside to those first-year situations was that once the word got out about how "weird" I was, I had to endure a lot of verbal teasing. I'd be walking across the parking lot or in the cafeteria and students would be yelling, "Buzzard Woman!" or calling me other ugly names. It wasn't until I was in my third year of college and got involved painting scenery at the school play that my college classmates realized I was good at something and they stopped teasing me so much. One of the unwritten rules that turn of events demonstrated to me was this: *people respect talent and like to associate with people who are good at something.*

As I got older, I learned another unwritten rule of friendships: *true friendships are built on shared interests, or shared ideas, or shared principles that you both hold meaningful.* There's always some common thread that binds you together. Just being the same age, or the same sex, or in the same class or going to the same after-school activity doesn't make a person a friend. Some of the other rules I learned during college and as a young adult are:

- Friendships take time to develop.
- People can disagree and still be friends—friends don't have to agree on absolutely everything.
- Friends are genuinely concerned about each other's feelings and thoughts.
- Friends help each other out in times of need.
- There are relatively few people who are your really close friends.

That last rule took me a while to learn, and is probably one of the more important rules to understand.

It's not until around middle school that one of the unwritten rules of social interactions kicks in and starts to really make sense: that *people often hide their true feelings from others.* Young children are honest in their words and actions. The world revolves around themselves and they see no reason to hide what they think or feel from others. As children age and their understanding of the different perspectives that make up the world develops, they quickly learn that disguising their feelings can be useful to further their own desires and fuel their needs. They also see that doing so is a socially prudent gesture at times, and learn that there are a myriad of reasons why people hide their true feelings: they don't want to hurt another person's feelings or they may be unsure about their own feelings and don't want to say or do something that is opposite their beliefs or principles. At other times people disguise their true feelings because they may be feeling an emotion that would be socially inappropriate to express in a particular setting. For instance, you may be raging inside at a comment your boss makes about you in the middle of a business meeting but you realize that acting upon it could get you fired. Or you're feeling deeply sad at the recent death of a friend while you're attending another person's wedding—a happy occasion for them and an inappropriate place for you to be crying in public.

These two examples illustrate an unwritten rule of social relationships related to the one above: *that children and adults can feel one emotion on the inside, yet act out its opposite.* To the literal thinking of some individuals with ASD, that is lying; they can view it in no way but that the person is being false.

Temple Explains:

Kids with ASD can easily be taken advantage of because they don't recognize when other people are lying, even when their lies are overt. They literally believe what they see or hear, no matter how illogical it may be. In their black-and-white thinking mind, people who act nice are nice. Period.

When these spectrum kids end up in situations where kids say something nice to them, and then do something nasty or hurtful, it's very illogical and confusing, so the meaning inherent in the social encounter never registers in their brain. They just keep going on with their rule-bound thinking and continue interpreting other kids' social behaviors as they see them. But they frequently become tattletales because of this, which only further alienates them from their peers. When I was growing up, Mother taught me to be a good sport and that being a tattletale was not good, so this wasn't a behavior I developed in elementary school. I also had pretty good self-esteem at the time the teasing started up, so for me there was a positive foundation to stand on when other kids were being unkind. I didn't believe everything they said about me; it was more a matter of trying to disregard their comments than my wrestling with negative beliefs about myself. Their comments bothered me, for sure; I wasn't immune to them. But my visual-logical mind held the images apart from the emotions, which I think really helped me get through those socially horrendous years.

When it comes to being teased at school, this same literal thinking that so many children with ASD exhibit makes it difficult for them to think in reverse and appreciate this unwritten rule of social interactions: *not all teasing is bad; sometimes teasing is a sign of interest and/or affection.* They're so rule-bound that whenever they get teased, they automatically think the person doing the teasing doesn't like them. They need to be taught about friendly teasing and how it differs from negative teasing and bullying and to recognize the signs that distinguish one from the other.

Sean, on the other hand, felt the sting of teasing and bullying in much more absolute, emotionally-based ways. His low self-esteem, coupled with his rule-based, rigid thinking, rendered it nearly impossible for him to intellectually process what was happening enough to even be able to ask for help.

Sean Describes:

I wouldn't be in the same financial league as Bill Gates, but I would be exceedingly wealthy if I had been given one dollar for every time during my childhood and teenage years that one of my parents came to me and said, "We want to help you, but you have to tell us what's going on," or any of its many cousins. This was especially true when I came home from school visibly upset, angry or on the verge of a meltdown because of something bad that had happened that day. My folks' frustration must have caused them at times to feel like melting down themselves because, despite their best and most soothing efforts, I never offered them information. This remained the case even when my mother stepped it up by getting down to my level, firmly grabbing a hold of both my shoulders and, with her face inches from mine, trying to get me to yield some clues so she could help me. Anything—a one-word response, a brief sentence, even a yes or no nod—would have been better than what I did, which was to move my head and eyes around and focus on anything in the room but her gaze.

There were several reasons I responded to her in such antisocial ways, but not among them was wanton defiance and general recalcitrance. Perhaps the biggest reason was my inability to organize a series of chronological and relevant thoughts well enough to describe what had taken place; I didn't even know how to attach words to the feelings I was experiencing. My boxed and literal thinking prevented me from being able to meaningfully relate the day's events to her or paint an accurate picture of what had happened. I knew I did not deserve to be bullied, ridiculed, hit, slapped, punched, tripped or tormented, but that idea was light years away from any logic that would suggest ways of stopping the bullying, including talking to someone who could help.

Another reason I looked everywhere but in my mother's eyes was because the acute pain of the day's experience was still so fresh that hearing all the bad things rehashed threw them with tidal-wave force back into my face. Having no perspective also caused me to think my parents would conclude that a certain amount of what happened was my fault anyway. After all, I was always getting reprimanded at home for things I had done that they said were wrong. Why would this situation be any different? Talking to her, or anyone, about other kids' cruel misdeeds also meant I'd have to face instead of deny them. I knew I didn't have the ability to describe those situations in words, so taking the paths of least resistance—denial and masking—seemed the best and only options. Why bother trying to discuss a bad day when my attempts would likely only cause me further aggravation? Another, perhaps more subtle reason, for my unresponsiveness had to do with self-image. My self-esteem was very low; even if I could verbalize what was happening, in my mind it would require a Herculean effort to rectify these wrongs that branched out in a dozen directions without a starting or finishing point. It seemed too futile to even try.

Most individuals with ASD want to please the people around them, their parents, teachers, friends, partners, coworkers and supervisors. This inner desire can manifest in many different socially appropriate and inappropriate ways, depending on their level of cognitive functioning, their thinking style and the repertoire of experiences they've had from which they can formulate conclusions. They can be easily led to tell a lie, out of a perception that the lie is what the person wants to hear. This can be especially disastrous if, as teens and adults, they wind up unknowingly involved in an illegal action and are being questioned by law enforcements officers uneducated on ASD. Adults with AS have confessed to crimes they didn't commit, because they felt doing so was telling the officer what he wanted to hear.

Understanding that people have ulterior motives, and that they can act out one emotion while feeling another, requires advanced levels of perspective taking (PT) and theory of mind abilities. To the child without PT, or with emerging PT abilities, this concept may not "make sense" to their way of thinking. And, when it doesn't make sense, it doesn't "stick" in their brain. Stop for a moment and think about that sentence and compare that way of thinking to how your own mind functions. Perspective taking arises from the fact that even when certain thoughts or situations are not directly applicable to you or your life, those thoughts, ideas, or aspects of a situation you may have witnessed find a home somewhere in your brain. Without ever having to consciously do anything, all those details get burned to your hard drive. Your brain files them away "for later," for a time when they may prove useful in deciphering a social situation or making sense of an unfamiliar challenge. It all happens for you on autopilot brain functioning.

Without PT abilities however, all those thoughts just disappear into thin air; they never get stored in the brain of the child or adult with ASD. They're MIA (missing in action) when a social situation arises for which that understanding may have been relevant. The less PT abilities a child has, the less information gets stored. The more PT abilities he has, the greater the number of details from a situation that get recorded. Can you now better understand why autism makes it so difficult to "make sense" of the world and why such a high degree of repetition and practice is needed in order for PT to develop? Unless an idea or situation is directly meaningful to the child, it doesn't register, and even if it does, he may get only 10% of the details the first pass. Next time a few more stick. In some cases, the data may be sticking, but the retrieval functions are faulty. The wrong information pops up, or information associations are atypical because there's still not a volume of experiences on the hard drive. The result can be obvious efforts on the part of the child to interact, but behaviors that are still mismatched to the situation.

For individuals with low or emerging PT, teaching more scripted actions that pertain to Rule #6 may be necessary while PT develops. Set up behavioral guidelines that can help children work through potentially dangerous situations. A more rote approach may also work better for the child who is a high visual-logical thinker. Use those strong analytic, investigative abilities to teach the child to problem-solve a social situation. Turn this learning into a "social experiment" or a "social puzzle" to figure out, with external motivations/rewards (if needed) to keep the child engaged in the process.

In matters of personal safety, err on the side of being too straightforward in talking about potentially difficult situations. Children and young adults with ASD may not recognize a risky situation when it's right in front of them, despite previous conversations with them. Their generalization skills can be weak, so that if conditions don't match perfectly, they miss the cues that signal potential danger, or that might raise concern that someone is trying to take advantage of them. For some children and adults on the spectrum, their black-and-white thinking, coupled with their own (often unrealistic) inner rules, overshadow even the most persistent efforts by parents and teachers to ingrain safety behaviors.

Sean Speaks:

During my twelve-year struggle to break free of autism, I clung to the belief that other people were good. I had a blind desire to see only the best in others. What people claimed was true about themselves and others must be true; if they appeared to act kind, they must be kind. These were some of the rules I lived by; these were some of the thoughts that cycled over and over in my mind. Unlike a typical child of twelve, all the "ifs, ands or buts" that would go along with these thoughts, that would allow me to gauge intentionality and truthfulness, were absent from my thinking.

I spent most of my teenage years through my mid-twenties liking everyone but myself. If someone smiled and seemed genuinely interested in me, then that was good enough. I could not imagine that people were not exactly what they claimed to be. I had no critical judgment and no common sense. My innocence, of course, made me extremely vulnerable.

When I was twelve years old, I was involved in an incident where a stranger I had been talking with for only a short while asked me to engage in oral sex with him. This man seems so nice and harmless, I thought, so he must be both. We live in a safe neighborhood and he is an adult, so why would he tell me to do something wrong? After the incident, however, I felt extremely uncomfortable, but didn't know why. On some level I sensed what he had done was wrong, but I was unable to figure out exactly what had happened or why it was inappropriate. After all, in my mind I was the one who was usually wrong; adults were right. I told no one what had happened to me because I could not possibly have found the words to do so. My parents didn't find out until about twenties years later.

Another time when I was eighteen, I had missed the last bus of the night home. Before I could call my parents to come and get me, a middle-aged man who looked friendly and trustworthy pulled up near the phone booth where I was about to make the call. He somehow sensed that I needed a ride and without hesitation I got into his car. It was a situation fraught with danger: he had been drinking, he started boasting about raping a woman recently. Luckily, I had enough sense not to have him drop me off at my house and I made it through the situation without harm. I accepted the ride and placed myself in danger with this man because I accepted him at face value. I had no ability, at age eighteen, to size up the situation, use common sense to sort out the details of the situation and process the "safety quotient" or listen to my instincts.

My autism interfered with my brain's ability to think in those ways. I'm thankful that, over the years, I wasn't taken advantage of in more serious ways and that my innocence and blind trust in people didn't lead to my being the victim of a serious crime.

My naiveté was one of the big issues my parents, through many months of talking to me into the wee hours, tried to help me tackle. They tried to get me to see, for example, that people could have many reasons for not telling the truth and a variety of motives for their actions. Mom and Dad were afraid that people would lie to take advantage of me or to get money from me. My parents did not want me to be cynical, but rather were trying to teach me an unwritten rule of social relationships: *weigh the words and behavior of others within the context of the situation before extending trust.* No matter how comfortable I felt seeing only the surface of what I was presented with, I could no longer deny that life was not simple. I also had to learn another unwritten rule related to that one: *you can't automatically assume that malice or evil is the motive when someone doesn't tell the truth.* Sometimes people lie, I learned, to avoid hurt feelings. It was a very slow, cumbersome and painful process to grasp the concept, perhaps best spelled out in the words of the song "Smiling Faces" by the 1970s R&B group The Indisputable Truth:

> *"Smiling faces, smiling faces sometimes, they don't tell the truth.*
> *"Smiling faces, smiling faces tell lies, and I got proof."*

Temple, on the other hand, with her visual-logical basis of thinking and processing, approached the realm of ulterior motives and assessing intentions in a characteristically analytic manner. Whether it's figuring out if the car mechanic is trying to rip her off, a co-worker is possibly sabotaging a project, or a newly-acquainted "friend" is really a friend after all, for Temple, it comes down to an algorithm.

Temple Explains:

Neurotypical people seem to have some inner sense of when people are lying or stretching the truth. Some people are really good at spotting deceit and others are not quite as good, but it's a sense they have that people with ASD really lack altogether. For me, with my visual mind and logical thinking patterns, figuring out if someone is telling me the truth or not happens like a computer algorithm. I have different variables I go through in my head and tick off the ones that apply and then figure out the probability that what the person is saying is truthful. I think like a goal-directed computer processor with the objective of calculating the best way to achieve success, whether it's on a project or getting one of my university students graduated. What neurotypical people refer to as "intuition" for me is a picture-based, logic-based mental process. It's not a feeling; it's an Internet search inside my head.

I start with an objective analysis of the variables, the most important one being whether or not a conflict of interest exists. I assume that people who have a conflict of interest are not going to give me accurate information and may be lying to a greater or lesser degree, or may have ulterior motives that they are not actively displaying. Conflict of interest also means that jealousy will probably enter into the equation, so I look at that. Jealousy often occurs in people who view me as an invader of their territory. On plant projects it was often the plant engineer; he felt I was doing his job. I assess the person's jealousy-quotient and apply that to the probability that the information he shares is accurate. Depending on the situation, I do any homework that I feel is necessary in order to gather related information before making a decision. For instance, if I'm trying to figure out whether or not I can trust a new car mechanic, I might ask some of his other customers, or look around his shop for licenses and awards he's been given, or whether or not he's a member of the Chamber of Commerce—homework like that. Based on the objective results, I'd assess the validity of what he's telling me, and whether there's a high probability he's lying. I use the same method whether it's a business or personal relationship.

Discovering that people had ulterior motives was something I spotted on one of the early cattle projects in my career. It was rooted in jealousy, and I can now spot that a mile away—the warning sign is the person at a project meeting who is very silent and not enthusiastic about the project. However, what was different about me is that I didn't notice it at first from a social perspective. I discovered it by paying attention to details in my surroundings and using my logical mind to piece it all together. We were having some problems with a piece of equipment; it kept malfunctioning. My mind hones right in on all the details, and because all of them are viewed as equally important, I noticed that every time I went to the bathroom, that's when the malfunction would occur. I found out another person on the project was sticking a meat hook into the piece of equipment because he wanted to make me look bad. We were almost at project failure mode, so I took a calculated risk. I wrote a little note to the boss and told him that one the guys was sabotaging the project. I knew I'd either save the project or get fired over it; that time it happened to save the job. Jealousy is a tricky thing to handle. So much depends on who's being jealous.

After that incident, I developed a few new work-related rules for myself; some of them are rules that are generally part of the hidden rules of the job. Let's say I'm consulting with a meatpacking plant and the plant engineer hired me. One of my rules is: *don't go over the head of the person who hired you, unless the project is going to fail*. That's part of respecting the *chain of command*, which is an unwritten social rule in every business setting. If a problem develops, talk it through with the person who hired you, or the person who's your boss, and try to resolve the issues. Another rule is: *if a coworker is jealous, give him a piece of the action*. I've found that involving the jealous person, complimenting him on his talents and making him feel needed in some way, usually diffuses the jealousy.

I did, however, get into some problems at work with telling management about what other employees were doing in areas that were not related to my project. It got back to them somehow and then the coworkers hated me. I learned pretty quickly to stop doing that. It became another sub-rule of mine: *don't tell management what other people are doing, just concentrate on doing your own job.* I think that's pretty much an unwritten rule of the workplace, because it's often repeated by managers, but it's a rule that more and more people keep breaking nowadays. It comes back to Rule 6 that this chapter is all about: Not everyone who is nice to me is my friend. People have become very cunning in the ways they deceive others on the job, and even people who have good social awareness can be fooled or not catch what they're doing. When they discover they've been taken advantage of, their response is to run to management and tattle, because they're angry, or hurt or their pride has been wounded. It's too emotionally complex for me to figure out. I just concentrate on what I'm doing and don't get involved in all of that.

On a personal level, another social rule I had to learn was that *relationships with other people are never perfect.* As I mentioned previously, I learned that perfection in design work is impossible. I also had to learn that this social rule applies to personal relationships as well. There will be disagreements with people and just as some projects are better than others, some relationships are better than others. I just have to try my best and at times, agree to disagree on certain subjects. I have friends who are great buddies when we build things together, but we avoid discussing religion or politics. That's another unwritten social rule I learned: *you can have a friend who has different beliefs without compromising your own beliefs.* Friends can be at different levels: I have engineering friends and animal behavior friends. These people are not deep-belief friends. There are few people I share my views with on sex, religion, or politics. I have learned that discussing these subjects may ruin a good friendship that's based on shared interest.

I learned these social rules not through emotional-relatedness, but by using my keen observational talents and then problem-solving the situation using a logical approach. Being able to do this is partly a function of having enough information on the mental hard drive to arrive at an educated, accurate conclusion. In high school I couldn't tell very well if someone was being truthful or not, or had an ulterior motive, because there wasn't a lot of data on my hard drive. There was nothing to search, nothing to use as an objective measure. Today, I may arrive at the same conclusions as someone using intuition, but my methods are different. They work for me and actually, I think they are sometimes easier to deal with because the analytic approach is one step removed from emotions and the mental confusion that often comes with them.

Temple and Sean have both learned to gauge the motives and intentions of the people around them, albeit in very different ways: Temple from a place of logic and social analysis, Sean from gaining emotional perspective arising from his ability to integrate his own feelings in relation to those of others. Progress for both of these successful individuals came slowly, but it did come for both of them. Many of the bigger steps in awareness of self and others came only once they became young adults.

Sean shares that as he was becoming more socially aware, one of the more eye-opening realizations for him was that even the social "professionals"—people whose field of expertise was psychology or counseling—didn't have all the answers when it came to understanding the intentions and motives of others.

Sean Explains:

I used many different methods as I tried to make a place for myself in the larger world. I decided I needed to read psychology books and practice to the letter what they recommended. Books about dating were the most interesting because I thought if I followed their advice, a girlfriend would soon be mine. I also tried to seek out positive people and pattern myself after them. During the many, many conversations I had with my parents, I tried to absorb and put into practice what they told me. I often had talks with myself in which I would repeat aloud what Dad and I had discussed until, I hoped, my mind and emotions would finally both "get it." The strategies I developed to turn myself into a happy person sometimes worked, but more often were painful and frustrating.

One particular incident that comes to mind, and further illustrates the blind adherence I gave to the opinions of others, was my effort to become more assertive. In the 1990s I grappled with a need to get better at dealing with conflict. I was tired of allowing fear, intimidation and low self-confidence to stop me from not figuring out, until after the fact, what I should have said or done in difficult or confusing situations— especially those in which I was being manipulated by others. I went to the local bookstore and, without passing Go or collecting $200, walked directly to the self-help section. There I found the book *When I Say No, I Feel Guilty*, a 1975 release by Manuel J. Smith, Ph.D., about assertiveness training that explained several specific techniques designed to stop manipulation and to effectively handle criticism.

Reading this book would catapult me forward, I predicted. After I finished it I had a formula to follow and I expected to be transformed— at once—into an expert in assertiveness. I never reread any book because I thought doing so would prove I was stupid and defective. But I reread entire sections of this one because I was determined to adopt its principles into my life—and fast.

After several months of trying to be more assertive and having limited success, I read in the newspaper that a four-week assertiveness workshop was coming to town. I immediately signed up and attended the workshop, but it only infuriated me further because I could not master the techniques the professionals were teaching. The result of the workshop was that, rather than becoming more assertive, I felt guilty and more autistic than ever.

As I painfully found out, there is a huge difference between simply reading a book or attending a lecture and being able to apply what it says. I continued to face social situations that were manipulative, but a lack of trust in myself still prevented me from clearly seeing what was going on until it was too late. Even more importantly, I was overlooking this important unwritten social rule: *no single person or book or workshop has "all the answers" we seek in understanding ourselves or the social relationships we encounter.*

Fortunately, since that experience, I have stopped thinking of therapists, counselors and self-help books—and of psychology in general—as providing absolute answers and concrete rules of behavior I had to follow if I were to be successful. I have learned to use what I read, or the advice I am given, as a guide, knowing that some suggestions may work for me and others may not. Another unwritten rule I've learned through these experiences is that *people love to give advice to others, and a lot of time it can be advice they don't necessarily follow in their own lives.* I don't have to blindly follow what other people suggest I do; I can use what seems appropriate for me and discard the rest.

In this final passage of the chapter, Sean offers further wisdom on recognizing deceit, manipulation and less-than-honorable intentions in others, this time in the deeply personal arena of emotional attachments, love and romance.

Sean Speaks:

Imagine this: You have just moved to an unfamiliar city where you have a new job. You have been given vague directions to the job site and on your first day of work, you get on the main highway, but see, much to your horror, that all the road signs are indecipherable. You don't know the speed limit, can't make out the name of the roads, you have no way of figuring out if the direction you're traveling is the right one, nor which exit you are supposed to take to get you to your destination.

This rather simple description echoes the level of confusion, the lack of awareness and the unfamiliarity of my surroundings that I experienced, not to mention the associated feelings of anxiety, anger, fear and depression, whenever I tried to figure out what people were saying to me and, later, why they said what they said and what they meant. When I was in my twenties, I was still lost socially—there was still so much I couldn't decipher about a social interaction. Whenever I talked with someone, I would later replay over and over what the other person had said to me. I would analyze the conversation to death and along with it, "analyze" myself into a bad mood.

For instance, one evening I went to dinner and a movie with a friend. We had a great time and I said goodbye as we parted. She, however, nodded, but said nothing. Suddenly the fun we had had all evening disappeared: What had I done wrong? Why didn't she say goodnight to me? What did that nod mean? Now that I thought of it, her smile when she nodded seemed insincere. My mood darkened and the evening was ruined.

Obviously, I still had a black-and-white picture of the way people should respond to me. My social behaviors had improved, but my rigid thinking patterns were stuck. If people failed to respond the way I expected, I assumed I had done something wrong or stupid. It never occurred to me that there were other perspectives than mine, and in fact, many possible, plausible different ways to interpret such an interaction.

I was in my early twenties before I learned a simple rule of social interactions that opened the door to greater understanding of others: that *people can and usually do feel more than one emotion at the same time.* It was inconceivable to me, for instance, that someone could be happy in general, yet furious with a specific incident, etc.—that two contradictory emotions could be operating at once in the same person. Or that a person could feel happy yet fearful about a new promotion at work or moving to a new city.

My myopic view of the conversational highway kicked into overdrive when it came to dating. Even into my thirties, I interpreted a woman initiating a conversation with me as a sign of her romantic interest and failed to see the many other possible meanings. I didn't understand a most obvious unwritten social rule between men and women: *friendliness is not necessarily a sign of romantic interest.* As a result, my emotions with women fluctuated wildly between euphoria and heartbreak—without taking a break at any points in between. Being so absorbed in loneliness, despair and desperation made it impossible for me to see things objectively. It didn't occur to me, for example, that the female clerk in the store treated me in a friendly manner because that was part of her job. Or that a waitress might stop and chat for a few moments with me because she had a gregarious personality. I didn't stop to reason that women I met might have full lives of their own, and I had yet to learn that when I approach a woman I should look to see if she has an engagement or wedding ring on her finger. The unwritten social rule that *you look for signs that a woman is married before you ask her out on a date*, wasn't yet part of my natural social functioning. I couldn't put all the different nonverbal and verbal clues together to arrive at a conclusion that accurately reflected the reality of the situation. My thinking was that much confused by my autism.

It took a long time to get better at judging situations I found myself in and to slowly gain the capacity to see the social clues and use common sense in deciding what to say or do. For years I continued to assume that everything that went awry was solely my responsibility. Although I didn't know it, a side effect of this rigid thinking was an inability to trust my instincts and intuition. This distrust—coming from the assumption that I would be wrong anyway—contributed to me getting into some bad romantic relationships and friendships and staying in them much longer than I should have.

ROMANCE AND HEARTBREAK

In the early 1990s, just when I thought I was savvy about dealing with others, I found myself in a situation for which I was completely unprepared. My hard-won common sense and healthy skepticism both left me and went south for the winter (and spring).

I was working at a nursing home in Ohio. One morning, I was sitting in the break room when a co-worker, Suzanne, sat down across from me. We knew each other only casually, since she had a management job. But on this particular day, we began to talk. To my surprise, I saw that she clearly wanted to go out with me and I could feel my insides glowing. I was still terrified to ask someone out on a date (a four-year relationship had ended a few years before and I was still feeling its effects) and this was the first time that a woman had ever approached me. Of course I'll go out with her, I thought, elated. I would be crazy not to.

Perhaps appropriately, our first date was on Halloween. We went to breakfast that morning and I immediately noticed how attracted to me Suzanne seemed. I also learned that she was a heavy smoker and I hated cigarettes. But the main thing was that she was paying attention to me and wanted to date me because I was special.

I quickly learned, however, that Suzanne was not what she appeared to be. She told me constantly that she was a "straight shooter," an open and honest person who always tells it like it is. Nevertheless, it took her a full month to reveal to me that she had a child. Also, she made me promise not to tell anyone else at work that we were dating. Then there was the matter of her age. Suzanne said she was thirty-two (I was thirty at the time), but a few weeks later she mentioned that she was thirty-five. Her age continued to jump mysteriously, yet when I pointed out that it kept changing, she simply said, "I'm just a few years older than you, but age doesn't matter."

If Suzanne disagreed with me or was angry about something I said or did, she responded in an oblique, roundabout way that completely confused me. Fred Astaire was one of her favorite performers and on occasion my "straight-shooter" girlfriend quoted lines from movies he appeared in—lines that were designed to make me see she was upset with me for some reason without dealing with the issue head on. She began to criticize nearly everything I said and did.

A month after we began dating she told me that her husband, whom she had left in North Carolina, had been physically and emotionally abusive toward her. She said that because of an incident she had been involved in, she could never return to North Carolina. I asked her to explain, but she refused to tell me anything more.

A few months later, our relationship began moving very fast—much too fast for me. She repeatedly told me that I was not to share with my parents anything about our relationship. I became increasingly uneasy because I started to notice that when we were together, the bad days outnumbered the good ones two-to-one, in a pattern I could predict. But I had no idea what to do, nor could I sort out what my feelings were.

My family began to notice that my behavior was becoming increasingly autistic. Constant tension and feeling on edge and lost most of the time caused some of my old habits to return and some positive qualities to go into hibernation. My mother and father commented that I had a frightened, set look on my face most of the time and that I walked stiffly. I rarely smiled; I seemed to have lost my sense of humor and ability to get others' humor. I made statements that I hadn't made since the early days of fighting autism, and I could not tolerate being wrong or making a mistake. I knew I was in over my head. Accepting it, though, was another story.

One night, perhaps five months into our relationship, Suzanne said she had decided it was the right time to tell me why she could never return to North Carolina. In return, I was not to tell anybody—not family, not friends, not anyone.

One night, Suzanne said, she and her husband got into a terrible argument and, she added tearfully, he had sexually abused her. After the attack, Suzanne continued, she went to the refrigerator, drank four beers and got into her car to get away from him. Speeding and drunk, she smashed the car into a concrete wall and was charged with driving under the influence. She then hired a local attorney who told her to leave North Carolina and never come back. Suzanne and her daughter had subsequently moved in with her parents in Pennsylvania.

After she finished telling me the sordid story, I did my best to be supportive and sympathetic. Mainly, I was truly flattered that she had confided in me. But I was also aware of doubts in the back of my mind. Had I been able to think clearly at the time, I would have had a lot of questions. Why hadn't she brought charges against her husband? Why was she so afraid to return to North Carolina to face such a minor charge? What kind of attorney would give her that advice? Didn't the North Carolina authorities have better ways to spend their time and resources than tracking down some woman who lost her head and wrecked her car by hitting a wall—especially if, as she claimed, no one was injured? Had she killed someone in the accident?

But I was not thinking clearly. Instead, I tried to swallow my doubts and pretend everything she said made sense.

One night in March, Suzanne and I went to a nearby mall. I went in with the intention of browsing while she shopped. But as we passed a jewelry store that was advertising its sale items, Suzanne stopped in her tracks. A huge smile crossed her face and in a childlike voice, she talked me in to going inside "just to look." A short time later I left the jewelry store with an $1,800 engagement ring.

"It's symbolic," she said. "It's the first day of spring and the beginning of a new chapter in our lives together."

I was struggling with conflicting emotions. She seemed to really love me, yet I was starting to realize that, for reasons I didn't understand, I was afraid of her. I now know that I was in love with the idea of being proposed to, but I was not in love with the person doing the proposing.

Later that evening we returned to my apartment and, at her urging, drew up a list of people we wanted to invite to our wedding, which she decided should be in August 1994. She drew a line down the middle of the sheet, which separated those she wanted to invite from the people I was to include. I felt like a deflated balloon as we sat at my kitchen table. I barely had enough energy to come up with any names. I knew in my heart that this would not work—that marrying her would be disastrous—and an encounter a month later and four hundred miles away put everything in perspective.

My mother and I were traveling to Hamburg, Germany, to do interviews for our book, *There's a Boy in Here*, so we met in the Newark, New Jersey airport. While waiting for our flight, we went to a coffee shop. Immediately after sitting down next to my mother, I let out an enormous sigh.

"What was that all about?" she asked.

"I won't have to see Suzanne for a whole week," I responded. "I'm so glad."

On the overseas flight, my mother pointed out that relationships are difficult for everyone for many reasons.

"But there's one thing that's easy," she stressed. "If you feel better and happier when you're *not* with Suzanne, the relationship isn't working."

Sure enough, my mother and I enjoyed several days in Europe, and at no time did I miss Suzanne. I didn't even think about her. Instead, I felt free, I had fun and I smiled and laughed easily. In short, I came back to life and my tension disappeared— all telltale signs that our relationship was in serious trouble.

For the next few months, my parents did their best to convince me that Suzanne was the wrong person for me, that I was obviously miserable and that, no matter how hard I tried to make it work, this was a relationship destined for failure. Marrying her would ruin my life and would cause, as my father put it, "the few good times you have with her to disappear."

I knew my mother and father were right but, as with so many things in my life, a chasm existed between knowing something and being able to accept it. For the last month of our relationship I was torn. I didn't want to hear what my parents were telling me because it confirmed that I had made yet another bad choice at a time when I was still trying to recover from making what I felt was a lifetime of mistakes. Yet at the same time, I was trying to figure out how to end it with Suzanne as amicably as possible. I had never broken up with anyone before. Fortunately, my common sense and ability to reason returned early from their vacation and in June 1993, I called Suzanne and said: "We need to end this relationship." I also asked her if she could return the ring.

She accused me of lacking the courage to give her this bad news in person—she was right and I was actually afraid of her— and told me she had been preparing to notify me later in the week that she was planning to break up with me anyway. As for the ring, Suzanne said she found my request an abomination. What a scumbag I was to suggest such a thing.

As difficult as it was for me to end an eight-month relationship with the only person who had ever asked me out on a date, I felt only minimally guilty and, in the end, enormous relief.

Obviously, you don't have to have autism to experience the ups and downs and often the heartaches that are a part of maintaining a romantic relationship. People who go through romances learn this unwritten rule: *having to break up with a significant other is painful.* But in my case, my fragile self-esteem and recurring need to believe people are what they claim to be made it that much harder to see things clearly and to know what I had control over and what I didn't—what was my fault and what wasn't. The most important personal rule of social relationships that this experience taught me was this: *having no friend or girlfriend is far preferable to having a person who's a constant source of negativity.* This was a major step forward for me.

READING MOTIVES AND INTENTIONS

Whether the relationship is one of romance, friendship or is a utilitarian function of daily living, some of the following unwritten rules can help you ascertain the motives and intentions of a partner.

- *There's a big difference between regularly going along with what another person wants to do and allowing yourself to be taken advantage of.* Pivotal questions to ask in any social occasion are: Am I doing this and spending time with this person because I want to or because I feel I have to? Do I feel in competition with the other person—that is, do I feel I have to constantly prove I'm right for that person to accept me?
- *Acknowledging your feelings of unease is a better relationship skill than is making assumptions* about something that you sense is amiss. Assumptions, I've learned, are far more often wrong than accurate and can be damaging. A true friend has never condemned me for expressing something from my heart or perspective.
- *Fear within any relationship is unhealthy.* Good relationships foster trust between the individuals and a sense of comfort, whether they are business or personal.
- *Lying is never a "little thing."* A person who, when caught in a lie, insists it's "no big deal" is probably not to be trusted in personal

or professional dealings. Ditto for the person who insists that your relationship be kept "a secret." Successful relationships are built on honesty and open communication.

Sean Continues:

Fortunately, in recent years I have had few people walk all over me. In the past, it was nearly impossible for me to know if a person was taking advantage of me because I wanted friends at any cost and could see nothing else. For many years, all another person had to do was show kindness and unconditional acceptance and I felt indebted to that person. Today I'm much more likely to rely on the opinions and judgments of family and other people whom I trust. I've come to learn an unwritten rule of social relationships: *trust the opinions of your close friends and family more so than you do a stranger's or a person you haven't known too well*. Now, for example, if I met a potential friend or date, I would be much less afraid to have that person meet my family and other friends so they could offer their views beforehand. If most or all of them had favorable things to say about the possible friend, I would spend more time with that person and try to strengthen the friendship. If, on the other hand, their comments were negative, I would back away from the person. I have done all of these things and the result has been finding people who enrich my life, not take advantage of me.

Another painfully learned unwritten rule of social relationships is *to be very, very careful to whom you lend money*. When I was fighting autism and desperately wanted friends, someone could have come to my door, claimed that his car was broken down and needed $100 and I would have given him the money, no questions asked. Today, I'm wary of people who make a habit of borrowing money and I don't feel comfortable blindly lending it. A good general rule is the less you know the person, the less money you should lend, if you lend any at all. However, this is an issue that can turn sour even between long-time friends. I nearly ruined a fifteen-year friendship with a woman named Helen over money. She asked if she could borrow $1,000 from me—money, she said, she needed to pay the tuition for her three kids to attend a Jewish school. I loaned her the entire amount and felt wonderful. Her coming to me for such a big favor validated in my mind how special I was to her. Joy turned to feelings of betrayal, however, when I asked her to pay me back.

Helen sent me money in $10 and $20 increments and it was several years before I received the entire amount. Accompanying each check was an impersonal note outlining how much she was sending and how much she still owed me. The notes, I feel, were intended to hurt me, but at least I got the money back—along with a healthier attitude and an appreciation for another unwritten rule related to money matters especially, but also to any other favors people ask of you: *it's easy to allow emotions such as sympathy or the desire to feel needed cloud good judgment.*

Recently I was in a department store and the sight of shoppers going up and down a set of escalators caught my attention.

At that moment, the movement somehow became symbolic of a theme that has repeated itself in my life. A warm thought of how many friends I have made in just the last several years washed over me. Another moment and the unwritten social rule echoed through my brain: *the more my rigid, unreasonable expectations of others have decreased, the more friends I have made and kept, and the more my happiness has increased.*

Every day, in every social situation, I try to look at the whole picture before me. I now realize that friendships and social relationships are not black and white, that they don't follow some prescribed set of rules that exist only in my own head, and that people are human, subject to mistakes and missteps just as I am. I have had people in my life who have hurt me several times, but who also possess attractive qualities and are otherwise kind. I have kept these friendships, but have modified them by sharing less time together or by having a friendship that is more casual. Like most everything in life, friendship can exist in degrees or along a spectrum. It wasn't until I was coming out of my autism and I was able to think in more abstract ways that this made sense to me. Today, some people are good friends, some are acquaintances, and some are individuals with whom I will never have more of a relationship than one defined by social small talk. That works for me because I've learned that *not everyone who is nice to me is my friend.*

2017 REFLECTIONS FROM SEAN

On several occasions, my girlfriend and I have spoken on our experiences with autism to a group of young adults with Asperger's syndrome in the Akron, Ohio, area, about an hour's drive from where I live. Invariably, at least a few ask about friendships and dating; over a few years, several have bluntly stated that they want a girlfriend but don't know how to start such a relationship or have tried and failed miserably.

It goes against my nature to give people advice. As such, I have never responded to any of these young men seeking a romantic partner by saying, "Well, if I were you, I would ..." Instead, I find it far more helpful to share my own background and experiences with relationships and hope they glean something useful from them.

In addition, the subjects of dating and intimate relationships are part of the general context of forming friendships, which is usually one of the core themes I address in presentations I give at autism conferences. Almost without exception, at least one mother will tell me before or after my presentation that her son wants such a relationship and that not having one is a major source of stress for him.

Of course, those on the spectrum take in and interpret information based largely on their learning style—whether they're visual or conceptual thinkers, for example. One of the core principles I try to stress is that forming friendships is a process that almost always takes time and requires both participants' contributions and cooperation. I also point out that, even if such efforts fail to materialize into a close relationship, they can result in a casual friendship, and that's okay too. Similarly, practicing playing a sport or a musical instrument may make one more proficient at the skill without promising a trip to Carnegie Hall or a call from the NFL, but can still lead to plenty of enjoyment and satisfaction. The image I like to use when I speak at conferences and other gatherings to drive home this concept of relationships is that of a series of concentric circles. This image likens itself to the degrees and levels of relationships many of us have, and it demonstrates that forming true friendships takes a lot more than someone simply acting friendly toward another.

A set of concentric circles starts with the smallest one in the middle. Then the farther out from the middle the circles get, the larger they become. The hierarchy of friendships works a lot like that. Most of us have more acquaintances and casual friends than close ones, so an easy way for people on the autism spectrum—especially the visual thinkers—to envision this concept is to imagine the relatively small number of those closest to us (usually husbands, wives, parents and close, lifelong friends) as being in the smallest circle and the larger number of acquaintances we might see regularly (co-workers, for instance) as occupying an outer, larger circle.

The more ubiquitous technology has become in our society, the more vigilant all of us must be. That couldn't be truer for young people and adults on the spectrum, largely because many of them have difficulty deciphering a person's intentions and motives, especially someone online who can't be seen. Many with ASD want to see the best in people and haven't developed the ability to exercise a healthy level of skepticism, or mistakenly think that being skeptical or critical is the same as being unfriendly. A wife abuser who communicates online probably isn't going to say something like, "I beat up my wife when she makes me mad and on a regular basis, but I also love walks in the park and going to movies." I like to think of the Internet in the same way as I do a vehicle. Neither is inherently good or bad. They can be highly effective ways to communicate and get around, respectively; on the other hand, they can be very dangerous if misused or used without taking proper precautions.

Sometimes, an inability to discern between what you should and should not reveal via the Internet can have dire consequences. "I had a student who met someone online and eventually was raped by several men. Low self-esteem, coupled with a lack of perspective taking and naiveté, can be the trifecta for being taken advantage of," warns Jennifer Schmidt, who teaches the Peer Spectrum social-skills course.

I can't stress it enough: It takes time to develop and cultivate long-lasting friendships. Many people nowadays are using the Internet for a myriad of social opportunities, including dating services, all of which are fine as long as caution and care are exercised. The combination of anonymous online interactions and a naïve person, especially one on the spectrum, can be dangerous, so I feel it's appropriate to include a list of tips from Milestones Autism Resources, based in Cleveland, Ohio, for staying safe online:

- Never provide passwords or confidential and personal information to someone you don't know, even a friend of a friend.

This includes your Social Security number, home address, bank and credit-card numbers and overall schedule.

- Refrain from posting anything that's derogatory or mean-spirited.
- Be careful not to post photographs that reveal personal information. Likewise, never post anything that is inappropriate or sexual in nature, because such pictures can spread online and be seen by many people. This can result in long-term backlash such as preventing someone from getting a job and, worse, damage to one's reputation.
- Realize that what you post is permanent. Even if you delete something, it's still out there in cyberspace.

POINTS TO KEEP IN MIND

- Teasing is a fact of life and as kids approach middle school, it intensifies. Remember to give equal time to the fact that not all teasing is bad—that kids tease each other as a sign of friendship and budding affection. Use movie clips, books and plays, and role playing to illustrate the verbal and nonverbal signals that distinguish "good" and "bad" teasing.
- Reinforce that "friendly words and actions" are not the same as being "friends." Check for comprehension frequently when a "new friend" is announced.
- Bullies target children who are alone or stand out from their peers as "odd," or "unaware." Make sure the school has a formal anti-bullying program.
- Teach nonverbal signs of interest/disinterest, physical clues that someone is lying, etc. Start with the concrete before moving to concepts like motive or intentionality.

- With very high-functioning AS individuals, whose perspective-taking abilities are developed, discussing concepts like "common sense" and "intuition" may have meaning. Keep in mind you may need to describe them in more concrete ways though, especially at first. For instance, in describing intuition, be sure to include the physical sensations that arise, in what parts of the body they are felt, in specific detail: increase in heart rate, pulse pounding, general uneasiness for no reason, fluttering sensations in your stomach, etc. Highly aware teens and adults can appreciate thoughts like, "If the situation 'feels' wrong, it probably is," better with the concrete tie-in made first.
- Relationships with other people are never perfect. A good relationship goes well most of the time, but not all of the time. Make sure this fact of life is made part of your conversation with the ASD child or adult.
- Make it a priority to teach stranger-danger safety skills in ways that the child's thinking can grasp. Use visuals to support the lessons.

RULE #7

PEOPLE ACT DIFFERENTLY IN PUBLIC THAN THEY DO IN PRIVATE

L et's face it. If people acted any way they wanted, at any time, in any setting, we'd be living in a chaotic, messed-up world. We wouldn't have basic structures that provide us with the essentials we need to survive, like food, clothing and shelter. Group dynamics require a set of rules that govern behaviors in order for the group to function. Whether the group is enormous—a society—or limited to a two-person interaction, what we can say or do in the presence of others has rules attached to it.

Rule #7 comes on the heels of the previous chapter and is linked to several of the ideas presented there: that people can think or feel in one way yet display a different behavior; that more than one emotion can be felt internally in any given situation; that a literal translation of behavior is most often an inaccurate one. It also calls up other rules: the importance of being polite in social settings and having good social manners, understanding honesty versus diplomacy and when unsolicited comments are best kept to yourself.

At first glance, this rule may seem so elementary, so simple that readers may question its value in our list of pivotal rules to teach children with ASD. Isn't it obvious, you may ask? Yes, it probably is to any neurotypical, but believe us that it is anything but simple wisdom to a child or adult with an autism spectrum disorder. Why? We hope by now, via all the repeated references we have made in previous chapters, you can answer that question easily yourself. However, for those "rigid" thinkers who may still need more practice, we once again point out the autism characteristics that will affect a child's ability to understand this rule:

- Literal interpretation of what they see: he looks happy therefore he feels happy. No contextual references.
- Literal interpretation of what they hear: he said he was happy, therefore he must be happy.
- Black-and-white, single-line thinking patterns: his brain only references the situation at hand; just like a Google Internet search on "happy" won't return any information on "sad" or any other related condition, neither does the rigid thinking process of the child with ASD.
- Impaired perspective taking: everybody thinks like I do; there's no data to call up that suggest there are multiple ways to interpret the situation.

Permit us to digress another moment from the rule at hand. By now we think it's highly probable that some (hopefully all) readers may be saying, "Yeah, I get it." But we continue to challenge you nonetheless. And this is why: until you can interpret the world around you from the autism perspective, internalize our ways of thinking and processing what we see and hear so that they become *your* second nature (not just an intellectual acceptance of information), you're still going to be teaching children, adolescents and adults from your own perspective, one that is inherently socially-conscious and emotionally-driven. When you can *easily* step outside that perspective, the manner in which you teach these individuals will dramatically change. When you can *easily* step outside that perspective, you'll "get" why the child reacts the way he does in any given social interaction and you'll be able to respond or adjust what you're doing or saying accordingly. When you can *easily* step outside that perspective, you'll understand how much is really missed in any interaction you label as "simple" and the resultant stress that creates. "Easily" only comes through practice. You expect us to learn how to *easily* exist within the social framework of the neurotypical world. We ask you to learn to just as *easily* step into ours. When that happens we'll all succeed. But it requires practice, practice, practice—*yours* as well as ours.

End of digression. End of your "teaching moment." (How does it feel? Sort of like a—lecture? Welcome to our world!) Back to Rule #7.

Temple often refers to herself as an actor in a play, and that analogy pretty much illustrates Rule #7: people "act"—they change their behavior in ways that conform to the public setting in which they find themselves. When Temple is alone at home, she understands she no longer has to act—she can do pretty much whatever she wants within the confines of her personal space. She is by herself; the space is "private." However, when she steps outside her home or other people join her in her home, she has to once again become the actor because her space has become "public."

Temple Continues:

The behaviors that are appropriate in private are different than those that are acceptable in public settings. This idea was demonstrated to me in very literal ways right from a young age. Mother clearly tied behaviors to settings in her teaching lessons. For instance, she made the distinction that messing up the living room was bad, but I could mess up my own room and it would be tolerated. Rather than teach me that "messing up the house was bad," she established context for the behavior: in this setting it's inappropriate, but in this setting it's allowable. She did the same thing with my stimming. When I was little, I was allowed a half hour after lunch and a little time after dinner during which I could stim freely at home; it wasn't allowed at the dining table or out in public. That's very concrete teaching and even though my thinking was inflexible at that age, the way she was teaching me planted the seeds of categories and subcategories in relation to time and place in my mind. That was very positive.

Mother was overall very good about looking forward and structuring lessons in a way that would help me be successful not just as a little child, but also as a teen and adult. She constantly tied behaviors to setting, and she constantly stressed being cognizant of other people and their needs (which is perspective taking). So, the public versus private issue was not one that was particularly difficult for me to learn and accept. Society had its rules and in the '50s and '60s, they were pretty strict social rules. People conformed and I learned quickly that I needed to do that too. Behavior had a consequence and some rules just had to be learned and accepted.

Many behaviors that fall under Rule #7 can be taught this way. Unwritten rules like, "Don't parade around naked in public," "Don't swear like a sailor in the boardroom," "Close the door when in the bathroom," and "Pick up your mess before leaving a public space," exist so that masses of people can function with each other. They provide guidelines, they define appropriate versus inappropriate behaviors so we can all live and work together as a society. Now, a person can do any of those things in private if he wants to.

As the old adage goes, "There's a time and place for everything." That's the value of this Rule: helping kids understand "where and when" behaviors are okay, that the context dictates what is acceptable to say or do. It comes back to drilling kids about manners, about appropriate social language and behaviors when in the company of others. It's about teaching them emotional control, that you can't always act out how you feel inside, based on the social setting. By nature, many autistics have black-and-white thinking patterns going on in their heads and need the repeated verbalizations that draw their attention to context. It's mental flexibility that will propel them to greater social understanding. That and repeated experiences that offer practice. Helping kids understand public versus private behaviors can be done in a structured, rote-type teaching environment for those with limited perspective-taking ability. The one caveat to keep in mind is this: be careful of using "rules" when teaching public versus private. There are few behaviors that are really *always* "private"—it depends on the level of intimacy among people who comprise a group. Adults are tempted to use the two-column teaching method, labeling a behavior as either public or private. When that's done, it reinforces the black-and-white thinking patterns, rather than promoting a more flexible mind and reinforcing attention to context. Don't underestimate the value of incorporating context and categories in even very young children. Save absolute rules for only a very few situations, generally where personal safety is involved.

What makes sense to me is to come back to the idea that all people are playing a part in the grand play that is life. I play my part: sometimes I play it one way, in other scenes my part is different. Sometimes I like the part I'm playing and other times I just have to act it out, whether or not I like it. The same applies for other people. And, that metaphor is relevant to the public versus private actions that I or other people exhibit. There will be situations where you're with people you absolutely can't stand, but you've got to be civil to them. The rule I have for myself is that I always try to be nice in any social interaction. That's my general "public behavior." In the privacy of my own home, I can rant and rave about anyone as much as I want, call people names, wave my arms around, stomp my feet in anger, whatever. That's "private behavior." If I acted that way in public, I would be creating negative consequences for myself. I dress in a socially appropriate way when I lecture or present at a conference. That's my "public image." However, socially acceptable dress does not have to be totally conventional; a person can be distinct and still socially acceptable. For instance, I wear my fancy western shirts for lecturing, which isn't conventional, but it still is acceptable. I often dress in old, worn, sloppy clothes at home, or let my grooming habits go for a day if I'm not going anywhere. That's "private behavior"—it doesn't impact anyone but me. The rule I've generated for myself is this: *the smaller and more intimate the social circle, the more private words and actions can be. The wider the circle, the more public/impersonal they need to be.*

There are dozens and dozens of specific unwritten rules about physical appearance, mannerisms, language, conversation topics, actions, etc., in public versus private settings to teach children and adults with ASD. Books and resources exist that attempt to itemize those and offer ways of teaching them. The take-home point to this chapter is to continually reinforce context while teaching the child these social skills so that mental flexibility and categorical thinking become second nature.

One aspect of observing the social interactions of others that was particularly difficult for Sean was understanding that the surface behaviors of people didn't always reflect what they were thinking or feeling inside. Passages in the previous chapter depicted Sean's thinking and his difficulty in understanding that people could feel one way and act another, or be experiencing more than one emotion at a time. He continues that train of thought here.

Sean Speaks:

As a young adult I wanted a girlfriend more than anything and was determined to get one. While I was trying to get a grip on social relationships, I was learning how elusive they often are. The harder I tried to find my place and get firm answers, the more everything slipped through my fingers. Unwritten social rules were everywhere, written in invisible ink; if only I had the magic solution to make them appear!

One day I came home from a nearby mall with a pained look on my face. My mother was visiting and could see how tense and upset I was. After asking me what was wrong, I announced that nearly everyone in the mall was holding hands.

"Everyone is in a great relationship but me," I said angrily. "You can't tell that, Sean," my mother calmly said. "You don't

know what you're really seeing."

"Yes they are. I see them holding hands, I see the evidence that everyone is in a happy relationship," I countered. "I only go with what the evidence tells me."

"Sean, you don't know what's going on in their lives. People are going to act differently in public," she said.

My mother and I had many talks about how I drew conclusions about relationships based on seeing only what was on the surface and how I made faulty assumptions based on that information. Behaviors people exhibited in public settings didn't always mirror what was happening between them at home, in private. I heard what she was telling me, but the residue of my autism and my rigid thinking patterns still lingered. I still saw only the surface of social situations and drew conclusions that reflected absolutes rather than acknowledging the emotional complexities inherent in social relationships.

Emotions are the back-seat drivers of how neurotypical people act in public settings. Even when boundaries of public versus private behaviors are clear, emotions can throw all of that logical thought into the wind. This is far more frequent with neurotypicals than it is for the rule-bound person with autism. However, we mention it to shed light on the difficulty it makes for people with ASD to learn public versus private words and actions.

Temple Explains:

My father was a highly unpredictable man when it came to his emotions. I was afraid of him because he'd blow up over seemingly unimportant things, like if the oysters he was served at a restaurant were too small. It was like being around a bottle of nitroglycerin all the time; I never knew when he might go off. Even though he would blow up over nothing, his temper was kept verbal. His social training prevented him from throwing things or hitting people. On the one hand I was trying to learn behaviors that were appropriate or inappropriate in public versus private settings, and on the other hand, here he was confusing the matter for me, acting in public in ways that I was being told should be reserved for private settings. My thinking was rigid enough at that age; when conflict like this kept popping up, it confused me enough that my mind would just shut down.

I hear from parents and teachers who think that telling kids that people act illogically will be too confusing for them to process. Yet, isn't it an unwritten rule of social relationships that *people aren't always consistent in what they say or do, even when they supposedly know better*? Children are going to feel the confusion when what you're teaching, the behaviors you're expecting of them, are being violated by others all around them. In my opinion, it's better to tell a child with ASD that people act illogically or that their emotions sometimes cause them to make mistakes, even when you're not sure they will understand. Pointing out the inconsistencies in others' actions also helps lay the groundwork for perspective to develop.

Taking this train of thought one step further, Temple expands upon the role that emotions play in deciphering appropriate public behavior, illuminating the almost unconscious way in which neurotypical people make allowances for emotional swings and know not to interpret literally the behaviors of others.

Temple Continues:

People have a "social face" they put on in order to interact with the people around them, and their emotions often dictate what mask they wear. For instance, people working in different professions are expected to act a certain way. A waitress and the grocery check-out clerk are expected to act friendly to customers; it's part of their job. But sometimes their personal moods affect whether or not they act friendly—even though their job description requires that "public behavior." Even though neurotypicals may agree that certain behaviors are "public" and others are "private" they quickly make allowances for others' behaviors, based on these emotional fluctuations—because they are shared experiences among them.

For instance, if you meet a person who is grumpy, and your exposure to the person is limited to that one encounter, you probably assume he's a grumpy person. Typical people do this all the time. They form a spot opinion, whereas the autistic person believes it as *truth*. However—and this is a major point—in the back of the neurotypical mind is a voice, a "second mind" as it's referred to, that draws attention to context and all the other probabilities that might contribute to this guy—any guy—acting like a grouch. They automatically and simultaneously assess the situation using their two minds; they use rational intelligence and emotional intelligence (see *Emotional Intelligence* by author Daniel Goleman). They form a conclusion yet understand that this opinion is not fact, not an absolute to use in all future encounters. It's "for now."

I don't think people with ASD have that second mind that provides two-way communication between rational and emotional intelligence. Some autistics process mainly from the rational mind, like I do. Some process mainly from the emotional mind, which might be Sean's way, especially when his autism clouded his thinking more. For the majority of people with ASD, it seems that a single channel is active.

The question becomes whether or not people with autism have both minds, and if so, how to activate both channels so they work together in interpreting the world.

So when confusion arises over behavior that is supposed to be private, yet is being displayed in public, the autistic person appreciates only the conflict. His mind wants conformity and the information he's processing is not giving him that. The response is akin to a computer glitch—information dump and reboot to regular processing.

Children need to be taught that all people—their parents, family members, teachers, the check-out person at the grocery store, the priest at church—have moods that fluctuate day to day, experience to experience, and that people's moods are often very illogical and unpredictable. So while it is true that people act differently in public than they do in private, and that being in the company of others requires a person to conform to the group expectations about behavior, people regularly fail to uphold that rule.

Nevertheless, people with ASD tend to blame themselves for social encounters gone wrong, which contributes to low self-esteem. They don't understand that sometimes the other person(s) in the encounter contributes to the demise of the social interaction. It's what people refer to as "emotional baggage"— their own positive or negative perceptions that influence their actions in any given social situation. That *people bring emotional baggage into a social relationship* is an unwritten rule that everyone accepts, but that is usually not pointed out to children with ASD.

It helps when parents and teachers point out these illogical, emotional responses that other people have, and explain that the behavior can interfere with a successful social interaction. Not all social situations are ruined because of a person's autism; sometimes it's the fault of the other person involved. However, we concentrate so much on teaching appropriate behavior and responses that we overlook teaching the child or adult that *all people in a social situation contribute to its success or failure*. The public behaviors of typical people are not always appropriate; regularly pointing this out helps the person with autism gain better social perspective and understand that social relationships require that all participants accept responsibility for their own actions.

Not only don't people always follow the rules that society dictates in regard to public versus private behaviors, they often don't "talk straight" in describing those rules, or in explaining the actions of self or others. Social language has a hierarchy all its own and oral versus written language makes it even more nuanced. Authors write with words that don't make sense to the literal minded person with autism. Public language has a level of formality based on the setting, from the highly formal orations of our government leaders, to the highly informal street-slang between two friends. People often say one thing in the company of others, then turn around and behave differently on their own. We've all experienced the employee who is the first to offer to help coworkers in the presence of his boss, only to be "too busy" to follow through when the coworker asks for help. People do indeed talk differently in public versus private settings. The confusion can be enormous, as Sean describes in the following two passages, and Temple offers to end the chapter.

Sean Begins:

The transition to high school had its pros and cons. On one hand, going to a large high school was less stressful for the same reasons going to school had always been: structured time blocks, concrete subjects like math and science to study, being able to better predict what to expect and being away from the tumult and turmoil that ceaselessly brewed at home. On the other hand, it magnified the social challenges I was already experiencing. Being one of more than 1,500 students meant many more sets of ears would be privy to negative information about me, and a larger pool of kids were available to join the rumor mill already in progress.

Shortly into the year, another aspect of high school that I couldn't have anticipated reared its head: academic expectations. With the predictability of an earthquake, I walked into English class and, after day one, realized the subject matter was light years removed from the English classes of years past to which I had grown reasonably accustomed. Before, English consisted mostly of learning the nuts and bolts of the language, like the parts of the sentence, using verbs well, knowing when to start new paragraphs and understanding what gerunds are. In other words, English was highly concrete and I had made reasonably good grades in the subject.

Now, as a ninth-grader, I was faced with the daunting and impossible challenge of learning to think abstractly, to interpret meaning and intention, to compare and contrast various perspectives. We were to read and critique short stories by writing about things like character development, point of view, tone, mood and what the author's overall grand idea was. I had no idea how to make sense of short stories because they were full of oblique and abstract devices such as metaphors and countless subtleties that implied more than they gave away. It might as well have been Greek, not English class; it all made so little sense to me.

It was a short time into the school year that my intense frustration, feelings of failure and tenuous self-esteem derailed further. Before, despite my inability to make friends, I was at least able to succeed academically. I maintained mainly Bs and Cs— and I had never failed a class, no matter how difficult. These early difficulties in English class told me that failure was about to enter a new realm.

My dad knew how anxious this class was making me, and he did what he could to make things easier. "Why the hell can't people just talk straight?" I angrily and sarcastically asked him one evening. Over the years he had told me to "talk straight" so we could get to the heart of some matter and resolve it more effectively.

I still didn't get it. I didn't understand that our actions and our words are framed by the social relationship or social setting we are in. These social boundaries, like fences, dictate what we can say or do when we're inside or outside the fence. There would be several more years of throwing textbooks in anger before I understood that English—and social relationships— were programs of study with endless levels of complexity. Mastery of the subject matter was going to take a lot more work than I could ever imagine.

Learning the rules of social relationships is a life-long process. You can be "inside the fence" and still encounter confusion, or make mistakes. Sean gives an example of such an instance when one bad decision lofted him back "outside."

Sean Elaborates:

Over the years, I have added many types of foods to my diet. I eat much more than the starchy cereals and plain hamburgers that saw me through my childhood. But no matter how diverse my diet becomes, the one thing that will never taste good in my mouth is my own foot. Discussing a private matter with someone else and then breaching that person's confidence in you is one of the best ways to ensure your foot is included with those hamburger and fries you're consuming. And in terms of Rule #7, and monitoring your public versus private behavior, you can wind up "eating crow" over the whole ordeal, too, while you're at it (meaning you've said something that you shouldn't have, and have to accept the consequences).

When I was in my twenties, I had a friend named Rebecca who thought she might be pregnant. She and her boyfriend, Larry, had been dating for a few years and I had spent time with both. One day, she came to me and seemed nervous. After reassuring me that her timidity wasn't the result of something I had said or done, she explained the real reason.

"Sean, I missed my period this month and have been waking up in the middle of the night more than usual."

"What do you think could be going on?" I asked.

"I think I might be pregnant, but Larry doesn't know. I'm afraid to tell him because I don't think he's ready to be a father just yet," she said, holding back tears. "We have talked about kids, but later, not sooner."

I was awash in mixed emotions. I felt bad because of her dilemma, yet I felt wonderful that Rebecca trusted me enough to not only share something this personal with me, but something even her boyfriend didn't know. After we talked awhile, Rebecca said she would find her own way to tell him her suspicions. I left, elated that the level of trust was so deep.

A week after I heard the news, Larry and I went bowling, and I still felt so good from Rebecca's confidence in me that I figured it wouldn't hurt to tell him the news. Larry, however, was less than elated when he heard from me that his girlfriend might be expecting. That mistake was far bigger than the gutter-ball I threw between the third and fourth frames—and led to much worse repercussions.

Predictably, my conversation at the bowling alley got back to Rebecca. She wasn't overly thrilled, either. What I didn't expect or understand was the intensity of anger she had toward me.

"I can't believe you would go behind my back! What we discussed was private. It was none of your business to tell him that," she said a day later.

"What did I do wrong?" I asked with a sick feeling. "I didn't mean any harm. I don't remember you specifically telling me not to tell him."

"All I can say is that I can't believe you would do that." And with that came the sickening click of the phone.

I was right in that she hadn't explicitly asked me to keep our conversation private. But she made clear, by her body language and tone, that she didn't want our talk to go any farther. Besides, Rebecca ended by saying that *she* would tell Larry, thereby implying not to break confidentiality.

Even though I had harmless motives, I caused quite a bit of harm in our friendships by breaking a cardinal unwritten rule: *you never—regardless of intent—divulge information meant to be private.* It made no difference to Rebecca that I told Larry because I was brimming at the news and was happy for them. The point was that it took a lot of trust and courage on her part to tell me, and she had made it clear that she would handle the situation from there. By intervening and breaking her confidence, I sacrificed a great deal of the trust they had in me. And another unwritten rule is that *trust is much easier to earn than to re-earn after it's been broken.*

It's akin to breaking a glass and trying to put it back together. It never is quite the same once it's been broken and mending happens a bit at a time. It takes much more effort to rebuild trust than to keep it in the first place, and listen up: some people will never give you a second chance to try. The best way for me to have kept my foot out of my mouth would have been for me not to place it in there to begin with. I'd prefer a plain hamburger instead.

2017 REFLECTIONS FROM SEAN

The other day I thought back to the many frustrating encounters between my mother and me over my inability to fully grasp the notion that the way people act in public and private often differs vastly. A recent conversation I had with a dear friend with whom I had gone to middle and high school brought these memories back to the surface. This friend mentioned many of the talents and abilities of her son, who is in his 20s and on the spectrum, in conjunction with his frustrations regarding dating and social opportunities in general. Specifically, when someone goes out with him socially, he often has great difficulty determining whether it reflects the other person's genuine interest in him or if it's out of sympathy. All of these things I can readily relate to, I told the friend, because I treaded that path repeatedly.

Today, however, I find this rule much less challenging to internalize and adhere to, mainly because of my long career as a journalist. Part of my job entails making my twice-weekly rounds to read daily police reports and compiling the salient points for our paper's crime blotter. I write about everything from those who have been arrested and accused of stealing video games from the local Wal-Mart to people who are charged with domestic violence. On a few occasions, I've read reports on people I know or am familiar with who had been accused of hitting and injuring a spouse during an argument that went too far.

When I saw those same people in public, though, they seemed perfectly content and normal; they gave no outward indication whatsoever that they were either unhappy in their relationship or capable of responding to disagreements and arguments with violence. And I have yet to meet a person who wears a T-shirt proudly proclaiming, "I abuse my spouse verbally, sexually, financially and physically, and I'm proud of it." In short, being continually exposed to such snapshots of people's lives behind closed doors has clarified the line between what others do and how they act in public versus in private, while solidifying in my mind that people can act perfectly normal in many social situations yet illogically and unpredictably in others. Most of us are fairly consistent in our daily behaviors, but that isn't the same as saying that we act and respond in exactly the same ways across the board.

Again, I think it's vital to teach and reinforce through social interactions and opportunities the concept that what one sees in a couple holding hands in the movie theater, for instance, may not necessarily represent the true nature of what typically goes on in their lives while at home. I've said it before, and I'll say it again: I have learned that it's far better to have no significant other in your life, even if it means some lonely times, than to be in a relationship that is toxic and damaging.

Temple Offers Her Own Perspective:

The children who are more rigid thinkers, who are very literal in their translation of their world, have trouble making inroads into social relationships partly because this literal translation extends also to language. Literal translation of the world alleviates the stress involved with risk-taking and "guesswork," and it provides some basis of order and predictability that appeals to children with ASD. Teaching children to think more flexibly, to get their brains to "see" the nuances of social language and social interactions is a very slippery slope, one navigated in a constant state of high anxiety.

I don't think most neurotypical adults appreciate the level of stress kids with ASD live with on a constant basis. Imagine having never skied before, and standing at the top of a triple Black Diamond expert run, one of most difficult expert ski runs. It's narrow, icy, with huge moguls and a near vertical drop. As if that's not bad enough, you know your balance is unpredictable and everything around you is uncomfortable: the ski boots, standing on skis, the poles in your hands, the bulky ski clothes, the sun in your eyes, the glare off the snow. Sheer panic sets in, because you realize there's no way you're going to get down that slope without hurting yourself. The real question is whether or not you'll even survive. Yet, you can't just stand there—you know you have to step off the edge. That's what daily social interaction can feel like for some kids with ASD. Sheer panic and no skill set to handle the interaction.

Now add language and communication into the encounter and it's even a more frightening experience. There's little that's consistent about people's language and communication. More than with their actions, people like to use language to express their individuality, to demonstrate that they're creative, or smart, to somehow distinguish themselves from others, or conversely, to align themselves or show empathy. There is nothing literal about communication, because tone of voice, inflection, and body language are all rolled up into it. What's made it even more difficult in today's culture is the liberal use of slang that is now commonplace. The social language of the 1950s and '60s had more structure and consistency to it. Slang that is "in" today can be "out" next week among teenagers. How confusing is that?

Growing up, I was never very good at understanding slang, or picking up on people's facial expressions or nonverbal body language. I could understand tone of voice, but that was because Mother used it constantly along with her language. I could tell when she was annoyed by the sound of her voice; I knew that I had better behave. Things that were subtle didn't register. Mother writes in her book about all the turmoil she experienced with my father while I was growing up. I didn't even know that was going on. Their public behavior and their private behavior were different. Their "public talk" was different than their "private talk."

That was the norm back then in society; couples didn't discuss their private relationship issues in public, even at home. My parents weren't throwing things, they weren't screaming or hitting. Any clues that they were not getting along were subtle. My sister picked up on it but I didn't.

As I mentioned in an earlier chapter, I didn't even know that people communicated with their eyes until I was in my fifties. I missed a whole language of public behavior that was going on around me. But my thinking in pictures actually made it easier for me to be less literal in interpreting idioms and metaphors. For instance, if someone said it was raining cats and dogs outside, that's the picture that would appear in my head. But it was easy to compare that picture to what I saw outside and know that they didn't match up. Logic told me that those words didn't actually represent reality, that they were a visual analogy. I do get some very funny visual images in my head, but I know they're not literal translations of what people are saying.

How does this all apply to Rule #7? It comes back to being able to think flexibly and know that the context of a situation affects the interaction. My *intelligence* tells me that people act differently in public than they do in private. Intellectually I know that unwritten rule exists within social relationships. Figuring out my own, or others' public versus private behaviors means analyzing the situation from the perspective of a social scientist. Even though I might not understand from an intuitive perspective that people communicate not just with words, but with body language, tone of voice, etc., I have learned, through observation, to recognize those signs and create categories on my hard drive to help me in social relationships.

For instance, I look at a person in a social interaction and watch his mannerisms. Whether he's animated or silent, if he leans into the conversation or sits back with his arms folded on his chest. Then I piece all the clues together with what he's saying and develop a hypothesis on whether or not he's putting on a "social face" out of politeness. It's the same with my own behaviors: I know that my own body language needs to support, rather than negate, my words. Most of the time my body language is pretty neutral; what I concentrate on is making sure it's not opposite what I'm saying. Again, that's all rote processing and analytic observation. My body language doesn't spontaneously happen through my emotions. There isn't that connection between thoughts and feelings like there is with neurotypical people.

When I was young, I couldn't interpret others' language and behaviors and monitor my own because I didn't have enough experiences to create refined categories about language and communication. I rotely understood public versus private behaviors; they were drilled into me as were other social skills. The more experiences I had, the more data I put on my hard drive from both my own experiences, watching others and reading books about social interactions, the better I became at noticing *when* and perceiving *why* people acted differently in public than they do in private.

It's helpful for adults to realize that for some people with ASD , an intuitive understanding of social language and behaviors may never develop. The "common sense" approach to public versus private behaviors may never surface. If a child's emotional relatedness is high, with practice this may become more second nature to him because by his very nature, his emotions are tied into his thoughts and feelings. But for other people who think like I do, it will remain a logic-based puzzle that is understood without a direct emotional tie-in. That's not to say we don't have emotions; it's more that emotions are one step removed from the interaction and are a separate component.

For us, being able to differentiate public versus private behaviors, or understanding that people's emotions and behaviors are not always 100% aligned may simply be a big, ongoing social experiment that exists to put more data on the hard drive and help us function better. Again, that's not bad; it's just a different approach to social relationships and understanding how to succeed within them. Highly social people instinctively put less value on this mode of functioning and hopefully, with greater awareness and understanding of how we think, these judgments will be released.

POINTS TO KEEP IN MIND

- Teach kids to "look beyond the surface" of people's words and actions to explore other possible meanings.
- People with ASD will use their logic to search for clues in their environment and then base their conclusions on what they see. Despite that ability to find the physical, overt clues they will often miss the intangible clues that are important to fully understanding the context. What is not happening is often as important as what is. Encourage them to take into consideration what is absent from the situation.
- Some private behaviors that are generally not appropriate public behaviors:
  - Don't "potty talk" (i.e., talk about bathroom bodily functions).
  - Don't talk about bodily noises.
  - Close the door when going into the bathroom.
  - Don't pick your nose in public.
  - Don't scratch your private parts in public.
  - Don't burp.
  - Don't discuss medical problems that involve the private parts of the body. Discussing a broken ankle is acceptable.

RULE #8

KNOW WHEN YOU'RE TURNING PEOPLE OFF

I t happens all the time when we're in the company of others. We say or do some little thing that doesn't quite sit right with someone around us. George tells you how much he loved a movie and you counter with, "It was the worst thing ever made," or you talk on and on about the latest segment of *General Hospital* to your friend Lucy who isn't in the least interested in soap operas. Other times the social faux pas carries a bit more heft to it: during a job interview you spend five minutes describing to your potential male supervisor why women make better managers, or during the middle of a meeting your express your strong disagreement with a coworker's suggestion in the form of a comment peppered with foul language.

Neurotypicals refer to it as being "clueless" or laugh it off as people who "put their foot in their mouths"—to inadvertently say things that irk their companions. But NTs have a sixth sense about this when it happens. They not only watch the slip-up, but form an opinion about its value in the overall scheme of the social interaction. Those who are a little less "clueless" also recognize the nonverbal signs that something has gone amiss in the social interaction. Body language, a shift in the other person's tone of voice or dead silence tell us we've done something wrong and we'd better repair the situation—and quickly.

The child or adult with ASD who functions with low perspective-taking ability and rigid thinking patterns misses this entire world of nonverbal communication. Oftentimes others around him are sympathetic to his blunders—it's so obvious that he's making every effort to interact. But for a vast number of children who "look" normal, but are still encumbered by the limited-perspective and rigid-thinking challenges of ASD (the higher functioning children, teens and adults on the spectrum) people respond very differently. They are quick to form negative opinions when these individuals "screw up," and slow to understand how deeply autism can impair the ability to process social information and respond in appropriate manners. When individuals with ASD do things that "turn them off" that negative impression lingers in their minds, and colors future encounters.

It's an unwritten rule of social relationships that *most people are quick to call your attention to what you're doing wrong and slow to praise you for what you're doing right.* There are all sorts of psychological reasons for doing so, ranging from petty jealousy to low self-esteem to never being taught a different way of interaction. We can act appropriately in ninety-five instances out of one hundred, and people around us will focus on the five things we did wrong—and with more vigor if they were directly involved in some way. It happens in personal and professional relationships and no, not everyone does it, but more people do it than not.

We chose Rule #8—*Know When You're Turning People Off*—for two reasons:

1. To draw attention to this pervasive but not necessarily positive trait of a large segment of mankind, the "Three Strikes and You're Out" rule, and
2. To draw attention to the fact that the older you get, the less praise you're going to hear from people around you for acting appropriately.

We spend our entire lives living under the unconscious global social rule: *do the right thing.* In ways large and small it sets the tone for how we relate to others, words we choose to say or keep to ourselves, decisions we make for ourselves and our families. Learning what constitutes the "right thing" is part of the process of living and we accept that it is a process, not an end point in itself.

As children, we receive a lot of praise for our efforts. It comes in the form of positive comments, new toys, being taken to favorite places, ice cream and cookies, and all sorts of different rewards. We get them from moms and dads, grandparents and family members, from teachers and next door neighbors. As we grow and develop, the rewards for good behavior diminish. As early as middle school we come face to face with another one of those unwritten rules that govern our social relationships: *teens and adults are expected to "know better," meaning once we are no longer children, adults expect us to have learned the social rules that govern group dynamics.* Acting appropriately no longer captures attention or praise; it's just expected. Doing the wrong thing is what captures the attention of people around you.

Turning people off is noticeable—it happens on the spot, and has repercussions that often last well beyond the initial situation and sometimes even after attempts to repair the situation have been made. There are all sorts of things that turn people off: aspects of our appearance, the words we use, our tone of voice and body language, personal eccentricities, personal opinions, not to mention the actions we take in response to other people. Standing too close, monopolizing conversation, poor hygiene habits, ill-timed remarks, and grossly inappropriate actions will generally call negative attention to yourself across cultures and settings, as will a host of other things that could easily fill a book of its own. As the old saying goes (and many old sayings exist because they echo an unwritten social rule), *"There's only one chance to make a first impression."*

Helping people with ASD understand first the obvious, then the subtler ways people turn off other people needs to be taught, starting at a young age. Many of the overt signs that you're turning someone off are shared from social group to social group, which is fortunate for people with ASD and makes this an attainable goal for most children and adults.

Temple Starts:

Mother instilled in me and my siblings from an early age that small talk was part of social etiquette and would open the doors to social interaction. We would be called down to meet people who came to the house and we were taught the correct way to make introductions, to say "Hello, how are you?" and answer questions that people might ask us. That was drilled into us as part of manners training. So, the idea that social interaction begins with some shared conversation was very natural to me, whether it was with my friends or my parents' friends, or when Mother sent me on errands to the hardware store or later with my coworkers.

As a little child, my curiosity about things spurred me into different situations that required conversation. For instance, if a new family moved in the neighborhood, I'd go over, knock on the front door and introduce myself. I knew how to do that and I wasn't shy to begin with anyway. Because I was smart and good at all sorts of activities, my friends and I always had things to talk about. You know, when you're working on a project, conversation about how to build it, paint it, play with it just naturally happens. That's why shared interests are such strong foundations for social interaction with kids on the spectrum.

I was so interested, though, that I had to learn not to be a pest. That's an unwritten rule of social relationships: *don't become a pest.* That turns people off. I'd want to go over to the neighbors' houses all the time and our nanny would say, "Don't wear out your welcome," which meant that the neighbors would not be happy to see me anymore if I went over there too often. She and Mother laid down a rule for me to prevent that; they'd limit how often I could visit one neighbor or another. That helped me learn not to be a pest, but it was gradual development. I didn't understand fully what she meant right away.

Mother also drilled into me another unwritten rule: that *asking people personal questions is rude.* So I knew better than to do that growing up, and I didn't turn people off that way. I remember one time when I was eight we were riding on a train and I got to talking to some nuns who were sitting opposite us about our trip to New York. That kind of social conversation was fine and was encouraged. But I knew better than to ask the nuns a personal question like whether or not they shave their heads under their habits. I was taught there were certain kinds of personal questions that were off limits.

My biggest problem wasn't turn-taking or sharing or asking inappropriate questions when talking with other people. Where I really turned people off was in violating the following two unwritten rules of social conversation: *1) don't monopolize the conversation* and *2) don't talk on and on about a topic that doesn't interest others.* At times I'd get on one of my talking jags. One time it was election posters—that got pretty boring pretty fast for my friends because no one found that interesting but me. Another time I fixated on the fun house at the Cheshire County Fair and talked about that over and over and over again until everyone around me was totally bored with it. I talked about these things because it was exciting to me to do so, which was internally motivating to keep talking about them. But being social with others requires you to be conscious of other people's interests too. It has to be balanced, like scales are balanced, for the social interaction to be successful for both parties.

What helped me most along the way was that a lot of people were *very direct* with me about what I was doing wrong. When I was young, my Mother or the nanny would tell me I'd talked enough about some-thing in very clear words, "Temple, that's enough about that subject." My friends would say things like, "Temple, stop talking about those stupid posters." My classmates would be blunt too, but in a less friend-ly way. They did it by calling me names. All through third and fourth grade I talked a lot and asked a lot of questions—way too many ques-tions—about anything and everything, not necessarily a favorite topic. That's how I got the name, "Chatterbox," they all called me. I'd ask other kids to name their favorite game over and over. It was a tool I used to get conversation going. But because my mind was still pretty inflexible, and I didn't have a lot of data on my hard drive, I'd ask the exact same questions over and over. That was a turnoff for everyone but me and my grandfather. He was a quiet, shy engineer who liked my questions. I asked him why the sky was blue or why tides go in and out and he would patiently explain. He liked talking about factual things.

When kids are young there's a natural tendency to ask questions. But for many kids on the autism spectrum it's an obsessive-compulsive physical urge to do so. Giving them lots of experiences so they have different things to talk about helps alleviate the extent to which they turn off their peers. So does making rules about talking about things. This is one instance in which the autistic person's rule-bound logic can help. Setting up the rule, "You can tell a story only once or twice to the same person," can be useful, but do recognize that for kids with little information to draw from, this can also produce a lot of anxiety. If they can't talk about their favorite topic, what else is there to talk about? Make sure the child has a variety of things to talk about before making this a rule.

In high school my mentors would be equally direct with me when I perseverated on a topic. When I went on and on about the fun house at the fair, I remember the headmaster saying to me, "Temple, you're really boring the kids. It's okay to talk about the fun house a couple of times, but after repeating it ten or fifteen times, nobody wants to hear about it anymore." I needed that feedback—and in words that were very direct.

There's a subtle undertone to those two rules I just mentioned about monopolizing conversation with a topic of interest, and it's a social rule all its own: *it's okay for members of the group to talk on and on as long as the topic interests a majority of the people involved in the conversation.* This happens all the time in normal social interaction. Teenage girls will spend hours talking about hair or makeup or the boys in their class. Boys will go on and on about sports—little boys and grown-up big boys. In a two-person conversation, each person needs to check for continued interest. But once there's three or more people involved, not everyone has to be equally interested for conversation on the topic to continue. I remember one time going out to dinner with a few pharmaceutical salesmen who spent three hours talking about sports themed nothing. There was no content to the conversation, no analysis of the game or discussion of the players or the coach's strategy. I sat there like a sociologist studying their behavior because to me, the talk was absolutely pointless. It really turned *me* off, but because all the rest of them liked the conversation, my opinion didn't matter. *The axiom that "majority rules" is true in a lot of social interaction, especially social conversation.*

LEARNING WHAT'S OKAY TO SAY

As I got older, I developed categories of conversation and within those categories I had rules about what's appropriate to talk about and what's not, what interests people generally and what will turn them off from the start. It depends on the context and who you're talking to, whether that person is a complete stranger, a person you just occasionally run into, or a close friend. Let's say I'm on an airplane and I'm sitting next to a complete stranger. I might say something about the weather, especially if the flight's delayed. Then I might tell them I'm going to a cattle meeting and ask about their destination, or what they do for a living. I've learned, through trial and error, that a general rule people follow is to *start conversation with generic subjects that most everyone feels comfortable discussing.* I know if I get right into talking about my research on the hair swirl patterns on bulls I'll turn off that person in a few seconds, and that will end our social interaction. However if I get into a really good conversation with the person I can eventually change the subject to my research. I might initiate this conversation with re-marks about careers.

Some of the "safe subjects" I talk about are the weather, our sur-roundings, recent movies, whether or not the person has pets, asking about any hobbies they have, etc. If I'm at an autism meeting, I know I can ask about different therapies or the school program, or books on ASD. One of the rules about conversation topics that seems to apply gen-erally in society is *there are three subjects you don't discuss with strang-ers and most people who are not close friends: sex, politics and religion.* People let their emotions get all tied up into those subjects which can result in volatile reactions that are sometimes hard to handle. I have close friends I can discuss those subjects with, but I don't talk about them with strangers. When I was in my twenties, I was obsessed with talking about the meaning of life. I did not realize that most people do not spend hours talking about such a deep subject. Today that's another subject I only discuss with a few very close friends.

People with ASD often want other people to know they're smart, or they crave social interaction to such a degree that they think immediately showing the other person how much they know will make them attrac-tive and encourage social interaction. It doesn't. People refer to someone who goes on and on like that as having "diarrhea of the mouth," which is a pretty disgusting metaphor, but good to keep in mind (especially for visual thinkers). That's how much you turn people off when you're rambling on and on about a topic that interests only you.

As with other social skills, learning the give and take of social conversation takes time. It's a gradual process that develops as you age and grow in social awareness. It requires you to be a social detective all the time: to take stock of the context of the situation, notice what other people are saying—or not saying—and what you do that turns people off. Then learn from it.

REPAIRING MISTAKES

I've certainly made my share of mistakes along the way and when I notice that I've said or done something inappropriate, I immediately apologize. When I turn off a person, it's my responsibility to try to fix the situation. It's another unwritten rule of social relationships that *quick apologies right after you've made a mistake repair a situation faster than trying to cover up or deny that you did something wrong.* It's best to acknowledge the mistake, say you're sorry and move on—especially with an etiquette/manners type mistake. People are usually pretty forgiving because we all make these types of mistakes from time to time.

For me, it took years of practice to get where I'm comfortable in my abilities to handle social interaction and conversation and not turn off people with what I say or do. I'm still learning. It's like that with other Aspies I know. Recently I ran into a good friend of mine who has her own electronics business. She commented that she keeps learning more and more every day about how to get along with people and notice what turns them off, or on. Some adults on the spectrum are looking for a magic bullet to understanding all this and there isn't one. It's a continual learning process.

As Temple mentioned, individuals with ASD are often eager to share their knowledge and expertise on a specific topic with others.

For some, it's a physical compulsion or internally motivating. For others, it's the only way they know how to engage in conversation. And for many of the emotionally-connected children or young adults with ASD, it can be a respite from low self-esteem, an attempt to capture positive compliments amidst a sea of constant negativity, either self-imposed or from others.

Sean Describes:

It's been said that knowledge is power. Certainly that was true for me as I progressed through childhood, my teenage years and into adulthood trying to make sense of a confusing morass of conflicting pieces of information and asymmetrical relationships between what people often said compared to their motives and intents. I used many devices to replace utter frustration and anger with comfort and control. When I still couldn't figure out what was going on around me—which was most of the time—I sought ways to rise above it all.

One of those ways was seeking knowledge. But it wasn't just any information; I had narrow interests and the more esoteric the fact, person, etc., the better. One such blossoming interest for me was jazz, especially facts about old and obscure jazz musicians.

I heard John Coltrane on the radio for the first time when I was fifteen. After moving to California, I began fusing my love for jazz with reading the *World Almanac*, a fact-lovers paradise in print. If I wanted to know the birthdates and deaths of many famous and not-so-famous jazz musicians, as well as the instruments each played, that information was only a page away. By age eighteen I had become interested in buying recordings made by only the musicians whose names appeared in the almanac and a favorite pastime was visiting record stores that specialized in selling out-of-print 33 rpm albums as well as 78s, the old breakable records that contained one song per side. That way, I would more likely remember the musicians' names—and use them as topics of conversation with people to show them how much I know.

One night my family and I, along with a few family friends, went out to dinner. I often hated these occasions because the bulk of conversations steered toward the music business (the business my parents were in) and I had nothing to contribute, which reinforced in my mind that I was small and insignificant. That is, I had nothing to add until now.

On this evening, I interjected at one point and asked my dinner companions if they had ever heard of Buddy Bolden, Freddie Keppard and several other musicians who were around in the previous century. All said no, which gave me the chance to tell everyone at the table when the musicians were born and what year they died. For once, I felt empowered instead of powerless. Here were people whose livelihood was vested in the music business and I was telling them about musicians whose names they had never come across. In addition, I included which instrument the given jazz artist had played and threw in a song title or two for good measure. My dinner guests looked rather confused, but I figured they were nonetheless extremely impressed with me. How many other kids my age knew about these remote and largely forgotten artists?

I had started this pattern of behavior a few years earlier, when astronomy was my topic of interest. How many teens, besides me, had ever seen Saturn's rings through a telescope? Whether it was jazz stars or heavenly stars I was telling other people about, the reasons to do so were the same: I wanted to impress those around me and in turn, go from feeling like a nobody to a somebody.

I was so busy in those days trying to fill voids in my life that I missed the social cues of disinterest and this obvious unwritten rule: *people don't like it when you engage them in uncomfortable situations without their consent.* I didn't realize when my words or actions were turning people off. If they seemed to be listening to me, or made sporadic eye contact with me, they were interested! I now know that in public social situations like the one I described they were simply being polite. By rattling off obscure names of musicians to people at the restaurant, I was giving them no choice but to listen; anything else they may have done would have been rude or otherwise socially unacceptable.

It would be years later before I understood an unwritten rule that neurotypicals learn in early childhood: *not all people are interested in the same topics; what's fascinating to one person may be utterly boring to another.* The reason those at the dinner table didn't know anything about the jazz musicians' history was not because they couldn't know it. They didn't know that information because, to cut to the chase, they didn't give a crap. The same could be said about radio and TV station call letters I had told my peers and others about, ZIP codes and other pieces of rote information I had acquired and that laced my conversations. It wasn't their lack of intellect; it was lack of interest.

Knowing when you're turning people off is crucial to any successful social interaction. No matter how much you prepare and practice, without learning some basic guidelines about what breaks apart a social encounter, you'll be floundering like a beached whale, with no way back into the ocean. If your desire is to attract, rather than repel, other people, let me offer some helpful advice about better ways to interact. I think they include:

- Having diverse interests. The more interests you have, the easier it will be to find people with whom you share things in common. Sorry, but I'll bet there are few teens out there (or anyone else under age ninety-five) who find Freddie Keppard's bio an interesting topic of conversation and pontificates on it.
- Asking questions. If there is one thing I have found true nearly all the time and in all social situations, it's this: People like to talk about themselves when given the opportunity. It's another unwritten rule of social relationships: *Asking questions sends the message you're interested in a person and what s/he has to say.* A related

caution in social interaction applies though: *Don't ask too many questions.* Asking questions is usually a good way to promote conversation and let the other person know you want to keep the interaction moving forward. Asking too many questions is viewed as excessive behavior.

- Using lead-ins. By this I mean good conversation openers and phrases that encourage the interaction to continue. These are things like, "That's interesting. Tell me more." They also include paraphrasing (without repeating verbatim) what the person told you. For example, someone tells you that she feels sad because her mother died or that she is overjoyed at getting an A on her test. You could respond with something like, "I'm sorry about your mother. I can tell you're feeling very sad. Tell me about her," or "That's great. I see how happy you are with your grade."

- Learning another unwritten rule of social relationships that took me a long time to learn: *being interested in others is an attractive quality.* Focusing solely on yourself and your own interests: bad. Giving time and attention to the other person and his/her interests: good. It's like being on a see-saw. To enjoy the experience, there needs to be movement up and down. By being interested in someone, that makes you more interesting.

Rule #8 is not just about social conversation, but our appearance and our actions. Nothing turns people off faster than poor hygiene: greasy hair, smelly clothes, body odor. While people may overlook a misstep in manners or still choose to interact with a person who has problems with communication, few will make allowances for a person who is unclean or unkempt.

Temple Speaks:

Grooming and hygiene issues will turn people off fast. It's an unwritten rule that *no one wants to be around another person who smells bad, no matter how smart he is or how much he can contribute.* Having bad breath or body odor from not taking a shower in days is a definite turn-off. It will alienate you from a group on the spot and those opinions won't change until you do something about yourself. Autism isn't an excuse for being dirty or smelly. If sensory issues are involved, there are all sorts of grooming products now to get around them: dry shampoos, soap towelettes, different flavored/textured toothpastes. Even if you wear the same three outfits all the time, keeping them clean is just a matter of soap and water and a little effort. Related to appearance are other behaviors that will turn off most people: picking your nose in front of others, scratching your privates, talking with your mouth full of food, hitting/slapping people around you, and displaying some of the private behaviors in public that we talked about in Rule #7.

Making a list of all the things people do that turn off other people would be an impossible task. It depends on who you're with, the size of the group, the age of the participants, the setting, and people's religious, economic and political viewpoints. However, when it comes to being aware of your own actions, and whether or not you're turning someone off, an overarching unwritten rule that these more specific unwritten rules fall under is that *each person is responsible for keeping the social interaction going, for monitoring his own words and actions in relation to the other person so that both people feel comfortable.* Related to this is an equally important unwritten rule: *most people won't tell you directly that you're turning them off—that they're getting uncomfortable with what you're saying or doing.* Instead, they do so via nonverbal cues. Being able to gauge when I'm turning someone off means being able to read their facial cues and body language to some extent. This was a skill I had to develop in myself; it wasn't automatic for me, nor is it for most people with ASD. It's an important source of information and situational clues, and is a teachable skill. Lots of good books and materials are on the market today that address this issue in a concrete and fun way.

For Sean, too, missing the nonverbal signs imbedded in social interaction was a common experience, contributing to problems large and small in interpreting the words and actions of others, especially with members of the opposite sex.

Sean Offers This:

When we moved to California from Ohio in early 1978, I took with me an intense interest in astronomy, which I alluded to earlier in this chapter. My parents had bought me a two-inch telescope through which I had seen planets and other celestial objects normally indecipherable with the naked eye. Shortly after getting settled into my new California life, I met a number of people with whom my parents worked or associated. They were very accepting of me and one of them, a woman in her late twenties with two young children and a husband, was someone I quickly became drawn to.

She lived one street from me and, later, when we moved, the couple bought a house across the street from us. So it became easy to visit her anytime I wanted. Among other things, I couldn't wait to share with her my profound and esoteric knowledge of the heavens and solar system. So intense was my interest that I spent school lunch periods reading my mother's college-level book on the subject instead of socializing with the other kids. Such information is fascinating to me, I figured, so she will feel the same way—especially since she is a friend.

Over time, however, it began to occur to me that her responses to what I was sharing weren't close to matching the enthusiasm I imparted in sharing it. I would tell her which planets, moons, etc., I saw the night before and be met with flat and generic replies such as "That's nice," or "Really? That's interesting." Each time I went to her home for a visit, it seemed as if she was becoming more easily distracted.

Many times I left with hurt feelings. Nevertheless, these feelings didn't deter me from using astronomical terms during a conversation the next time I saw her. And each time I did so, she appeared to become more distant from me, rarely if ever asking questions relating to astronomy.

My hurt feelings soon turned to anger toward her. How could someone claiming to be a friend not be interested in what meant so much to me? Eventually, I withdrew from her and my now familiar pattern of ignoring people who didn't meet my expectations kicked in. This, of course, negatively affected our friendship. I sensed that I was boring this friend—the nonverbal cues were not completely lost on me—but accompanying my suspicion was the belief that the more I talked about what I was interested in (perhaps sharing, for example, information about a different planet), the more she would "come around" and become interested. Instead, it always produced the opposite effect. I remember several times being at this friend's home and her getting up in the middle of a conversation. I took her lack of interest personally and became more desperate to keep her focused on me.

For many years, I never thought to ask someone with whom I was in a social situation, "Are you interested?" My black-and-white thinking prevented me from being able to reach beyond my own needs. And I probably would have been devastated anyway had I received the answer I didn't want to hear.

There are numerous ways to tell if you are turning someone off other than the person bluntly saying, "I'm not interested in you. Get out of my face!" Most people don't want to hurt others' feelings so they will exhibit a variety of nonverbal behaviors if in a situation that's boring or offensive to them. Some physical signs may include:

- Fidgeting with some object nearby.
- Appearing distracted and giving only glancing eye contact.
- Responding with flat affect, meaning there's little variation in their tone of voice.
- Getting up frequently or constantly shifting one's weight.
- Yawning or showing few facial expressions.
- Looking angry, irritated or confused.
- A noncommittal attitude or not asking open-ended questions. These are questions that require more than a simple yes or no response.
- Looking at a clock or wristwatch or cell phone.
- Silence or little participation. If you're making all the effort and the other person is making little or none, then it might be time to do the highway thing.

On an intellectual and social level, many higher functioning people with ASD are able to recognize when they are turning people off in social interactions, but because of physical issues are unable to control their behaviors well enough to stop doing so. They become locked in a spiral of saying or do things that alienate others, then trying to make amends to repair the situation. After a while, even the most tolerant people tire of the pattern and the relationship deteriorates into nothingness. Temple shares her experiences growing up with recurrent panic attacks and how that affected her ability to act appropriately.

Temple Speaks:

Sometimes turning people off happens despite what a child or adult "knows better" about social interaction. He may have a strong desire to "fit in" from a practical or logical perspective or may be highly emotionally connected, yet reasons outside his mental framework compel him to say or do things that alienate people. It may be that the environment becomes overwhelming to the point that a meltdown in behavior occurs. As I've mentioned before, until sensory issues are dealt with in a child and he can work through them (either himself or through a sensory diet set up for him by others), social competence will fall by the wayside. It's just impossible to concentrate on making appropriate social choices when your senses are going haywire, no matter how much training you receive.

Or, puberty might be the culprit. Adolescence is a time when kids hone in on their similarities and differences in an attempt to define their own personalities. They begin to disassociate with their parents and gravitate toward fitting into their own peer group. The desire to belong is strongly felt and social groups and cliques take on a new level of importance. For the child with ASD, the social chasm widens at this stage of development as neurotypical peers become less forgiving and more prone to alienating children who are odd or don't fit in. Hormonal changes are sometimes coupled with other physical changes that make fitting in not only difficult, but impossible. The result? The child keeps turning people off because he can't help it. Pharmacology rather than psychology may be the answer for some of these teenagers.

For me, puberty brought with it panic attacks—daily and pervasive panic attacks. The morning would start out okay, but between lunch and dinner time, panic was my steady companion. At that time, I didn't know, nor could I figure out, what was going on with me. I now know it was based on cortisol rhythms in my body. But back then, it was like living in a constant nightmare. Think of your worst phobia and imagine having to face it on a minute-by-minute basis. It was like that. We'd go into daylight savings time and that change would make the panic attacks worse. Any change made them worse. That's totally irrational, I know, but that's what it was like. When I was a little kid, if someone asked me what I'd wish for if a genie granted me three wishes, my first wish would be to be able to fly. As an adolescent my first wish was to get rid of the panic attacks; they were that severe.

The confusion didn't deter me from trying to figure out what was wrong with me, though. I was a problem-solver and these panic attacks needed to end. This was the early '60s—I didn't have a library readily available to me, and the Internet didn't exist. Any self-help material I could get my hands on was Freudian based—everything in life purportedly resulted from some injury to a person's psyche. I spent years trying to psychoanalyze myself, telling myself that if I could just figure out my psychic injury, the panic attacks would go away. Well, of course there wasn't any. It was defective biology made worse by hormones.

It was a strong motivation to read and learn a lot about psychology and many things I learned were actually helpful. But it wasn't until I was in my early thirties that I discovered antidepressants—the magic pills that made those panic attacks stop. Up until then, all through my twenties, I had a lot of nervousness going into social situations. The medication reduced that nervousness and made it easier for me to look at the context of the situation I was in, to notice clues, and to learn the rules that were at play in different social settings. The medicine didn't make me instantly social; but it did make it much easier to notice when something was amiss. Without the constant anxiety and fear, I could give more attention to social interaction. My "fitting in" skills improved and I was better able to interact in ways that contributed to, rather than detracted from, social success.

Parents and teachers who notice a behavior shift as children move into their teen years—the child becomes more agitated and it seems like he's always on edge—may want to consider adding medication to his intervention program. I say "adding"; medication should never be used as an easy-fix where dietary, behavioral and/or social interventions may accomplish the same end result. I talk about this in detail in *Thinking in Pictures*. For me, anxiety worsened throughout my twenties. For other people on the spectrum, this doesn't happen; they are calm and do not need medication. Autism is highly variable and some teenagers and adults need medication and others do not. Antidepressant medication such as Prozac (fluoxetine) and Zoloft (sertraline) help many high-functioning people and for these people, doses often have to be lower, not higher, than for normal people. Some spectrum individuals need one-third to one-fourth of the starter dose. Too high a dosage will result in insomnia and agitation. I've noticed with the people I've met over the years, both on the spectrum and within the meat packing industry, that visual thinkers often times have horrible anxiety problems. For them, medication can literally change their lives.

Parents who are hesitant about putting their teenager on medication can try a gluten/casein (wheat/dairy) free diet first. Another thing that helps alleviate anxiety is a good exercise program. Some teens will function better with just the diet, others will need all three options: diet, exercise and medication. I used to be hot and sweaty, hunched over and rubbing my hands all the time from these panic attacks. It certainly didn't help me "socially, and turned some people off enough that they limited their social contacts with me, I'm sure. The combination that works for me is a small dose of antidepressant combined with a regular exercise program. The exercise enables me to function with a low dose of medication. I have found that the Aspies who have been successful adapters have figured out how their biology affects their ability to play their part in social relationships, and have found the combination of science and psychology that works best for them. It's an issue that should be considered as part of any teenager's or adult's intervention program.

Finally, low self-esteem and a rigid mind often keep one thought spinning within the minds of some people with ASD: "I'm the one at fault all the time." While it's important to know the signs of disinterest in another person and to recognize when a word or behavior offends another person, some adults, in hindsight, realize that their rigid perception of themselves growing up was often worse than the reality of the situation in the minds of those around them.

Sean Shares:

During the last several years, I have run into many of my high school classmates. I felt at the time that my behaviors put them off to a degree that most of them hated me. Now I realize my perceptions of reality were wrong all along. As I've learned, many of them remember me as quiet, shy or introverted, not weird or defective.

In 2001, I attended my twenty-year reunion and was amazed to learn that none of these classmates had held onto negative impressions and memories of me. Most of my humiliation and feelings of alienation came from what I perceived was contempt and judgment on the part of those kids. In social relationships, an unwritten rule that many people have trouble accepting is this: *we often judge ourselves much harsher than other people judge us*. Meeting those old school mates washed away a whole trunk full of painful memories. As a result, nothing from those painful, difficult years adversely affects me now.

2017 REFLECTIONS FROM SEAN

As mentioned earlier, the Internet and social media websites are wonderful tools for communicating in an infinite number of ways. They provide a powerful means by which to share ideas, make plans with one another and quickly learn facts about people, places and countless interesting things. Want to know where your favorite movie was filmed or more about the world's most dangerous insects? A quick Google search will have some readymade answers for you.

But with all of that comes a dark side, namely the fact that the age of instant information also offers platforms and anonymity for people of ill will to viciously attack others whose views and perspectives they disagree with. And far too many websites have been created for angry people to put forth conspiracy theories with no repercussions to them, all of which has, in my estimation, blurred the distinction between facts and lies while making it harder for many people to know whom and what to trust. The more a lie—or "fake news"—is told and spread, the more legitimate and "true" it appears to be as it takes on a life of its own. This can be potentially disastrous, as when a man named Edgar Maddison Welch drove hundreds of miles from his North Carolina home a month after the 2016 presidential election to shoot up a Washington, D.C. pizzeria. Welch's actions stemmed from a self investigation he was doing on Hillary Clinton based on a conspiracy theory he had found online and completely believed. These days it often feels like everything is real, yet nothing is.

What does all of this have to do with learning social etiquette to make one more attractive to others? For me, the negative fallout from what I see as a monumental loss of civility in our society paired with the rise of overt expressions of hatred and acts of violence has caused me to re-examine myself in certain ways. One of those is a recent commitment I've made to double down on efforts to further improve my active-listening skills.

As I alluded to earlier, mastering this ability is always a sure-fire way to attract others for many reasons. For one, it means using your heart, mind and ears to listen to and take a sincere interest in another person. It's much more than simply hearing another's words and responding in kind, trying to win an argument or convincing others that your point of view is the right one. It's also the best conflict-resolution tool we have.

As a University of Colorado Conflict Research consortium puts it, "Active listening has several benefits: First, it forces people to listen attentively to others. Second, it avoids misunderstandings, as people have to confirm that they do really understand what another person has said. Third, it tends to open people up, to get them to say more."

It goes on to mention that if those engaged in a conflict know that their feelings are being validated and they're genuinely being listened to, the chances of developing a deeper dialogue and finding a solution become greater.

We have a strong, innate desire to want to "win" a debate or conflict, so the temptation to simply wait for the other person to finish before speaking can be extremely strong. Just focusing on what you're about to say, however, causes you to unconsciously tune out the other person and miss opportunities that could lead to relating on a deeper, more intimate level and finding common ground.

In a real way, what I view as a loss of societal civility and respect for one another has provided added fuel for me to further recognize and curtail my own occasional tendency to get in what I wish to say at the expense of truly listening to the other person. For nine years, I have volunteered at our local crisis-intervention center, where I have spoken to people on the phone who have been on the verge of suicide and who are trying to deal with various crises. And I can say without hesitation that using active-listening techniques sends the message to others that it's okay to feel as they do, that they're not being judged and that I accept them where they are. It also has likely saved lives.

If you want to be attractive to others, learning, practicing and applying this gift will go a long way.

A caveat to mastering the art of active listening is that we must recognize that, as a general rule, people enjoy talking about themselves. I'm not implying that they are selfish, but it's true that most of us want others to be aware to varying degrees of our talents, accomplishments, triumphs and, perhaps to a lesser extent, our trials and tribulations. So it's crucial to teach those on the spectrum the importance of picking up on body language and nonverbal cues, which, as mentioned earlier, constitute at least 90 percent of our communications.

Jennifer Schmidt works with her Peer Spectrum students on things such as knowing how to stay on track when with others. If another person is making eye contact, leaning slightly forward and asking open-ended questions, then it's a safe bet they're interested in hearing more about a given topic. Conversely, if the person is looking at an iPhone more than at you, squirming around or changing the subject, then that's probably the time to shift gears by ending the conversation or switching topics.

"I teach students to ... ask people questions about themselves or what they are interested in to ensure that they are not monopolizing the conversation, especially if the topic is an area of interest," she says.

POINTS TO KEEP IN MIND

- People tend to focus on the negative and overlook the positive. A child can act appropriately nine times out of ten and people around him will hone in on the one thing he does wrong. Accentuate the positive!
- Perhaps second to grooming/hygiene issues as an immediate turn-off is violating social rules concerning "personal space." Teach the child about this in whatever way meshes with his level of relating, i.e., a social rule might be to stand an arm's length away during conversation.
- Children and adults with ASD are generally unaware of their own nonverbal actions and the messages they send to others. For instance, they may not know they're talking too loudly or in a monotone or so softly they're barely audible. Videotaping helps them get a concrete picture of their own nonverbal behaviors.
- Many AS adults who report success and a tolerable level of social comfort later on in life attribute much of their success to mentors who acted as personal coaches or patient adult-skills instructors. Consider hiring these individuals to help AS/HFA teens, young adults or adults just as you would a language specialist or academic tutor.
- Another turn off is the "know-it-all child." Spectrum children and adults are known for their remarkable memories. As positive as this trait can be, it can also backfire when they use this "total recall" inappropriately, bringing up past mistakes, correcting others on inaccurate facts, or sharing private information in public. The intention is usually not malicious, but rather to demonstrate their intelligence. Keep that in mind; don't react negatively or make judgments. Simply explain context and why the action was inappropriate.

- Be clear and precise when teaching a child with ASD about situation repair or pointing out how his actions affect his social partner. For instance, a child who doesn't recognize when it's time to stop talking about his favorite subject and give his partner a chance to talk may need to be told very clearly—almost bluntly—to change the subject. Use visual tools like a Turn Taking card that children pass back and forth.

- Children/adults with low perspective-taking may think that their physical presence is enough to let people know they are interested in conversation or interaction with others. Be sure they understand that more is needed.

- Encouraging the child to use his special interests as a springboard to social interaction is great, but alongside that lesson teach the child to spot check interest by asking "Is it time to talk about something else?"

- Learning to be an active listener can be a good strategy to add to your social toolbox so you don't turn off others when in their presence.

RULE #9

"FITTING IN" IS OFTEN TIED TO LOOKING AND SOUNDING LIKE YOU FIT IN

"**H**e just doesn't fit into our social circle. His mannerisms are rude."

"Her work habits are fine, but have you noticed what a loner she is? You'll never catch her around the coffee pot in the morning, chatting with the rest of us."

"Hey, have you seen that new guy in math class? Where'd he get those clothes he wears? What a dork!"

Social conformity opens the doors to group interaction. And, while we don't want to make people with ASD into something they're not, people with ASD have to be taught—or as adults they need to accept—this unwritten rule of social relationships: *the outside package is just as important as what's inside.* Before you even get close enough for conversation, people are forming opinions of you based on what they see. Think back to the previous chapter about things that turn people off. A lot of them have to do with that outside package—the way you dress, the manner in which you carry yourself, your total outward appearance.

Autism makes social interaction difficult enough, especially once you do get to the point that you need to say something, when conversation is needed to keep the encounter unfolding. Arriving at the scene

---

with two strikes against you will, more often than not, find you striking out at the plate. Do that a few hundred times and no team will want you as a member.

Dressing to fit in is a skill that reigns supreme during adolescence and takes on a decidedly more civil tone once kids age out of school. That's the good news. The bad news is that dressing to fit in is such a critical part of middle and high school, the peer "fashion-police" are ever vigilant during those years, that this must not be overlooked by parents and teachers in working with adolescents with ASD. From a social perspective, it should even be built into a student's IEP goals. Even sensory issues can be accommodated; there are so many clothing options available today, and trends change so quickly, that most teens with ASD can find a style of dressing that allows them to fit in and be comfortable.

Temple Comments:

An important aspect of Rule #9 applies to fitting in by wearing clothing that is situation appropriate, neat and clean. It doesn't mean everyone has to dress like clones of each other, but it does mean learning a couple of rather important unwritten rules:

- People form impressions about you based on the way you dress.
- During the highly social years of middle and high school, dressing outside the norm will make you the subject of teasing and bullying, absolutely and always.
- Society expects you to follow the formal or informal "dress code" for the event or the setting. When you're young, society expects your parents to take care of this for you. As you become a teen or adult, society expects you to master this grooming basic.

That first unwritten rule may seem unfair—that the way you look is apparently as important, or in some instances, more important, than your personality or your intelligence. But it's a fact of social interaction that just has to be accepted; it's real life in action. Learning how to dress appropriately is pretty easy to do, though, and there are lots of people and resources that can help. You can look at what people in your age group are wearing in magazines; there are books about dressing for success in the workforce; you can ask coworkers to help you modify your wardrobe or most clerks in clothing stores are willing to help you put appropriate outfits together. And, there's always observation, whether it's of classmates, coworkers or special occasion situations. Like it or not, other people view what you wear as an expression of who you are, your personality, and how you view yourself.

For instance, as an adult I adopted my western themed shirts and pants style because it worked for me from a sensory perspective, it fit into my line of work, and I liked it. It might be called eccentric, but I've learned to make it work within social boundaries. I have expensive, very dressy shirts and pants for more formal occasions and other shirts and jeans to wear when I'm out on a construction site. I don't own a dress. To keep my sensory oversensitivity under control, all jeans are washed several times before wearing and I wear old, soft t-shirts under the dressy shirts. Another example: I met an astronomy professor who was an Aspie. He had long hair, but it was clean and pulled back into a neat ponytail, and he wore nice blue jeans and a really cool astronomy t-shirt when he was teaching. That was fine. He was a science nerd and proud to be one. He was very good in his field, and his dress was appropriate for the college setting. He may have been eccentric, but he wasn't sloppy. That's the difference in whether your appearance helps you fit in or not as an adult.

When I'm meeting a new client, I make sure to look my best, because here's another unwritten rule: *first impressions are lasting impressions*. If you blow the first encounter—you arrive dressed inappropriately, you say something really wrong during the first few minutes of chitchat, or your behavior is obviously odd in some way—it's an upward battle to change that person's mind about you. Again, not fair, but reality. So, I take extra care to pick out appropriate clothes, go over in my mind what to say, and watch my mannerisms during that first meeting. The total picture has to work. Just looking the part isn't good enough to keep the social interaction progressing smoothly. If you can't do the meet-and-greet thing or control your own behaviors that will create a negative impression too. But never underestimate the power of looking like you fit it.

People with ASD do have sensory issues that need to be taken into account, but there are so many clothing options available now that most of the time, this can be circumvented and appropriate styles can be found nevertheless. Trouble arises because a lot of Aspies themselves don't place much importance on what other people wear or how they look, and consequently they don't pay attention to hygiene, they dress like a slob or wear mismatched clothes, or clothes that don't fit. Whenever I see an Aspie peer who is doing that I get right on them. People did that with me, and even though I didn't like it at the time and it hurt my feelings, I realize now that it was a big help for me in the long run. You can be angry about social expectations, over how you should dress and not want to conform, and you'll keep turning people off. That's a choice you can make, but if your goal is to have successful social relationships across various settings, you need to get over that anger and just accept the fact that how you look is part of fitting in. Eccentric is okay; being a slob is not. And note that this isn't an expectation for only those of us with ASD; this same "rule" applies to everyone in a particular situation. If you work in a suit and tie environment, you wear a suit and tie, autism or no autism.

Another unwritten rule about how you look that I only learned later in life is that *people treat you differently—better—when you respect the dress code of the setting.* For instance, I've learned that when I dress up at the airport I'm more likely to get an upgrade. I used to wear pretty sloppy clothes when I traveled, but I no longer do that. I'm treated differently when I look nice and there are tangible benefits to doing so. Also, people are recognizing me more often now since the release of the HBO movie, *Temple Grandin*. Almost every time I fly somewhere, someone recognizes me and comes over to talk, so I don't want to be seen in the airport looking sloppy. That would not create a good impression. When you take a bigger role within a community, like the autism community, or gain recognition professionally, there's a certain social responsibility that comes with that in relation to the impression you make on others. You have to be more careful about what you do and say and look like. People expect that of you. It's another one of those unwritten rules of social relationships: *the more recognition you achieve for your efforts, the more careful you have to be to look and act that part.* It takes a lot of self-monitoring.

"Looking the part" to the point of semi-conformity seems to be most important during the middle school years, partly because this is a time of social-emotional development in a typical child, when he aligns himself with his peers in an effort to establish his own identity and independence apart from his parents. Dressing too far outside what other peers consider fashionable that year (or season) will quickly single out the child for harassment and bullying. Once the adolescent makes it through these years and into being a young adult, the pressure to do this lessens dramatically. After adolescence, diversity becomes more respected and acknowledged, and individual styles (again, within the broad social conventions) are viewed in a better light.

While it's apparent that Temple's approach to dressing arises from her logical, goal-oriented thinking patterns, Sean's struggle with looking good arose from a much more deep-seated emotional well of low self-esteem.

Sean Shares:

I didn't spend any time during my middle or high school years trying to make a fashion statement, but had that been my ambition, I would have been grounded before pushing back from the gate. I consistently failed to follow the first step of "looking good," which was to check my appearance in a mirror while getting dressed and before leaving for school each morning.

It wasn't that I forgot that basic piece of etiquette; it was that I deliberately avoided it. The reason was simple yet complex: I usually hated the person staring back and didn't want to look at him. As a result, I might as well have been a blind person trying to improvise the art of dressing and looking presentable, and the times I left for school looking good were more attributable to luck than a conscious effort on my part to ensure that that was the case.

My aversion to mirrors was so strong that for years I turned my head whenever I passed one. When I was in situations that required me to be next to one—like getting dressed—I looked above my reflection, to the side, at my lower body, anywhere but at my face. I remember a few occasions during my mid-teens when I made a conscious (and painful) effort to force myself to look at my reflection only to literally turn red with embarrassment. I couldn't stand how I looked, how tall I was (I thought I towered over kids, another way I stood out) or what I was forced to be reminded of each time I took a peek. As I've mentioned in several places already in the book, I was convinced that I was an inherently bad person; looking in a mirror threw that reminder back in my face, literally.

It's difficult to emerge from home looking your best when you have an acute case of mirror aversion combined with low self-esteem. For years I was teased and tormented in school for a variety of reasons. I realize that shortly after I arose each morning I helped set the wheels into motion to ensure this was a staple of my school day. Even before laying eyes on the day's first tormentors, my mother was using every means she could think of to get me to look at myself as I got dressed ("You have to look at what you're doing," "People notice how you look," "If you want to make friends, you have to look presentable"), only to have me still reach the front door in the morning with my shirt collars up and my self-esteem down.

On days that I left for middle and high school looking okay largely because of her efforts, I usually came home looking anything but. That was because I had gym class most days, and on those days I was required to dress, undress and take a shower. Since I didn't have my mother guiding me, and had a limited amount of time to dress before the next period's bell rang, I did so hurriedly and away from a mirror that could keep me on course. I had greater motor difficulty with shirts that had a lot of buttons, especially smaller ones, and cuffs. In addition to mismatching the buttons to their proper holes, I often put on my shirt without having dried my back. I was a prime target for those who enjoyed making fun of me.

When I was made fun of I stewed inside, but rarely retaliated or thought about changing my behavior or learning the art of dressing. Instead, I took my pent-up fury out on the object I perceived was responsible for creating the conditions that allowed the incident to occur. In these instances, the shirt or pair of pants were to blame.

If shirts with buttons were hard to put on each morning, they were even more of a challenge to remove. When I came home, I tried to get them off not by unbuttoning each button, but by lifting them over my head. This way, I reasoned, I will get the process over with faster. If such shirts didn't slide right over my head, my anger was unleashed and I ripped the buttons off, often throwing the shirt or pants away. Later, when I cooled off, I placed the clothing article at the bottom of the waste basket and put trash over the "offending" item hoping no one would notice. Someone always did, however.

As if all of that wasn't enough, there was the sore issue of letters and numbers. I steadfastly refused to wear any clothing item that had writing on it. I had several shirts that contained logos and various expressions, and those were the ones that collected cobwebs in the drawer or closet. As a result, I constantly wore the same four or five shirts, the ones that were solid or had little color variation, regardless of whether they had holes worn into them or how they matched the rest of my outfit.

One day midway through eighth grade, my mother had had enough. I had a blue pullover shirt with red stripes that I wore a lot, and after wearing it for the fifth consecutive day, my mom let her feelings be known.

"Take that off!" she said at the bottom of the stairs when she saw me coming down.

Without saying a word, I returned to my room and replaced it with another shirt I wore nearly as often.

As I look back on those years, I realize that not only did I have no idea how my own clothing worked, I also had no idea about how other people dressed and why. People wore certain color or pattern combinations, for instance, and I hadn't a clue about those. Also lost on me was the concept that, like certain behaviors, many types of clothing were appropriate in one setting and not okay in another.

I remember my grandmother's funeral when I was fourteen, and that the men wore suits, ties and dark shoes, and the women attended wearing dresses and good-looking shoes. At the time, however, I didn't know that such attire was appropriate for the sad occasion. Had my mother not picked out my outfit beforehand, I might have gone wearing what I wore around the house, even though it was February.

A person's appearance, going for a job interview and taking someone out on a first date have one thing in common: They speak to the importance of first impressions. When I got older, during the time I was overcoming my autism and still had difficulty with some dressing issues,

I began to justify my refusal to take the extra time to look presentable by saying that true friends would accept me for who I am regardless of how I looked. As I learned, however, there's no relationship between people's unconditional acceptance of me and their being turned off by my poor appearance. Entering a social situation looking unacceptable is unattractive to others, regardless of how well they know the person with the turned-up collar and uncombed hair.

I don't know if I fully subscribe to the saying that the clothes make the person. I do, however, buy into the idea that the clothes set up impressions about you in other people's minds. So when it comes to getting dressed and wanting to create a good impression, I recommend:

1. Asking for help if you're unsure about how an article of clothing looks with something else. On several occasions, I have asked my girlfriend if a particular shirt is color-coordinated with the pair of pants I have on. Asking someone else doesn't mean I'm stupid or don't know better; another opinion can help you think of something you hadn't thought of before.
2. If anything, taking more, not less, time to look your best.
3. Paying close attention to hygiene. That means showering daily, washing your hair with each shower, if needed, and always using deodorant.

I take great pride in dressing each morning and looking my best for whatever the day may bring. It's one of those unwritten rules that abound: *looking good creates a positive tone to the social interaction and sets the stage for fitting in with those you encounter.*

Temple offers a few other unwritten social rules she's learned about looking and acting like you fit in.

Temple Says:

There are lots of common, everyday social skills that people in general exhibit in order to get along with each and fit into society or a particular social group. For instance, here's some unwritten rules about "fitting in" that I've learned from my experiences:

- *People who are polite and cheerful will have an easier time getting along in the world.* That may not seem fair, but people like people who are generally happy.
- *Good manners are a must.* I know I'm repeating this over and over throughout the book, but that's because they open so many doors to social interaction. I can't impress strongly enough upon the parents and teachers reading this book the importance of drilling these basic social functioning skills into the child. Like the Nike ad says, "Just do it."
- *Social interaction is a two-way street,* which means that you're going to need to extend yourself out to others; to fit in you must initiate social contact some of the time.
- At school or on the job, *greet your peers at least once each day.* It can be a simple gesture: make eye contact (or if that's too difficult, just look at the space between their eyebrows) and say, "Hi, how's it going?" or even just "Hi!"
- *Actively try to engage in some small talk with peers you interact with on a daily basis* (lab partners in science class, homeroom students, coworkers, etc.). While it's not necessary to form friendships with all of these people, some social interaction is needed if you are to be viewed as fitting into the group.
- *Act the way you want people to view you.* Be friendly if you want friends. Be cooperative if you want cooperation from others. Acting depressed won't attract happy people to you.

I've used the analogy lots of times before that we're actors in a play that is life. An important caveat to keep in mind is that *society is one of the directors of this play*. Society sometimes dictates the role you play in a certain scene, or how you're supposed to play it. We don't always get to do it the way we want to. There will be times the director requires we perform a certain way: that's how life is, too. We're expected to rehearse the part and learn to perform it—going through the motions even when we might not agree, or understand it 100%. It is an unwritten rule worth repeating: *Sometimes you just have to learn to perform the behaviors that allow you to fit in, like it or not.* This is troublesome for many of my peers with ASD. They want to be the sole director of their play. That's impossible if you want to exist within any society and interact with others. It's a group effort and you have to abide by the group rules.

In the following passages Sean echoes Temple's words and moves forward to the second part of fitting into a social encounter: chitchat and small talk, which he refers to as the social glue of interaction.

Sean Speaks:

If you have ever attended a Major League baseball game, much of your excitement probably comes from the knowledge that you're seeing the best and most well-known players battling it out. Most of the top ball players have a knack for making tough plays look effortless and easy. Batters hit balls coming at them at 90 mph or more; infielders catch line drives that, if hit my way, would cause me to wonder whether my Blue Cross is paid up before I ducked first and asked questions later; and they perform in front of thousands of people every day.

But if you get to the ballpark, say an hour before game time, you also notice something else: the same players who make it look easy on the field are taking batting practice, doing stretches and other calisthenics and going over the same skills and drills they likely learned back in their days of Little League. In other words, these professional baseball players don't just take their positions, pick up a bat and go at it. Even after more than a month of spring training, they still practice and refine their abilities before all 162 regular season games. And the key to their success in the Major Leagues can be summed up in two words: making adjustments. The rules of the game are the same; it's being flexible in playing each game that results in a win for the team.

I use this example to illustrate what I see as parallels between baseball and social skills. It took me many years of trial and error as well as pain, heartbreak and difficulties to learn what I have learned about relating well to people. One unwritten rule is this: *Whether or not a person has autism, fitting in socially requires that we each play by certain rules that form the structure of our society.* Within that framework, however, we each bring individual skills and talents that create the team's personality. An equally important unwritten rule that is often difficult for the person with ASD to grasp is that *fitting in requires that I keep making adjustments to the interaction, based on the context of the situation in which I find myself. In essence, I adjust to the situation* instead of going into a situation and expecting it to adjust to me.

Like the player who undertakes batting practice before the game, I "warm up" to many social situations, as opposed to going into them full steam and with a mental "map" of how I want them to go. Not only were most social skills ones I understood much later than most people, but I also had to learn what a friend of the family refers to as the "social glue," that is, words and phrases that cause people to feel comfortable around you and keep a conversation "glued" together and moving forward.

Chitchat and small talk are the glue. They are not necessarily the same as meaningless bantering or other types of idle conversation, however. Both are about more than filling time by simply discussing with a stranger in the supermarket the weather (although that can be okay, too) or the latest blockbuster movie. Chitchat can be a valuable social tool; in it is a gold mine of catch phrases and early opportunities to create a favorable impression, thus setting up the possibility of hitting a homerun with another person or a group. It can lay a foundation for a friendship or other healthy relationship to be built. Allow me to use a few personal examples to illustrate my point.

SAM BARZILLO

At the beginning of seventh-grade, I somehow found the courage to do something uncharacteristically risky. I was proud of myself because during the first week of school, I initiated a conversation with a pupil seated directly behind me. We were seated in alphabetical order, so I was easily able to talk to Sam Barzillo by virtue of location. This simple act was nearly unprecedented, partly because I felt comfortable only with teachers and adults at school and rarely with those my own age. The few times I did initiate an interaction with another child were almost always an extension of or variation on one of my compulsions, which, of course, was the antithesis of an offer of friendship.

But on this occasion during homeroom, I found it within me to garner the courage to turn around and start talking to him. Even so, I did it only within a very narrow comfort zone. I was just a step or two away from stressing out—and dealing with this stress in classically autistic ways—if he crossed a line that forced me out of the zone.

Sure enough, that is exactly what happened. Sam, no doubt sensing that I was making an overture of friendship toward him, responded back to me in kind. However, the interaction quickly moved into uncharted social avenues for me. I didn't understand that a back and forth banter about generic subjects was needed for people to become comfortable with one another. My communication arsenal didn't include the friendly "I'd-like-to-get-to-know-you" conversation openers that most kids pick up with ease. The whole idea of small talk was foreign to me; all talk was big talk and carried with it unspoken opportunities for pushing me outside my comfort zone.

I withdrew from Sam and began ignoring him, most likely reinforcing in his mind that I wasn't friendship material after all, but a weirdo who didn't know the first thing about fitting in. Not surprisingly, a potential friend became another tormenter, and my interactions with Sam evolved into needling and bullying that plagued me and intensified over the next two grades. Had I understood that the game of friendship requires that I step up to the plate with at least a few basic skills under my belt, Sam and I might have become teammates. As it was, my lack of skills resulted in my remaining a team of one.

MY CHITCHAT EXPECTATIONS OF OTHERS

When I lived in California and was seventeen, my parents took me to see a play at the Victory Theater in Los Angeles. My folks heard about the performance through its director, whom my mom and dad knew casually. After the curtain went up and the final applause died down, we stuck around so they could thank the director, meet her husband, and have the two meet me. Little did the director realize that the real drama of that evening was yet to come.

"I'd like you both to meet our son, Sean," my mother said to the director and her husband.

What followed was not the customary "Nice to meet you, too," or any related variation. Instead, I responded by taking a large step backward and following that up with silence. I didn't smile or in any way indicate I wanted anything to do with this couple. Did I instantly dislike them? Was I deliberately being mean? Did I have a vendetta against this man and this woman who let us see a play for free? The answer to all three was no. Nevertheless, my actions portrayed a boy who was cold, rather hostile and unresponsive, and they undoubtedly wondered what was wrong with me.

Even though I had not set out to be unfriendly, these two kind people had no way of knowing what was going on behind my inappropriate reaction. Nor were they obligated to figure it out. During this time in the late 1970s, my self-esteem was more fragile than fine porcelain and even the slightest failure or negative reaction from someone—*real or perceived*—shattered it. To compensate, I developed a mask of sorts to handle the low opinion I had of myself. When I met new people, I waited for them to approach me and *prove* I was special. I wanted them to make me feel okay about who I was. This caused me to go into these situations with expectations of how people were to greet, respond and pay attention to me (all of which were unrealistic), and when they "failed" to "validate" that I was a terrific person, I reacted with coldness because, without any of these people knowing it, they had "shattered" what I was trying so hard to preserve.

Again, what should have been routine greetings turned into vicious circles because I reacted as I had, causing those who met me to sense something was wrong with me without knowing what. That in turn caused people to avoid me because they didn't know how to handle such unusual and unexpected behavior. I interpreted their avoidance as not caring about me, which deepened my resentment and caused me to become even more obstinate.

THE PRICELESS VALUE OF SMALL TALK

It was in my junior year of high school that I experienced my first-ever peer group social situation. I, my sister, and three other of my high school classmates went out to dinner after school one afternoon. I had a lot of trepidation initially because I had never gone out with anyone my age before, yet part of me was excited because I was entering uncharted waters.

During the dinner, the other three teenagers were kind to me and made efforts to include me in the conversation. I didn't know how to use lead-ins to start a conversation with anyone, so I mostly sat back and tried to appropriately respond to their overtures. I was pleasant to them because I wanted friends so badly and even though the meal was punctuated by many awkward moments, the group didn't seem fazed and continued to reach out to me. I suspect they knew I had autism.

Overall, the evening went well and I came home thrilled that, despite every fiber in my body telling me not to go, I overcame my fear. But when I now look back on that evening, I recall what was missing from my social repertoire: small talk and conversation openers, the keys that open doors to social relationships.

So what's the big deal about chitchat and making small talk with people? Why not just skip over the preliminaries and cut to the chase already? I have found that it makes no difference whether you have known a person for two minutes or two years; such "social glue" is valuable because it:

- Creates in the other person an early impression of you. Meeting someone, making eye contact, smiling and simply saying things like "How are you?" "That's a really nice outfit you're wearing," "Hey, you look great," etc., tells the other person you're open and approachable. Many solid friendships I now have began with chatting in some form; indeed, it's how all friendships start out.
- Makes it easier to continue the social interaction with another person. Simply saying, for example, "My, that tie looks good on you," pays a compliment to the person, and it's an unwritten rule of social interaction: *most people enjoy receiving compliments.* Compliments also open the door for the conversation to go in many possible directions. Maybe you have a tie that looks like the one the person you have just met is wearing and a conversation can come from that. Perhaps that statement or one like it could

spawn a conversation about ties, which can lead elsewhere. One time at work, I ran into a co-worker who was wearing an ostentatious checkered tie and I went up to him, unprompted, and said, "I love that getup you're wearing. I'll be the first to admit that I don't have a tie exactly like that one." The other person laughed and we parted with good feelings. So a few words or a single sentence can lead a conversation in any of a million directions—all desirable ones—instead of having it stall at each red light like a poorly tuned car.

- Allows interactions with people to run more naturally, smoothly and rhythmically. Somehow, simple chitchat often puts people at ease and when you do get to the more serious topics (asking someone on a date, for a favor or countless other possibilities), it doesn't seem forced.

- Shows interest. Remember, it is more attractive—and you make a better and longer lasting impression—to show interest than to try so hard to be interesting.

For years, I reacted to uncomfortable situations with silence. During the same time, I clung to the mistaken notion that silence was just that—a void, empty of meaning. Regardless of how hard I tried to remove myself from that uncomfortable situation by retreating into myself, I always gave off something negative that those in my presence felt and picked up on every time. In itself, this is another unwritten rule of social interaction: *being silent is a form of communication all its own.* There are appropriate and inappropriate times and places for being silent. Inappropriate silence speaks volumes and the old adage, "silence is golden" doesn't always apply.

People subjected to my coldness and silence backed off not because they were uncaring or unfeeling, but because they didn't know what else to do. They may not have known what was ticking inside my head, but they certainly were privy to the fact that something was amiss.

And throughout all of it, one unwritten rule of social relationships stood strong: no one wants to be around someone who consistently gives off negative energy. Each time I stepped up to the plate with that response, I struck out.

Some of the social rules of chitchat are more nebulous.

Temple Points Out:

Sean has offered a lot of good information on the value of chitchat in social interactions, and his personal examples demonstrate how it can make or break social relationships. In my experience, there are a few other related unwritten rules about making small talk that I think are important to discuss. One is this: *people chitchat as a way of being polite with each other in social settings, but many people don't expect you to thoroughly address a question, or even be 100% honest in your answer.* This does vary from person to person, and it depends on how well you know the person. But for instance, the stranger who says, "Hi, how are you?" isn't expecting you to talk on about the fact that you just had the flu and the doctor gave you a shot and you were throwing up for three days. The appropriate response is a short, "Fine," or you might say, "I've been sick but I'm feeling better now, thank you." This is a time when 100% honesty can be a turn-off if you launch into a detailed description of your ailments.

Here's another unwritten rule about small talk: *the less you know the person, the more the conversation is comprised of short, generic questions and/or statements.* Social conversation unfolds, like a flower unfolds its petals in the sun, based on how little or how well you know the person. With strangers, questions and answers start out short and generic. They go back and forth as people gauge interest in each other and surmise how much they might have in common. Back to the stranger on the airplane who I talked about in Rule 8: after the initial introductions and chitchat about where we're both going, I might next talk about some travel war stories of mine and test if that's a subject of shared interest. Most people who travel a lot have them. I keep the story short until I can see if the person's engaged or not. Short, one word responses like "interesting" or "really?" or "hmm" indicate disinterest, as the person isn't asking another question or offering any information back to me of his own. If I want to continue with our interaction, I might try another topic. One sure sign that he wants the conversation between us to end is when he starts reading a magazine, or unpacking his laptop, while I'm still talking. At that point, I know he's no longer interested. Now, I don't take that personally, and automatically assume I've done something wrong. There could be lots of reasons that have nothing to do with me.

With someone you don't know very well, polite chitchat is the starting point to conversation. It can lead to more meaningful exchanges if you both hit upon a topic of mutual interest. Or, the social interaction can be no more than chitchat. Either way, it's a skill that when mastered, lets you fit in with all different types of people, across different settings and cultures. It's a universal unwritten rule of social relationships.

Humor is next on the list of ways to fit in, and one of the most difficult social skills to master. It's highly context driven, demands a good ability to read the situation and the responses of other people (both verbal and nonverbal), and to be successfully used, requires spot-on timing. Sean has accepted the challenge of conveying the pitfalls of using humor and eventually feeling the power of it as a conversational vehicle to fit into a social group.

Sean Speaks:

In the mid-'70s, I was fascinated with the popular television show of that era, *Gilligan's Island*. Each day at 4:00 PM I was counting on the silliness of Bob Denver and the other characters to be my ticket out of unhappiness. I spent an unusually large amount of time that year at the kitchen table, turning on the tiny black-and-white screen to memorize dialogue and become funny.

Besides air, food and water, I needed a sense of humor, and I was willing to try any means necessary to achieve it. Nothing else was working to get me out from under the heavy burdens of unhappiness, low self-esteem, suicidal thoughts and fantasies and unpopularity at school, so I figured that developing the ability to make others laugh would dramatically shift their opinions of me from negative to positive and counteract the effects of bullying and emotional pain. Humor would be my free pass to fitting in with my peers.

My plan was the essence of simplicity: just take note of and memorize those chunks of dialogue that result in audience laughter and use them myself in conversations with people at home, school and elsewhere. Even in the haze of autism, I knew this unwritten rule among social partners: *funny people are attractive people.* And in my case, an ability to get my middle school classmates laughing harder and longer would go a long way toward reversing a self-history fraught and littered with despair and suicidal ideations.

I never spent a moment of my teenage years wondering about the show's lack of reality, how the seven people functioned as they did in such a setting and kept their sense of humor and wits when faced with the world's worst luck. Nor did I stop to wonder how the three women stayed so beautiful and proper without the barest essentials at their fingertips, like electricity to wash their beautiful and proper clothes. It never occurred to me to question how that many people, stuck indefinitely on an island I literally thought was real and in the middle of the South Pacific somewhere—so real that I once tried to find it on my globe—could never run out of supplies.

In much the same way, I was identifying various television commercials I found funny to pick out those delicious bits of humor that would make me equally appealing to my classmates. These included the ads for Kool-Aid® drink mix and Sugar Crisp® cereal. Here I went a huge (and sometimes painful) step further by trying to imitate the character's movements, as well as tone of voice and articulations. I remember the person dressed up as the Kool-Aid pitcher breaking down a wall and making his presence felt and I tried, at home and at school, everything short of putting a life-size hole in a classroom wall to mimic that opening scene. So now I had two ways to add to my humor arsenal. I would surely fit in now at school. How could I miss?

Unfortunately, I went 0-for-2. Instead of throwing a dart and hitting the bulls-eye, I was unwittingly tossing a boomerang. The very things I thought should be funnier through repetition were the same pieces of script that were increasingly driving people around me crazy and further alienating me. In a short time, my sister Meg got to where she couldn't stand the sight or sound of these and other commercials and my family's opinion of *Gilligan's Island*, poor at the starting gate, plummeted. Not only was no one in the family laughing, but they were also getting angrier. I couldn't understand how someone else could view something that was hilarious to me in any other way than how I saw it.

Likewise, I had no way of being able to judge whether those who did laugh at my antics were laughing with me or at me. Laughter was laughter and was always accompanied by a smile, both of which meant something good. It meant that whoever was laughing was finding me funny, period. Even though I could sometimes sense if someone's laughter was meant to convey, "You're weird" instead of "I think you're funny and I like your humor," I couldn't definitely rely on any internal signs or signals to clue me in to what was going on.

Unfortunately, as time went on and my humor value dropped, it became painfully clear that two things were happening: one, the arguments, not laughter, between me and my family were accounting for the bulk of decibels at home and two, the scant number of kids who seemed to like me was decreasing. I could tell that I was more and more in disfavor at school because many kids would preempt or try to one-up me. They would mock me by repeating snips from the commercials or other sayings I came up with on my own before I opened my mouth. And I had no idea how to be funny or where to go with it when I was in the position of having to respond to what someone else said; my attempts at humor relied solely on my initiating them and the humor unfolding in a carefully scripted manner. In these situations, I would become visibly frustrated and red, which would only act to spur them on—turning an opportunity for humor into yet another source of torment.

I had no way of knowing it at the time, but the chief culprits for humor dissolving into misery were not my lack of material or exaggerated movements per se, but my inability to put anything in perspective, as well as an abundance of literal and boxed thinking. Such a mindset told me that all I had to do to be funny—and win the hearts of hundreds—was copy what was viewed as funny on TV. After all, if a given character said something that led to laughter, then it stood to reason that repeating those words would yield the same results. Nevertheless, what this mindset prevented me from getting was one of the unwritten rules of social relationships: that *humor only works in context*. Yes, a certain chunk of dialogue may be hilarious in one setting, but the precise words or actions in another context may be insulting, hurtful or inappropriate. Calling someone names on a TV show may be funny to those looking in, but doing the same thing in the wrong setting is more likely to get you punched than make you popular. And repeating the same joke, commercial or dialogue to the same person makes it less funny—something that took me a long time to understand.

Copying other people—whether from television shows or real life—in order to fit in never got me what I truly wanted. Instead, it got me into trouble with myself because I had to live up to impossible and unreasonable expectations that caused enormous disappointment, anger and heartbreak. The important caveat of Rule #9 I learned, that is in itself another unwritten rule of social relationships, was this: *I can dress like others, talk like others and act like others in an attempt to fit in, and a measure of that is needed in order to do so. But long-lasting social acceptance comes from liking yourself enough to let your own unique personality shine though. That's how you truly fit in.*

It took me a long time to realize that spontaneity is humor's lifeblood. When I got older and was beginning to emerge from my shell of autism, my sense of humor was blossoming. However, even then I still went into a given social situation planning ahead what I would say to make those I interact with laugh. I would play in my head something I thought was funny and would come home in the evening disappointed or feeling at a loss if I forgot to say it. The same feelings—along with a shot of embarrassment—resulted if I did manage to say what I thought were the humorous words only to be met with a cool or tepid response or no laughter. I took such dashed expectations personally. I still didn't comprehend the importance of being spontaneous in such situations and still had a long way to go to learn that humor is not something one can usually "plan."

Through this journey to develop my sense of humor, I learned a very important lesson, an unwritten rule that applies to using humor in a relationship: *never use sarcasm or any other style or form of humor to deliberately hurt someone or at their expense.* That's never funny and will end a social interaction quicker than anything.

Here's another unwritten rule that became apparent to me as I emerged from my autism: *Being able to laugh at your own gaffes, miscues, mistakes and shortcomings certainly helps maintain—and in some instances, repair—a social relationship.* For me, perhaps this was the hardest thing of all to learn—and it's something I still on occasion have to remind myself to do. It also goes a long way toward diffusing a potentially negative situation before it can ruin an evening, date, dinner or day.

It's not been easy to learn these and many other social-emotional life lessons. I had to go through years of trial and error and literally start by taking Relating to Others 101, which had watching how people greet each other, smiling and looking natural and laughing appropriately on its syllabus. I've discovered that having an ability to make others laugh and spread joy that way is a valuable means to fitting in with others. But humor, in and of itself, is not an end to strive for. The end is being able to establish positive, vibrant, healthy and long-lasting relationships with people on many levels.

2017 REFLECTIONS FROM SEAN

As was the case with becoming more adept at navigating through Rule #7, my journalism career has provided the perfect set of opportunities to more fully grasp and appreciate the link between fitting in somewhere and appearing as if I do. Knowing what to do and how to conduct myself after having been asked to cover an event, a meeting or other public gathering for our newspaper has a lot in common with knowing how to prepare for a social outing, and a key component of both is having the ability to keep an open mind. If I cover, say, a county commissioners' meeting, I go into it open-mindedly and base my story on what's most newsworthy, along with what I feel will be most interesting to our readers, not necessarily on what I personally might think is most important or captivating.

Likewise, this is how I try to approach social situations. For one, I love to make others laugh – without striving to be the center of attention – but at the same time, I have to take into account that not every social gathering lends itself to laughter. I may be in a wonderful mood, but the overall tone of a given setting could be somber and sad, so obviously it's up to me to make the appropriate adjustments, which may mean trying to help others feel better instead of trying to inject humor. Any social gathering is, by definition, a collection of what everyone brings to the table, and I have only a finite amount of control over a setting.

Following this trajectory does not mean pretending to be something you're not or betraying your true self. It entails adjusting to the myriad of situations that life throws your way, which leads to further personal growth.

In her Peer Spectrum classes, Jennifer Schmidt points out to her students the subtleties of this social rule, things that most neurotypical people adapt to but are often confusing and challenging to those on the spectrum. Through outside class activities and field trips in a variety of settings such as the local mall, she ensures that her students on the spectrum learn that this social skill also depends heavily on who is part of the equation, how well others in the situation are known, the participants' ages and the environment. Taking into account that complicated, nuanced social opportunities can be highly confusing and frustrating for those with literal, black-and-white thinking patterns, Schmidt also uses role playing as a means to help her students grapple with this concept so they have the tools to better fit in wherever they may be and whomever's company they may keep.

POINTS TO KEEP IN MIND:

- Neurotypical people often throw out questions as part of "social chit-chat" that they really don't want a long or involved answer to. Be sure to share that caveat when teaching aspects of social conversation.
- Sensory issues can interfere with appearance and grooming; find age-appropriate ways to help the child fit in while still working within their sensory sensitivities.
- Teaching age-appropriate language to fit in will mean also teaching children the slang words and expressions, whether or not the teacher/adult feels they are "right."
- Fitting in requires the ASD individual to adapt to social convention; at times the rules may seem silly or unimportant to him. Remind the ASD individual that sometimes it's just the "part" he needs to play in order to be a part of a social group/interaction.
- Respect the ASD person's individuality and help him express it within socially accepted boundaries. Changing him into a neurotypical "clone" is not the goal of intervention.

What is "humorous" varies from culture to culture, from company to company, teacher to teacher, etc. It's highly situation and context driven—and will be difficult for the child with ASD who thinks literally to appreciate.

RULE #10
PEOPLE ARE RESPONSIBLE FOR THEIR OWN BEHAVIORS

Social interaction requires some level of personal responsibility in order for the parties involved to achieve success. Neurotypicals naturally understand this and the tides of conversation (talk, listen, silence) or interaction (action, response/no response) ebb and flow between partners as they engage with one another, whether it's a two-person interaction or a large group function. Each person acknowledges responsibility for keeping the social exchange moving along at whatever pace the group deems appropriate, and stepping in with social repairs when the interaction goes amiss.

While all people generally acknowledge that they are socially responsible within an interchange, not all people accept that responsibility and act upon it accordingly. Emotions get in the way, personal definitions of what level of involvement is needed differ. Some people are more self-motivated than others. And, this is ever a dynamic interchange: rarely do situations repeat themselves in exactly the same way. In one interaction Wayne takes a leadership role, steering the group to success and in another situation Mary does so, or it's a joint effort among several participants.

How much or how little people actively engage in a social situation is a choice left to each participant. Society doesn't set hard and fast rules that apply across the board because each social exchange is so unique.

However, group members do begin to apply labels to people over time, based on a member's level of social interaction with a specific group or groups and the nature of the involvement. Social butterfly, loner, social-climber, recluse, all-around-Joe, leader of the pack, and worker-bee all describe various levels of social engagement applied to people. Depending on a person's individual code of ethics and morals, these are viewed as positive or negative labels.

Whether you think of it as psycho-babble or psychological truth, an oft-repeated mantra of social relationships is this: *"The only person you can ever change is yourself."* Accepting personal responsibility for how well you do or do not fit into social groups means acknowledging that personal effort is required in cases where your skills don't match your aspirations. Just as we mentioned at the end of the previous chapter, becoming socially aware is a life-long learning process; a never-ending play that provides the backdrop against which we practice and perfect ourselves. Temple has an interesting opinion on how this realization plays out within the autism community.

Temple Speaks:

There's a lively debate going on today within the ASD community about how much people on the autism spectrum should have to adapt to the world around them, and how much the world should be adapting to the ASD person. Rule #10 is tightly wrapped up in all of this debate, as are many of the related rules involving personal responsibility and emotional control.

Interestingly enough (and mirroring the black-and-white thinking patterns that are characteristic of the disorder), there are Aspies who feel "everyone else" should do the conforming and changing, and that people with ASD are just fine the way they are—no changes needed, no interventions required. This is an extreme perspective that in my opinion does not take into account the entire spectrum of individuals with autism, and especially disregards the needs of those who function on the lower end of the autism spectrum.

I've mentioned this in other spots in the book, and repeat it here: the goal of any intervention program should be to provide the individual with knowledge and practical tools to help him succeed within the world around him. The goal is not to make a person with autism "normal" or "typical," to transform him into someone he is not—we'd have a whole lot of uninteresting people around if we did that—but to enhance his strengths and teach him to maneuver around his difficulties. But fact is fact, and the unwritten rule that is at the heart of this chapter echoes loudly here: *People—all people—who participate in social interactions are responsible for their own behaviors.* You can choose to live as a hermit, in a cave in the mountains and let your autistic characteristics run wild. But if you choose to live in a house or apartment and eat food that you buy in a grocery store, or wear clothes that you purchase in a store, you're going to have to interact within social groups to one extent or another. That means social responsibility kicks in.

I think some of the high-functioning people with ASD who want to be engaged too readily accept total responsibility for the success or failure of a social relationship. That's a huge burden on their shoulders—one that is largely self-imposed—but monumental nevertheless. Couple that with their absolute thinking, and the task of taking responsibility for social interaction looks so enormous, and so intense, that it deflates motivation to try. Sean has mentioned it over and over again in this book. People like him who are emotionally-related, especially as a child, can't see through the dense fog those emotions create. For me it was different. My visual thinking and logical reasoning mind wasn't clouded with my emotions anywhere near as much as it was with Sean. That's what makes our two paths so interesting; we both ended up as happy, independent, functioning adults.

It's important for us, as teachers and guides, to frequently reinforce to adolescents and adults that all the troubles in social relationships are not their fault. You are not responsible for the things I say or do, or what the check-out clerk at the grocery store says or does, or the thoughts and actions of your teachers or our Congressmen—but you *are* responsible for your own. Hidden within that rule are a few others that are equally and actively at play within social relationships:

- Don't blame others for your own mistakes.
- Human emotions are grossly illogical at times—most of the time.
- You can't control your feelings; you can learn to control your responses.

Dr. Leo Kanner, the person who first described autism in 1943, stated that *the people who adapt best to the world realize themselves that they have to make some behavioral changes in order to fit in.* That was true for me and I'd venture a guess it's true for any of my spectrum peers who are living independent, successful, happy lives. That doesn't mean we no longer struggle, that we no longer face daily challenges, that we no longer continue to learn and become "more skilled" at this role we play. What it means is that we have accepted that we, ourselves, are responsible for learning how to survive in today's world. Our lives are what we make them—hell or heaven—and some of us have to work pretty damn hard to achieve even a mediocre existence.

You may think that's unfair; I agree, it's not fair. But that's another unwritten rule of social interaction: *life is not fair and things don't always turn out the way you'd like them to.* You can either decide to find ways to fit in, or you can keep getting fired from one job after another, or losing one friend after another, or spending your entire day locked in your apartment in front of a computer. Some kids try hard and keep trying, despite the mistakes they make. Some kids try hard and then give up. Some kids don't try very hard at all. Basic personality characteristics are a force in kids with ASD, too. Even the "perfect intervention program" will only go so far if the child has "lazy genes."

Blaming people around you for not understanding your autism, or expecting people to give you a break because you're different is often an excuse for not wanting to do the hard work you need to do. People who aren't on the spectrum use these excuses all the time. Do you think that television shows like Dr. Phil would be so popular if people knew how to act and interact successfully all the time? *Life is a learning process for everyone.* If you want to change your situation, change yourself. If you keep getting fired from one job after another, change what you're doing, get help from others if you need it, see a psychologist or make an appointment with a career counselor. If you think the world is against you, that perception will affect your thoughts, your actions, your words and ultimately, the reactions you get from people. It can be a self-fulfilling prophesy.

Some people on the spectrum have problems with obeying authority figures, such as a policeman or their boss at work. Maybe you do not think the situation is fair, but in some situations, you just have to obey. For instance, police you *always* obey very politely. Bosses, well, it's a fact of life that if you work at a job, you're probably going to end up working for a "bad boss" at one point or another. There are two kinds of bad bosses: 1) jerks who most employees hate and 2) bosses who are nice to neurotypicals but don't like Aspies. Either kind may be impossible to work with, but don't give up right from the start. People on the spectrum function better with a sympathetic boss who appreciates their abilities. Even with the best boss, you will still have to do some things you do not want to do, or some tasks you hate doing. All employees encounter this. It's important to differentiate between tasks you just don't want to do and tasks that are extremely difficult for you, due to sensory problems or executive functioning challenges. When those issues crop up, talk to your boss and explain why a certain task is difficult. For instance, multi-tasking is generally hard for Aspies because of the way their brain connections work. Try to problem-solve with your boss to find a solution you can both live with.

The issue of "fairness" for me, in my logic-based brain, is essentially an If-Then computer sequence. I think my way of mental processing makes it easier for me to conform than an Aspie who has a strong emotional makeup, who has emotions more wrapped up into the equation. *If* I wanted my job, *then* I had to change certain behaviors as a young adult. *If* I wanted to keep a certain client who was demanding or pushy, *then* I had to learn how to deal with his nervousness and tantrums. *If* I wanted to be a team player on a job, *then* I needed to learn how to work through employee jealousy. *If* I wanted to give interesting autism presentations, *then* I had to learn better public speaking skills. *If* I wanted to develop friendships with people, *then* I had to learn friendship skills.

There's one If-Then logic statement—you could say it's the prime statement of all—that people operate under: *IF you want to be a player in the world, THEN you need to learn your part.* It's one of those statements that looks so simple, yet has hidden within it layers and layers of nuance that make learning it and all its variations an endless task. Another unwritten rule of any social relationship, whether it's personal or professional is this: *Functioning in the world is a lifelong educational process. Life is a process, social interaction is a process; there's no "end of task" to strive for, no one magic bullet that, when learned, turns social confusion into social understanding.* People on the spectrum seem to miss that—or not acknowledge it, or simply are never taught it. Not only are they not taught it, but they are not taught that it's okay—*there's no end point.*

Having autism isn't a "free pass" to act in any way we feel, in any situation. We've said that before. Here's another one of the unwritten rules: *life is compromise; we all have to do things in our lives that we don't necessarily want to do.* Everyone has to compromise, whether on the spectrum or not. It's part of our personal and professional relationships. That means that probably on a daily basis we're all going to have to do things we don't really enjoy, or sometimes even like, as part of that compromise. If you're a brilliant math whiz in a first year teaching position, you may not enjoy grading all those papers, but you do it until you become better known in the university and get a teaching assistant. If your social skills are preventing you from getting that computer programming job you know you can do, and you start out as a file clerk in the company mailroom instead, you can be angry and act inappropriately and get fired from that job, or you can do the tasks you feel you're much too smart to do, and at the same time learn to better control your emotions and prove that you can handle more responsibility. If you do this, you may just get that promotion to the position you want.

We each are responsible for our own behaviors and the consequences they elicit—good or bad. That's why it is so important for parents to hold young child accountable for their behaviors and to implement good, sound parenting strategies at home with their children. It's never too soon to be teaching children with ASD the boundaries of acceptable and non-acceptable behavior, and more importantly, that behaviors have consequences. Of course, this is said with the understanding that parents are able to distinguish those behaviors arising from sensory overload or other autism-related challenges, such as anxiety or social misunderstandings, and deal with them through intervention and not as a behavior challenge.

2017 REFLECTIONS FROM TEMPLE

Be Careful Online

Since this book was first published, the use of social media has exploded. One bad feature of social media is that people sometimes write nasty things to each other. A good rule to keep in mind when you see such comments is not to respond to them. When people write rude stuff to me, I block the sender and delete the post. It is best not to respond.

Another thing you must remember is that social media is not private. Nothing online is private!

If the thing you want to write is not fit for your grandmother to read, do not write it or send it.

The following activities are not private, regardless of the situation:

1. Instant messages on your phone
2. Emails
3. Facebook or any other social media
4. Voice mail
5. File sharing sites
6. Multi-player games

All communications can be tracked. That is why you must never threaten or say anything that could be misinterpreted as criminal behavior online.

Everything you do online is preserved in the cloud, and it can be tracked back to your phone or computer. A site may tell you that your photos disappear, but they always remain in the cloud.

I am not trying to scare you or prevent you from using online communication. Just remember that everything is a public forum.

You also must be careful to avoid accidentally getting involved with activities online that could get you sent to jail. Teenagers often get interested in sex, but you must not do anything involving sex online. Dating sites must be approached with great caution. Some are well regulated and relatively safe, and others are dangerous territory. You need to talk to people you can trust—BEFORE doing anything like this online.

When in doubt, it is often best to pick up the phone and talk to somebody instead.

Sean Says:

During the explosion of trashy talk shows in the 1990s, there was never a moment that I didn't despise all of them. I didn't have to watch these shows to know that they were detestable any more than I needed to get hit by a car to realize such an experience would be painful or lethal. Aside from hating the fact that they encouraged an assortment of trashy people to display an array of antics such as chair throwing, verbal spewing and terrible manners, I resented Rikki Lake, Jerry Springer, Maury Povich and (fill in the blank) because of the not-so-subtle message they not only drove home, but glorified: that it's hip, cool and glamorous to blame someone else for whatever goes wrong in your life. I'm convinced that many of these programs are in part responsible for creating the litigious society that has flourished in recent years.

What lies at the heart of my animosity is that each of the talk shows undercut or completely went against the grain of an important unwritten rule of social relationships that I learned—made all the more difficult because of my struggles with autism. The lesson was a simple one, at least in concept: *Each person is ultimately responsible for his or her own behavior, happiness and well-being. When something goes awry in our lives, it's generally up to us to fix it, not someone else.*

That's certainly not to say that people don't cause problems for each other or that there shouldn't be ways to redress wrongs. If I'm sitting at a red light and another driver slams into the back of my vehicle, I should have every right to collect and, if injured, have my medical bills paid. If I buy a product later determined to be faulty, then the manufacturer should be responsible for what went wrong, and I should be compensated in some way.

But these and similar occurrences are the exceptions in life, not the rule. Most people's unhappiness is not solely the result of forces beyond their control; much of it, I've learned, comes from how we handle what's dealt us. In other words, another unwritten rule subtlety imbedded within the first is this: that *attitude goes a long way toward determining one's satisfaction and happiness.*

This lesson certainly didn't come to me automatically, though. It took me many years to see that I, and I alone, am responsible for my behavior as well as my feelings and how I choose to express them.

Many otherwise pleasant social situations for me were ruined, especially when I was in my twenties, because I was fighting against autism and didn't yet understand how my negative moods affected those around me and colored my interactions with people. I spent a lot of time during those years looking inward and trying to figure out how to fit in and make sense of what I had missed growing up. Accompanying my growing awareness was enormous self-rage, which resulted from seeing firsthand what I had missed, knowing I had a lot of catching up to do, and realizing what my behavior did to other people. All of this made me feel quite defective. And it surely impacted my mood much of the time, clouding my ability to see another one of those unwritten social rules: *no one wants to be around a person who is angry, morose or depressed much of the time.*

My dark moods, which were nearly always the result of being angry with myself, also made it much harder to learn to be in the moment, socially. Compounding this situation was the fact that these were feelings directed toward myself, not anyone else. Therefore, I rationalized, why should the other person have any reaction—except sympathy or understanding—to how I was feeling? I believed that my moods didn't negatively affect other people unless I was angry with someone.

It took very little to trigger one of these moods. I got furious with myself if I mispronounced a word, for example, and the mood persisted like a dark cloud hanging over me. And within social relationships this unwritten rule applies: *unresolved negative emotions only get stronger as time goes by.* I couldn't push the anger aside and get out from under; it wasn't uncommon for the feelings to last for hours. If during those hours I was in a given social situation, I would spend the time replaying over and over whatever I was upset about instead of savoring the moment and shaking off the mood. All that did was solidify the anger by reinforcing that I was stupid, etc., and all the people in my company knew was that I was unpleasant to be around.

What kept the vicious pattern going was misreading what I was seeing in such instances. If I caught wind that someone didn't want to be in my presence, I interpreted their reaction as disinterest in how I felt. If they truly cared, I incorrectly reasoned, they would try to help me feel better. As I have come to learn, however, that's not the way it works, as this example illustrates.

One day after school I walked to the recording studio where my mom and dad worked. I was in a bad mood from having done poorly on a test earlier that day and I brought the mood to the studio with me.

I entered and saw my mom talking to two people, both of whom were co-workers and family friends. I made eye contact with the three, but kept walking toward the back of the building and breezing by all of them without acknowledging anyone. A few minutes later, my mom caught up with me.

"Sean, you didn't say hello to Marcia," she quietly said.

All her logical reaction to my antisocial behavior did was serve to further infuriate me. With that simple statement, she violated one of my cardinal rules of that time, which was that I was never to be corrected.

I was breaking free of my autism and wanted to be in total control of myself. With that, I angrily shot back, "I should know that by now!" referring to the basic social graces.

Shortly afterward, we all went out to dinner. By now my mood was worse because not only was I still angry about the test, I was upset that I had acted impolitely and then been corrected as soon as I walked through the door. I sat at the restaurant stone-faced and turned away when someone addressed me, and spoke to no one throughout the meal. I was especially incensed with Marcia, whom I blamed for making the situation at the studio possible.

Yet undulating underneath was a very strong undercurrent at cross purposes with what everyone in my company was seeing. I was crying out for their attention. I desperately wanted people to pay positive attention to me and I expected Marcia to ask me what was wrong to confirm that she cared about me. I got satisfaction from people asking me about my feelings and I felt it was *their* responsibility to pay attention to me until I was out of my negative mood. And I spent the entire meal waiting for her to ask. Instead, the food came but the question didn't.

However, when people did ask me what was wrong, what was bothering me, etc., I almost never responded to them. An old adage is a relevant social rule here: *Three strikes and you're out!* Most people will give you the benefit of the doubt a few times, and after that, if you don't take responsibility for either changing your behavior or repairing the situation, they lose interest in further social interaction with you. Or they make negative assumptions about your abilities: "He's lazy." "He won't try." "He's too stupid to know better." So it was here. My silence caused them to quit asking, which in turn, confirmed to me that they didn't care anyway. It seemed nothing could break this twisted scenario. I had no way out largely because I had a total inability to read people's signals or make sense of their actions, let alone their reactions to me. Scenes like this played out repeatedly during my late teens and through my twenties. They alone could fill a book.

How did I react to these scenarios as they played out over and over? I went to the other extreme by trying to bury the feelings and completely deny them. I pretended everything was wonderful, and this was reflected by an "artificial look on my face," as my mom calls it, and a slight elevation of my tone of voice. By pretending all was well when it wasn't, I was only making those who were trying to help me more frustrated, which in turn had the effect of increasing my anger. Not a good solution, in my estimation.

My parents tried for years to get me to see the value in admitting to however I felt—taking responsibility for my feelings and behaviors— and moving on. What prevented me from admitting to my true feelings was the conviction that doing so would bring everything to the surface and cause me to be overwhelmed by it all.

I realize now, however, the value in what my mother was trying to teach me, and, indeed, that it echoes an unwritten rule at work within relationships: *People are more accepting of your shortcomings if you are honest about them. Dishonesty will generally make a situation worse, not better.* In all the times I have been honest about my feelings and admitted something unpleasant, the situation has been easier to deal with, and ended up more positive. I have always felt better and have been able to move on. This has been true whether I'm with parents, friends, dates or any other social contacts. Coughing up unpleasant feelings has many benefits. They include:

- Allowing yourself to be open to another point of view or perspective you probably hadn't thought of. Being consumed with anger or unhealthy ways to handle it prevents such openness and clear thinking.
- Seeing that it's okay to feel upset, hurt, angry, etc., and that it's how you express them that ultimately matters.

- Getting closer to taking constructive responsibility for changing whatever is at the root of the problem, if possible.
- Moving past the situation a lot faster.
- Often, seeing that what seemed so huge was really quite small or insignificant.

Here, I'm not talking about situational anger that naturally results, for example, if someone steals from you, or about clinical depression.

But for the most part, how you handle emotions goes a long way toward determining if you're attracting or alienating those around you. It's a lesson I had to learn the hard and painful way.

2017 REFLECTIONS FROM SEAN

"The world can use … more solvers and fewer blamers; more folks showing a better way and fewer folks complaining about how much better things used to be; more folks offering help and fewer folks wringing their hands about the problems; more hope bringers and fewer hope killers."

I think this quote by Steve Goodier, an ordained minister and author of several books on personal and spiritual growth, offers powerful insight into and a good remedy for what I see going on in our society as the blame game on steroids. So many people—from the unhappy business executive who was passed over for a promotion to our next commander-in-chief—would rather blame others for their troubles (real or perceived), poor decisions, inadequacies and lack of fulfillment than look inward to see what can be fixed or adjusted to make their lives better. As most of us know, it's far easier and more convenient to blame someone or something else than to take stock of oneself and make a commitment to make inner repairs. This tragic reality flies squarely in the face of what my parents drummed into my head and that I try daily to live by—that we are responsible for our own behaviors, choices and happiness.

Exacerbating today's "happiness and personal-responsibility crisis," as I call it, is the Internet. It offers a platform for people who feel marginalized and disenfranchised to express their anger without requiring them to spend time figuring out how they can be proactive in remedying their problems. Someone who lost a job can easily go online to tell anyone who will listen that the job loss was the fault of undocumented workers who come to our country to "steal our jobs." And the blame game impedes those engaged in that irrational, narcissistic pattern from taking proactive steps to ameliorate the problem. To a large degree, this circular, self-reinforcing, toxic stew is anathema to healthy personal and business relationships. And it has poisoned our political system.

A 2012 article in *Psychology Today* describes four false beliefs that feed the blame game: someone else must be at fault for whatever goes wrong, others' malfeasance makes them less worthy of respect, it is permissible and justified to treat those others with contempt and disdain, and the person at least partially responsible for a situation is absolved of any culpability. Sadly, all of these are playing out regularly today in all walks of political life, and they are antithetical to what we should be teaching our children about self-accountability, regardless of whether they're on the autism spectrum.

Other ways in which engaging in this problem-solving choice is so destructive is that it blocks openness with others, creates added resentment and tension and never results in constructive change or additional personal happiness. As the PT article further points out, "[The blame game] has been responsible for mass casualties of war, regrettable acts of road rage and, on a broad, interpersonal level (social, familial and work-related), a considerable amount of human frustration and unhappiness."

When it comes to engaging in this self-destructive, zero-sum game, those on the autism spectrum aren't immune, though the dynamics are quite different. According to a recent study by neuroscientists with the Massachusetts Institute of Technology, many high-functioning adults with autism have difficulty applying theory of mind (the ability to attribute mental states to oneself and others with the understanding that other people have beliefs, ideas and perspectives that differ from one's own) "to make moral judgments in certain situations." The study also notes that adults on the spectrum are more likely than their neurotypical counterparts to blame someone for unintentionally harming another.

"This shows that their judgments rely more on the outcome of the incident than on an understanding of the person's intentions," says Liane Young, one of the study's authors.

I can relate to this study's main premise, because it largely describes some of what was going on with me mentally when I was a child and young adult. But despite this huge gap in my understanding of others' actions and motives, my parents continually tried to get me to see that I was still responsible for my own.

In the end, it doesn't matter how much more advanced technology becomes, how frequently the forty-fifth president threatens to sue others who anger and criticize him, how often those who commit domestic violence blame their spouses for the abusers' behavior or the degree of belligerence students who didn't study and failed a test express toward their instructors. The bottom line is the same: We are responsible for our decisions, actions, reactions, behavior and overall happiness. It's a life lesson I learned long ago—one that I remain convinced will make our lives and society stronger and better.

It is adults who create the environments that teach children the early lessons of personal responsibility for their actions. Throughout this book we've urged parents and teachers to use clear, concrete behavior principles with children, to link behavior with consequences, and to be diligent in teaching children appropriate behaviors, rather than calling attention to what they do wrong without teaching a replacement behavior. Laying the groundwork while the child is still very young instills behavior patterns that will help the child as he grows up.

Temple Shares:

I don't think Mother intellectually recognized how good of a "behavior specialist" she was with me as I was growing up. Lots of the things she naturally did are now recognized as integral components of a positive behavioral support plan—if you want to use more technical terms. So while she made it clear that I was responsible for acting in appropriate ways in different situations, she was equally adept at understanding that sensory issues were a major factor and some tantrums were caused by too much overstimulation. She knew noise was a real problem for me and if I was in sensory overload, she'd remove me from a situation, no questions asked, no further expectations that I behave. For instance, if I started acting out while we were at the circus, Mother knew it was time to go home; I was in overload. However, if I was testing boundaries or acting out for other reasons, as all kids do, she just wouldn't let me get away with it.

She maintained high expectations of me, too, which in the long run fostered development and progress in many different ways. Mother wanted to keep me out of an institution and the way she could do that was to make sure I acted appropriately. It was like having intensive ABA therapy when I was young, without knowing she was doing that. Lots of repetitions and teaching using many different examples, lots of trials; really clear, consistent application of rewards and consequences. So I learned to get through church on Sunday, and to act appropriately at the formal Sunday dinners at Aunt Bella's and Granny's. But I was allowed to do certain little things after dinner that helped me stay in control. There was a big long hall in Aunt Bella's apartment with a large mirror at one end. After the formal lunch I was allowed to run up and down the hall so I could watch myself get big in the mirror. As long as I kept my running confined to the hallway, I could run up and down that hall all I wanted. That's what helped me keep self-control: having outlets like that to express my behaviors in ways that were accepted and okay.

Physical exercise is a great stress reliever that parents and teachers pay too little attention to nowadays. They use computer time or playing with toys too much as reinforcement, when getting kids up and running around might help them more in the long run to self-regulate. When we visited Granny's apartment I was allowed to run up the stairs once and do what I called "beat the elevator." It was a slow elevator and I could run up five flights of fire stairs faster than the elevator. When we went to Granny's I was allowed to do it once when we first arrived, and I was allowed to do it once upon leaving. This was motivating to me to keep my behavior in control while we were at Granny's apartment, but it was also a very physical energy release.

Children grow into teenagers and teens into young adults. As parents lose the ability to motivate their child's behavior through discipline, young adults struggle to control their own behavior, good and bad. As Sean has so frequently described, his feelings of low self-esteem and worthlessness rendered him responsible for every social mistake he made and the anger and resentment that arose internally. Anger becomes a pervasive, powerful fire fueled by the illogical thoughts, unrealistic expectations and confused emotions of many adolescents and adults on the spectrum. For Sean, anger was often a roadblock of such enormous proportions that it brought him to a standstill, unable to figure out how to maneuver around it. For Temple, it became an obstacle that merited analysis and solution, which she accomplished.

Temple Shares:

I think one of the reasons more adults with ASD "act out" in today's world is that they are angry that the world is so difficult to manage. Their anger can be self-directed, which often results in depression and withdrawal from society. In other cases, the anger may be directed toward others through a stubborn refusal to conform to society's rules and/or by blaming parents, teachers, or society as a whole for their unaccepting attitudes toward people who are different.

People involved in social interactions all recognize the unwritten rule: *anger can be a very destructive emotion in all facets of social relationships.* It is probably the one emotion that Aspies have the most trouble controlling. I had an anger problem growing up, but my intense interest in certain things motivated me to learn to control it—otherwise I lost privileges that fueled those interests. Other people provided behavior management that helped me learn, albeit in a rote manner, to control my anger when I was young and through my school years. Sometimes it worked; other times it didn't, as evidenced by my being expelled for throwing a book at another girl during one of my angry outbursts.

As I moved into young adulthood my ability to think in flexible ways and perceive the thoughts of others helped me realize that unless I learned to maneuver around my anger, I could kiss my career goodbye. Anger is simply not tolerated in the workforce. If you have a big blow up with a boss or coworker or during a meeting with a client, that's the end of your job. The same is true in situations with law enforcement. Going off on the policeman who has stopped you along the highway can land you in jail.

I switched from anger to crying in order to control my emotions on the job; it was my solution to the problem. I did a lot of crying back in those days out in secluded spots of the stockyards because my anger often got ignited. Girls can do this, but guys have a harder time learning to control their anger, as crying isn't an option for them. Anger is a real issue in today's world, not just with Aspies. I recently learned that one of the major computer tech companies is hiring their programmers out of the military. These people come to the job with a solid work ethic, they understand chain of command, they have been taught to handle their anger. Lots of people are really intelligent, but it takes more than just book smarts to get and keep a good job. Anger management is high up on the list of desirable qualities in the professional job force. Plus, in social-emotional relationships it's equally important to be able to control your anger. No one wants to feel fearful of another person's emotional outbursts.

Adult Aspies can be very creative when it comes to finding ways to manage their anger. Many of them have devised very clever ways to diffuse their anger before it causes an emotional outburst. For some it's converting the anger to something humorous in their own minds. For others, it's learning coping techniques. Anger management seems to be such an important topic within the adult autism community that we interviewed a few peers about anger and anger management. Following are comments from people on the spectrum about ways they handle anger.

Temple on Anger Management:

People who drive gas-guzzling SUVs really get me angry. I might put signs under their windshield wiper that said, "GAS HOG! OINK! OINK!" Or, I might put a pig nose on their car as a hood ornament, and then make a custom license plate holder that I could slip over the existing plate. The top part of the frame would say "OINK! OINK! I'm a gas hog," and on the bottom of the frame there would be a pig's tail. And on the back of the license plate I'd have the name and phone number of an environmental group and statistics on oil and energy conservation. That would convert my anger to humor; even just thinking through the scenario would help. But I'd never damage their car; that's off limits in my set of principles and morals.

Other ways I manage my anger are listed below:

- Antidepressant medication. It reduces anxiety and irritability that can make anger harder to control. I take an old-fashioned antidepressant, Norpramin (desipramine). Many other people find that Prozac helps them control anger. Use low doses.
- Switch emotions; from anger to humor or anger to crying (in a private place). This is how I stopped getting into fist fights when other teenagers teased me in high school. When I get frustrated with a computer, a cell phone or other device, I cry instead of throwing it against the wall. I absolutely have to switch emotions because I find it very difficult to modulate the intensity of my emotions. Once, when a project failed, I cried for two days.
- I do *not* have pent-up rage inside me that simmers and boils. I had to just "turn off" anger because it is so difficult to control. That's why the emotion substitution was so critical. I experienced fear as a nonstop emotion until I took the antidepressant. The medication greatly reduced that feeling.

- Regular vigorous exercise helps me sleep and remain calm.
- I avoid situations where a person may try to deliberately make me angry. I avoid emotional conflict with other people as much as possible. If provoked, I walk away.
- If somebody writes me a nasty letter or email I have learned never to respond in anger. I calm down first and use logic and diplomacy. Treat an email as though the whole world will read it.
- If a client has made me angry I sometimes have a private "bitch session" either by myself or with a good friend and think up the most inventive combination of swear words to describe the person. I finally end up laughing.
- On the job I remember to always be "project loyal." My job is to complete a project I have designed and make it work. I had two big projects where the client was a control freak and he kicked me off the project before it was finished. I continued to manage the project by having secret phone calls and meetings with the client's employees. I must admit that it was a thrill that I was clever enough to work around that guy. In the engineering world, there are "techies" and there are "stupid suits," meaning management type people. The techie motto is that the project is the coolest thing in the world and making it work makes us happy.
- The most important part of anger management for me personally is having lots of interesting things to do with interesting people. Self-esteem for me is gained through doing projects and other activities that make real improvements. I am happy when a project works or when I am able to implement programs that make the world a better place.

ROBERT S. SANDERS, JR. ON ANGER MANAGEMENT:

As far as my AS making me angrier than most people, I would say that it doesn't, that I have known clinically normal people to get much angrier about things than I do. Most of us learn to control anger, especially at critical times. For example, if a cop pulls you over and yells at you or abuses you, it's wiser to hold back the anger that you would love to unleash onto him at full force, to avoid being hauled off to jail! Holding back anger in that type of situation is very difficult, but necessary. There are other times (safer times) when I have expressed my anger or dissatisfaction at something, even to the point of making scenes—for example, expressing dissatisfaction at someone smoking in a public place where the rest of us are trying to breathe.

There have been times when I've expressed my anger in other, more creative ways. One time I wrote a letter on tin roofing to a woman who lived in a small town in Mexico, so she couldn't tear it up and throw it away. She had falsely accused me of stealing, and was making my life miserable with the authorities, and wouldn't even let me talk to her to clear up the situation. I also thought to anonymously call her from a payphone several times from out of state and play ELO's "Evil Woman" each time! Plus, for the damage she did to me with her defamation, I created some bogus flyers depicting her and her husband running a prostitute business! If one day she does me really serious harm, I am poised to scatter those flyers all over that town, and flee fast! Russia and the United States have their nuclear weapons. I have my flyers.

What this goes to show is that ASD people sometimes hurt back and in very clever ways. Yes, there have been times when I have been "stuck" in negative thinking patterns about certain other people who have wronged me, and sometimes I have remained angry at them. Those are what are known as grudges, and some people hold onto grudges for lifetimes. I don't hold grudges nearly as much as I used to, thanks to utilizing various ways of laughing off the anger and resentment toward those who have wronged me. For example, one clever anger management tool I have utilized is creating bogus course outlines with certain themes or a major course of study for a four-year curriculum in university, complete with appropriate course numbers, credit hours, labs and related seminars. For instance, I've created courses such as:

- Speech I: Long Talk Techniques
- Speech II: Knowing it ALL
- Speech III: Hearing Oneself Talk

- Arrogance I: Ignoring Others
- Arrogance II: Insulting Feelings
- Arrogance III: Belittling Others
- Arrogance IV: Snippy Answers
- Seminar: Put-Down Remarks

- Science of the Back I: Indifference
- Science of the Back II: Arrogance
- Science of the Back III: Egotism
- Science Labs: Scoffing Techniques

These course syllabuses are great release vehicles as I create them; I find myself laughing at each clever bogus course name that I conjure up!

There are many anger management tools, as the above examples point out. I don't feel that AS individuals always have to conform to the norms of social rules of conduct, but at the same time, it's not useful to any of us to carry our anger too far.

Robert Sanders, Jr. is a person with ASD, single, and in his late thirties. He has a degree in Electrical Engineering, lives in middle Tennessee, and makes his living as a writer of science fiction books and a nature photographer. As a young child, his most prevalent autism characteristics were repetitive play, sensory sensitivities, being fixated on certain toys, and a lack of communication and developmental social skills until age seven or eight.

Today Robert likes to travel and spends his winters living in Mexico. He is fluent in Spanish. He enjoys exploring, hiking, camping and bicycling. Aside from his many sci-fi novels, he is the author of two autism books: Overcoming Asperger's: Personal Experience & Insight *and* On My Own Terms: My Journey with Asperger's, *the latter of which he also translated into Spanish (*En Mis Propios Terminos: Mi Jornada con Asperger's*).*

JENNIFER M^cILWEE MYERS ON ANGER MANAGEMENT:

The main way I have been able to deal with anger is through a cognitive-behavioral approach and by studying human behavior. This way I have been able to learn not to trust my anger—that is, I have learned that rage is a false-faced emotion which usually does not accurately reflect reality. By working very hard on learning that rage is a false and *nonfunctional* emotion, I've learned 1) not to express it so often (walking away from situations when possible, or promising myself a chance to yell and stomp later, when I'm alone) and 2) not to blame others for my rage. Even legitimately bad behavior on others' part does not justify rage behaviors, therefore I make my apologies and reparations without referring to the behavior of the other person(s).

If there are real issues in the relationship or situation, I deal with those completely separately from the reparations process. This prevents getting into the cycle of an apology turning into another rage.

By the way: I know that it is quasi-acceptable for women to cry when they are angry, but I *hate* to cry in public, so I will avoid it unless I cannot prevent it. Because of this, I have developed both preventative and on-the-spot techniques for coping with anger, some of which follow:

Preventative Measures

- Anyone who, like me, has had both a long-term anger problem and long-term problems with depression, anxiety, and panic attacks has *got to* look into getting an appropriate dosage of an antidepressant. The one I use, Imipramine (Tofranil), has the added advantage of fixing my insomnia (I get real sleepy right after I take it).
- Things that severely stress the body make me more likely to get angry. Eating nutritious food, limiting junk food, and keeping hydrated all help me stay on an even keel and less likely to erupt.
- Also, if I know I'm under a lot of physical stress of this kind, I avoid or postpone confrontations where possible. If I get an email from someone who annoys me when I'm going on not-enough sleep, I try to put it aside and don't answer it until the next day (if possible).
- I also find that regular vigorous exercise greatly reduces the chance of me blowing up.

On-the-Spot Techniques

- It has taken a long time, but I'm getting moderately good at self-awareness. Because of this, I can often tell when I am starting to build up anger. At that point, if possible, I will try to absent myself from the situation to take a brisk walk.
- If I have to stay where I am, I try to reduce how much I speak. The more I talk, the more likely I am to say something I'll regret.
- I can't promise myself I won't blow up at all, so I make little deals with myself. I tell myself that I will not blow for the next two minutes. Then I try to do another two minutes, and so forth. I can often handle small increments of time.
- I try to breathe deeply and slowly. If I'm in a situation where I can take really deep breaths without calling attention to myself, I do so.
- Having a Harry Potter or Disneyland item in my pocket that I can

touch can help me calm down. I wear an official but fairly subtle Harry Potter watch so I can glance at it as needed.

- After dealing with someone who makes me angry, or when I'm in a rage at the world in general, I will write down all of the things I think I should do about it and the particulars of who is *wrong* about things. I then put these notes away for consideration after a good night's sleep. This way I know I will still remember all of the "brilliant" thoughts associated with my anger and will be able to make use of them later. When it is later, I usually realize that all of my ideas were pretty unrealistic and overwrought.
- Repeatedly writing down my thoughts while I'm angry and reviewing them when I'm no longer angry has taught me that when I'm really angry, I come up with really stupid ideas. This helps me deal with my anger, as I no longer am able to retain the adolescent view that my anger is righteous and good.

It is vital for people with AS (or at least for me with AS) to remember that anger is not your friend. I have "talked" online with several Aspies who told me they have a "right" to be angry at the world. The problem with that is that hanging on to your right to be angry hurts you and doesn't benefit you in any way to make up for the hurt. Despite what you may think, the unwritten rule in social relationships stands: *Anger hurts the angry person, not the person you're angry at.*

Also, *no one* ever changed their mind because someone yelled at them. Arguing and yelling are the worst ways to change someone's mind. It never works. If you rage at someone, they won't be stricken with remorse for how wrong they are; they just will think you are a jerk.

If you allow your rage to rule you, you will become your own enemy. Not only that, but you will be stooping to the level of the people you dislike most. Lashing out at people in a rage is just as mean and nasty as any of the unfair things people have done to you.

It is also very important to understand the "fundamental attribution error." This is the tendency of all humans to overestimate how much people's behavior comes from their basic personality and to underestimate how much of people's behavior comes from situational influences.

For example, if I accidentally cut someone off and they flip me the bird, I think, "Wow, that guy is a total jerk!" If I get cut off, I think "Wow, that guy is a total jerk!" The reality is that bad driving may come out of being in a hurry or missing something in one's blind spot, and is not personal in nature. Whether someone drives well in all situations does not tell us anything about who they are as a person, but we almost always assume it does. We "know" that the guy who cut us off is a jerk, but he may just be in a frantic hurry because he needs to get to the next rest stop.

If people make mistakes or don't know the "best" way to do something, it is not necessarily because they are stupid. They may not see the situation the way you do. They may have either more or less information about a situation than you do. In other words, their mistakes may well have a lot more to do with the situation (what information they have gotten) than to who they are inside (probably not just a stupid jerk, although some of those definitely exist).

In other words, just because someone is making you angry doesn't mean they are a bad person or stupid. Just because someone is making you angry doesn't mean that they richly deserve to feel the full force of your righteous anger. Err on the side of caution whenever possible in these situations. Studying human behavior helps me to accept the fact that humans are, well, human.

Letting anger and self-righteousness dictate your life sucks. Many people with AS do not seem to understand this. It has to be explained very carefully and in a gentle, non-accusatory way. Sometimes even the best explanations don't help. For me there came a point at which I had to decide which I loved more: my self-righteousness or my happiness. You can't have both.

Over the years, I've also come to the conclusion that you can't blame people for not understanding Aspies any more than you can blame a dog for sticking it's nose into your crotch area. A whole lot of them just don't know any better.

Jennifer McIlwee Myers was diagnosed with AS at the age of thirty-six in 2002. As a child, she couldn't figure out how to play with other children, but was fascinated by reference books, Fred Astaire, and the Algonquin Round Table.

Jennifer is a writer/speaker with a BS in Computer Science who can write a software manual faster than anybody. Her hobbies include Disneyland Pin Trading (Haunted Mansion), pre-1970 horror movies, Harry Potter, and rearranging her books.

Jennifer has been married to Gary Myers for eleven years. They met at a science fiction/fantasy book discussion group, where he wowed her with his encyclopedic knowledge of horror films and early 20th century fantasy literature.

Jennifer works from home so she can control her sensory environment and work odd hours; this allows her to work around her chronic insomnia.

KATHY GRANT ON ANGER MANAGEMENT:

As a person with High Functioning Autism who is forty years old, I tend to handle anger in two different ways, depending on the setting. I get very physical and violent when I get angry at myself in the privacy of my home. The safety and anonymity of being at home gives me permission to let my anger loose. I get the angriest at home when I lose things I need. I know all the dates in Russian history, but I can't remember where I put my glasses, keys, or bus pass. Late last year, I lost my bus pass and credit card for a whole week. I became so angry with myself that I broke the phone by pounding it on the desk over and over for a couple days. In 2001, I kicked a hole in the wall because I was mad that I was going to be late for an appointment; I hate being late for anything! The hole is still there below the window. After these incidents, I usually feel bad and exhausted, but then I am not angry any more.

In social settings where I am just as angry, I am, however, not as violent. I grew up in fear of my father's anger, and I don't want people to be afraid of me. So when I am in front of people, I control myself more. When I'm angry in a social setting, I sometimes do yell and scream, but I do not become physically violent. If I yell and scream in public, it is usually not directed at a particular person; if it is a person I know, of course I will apologize profusely after I calm down. I know there are times when I can't yell and scream, and in those instances I usually just give a nice Klingon growl to myself, or I just stuff it.

A few years ago, I experienced anger with my advocate over the issue of me not taking my meds. I felt like I was being bossed around and I was angry. I didn't do anything but yell because I didn't want to lose the relationship with her, so my anger turned passive-aggressive. After I become passive-aggressive, my anger can be manifested in funny ways. In this instance, I would withhold information from her, but still expect her to help me with things, even if she didn't have enough information to go on. The only person I hurt with that reaction was myself.

How I handle my anger tends to be dictated by the situation and how safe I feel in controlling it or letting it loose.

Kathy Grant is an active, independent forty-year-old woman with autism living in Denver, CO. Although she learned about her autism at age twenty-one, she wasn't formally diagnosed until age thirty-six.

Growing up, Kathy had strong fixations on all sorts of topics, ranging from numbers (she knew her times tables up to 12 x 12 by second grade) to foreign countries. Even today, she retains an avid interest in Russia. Kathy also deals with sensory issues: she has auditory processing difficulties (she can partially read lips to compensate), and has no depth perception, which is why she doesn't drive a car.

For the past four years Kathy has worked part-time as a respite provider through Catholic Charities for a family who has a young adult with autism. She is also an active volunteer in her community and her church. She was married and is now divorced, and travels abroad as much as possible. Her hobbies include collecting flags, icons (religious pictures), her two cats; she is an avid Battlestar Galactica fan.

JERRY NEWPORT ON ANGER MANAGEMENT:

ASD folks are no strangers to anger. They have lots of reasons to grow up into angry teens and angrier young adults. Put yourself in their place. Imagine yourself being teased, constantly misunderstood, abused in the name of therapy and often genuinely confused and overwhelmed by it all—not just a few times, but hundreds, if not thousands of times. It is no wonder that I know many adults with ASD who are literally paralyzed by their anger.

A life is a terrible thing to waste. I know very talented people on the spectrum whose adult life consists of the Internet, broken up only by occasional trips to cash the latest public assistance check. Their lives could be so much more. It saddens me that they are so angry at the world and themselves that they have shut their life down in this way.

ASD doesn't give people a license to act in physically or emotionally destructive ways or opt out of the "work" we all need to do on ourselves. ASD makes the road a tougher one to travel, for sure, but it isn't an out to having to explore inner feelings and come to terms with the place autism has in your life. The autism isn't always to blame: If you took away the autism, you might still be an angry person! Autism is only part of who you are. We can get angry, but we have to know there are consequences.

If I have to become the "Dr. Phil" of ASD to make this point, I can think of no higher calling.

Accountability, I believe, is one of the best things to teach our people. It may mean a different consequence is applied than that given to someone without the challenge of ASD, but there must be a consequence when we do something unacceptable. If someone feels, as too many of my Internet peers do, that his condition justifies any behavior, the concept of consequence and civility goes out the window.

Of course, I also believe that supportive services are a key to helping our community deal with anger issues. There are many reasons and ways to be angry; some are constructive, while a whole lot of those better known are destructive. Anger management education is taught by probation departments to people who get into trouble—we shouldn't have to land in jail to get help.

We can provide our own support. I have started and seen many peer support groups. They are more effective than Internet groups in which people are detached from their group mates. It is a lot harder to use "I have ASD" as an excuse for angry behavior in an actual room full of people who can all say the same thing! I remember my first group when it had to vote a member out who repeatedly did threatening things. At a steering committee meeting, one of my peers shrugged his shoulders and said, "You know, even we have standards."

There are some excellent resources to learn how to work with our anger, to understand what causes it and how to manage it. Tony Attwood, a friend and fellow writer, is a proponent of Cognitive Behavior Therapy (CBT). Cognitive-behavioral therapists teach that it is our thinking that causes us to feel and act the way we do. If we are experiencing unwanted feelings and behaviors, it is important to identify the thinking that is causing the feelings/behaviors and learn how to replace this thinking with thoughts that lead to more desirable reactions. CBT helps you control feelings instead of being controlled by them. Some of my support group peers swear by this approach. Tony also has other resources available to help with anger at his website, www.tonyattwood.com.au. For more in-depth information about CBT, visit the website of the National Association of Cognitive Behavioral Therapies, www.nacbt.org.

On a personal level, my anger still gets me in trouble. Despite a lot of work I've done in this area, I still have to keep "aware" of my anger and work through it. I've done a lot of thinking about why I get angry in the first place. How much of my anger issues comes from old stuff that can't be changed and therefore should be let go of, or accepted? How much anger is the result of unrealistic goals or unrealistic expectations I have of others?

Another lesson I've learned is to not surrender so easily to the anger impulse. I call it the "three second rule." Many times I avoid stress now by not immediately responding to something that is momentarily unpleasant. Three seconds go by, I find myself still alive. Those three seconds give me space for a new thought to surface: maybe it isn't so bad as it first seemed.

Anger management is a hugely personal subject for my ASD peers. There are good resources available but each of us must take the first step to recognize that a problem exists. We must recognize anger, understand it and gain control of it so it doesn't control us. More than anything else, we need to accept responsibility for angry behavior and how it affects people around us. For many of my adult and teen peers, this is issue number one. It can and must be dealt with if they are to live to their best potential.

Jerry Newport, fifty-six, always knew there was something wrong with him. But as he was growing up, he didn't know what it was. "I was just Jerry," he says. "I was just odd, eccentric ... almost normal." He graduated from the University of Michigan, but spent the next twenty years drifting from job to job. He was a taxi driver, a messenger, a clerk, busboy and delivery man.

Jerry was diagnosed with Asperger's Syndrome at age forty-seven, after seeing the movie Rainman *and realizing he shared many of the character's odd traits. Once diagnosed, he went on to start a support group for adults with ASD.*

Today, Jerry is still affected by autistic challenges: a sensitivity to light, sounds, smell and touch, and difficulty making eye contact. He is an accomplished author and presenter on autism issues, and drives a cab in his hometown, Tucson, to 'pay the bills.' The motion picture, Mozart and the Whale, *is based on his life. Jerry's hobbies include caring for his menagerie of pets that includes more than ten birds and an iguana.*

What these passages on anger management all have in common is that these adults with AS have recognized their anger, taken responsibility for it, and problem-solved ways to diffuse it and understand why it happens. Temple shares further thoughts on emotional problem-solving as a necessary skill to resolve conflict in life, no matter what causes it.

Temple Says:

It wasn't until I was in my fifties that I was able to problem solve emotionally laden situations, by myself or with my adult friends. For me, problem solving is problem solving, whether it's about emotions or fixing a piece of equipment. I approach it in the same way, because of the way I think and process information. Problems involving emotions are a lot harder to figure out, however.

Let's say a friend is telling me about a problem he's having with another person. First, I ask for all the details: who said what, when, background information—data. Step one is gathering data about the situation. Then I look for patterns; in this case it might be behaviors or attitudes that keep cropping up in one or both persons. Next, is there any social-emotional research on the issue at hand, either in my own databank, or books or articles that might offer some help? Even with emotional issues, there's generally some factual knowledge about people's behaviors, or their intentions, or perspectives that can increase our understanding of our emotional responses. I'm sort of like Mr. Spock on *Star Trek*—analyze the emotions and responses to start with and then form a hypothesis about what's going on and then brainstorm possible solutions. What's interesting is that taking one step back from emotions and approaching a situation in a more analytic manner is often very, very helpful—even for people who are highly social.

Here's an example: I had a friend whose brother got killed and she was very upset over it. She didn't think she could handle how badly she felt. One of the things that helped her was my telling her that grieving takes at least six months before you start to feel better. That's what research shows. The average person in a situation like hers is upset for six months but then you start getting over it. It doesn't feel that bad forever. You need to grieve, though; there is some research that shows that giving drugs to prevent grieving is actually a bad thing to do. So we talked about this and it helped her to know that in time her pain would lessen. The brain responds to facts; that's the way it works. Cognitive behavior therapy, a process that noted Aspie Jerry Newport talks about often, and that AS expert Tony Attwood has a couple of books about, is proving very helpful to many adults with ASD. It links thinking to emotions, looking at the facts of the matter and using that information to see our perceptions and behaviors differently. That's how my mind works: always the social scientist.

Being responsible for your own behaviors means problem solving situations in order to determine what to say, when to say it, and how to act as each social situation unfolds. Each day I'm faced with situations that are easy or more difficult to figure out. While children do need to be taught specific social skills, the process of problem solving teaches the child about applying those skills in increasingly more refined ways, based on the context of the situation.

Absent the ability to problem solve, all the information on his hard drive is like a billion bits of independent data without any mechanism to access them in a logical manner. It's like the Internet without a search engine, without Google. Google provides a means to problem solve; it's a way to make sense of all the data, to relate it to the keyword search. That's an important skill for a child with ASD to learn; it's a tool he will use for the rest of his life.

Temple also points out that for many adolescents and adults on the autism spectrum, especially the higher functioning individuals, conventional and alternative therapies may be needed to help control highly destructive emotions, like anger and depression.

Temple Continues:

For some people on the autism spectrum, Rule #10—being responsible for your own behaviors—will be impossible without the addition of medication and/or alternative therapies. As I've alluded to in other parts of this book, people with ASD can live within a world of sensory sensitivities, severe anxiety and fear that impedes their ability to function in a socially appropriate manner. For some of these individuals, a special diet, such as GFCF (gluten-free, casein-free), can make remarkable changes in their ability to remain calm, and attend to the social clues in their environment. Auditory training for hearing sensitivities, Irlen lenses for visual problems, and different tactile therapies can help calm overactive senses or stimulate lethargy in people with ASD. Different environmental accommodations within the workplace can help, like asking for different lighting or requesting that the ring tones on telephone be changed. One of the unwritten rules of social interactions that

I've discovered applies here though: *in most instances, if you need help, you need to ask for help yourself.* Most people are genuinely interested in helping, but you need to do the asking to set the process in motion. If you wait for them to offer help, you'll just wait. It comes back to being personally responsible for your behaviors.

There is a segment of the autism population for whom anxiety problems are so severe that life revolves around trying not to have a panic attack, and also a segment for whom anger is ever knocking on the door of their emotional control. When all of your daily attention is focused on avoiding a panic attack or keeping your anger in check, or your depression is so severe that you can't even get out bed, it leaves little effort left for being social. You just can't attend to anything else; you don't care about attending to anything else. Often, biology rather than psychology is the culprit. That was me. My social skills got better and my ability to see the social interactions going on around me improved significantly when I started taking antidepressants to control my anxiety. Even my physical mannerisms (my handwringing, my hunched-over walking) calmed down, making me look more like I fit in, so people responded to me more positively. Two of the three Aspies who offered their insights on controlling anger mentioned taking medication.

Medication usage is a personal choice, and I don't advocate it as a first-line treatment option. I also don't recommend it being used for children. However, there are some teenagers and adults whose social life will improve greatly once their nerves get calmed down. For some, a special diet will be enough. For others, more is needed. Oftentimes the combination of special diet and medication is the turning point.

Finding the right medication and the right dosage is imperative, and should be only done under the supervision of a medical doctor. It often takes time to find the right combination. Take care that the teenager or adult is not being given too high a dosage, which is often the case when the physician is uneducated about ASD . He'll either start out with too high a dosage or up the dosage when he notices that a little bit is helping. For instance, too much Prozac often gets Aspies agitated again, and the doctor will then prescribe a tranquilizer or another drug instead of cutting back the dosage.

Noted Aspie writer and speaker Donna Williams discovered that diet, coupled with a tiny bit of medication, enabled her to tolerate big convention centers well enough to be able to speak before large groups. Without the diet and meds, she couldn't even go near a convention center. She took responsibility for her life and found a solution that works for her; that's really a wonderful thing.

Being responsible for your behaviors requires a holistic approach, whether it's a parent or teacher working with a child, or an adult trying to live and work independently. Any approach needs to take into consideration the person's mind, body and spirit, or basic personality, along with the environment in which the child lives, learns and plays. There are some high-functioning AS individuals who absolutely do not need medication. They're calm and their social learning needs can be taken care of through behavior modification approaches, cognitive therapy or other autism-related, social-emotional interventions. For others, anxiety and sensory issues are major considerations, and arise from a biological basis. Yet these needs often go unattended, or take a back seat, to behavior modification and academic approaches. Until the anxiety and sensory issues are taken care of, social understanding, self-control and academic success will be difficult, and sometimes impossible, goals to achieve.

POINTS TO KEEP IN MIND:

- Never underestimate the amount of stress individuals with ASD live under *constantly*. Sensory oversensitivity can make school or office environments highly stressful. The problems will vary greatly from individual to individual.

- Use positive behavior principles and good behavior modification techniques:

  - Adopt this mantra: All behavior is communication—what is the child trying to say?
  - Distinguish between "I can't do it" (lack of knowledge, skills) and "I won't do it" (I know how, but choose not to).
  - Remember: All behavior has a function to the child or adult.
  - Look first to the environment as a source of the inappropriate behavior. Is it sensory unfriendly?
  - Periodically do a reality check. Ask yourself: "Is this behavior I'm trying to teach really necessary?" "Is the obsession I'm trying to eliminate really that bad?" Sometimes parents and teachers want a behavior to stop because it bothers *them*, not the child or everyone else.
  - Accentuate the positive! Let the child know what he does right, too!

- Verbally and visually reinforce that the child/teenager/adult is responsible for controlling his behaviors. Some individuals are never told this!
- Children are very, very literal in their interpretation of language. Be careful when working on behavior that you don't confuse the child with your own verbal miscues. Asking a child to "tidy up" his room may not make any sense to him. Make sure to explain what "tidy up" means—then keep in mind that if you left anything out, the child won't be able to understand that! He'll do just what you tell him to do—he can't interpret that you really might have meant more than that.
- Is your social expectation for the child too high for his own personality? Not all individuals with ASD want to be the life of the party or the center of social interaction. Many like spending time by themselves and are happy and contented when doing so. Respect the individual and his choice for social interaction. Distinguish between the child

who is alone because he lacks the skills to interact, and the child who has the basic skills but prefers to spend more time alone. Don't be a pushy parent!

- Feelings change from day to day, sometimes minute to minute. This is no less true for people with ASD. Watch yourself if you're expecting them to display an unchanging level of emotional control. Neurotypical people give themselves the right to experience fluctuating emotions; make sure you are extending it also to the person with ASD.

- Teach emotional problem-solving alongside specific behaviors. Younger children need to be taught specific behaviors, but as the child ages, emotional problem solving will benefit him on a life-long basis. The value of Rule #10 is in the process, not the end product.

- Keep in mind the on-off nature of emotional expression in ASD individuals. Adults with AS can explode and then be done with the emotional expression. The fact that their behaviors may linger on in the minds of their NT counterparts is often lost on them. They may overlook the need for emotional repairs to be made in a relationship because the impact of the outburst is no longer part of their perceptual framework. Their response, "What's the big deal?" may make them seem uncaring or lacking in empathy, especially when coupled with their inability to pick up the nonverbal cues that a friend or co-worker's feelings are still tender.

- Their strong desire to "get it right" in social interaction produces an exorbitant amount of stress. Some children try so hard to keep themselves together at school that as soon as they come home, their behaviors erupt. Or they retreat into isolation in order to unwind from the day. Yet, often parents hold high expectations that they interact socially at home, or they enroll their kids in after-school social activities that further tax their limits. Be careful of thinking, "Well, he behaves so well at school, why can't he do that at home (at the gym/in the social skills group, etc.), too?" Planned breaks, a sensory safe place, or a less-active schedule may be needed for this type of child.

- Teach children and adults to monitor their self-talk, i.e. the things they say to themselves in social situations.
- Help them replace the more common negative self-talk with positive alternatives.
- Children and adults manifest their anger/anxiety/stress in two major ways: active outbursts or passive withdrawal. It's not just the explosive and emotionally demonstrative ASD person who needs our help. The silent, socially-avoidant, passive individual deserves it equally so, but is often overlooked.

TEMPLE'S EPILOGUE

I think lots of parents and professionals overlook the fact that I didn't always function the way I do now, even as a young adult. When it came to looking and acting like I fit in, some things about me were okay, but lots of things about me were still very weird. It's not like I had early intervention and then came out of my autism and could function, go to college, graduate and get a job. That's not how it all happened. All the unwritten social rules offered in this book, and others, were learned over time, using my logical, visually-based mind.

At age twenty-seven, when I worked at both the Arizona magazine and a construction company, I knew enough manners and basic social functioning skills to be able to fit into the work environment—barely. The boss who hired me was an odd guy himself, but he knew I was smart and he recognized talent; he hired me strictly based on my drawing ability. If I hadn't had those drawing skills, there's no way I would have been hired based on my other abilities. Once at the magazine, I started off writing articles for free and then they started paying me a little bit for pieces I wrote. I'd been there maybe two years when the magazine was sold, and the new boss thought I was really weird. The only way I saved my job was putting together a portfolio of what I'd written over the past two years and showing him. Otherwise, I would have lost that job, because I was weird. This was before I discovered antidepressants at age thirty-three that alleviated a lot of my visible autistic symptoms. I walked kind of hunched over. I would talk really loudly and in a mono-tone; people would tell me I sounded like I was always out of breath. I went about constantly rubbing my hands because of the pervasive state of anxiety I lived within all the time. I dressed like a slob and didn't have good hygiene. That's certainly not the picture of a person the typical world would say fits into society.

Learning to be part of the social world around me is an ongoing process; I keep learning and doing better all the time. It's going to be that way for most kids on the spectrum. There's not a magic turning point after which things will become natural and effortless—it's a process. Some adults seem to be searching for a "single something," a key that will open the door to the child's understanding of the world around him. That's not how it happens. Fitting into society in ways that foster positive social interactions is a series of doors, each with its own key. Flexible thinking opens lots of doors, as does being able to understand another person's perspective. They're master keys, but there's never going to a single key for all the doors. Then there's self-esteem and motivation; they're personal characteristics that keep the doors propped open so the learning and awareness can flow from one room into another. Otherwise, some of those doors you open just swing closed again. Teaching and learning goes on and on throughout life—it's the same for people with ASD as it is for neurotypicals. However, I do want to say that medication was one of the things that made success possible for me, because it stopped the debilitating panic attacks. Not everybody needs medication but I am one of those who do. For me, socialization is impossible if I constantly feel like I'm being attacked by a lion. Consider that your own child may be experiencing as much anxiety and fear as I did.

To me, "success in life" is defined by my job, my friends, my contribution to society, not by becoming emotionally related so that feelings become my prime motivator. I hope this book has opened many doors in your own mind about the very different thinking patterns that are characteristic of ASD.

SEAN'S EPILOGUE

When I was twelve, I was convinced I would grow up to be a criminal and spend most of my adult life in prison. One of my fixations was on Charles Manson and his murderous "family" because I felt that his fate would soon be mine, and I needed to compare myself to someone I perceived as worse off than I.

Thankfully, that prediction didn't come true.

My parents couldn't imagine what I would become—that one day I would be able to live independently, handle money, hold down a job, own and be responsible for a vehicle, live in and maintain my grandparents' family home and have successful relationships. In the early 1990s, my mother and I had our first book published, *There's a Boy in Here,* something that opened the door to many opportunities that would otherwise have been unavailable to me. Those included giving presentations to and meeting many terrific people, and using my experiences to help them in dealing with their children's autism and challenges. Another was seeing much of the world in my travels.

Seeing my life in print also allowed me to forgive myself for what I felt I had put my family through. The process gave me an objective perspective on my difficulties related to autism, a point of view that replaced blame, guilt, anger and other emotional baggage.

Now I get my greatest pleasure in doing things that require me to look outward. I have been a Big Brother with the Big Brothers/Big Sisters organization, a prison mentor and a volunteer at a local animal shelter. I currently work full-time at our local paper as a copy editor and reporter; I often have to interview people, which requires initiative on my part. To do both jobs well, I have to look at events from different angles and weigh them, and do the same with others' work—all skills that represent the opposite of what I was like with autism.

Fortunately, fear is no longer a negative force in my life. What drives me now are interests, goals and curiosity. I love to travel, meet people and be in a challenging job in which no two days are identical.

I've reconnected to my past in many ways. Thankfully, what's now missing from that connection is the pain.

REFERENCES

Antshel, K., Zhang-James, Y., Wagner, K., Ledesma, A., & Faraone, S. (2016). "An update on the comorbidity of ADHD and ASD: a focus on clinical management." *Expert Review Of Neurotherapeutics*, 16: 279-293. http://dx.doi.org/10.1586/14737175.2016.11 46591.

Aron, A., Fisher, H., Mashek, D.J., Strong, G., Li, H., Brown, L.L. (2005). "Reward, motivation and emotion systems associated with early-stage intense romantic love." *Journal of Neurophysiology*, 94: 327-337.

Baron-Cohen, S. (1995). *Mindblindness: An Essay on Autism and Theory of Mind*. Cambridge, MA: The MIT Press.

Bolick, T. (2001). *Asperger Syndrome and Adolescence: Helping Preteens and Teens Get Ready for the Real World*. Gloucester, MA: Fair Winds Press.

Courchesne, E. et al. (2004). "The Autistic Brain: Birth Through Adulthood." *Current Opinion in Neurology*. Vol. 17: pp. 489-496.

Dunn Buron, Kary. (2007) *A 5 Is Against the Law*. Shawnee Mission, KS: The Autism Asperger's Publishing Company.

Grandin, T. (1999). "Social Problems: Understanding Emotions and Developing Talents." From the website: www.autism.org.

Grandin, T. (2001). "Lose the Social Skills, Gain Savant Skills?" *Autism Asperger's Digest* magazine. September-October 2001.

Grandin, T. (2002). "Happy People on the Autism Spectrum have Satisfying Jobs or Hobbies." *Autism Asperger's Digest* magazine. March-April 2002.

Grandin, T. (2002). "Teaching People with Autism/Asperger's to Be More Flexible." *Autism Asperger's Digest* magazine. July-August 2002.

Grandin, T. (2003). "Teaching Concepts to Children with Autism." *Autism Asperger's Digest* magazine. November-December 2003.

Grandin, T. (2003). "Disability Versus Just Bad Behaviors." *Autism Asperger's Digest* magazine. May-June 2003.

Grandin, T. (2005). "Learning Social Rules." *Autism Asperger's Digest* magazine. January-February 2005.

Grandin, T. & Duffy, K. (2004). *Developing Talents: Careers for Individuals with Asperger Syndrome and High-Functioning Autism*. Shawnee Mission, KS: Autism Asperger's Publishing Company.

Grandin, T. & Moore, D. (2016). *The Loving Push*. Arlington, TX: Future Horizons.

Grant, K. (2005). Private email communication.

Grzadzinski, R., Di Martino, A., Brady, E. et al. (2011). "Examining autistic traits in children with ADHD: Does the autism spectrum extend to ADHD?" *Journal of Autism and Developmental Disorders* 41: 1178. doi:10.1007/s10803-010-1135-3.

Grzadzinski, R., Dick, C., Lord, C., & Bishop, S. (2016). "Parent-reported and clinician-observed autism spectrum disorder (ASD) symptoms in children with attention deficit/hyperactivity disorder (ADHD): implications for practice under DSM-5." *Molecular Autism Brain, Cognition and Behavior*, 7: 7. doi: 10.1186/s13229-016-0072-1.

Katz, I., Yellen, A. (2000). *Social Facilitation in Action*. West Hills, CA: Real Life Story Books.

Lichtenstein, P., Carlstrom, E., Rastam, M, Gillberg, C., & Anckarsater, H. (2010). "The Genetics of Autism Spectrum Disorders and Related Neuropsychiatric Disorders in Childhood." *The American Journal of Psychiatry*, 167: 1357-1363.

London, E. (2014). "Categorical Diagnosis: A Fatal Flaw in Autism Research?" *Trends of Neuroscience*, 36: 683-686.

Meyer, R., Root, A., Newland, L. (2003). "Asperger Syndrome Grows Up: Recognizing AS Adults in Today's Challenging World." From the website: www.aspires-relationships.com.

Miller, B.L. (1998). "Emergence of Art Talent in Frontal Temporal Dementia." *Neurology.* Vol. 51: pp. 978-981.

Moyes, R.A. (2001). *Incorporating Social Goals in the Classroom.* New York, NY: Jessica Kingsley Publishers.

Myers, J.M. (2005). Private email communications.

Myles, B.S., Trautman, M.L., Schelvan, R.L. (2004). *The Hidden Curriculum.* Shawnee Mission, KS: Autism Asperger's Publishing Company.

Newport, J. (2005). Adapted from "Horses Get Angry Too; But Angry Horses Win Few Races." *Autism Asperger's Digest* magazine. January-February 2005.

Prizant, B. (2016). *Uniquely Human.* New York, NY: Simon & Schuster.

Rakovic, P. (2005). Private email communication.

Reiersen, A. (2011). "Links Between Autism Spectrum Disorder and ADHD Symptom Trajectories: Important Findings and Unanswered Questions." *Journal of the American Academy of Child & Adolescent Psychiatry*, 50: 857 – 859. doi: http://dx.doi.org/10.1016/j.jaac.2011.06.012.

Reiersen, A., and Todd, R. (2008). "Co-occurrence of ADHD and autism spectrum disorders: phenomenology and treatment." *Expert Review of Neurotherapeutics*, 8: 657-669. http://dx.doi.org/10.1586/14737175.8.4.657.

Rogers, S., and Dawson, G. (2009). *Early Start Denver Model for Young Children with Autism.* New York: The Guilford Press.

Ronald, A., Simonoff, E., Kuntsi, J., Asherson, P. and Plomin, R. (2008), "Evidence for overlapping genetic influences on autistic and ADHD behaviours in a community twin sample." *Journal of Child Psychology and Psychiatry*, 49: 535–542. doi:10.1111/j.1469-7610.2007.01857.x.

Rogers, S., and Dawson, G. (2009). *Early Start Denver Model for Young Children with Autism*. New York: The Guilford Press.

Sanders, Jr. R. (2005). Private email communication.

Winner, M.G. (2002). *Thinking About YOU Thinking About ME*. San Jose, CA: Author.

Winner, M. G. (2004). "Perspective Taking Across the School and Adults Years for Persons with Social Cognitive Deficits." *Social Spectrum* newsletter, Vol 4-03/04.

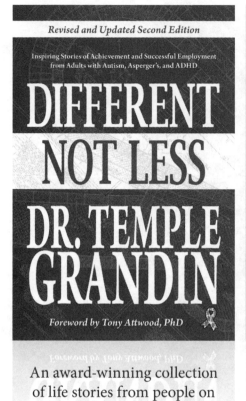